US Defense Politics

This book provides an accessible overview of US defense politics for upper-level students. This new edition has been fully updated and revised, with a new chapter on veterans and new material on topics such as cyber warfare and lobbying.

Analyzing the ways in which the United States prepares for war, the authors demonstrate how political and organizational interests determine US defense policy and warn against over-emphasis on planning, centralization, and technocracy. Emphasizing the process of defense policy-making rather than just the outcomes of that process, *US Defense Politics* departs from the traditional style of many other textbooks.

Designed to help students understand the practical side of American national security policy, the book examines the following key themes:

- US grand strategy;
- who joins America's military;
- how and why weapons are bought;
- the management of defense;
- public attitudes toward the military and casualties;
- the roles of the president and Congress in controlling the military;
- the effects of 9/11 and the Global War on Terror on security policy, homeland security, government reorganizations, and intra- and inter-service relations.

The third edition will be essential reading for students of US defense politics, national security policy, and homeland security, and highly recommended for students of US foreign policy, public policy, and public administration.

Harvey M. Sapolsky is Professor of Public Policy and Organization, Emeritus, at Massachusetts Institute of Technology (MIT), Cambridge, Massachusetts, USA, and the former Director of the MIT Security Studies Program.

Eugene Gholz is Associate Professor at the Lyndon B. Johnson School of Public Affairs at the University of Texas at Austin, USA.

Caitlin Talmadge is Assistant Professor of Political Science and International Affairs at the George Washington University in Washington, DC, USA.

US Defense Politics

The Origins of Security Policy

Third Edition

**Harvey M. Sapolsky,
Eugene Gholz and Caitlin Talmadge**

Routledge
Taylor & Francis Group

LONDON AND NEW YORK

First published 2008

This edition published 2017
by Routledge
2 Park Square, Milton Park, Abingdon, Oxon OX14 4RN

and by Routledge
711 Third Avenue, New York, NY 10017

Routledge is an imprint of the Taylor & Francis Group, an informa business

British Library Cataloguing-in-Publication Data
A catalogue record for this book is available from the British Library

Library of Congress Cataloging-in-Publication Data
Names: Sapolsky, Harvey M., author. | Gholz, Eugene, 1971– author. |
    Talmadge, Caitlin, author.
Title: US defense politics : the origins of security policy / Harvey M.
    Sapolsky, Eugene Gholz, and Caitlin Talmadge.
Description: Third edition. | New York, NY : Routledge, [2017] | Includes
    bibliographical references and index.
Identifiers: LCCN 2016037048 | ISBN 9781138657618 (hardback)
    | ISBN 9781138657649 (pbk.) | ISBN 9781315621227 (ebook)
Subjects: LCSH: National security—United States. | Civil-military
    relations—United States. | United States—Armed Forces—
    Appropriations and expenditures. | United States—Military policy.
Classification: LCC UA23 .S2582 2017 | DDC 355/.033573—dc23
LC record available at https://lccn.loc.gov/2016037048

ISBN: 978-1-138-65761-8 (hbk)
ISBN: 978-1-138-65764-9 (pbk)
ISBN: 978-1-315-62122-7 (ebk)

Typeset in Times New Roman
by Swales & Willis Ltd, Exeter, Devon, UK

Printed and bound in the United States of America
by Edwards Brothers Malloy on sustainably sourced paper

To Karen, Rose, and Steve, our support and inspiration

Contents

Figures

Tables

Boxes

Preface

We are motivated to produce a third edition for *US Defense Politics* to provide the needed updates on American defense policy, but also by the desire to expand the discussion of interest groups affecting US defense spending and the role of the president's own staff in making defense policy. The US is involved in a long war against the terrorists who had their big day on 9/11 and those who have followed them. There are constant developments in this war, some of which need to be recognized in this book on the making of US defense policy. We do not chronicle that war or defense policy in general, but we want our readers to understand how a long war affects the topics that we do focus on: the policy-making process, the institutions of government, and the politics of defense.

The interest that we highlight, giving it its own chapter, is that of America's 20 million-plus veterans and their dependents. Some believe that the United States neglects its veterans. Not us. In order to explain how veterans are treated, we have expanded our discussion of the pay and benefits of the active force. This gives us a framework then to discuss those who leave service and their needs and opportunities – trends in benefit claims, the politics of veterans' organizations, and the expectations for reforms.

Centralization is a policy trend that we lament in several parts of the book. There is no more obvious example of centralization than the growth of staff and authority for foreign and defense policies within the White House. In the new chapter on the president, we examine the cause of the trend, its manifestation, and its potential consequences. Breaking out our treatment of the president's role into a separate chapter in this edition allows us to highlight the National Security Council, but it also to gives us an opportunity for greater coverage of Congress, interest groups, and their roles in defense policy.

In other chapters, we have expanded coverage of privatization of intelligence and policies to respond to cyber threats – new areas of significant interest in US defense politics.

Some question America's role in managing global security. At home, the costs of the task bump against the demand to spend on domestic priorities. Overseas, those subject to America's actions, policing the world, are also increasingly unhappy. Our work shows how hard it will be for the Americans who plan and execute the policing to give up the job. A quarter of a century after the Cold War, the American defense enterprise is still thriving. The radar still sweeps the globe, looking for a challenger.

Acknowledgments

Several colleagues helped us understand important aspects of US defense politics and policy through their willingness to share and debate ideas with us. We thank Owen Coté Jr., Michael Desch, Jaymie Durnan, Charles Dunlap Jr., Etienne de Durand, Benjamin H. Friedman, Brendan Green, Philip Hahn, Kathleen Hicks, Colin Jackson, Ron Kurjanowicz, Brett Lambert, Austin Long, Thomas McNaugher, Neal Orringer, Barry Posen, Om Prakash, Daryl Press, Stephen Rosen, Russell Rumbaugh, Jeremy Shapiro, Michael Schrage, Stephen Slick, Ron Stoltz, Earl Walker, Sharon K. Weiner, Sanford Weiner, and Cindy Williams.

We also learned much in discussions with the many fine US officers who served as military fellows at the Massachusetts Institute of Technology (MIT) and Harvard University, most especially Robert Durbin, Michael McKeeman, Michael Trahan, B. Don Ferris, Michael Wehr, Greg Hoffman, Thomas Schluckebier, Al Kirkman, Gregg Martin, Russell Howard, Samuel Perez Jr., John Turner, David Radi, Richard Reece, Michael Hodge, Edward Rios, Lenard Samborowski, Louis Lartigue, Michael Smith, David Winn, Kevin Bensen, Thomas Hanks, David Mollahan, Mary Whisenhunt, Brooks Bruington, Raymond Coia, Christopher Conner, George Bristol, Van Gurley, Scott Henderson, Patrick Stackpole, Thomas J. Gordon, and Ryan Jeremy Bernacchi.

The team at the Security Studies Program, most especially Magdalena Reib, now elsewhere at MIT, and Lynne Levine, was, as always, crucial to our ability to get anything done. We also thank two research assistants who contributed to the second edition: Russell Spivak at MIT and Christina Caan at the George Washington University. Russell, we should note, is not only an outstanding student but was also Captain of the MIT varsity football team. Yes, there is indeed such a team. Eugene Gholz is also grateful to James McAllister and Williams College's Stanley Kaplan Program in American Foreign Policy, which provided a wonderful spot for a visiting professor to work on the third edition.

We would also like to thank *Air Force Magazine*, published by the Air Force Association, for permission to use charts reproduced in Chapter 5 of the text, and the Blue Angels and Boeing for the third edition's cover picture.

1   Enduring questions, changing politics

This book is about how the United States prepares for war by raising, maintaining, and equipping military forces. It will describe how American political leaders decide upon a national security strategy and the specific size and kinds of military forces the nation will field. And it will explain how the United States finds its enemies, fights wars, and deals with their consequences, foreign and domestic. It will cover the organization, management, and politics of American national security policy.

The subject is at the forefront of citizens' engagement with their government. After all, according to the Enlightenment theories of a "social contract" that so influenced America's Founding Fathers, national defense is the reason to have a government to begin with. Although modern Americans debate the legitimacy of many other ways that government may also contribute to the commonweal, essentially everyone agrees that providing for the common defense is its first obligation. Americans look to their government to ensure their physical security, to prevent foreign powers and overseas chaos from disrupting their prosperity, and to recognize and encourage their various expressions of individual liberty. National security encompasses these three core aims – and from time to time, some others as well.

Defense policy issues account for many of the policy issues most prominently discussed among Americans. Presidential candidates are always asked about what they think are the gravest threats to US security and whether the existing defense budget and policy choices are the best way to address them. As you will learn in this book, though, neither their broad campaign statements about national security nor their seemingly detailed plans intended to show off their knowledge and expertise are directly implemented once candidates win their elections. For good reasons, presidents are only one important member of the complex cast that makes national security policy. They have to deal with Congress, the military, think tank experts, advocacy groups, the defense industry, and of course the ever-changing views of the public, informed, more or less, by the 24-hour news cycle and the never-silent Twitterverse.

The politics of national security extend well beyond decisions about how to respond to foreign policy crises. To be sure, defense policy debates sometimes focus on issues such as the complex question of whether it serves the national interest to send American ground troops to fight in Syria, whether against fundamentalist Islamist terrorists like ISIS or against nasty authoritarian leaders like Syria's President Bashar al-Assad. The substantive analysis of the ways and means of such an intervention is important, and experts claim that they can divine the objective truth about national interest. But in practice the national interest is a very slippery concept, and different people with different personal values define the national interest in different ways. Politics within the United States give us our national security decisions, and many other prior decisions about defense policy create conditions that strongly influence, if not determine, the choices about specific interventions such as Syria. It is the day-to-day arguments about defense investment, organization, and management that set the stage, and the day-to-day decisions about defense politics are themselves controversial and consequential on their own terms.

This book highlights those day-to-day decisions – how they get made, what they have been, and why they matter. Outside of crises, organizations rather than individual personalities have more influence on policy. Their default routines, known as standard operating procedures (SOPs), and their own political interests can influence important decisions, especially those that take place below the radar of public, presidential, or congressional attention. In the day-to-day functioning of government, including in military affairs, the president is powerful but not unchallengeable. Even wars have elements of choice, and presidents rely on expert advice furnished by military leaders and on congressional allies to help rally public support. Those advising senior officials through positions in the National Security Council (NSC), in the Intelligence Community, on Capitol Hill or over at the Pentagon – that is, those parts of the security apparatus that have been built up in Washington, DC, over the decades since World War II – can be especially influential by framing arguments and assembling evidence. All of these organizations influence policy-making and need to be considered in any study of security policy.

The investment, organization, and management themselves matter. For example, recent secretaries of defense (Gates, Panetta, and Hagel) have complained that President Obama's National Security Staff has taken on too much of the secretary of defense's policy-making role, centralizing decision-making in the president's bloated-but-still-easily-overwhelmed personal orbit, and reducing the opportunity for people with military experience and institutional memory to influence the decisions. Are their criticisms right? Are they fair?

Meanwhile, the military itself is in the process of rapid social change, in particular opening opportunities to women and gays. Have those reforms been implemented as rapidly and effectively as they could have been? The military also faces social challenges, including sexual assault and suicide. Are its policies to handle those problems responsive and effective? The answers tell us something important about the military's role in American society.

Separately, Americans worry that their government is getting away from them – that it spends too much and achieves too little. Defense spending is one of the biggest components of the federal budget, vigorously supported by Americans' patriotism and lasting trust in the military as one of the few effective institutions in American government. As Americans seek to cut government spending, they clash over how (or whether) to allocate a share of the cuts to defense. The automatic mechanism that Congress imposed to actually enforce budget cuts, "sequestration," has become a hated epithet in the defense policy world, where many view it as non-strategic and dangerous at a time that they see mounting threats to US security. Is sequestration really as bad as people say, or are the complaints just the normal pushback of bureaucrats and pork-barrel interests who have grown accustomed to the cushy life in a profligate national security state?

This book explains these and other recent important American defense policy issues, not just because the issues are themselves important but also because they help us to learn about the broader framework and processes of US defense politics. It provides some balance to the study of security policy as it is currently taught in most colleges and universities. The common approach is to focus on international relations, without much consideration of the domestic politics that influence them. This perspective frequently considers states' "regime type" – that is, whether they are democracies or not – but often does not delve further into democracies' processes and concerns in choosing their national security policies. It worries about the international balance of power much more than the domestic one.

This limitation would not matter much if the students of domestic politics and policies paid serious attention to national security issues. But they usually do not. For them, the politics that hold interest, especially in the United States, are those affecting social welfare, racial inequality, the causes and consequences of globalization, elections, and other internal issues. When they look for comparison to the politics or policy in their areas of interest, they look abroad for the contrasts and similarities, not to the national politics of defense, and they tend to overlook the role of defense in Americans' consideration of those issues. They compare US and European health policies or US and Asian trade policies but never US business–government relations in defense and non-defense industries.

The topic of civil–military relations is central to this book – defined in the American context as the relationship between elected civilian leaders (the president and Congress) and professional military leaders (generals and admirals). Unfortunately, most of the work on civil–military relations focuses on explaining coups in the zone of instability that is much of Africa, Latin America, and Asia. It has little to say about stable societies such as the United States, where no one fears that the military will take power. A general rebelling against the government occasionally makes for a good movie plot (*Dr. Strangelove* features just such a story) but finds no reality within the actual American officer corps. And the fear that military leaders are uniformly hardliners, who no matter the situation will advise an aggressive military solution to the nation's problems, is also a Hollywood exaggeration. As generals and admirals know, wars destroy organizations and give reason for civilian leaders to interfere in military affairs. Better just the threat of war, as far as they are concerned.

Ultimately, the literature on civil–military relations downplays the most important question for the American context: how can the president get strategic advice from the professional military – preferably a menu of options from which the president, elected by the people for this very purpose, can choose, but not so broad a range of options as to produce cacophony and incoherence? Military officers need to engage constructively in advising civilians and the public about security threats and appropriate national strategies to counter them. They also need to be responsive to civilian direction even when policies work against their service's interest or that of the military as a whole – indeed, we hope that they will advise the political leadership to cut back military expenditure in American society when benign international conditions warrant those policies. That responsibility throws the military into the political mix with other sources of advice, and it also emphasizes the military's multiple other political interactions beyond those with the president, not the least of which is the armed services' own rivalry among themselves for prestige and relevance. The services (the Army, Navy, Air Force, and Marines), the Office of the Secretary of Defense (OSD), and other units of the government, including the Office of the President, are political institutions with organizational interests and pathologies of their own. We will help you understand them in this book.

The work on business–government relations is another literature that is relevant to this book. Strangely, the defense industry is hardly ever considered in academic discussions of business–government relations, although the "military–industrial complex" is often the bogeyman of journalistic investigations and conspiracy theories. The lack of systematic analysis is surprising, because no industry is more heavily regulated than the defense industry, and the government is, through the armed services and related agencies, the only buyer of many tens of billions of dollars' worth of weapons, equipment, and related services that this industry sells each year. Much of the federal government's support of research and development efforts is channeled through defense firms, whose work has been at the cutting edge in several fields such as aeronautics, satellites, remote sensing, robotics, simulations, and data processing. The military buys more, hires more, and uses the private sector more than any other part of government. We will explain why the military favors the use of contractors for many of its support functions and with what consequences. Do contractors gain undue influence on national security policy? Who else has a say in how America spends defense dollars and fights its wars? You will find out.

Though their work is complex and sometimes classified, militaries, especially the US military, take pride in their histories, seek to create and follow traditions, commission and attract many studies, keep good records, and are central to major security policy decisions. In contrast, business firms usually ignore their histories, limit access to records, shun probing outsiders, and prefer to claim limited or no roles in public policy decisions. Understanding the information militaries provide requires a trained eye, but the material is there for examination.

There are myths to explode. We will be surprised and disheartened if when you have finished reading this book you still believe that the F-35 fighter aircraft or the AH-64 attack helicopter is being bought only because it is made in 49 of the 50 states or 367 of the 435 congressional districts. And, yes, Congress has met a weapon system that it did not like – more than one, in fact – despite the obvious political incentives to preserve defense industry jobs and to grandstand by voting "for" national security. Politics play a central role in weapons acquisition decisions, but a much more complicated and subtle politics than the handy – but wrong – state or district count implies.

Weapons' quality and efforts to reform the acquisition process are another fruitful source of myths about national security. In the past, critics often complained that the defense industry overcharged for "gold-plated" equipment with unnecessary, deluxe features; today, the complaint has changed to allege that defense firms peddle old technologies long left behind by the commercial marketplace. In truth, there are reasons why the armed forces buy the weapons that they buy and why they follow Kafkaesque acquisition regulations. We will learn why the result of that process, expensive as it is, is worthy not only of our scorn but also of our admiration.

Our goal, though, is to do more than get rid of the easy answers. We want to equip readers with analytical concepts that will allow them to have a very good understanding of not only past defense decisions but also future ones. We seek to provide a framework for analysis, not a description of historical actions and the leaders associated with them. Certainly, parts of the book will relate historical events, both to familiarize readers with key events and changes in American defense policy – the "coin of the realm" – and to present examples and evidence to support our interpretations. But the book's goal is broader than offering a historical account: we will help you discern the recurring patterns behind events and give you tools so that you can recognize those patterns in the future. Politics – the way that politicians, government employees, and regular citizens adjudicate their differences about values and priorities – confront an ever-changing array of specific issues, but most of the debates actually reflect underlying questions that endure.

The framework is what makes the book most useful for the future, because the details change frequently. It is, as the cliché says, "a very uncertain world" in which we live. Who would have predicted in 1981 that the Cold War would end within the decade, and peacefully as well? Who would have predicted in 1991 that a decade later the United States and its North Atlantic Treaty Organization (NATO) allies, including nations that once were members of the rival Warsaw Pact, would be fighting side by side in Afghanistan? And who in early 2001 would have predicted that the American defense budget would soon reach the heights achieved in the Cold War, but without America facing a rival that could be truthfully labeled its military peer? We do not expect our readers to become fortune-tellers. Rather, such

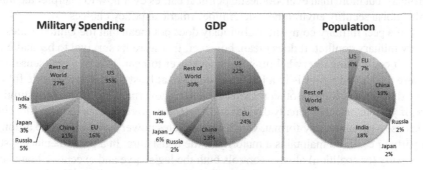

Figure 1.1 American dominance: military spending, GDP, and population pie charts

Sources: All data are for 2014. Military expenditure data are from SIPRI; GDP and population data are from the World Bank's World Development Indicators, updated June 2016.

concepts as the defense budget cycle, the temptations of empire, the desire to free-ride, and the congressional fear of responsibility – all to be explained later – will give our readers a good and useful set of tools with which to understand recurring themes in US defense politics and policy. Readers will even be able make broad predictions about the future based on the framework, and they will better understand the consequences of reforms that change the balance of power among the individuals and organizations that influence US defense policy.

Thoughts about comparison

The United States has long been a global power, but it was not until World War II that it became committed to using its power to shape the international system. World War II finished what World War I started: the demotion of European nations from the status of global powers. Then the Cold War pitted the United States against the Soviet Union. The eventual collapse of that overextended, decaying dictatorship left the US standing alone.

The scale of US power dwarfs other countries', and it differs dramatically in both how it is generated and how it is used. The United States now spends more on defense than most other countries combined (see Figure 1.1). It invests six times more in defense research and development activities than the rest of the world (e.g., designing military aircraft, testing new weapons, and seeking better military communications gear and sensors), and it has sustained its high research and development (R&D) spending for more than six decades. The US Navy is about ten times bigger than the next largest navy, which happens to be its close ally, the Royal Navy. The United States has four air forces, one for each of its armed services, and all are very capable. Its military power draws on a vast resource base: a gross domestic product (GDP) of well over $15 trillion that accounts for nearly a quarter of the world's economic activity. And America has no peer in terms of its global cultural influence. The American way of life – an apparently enticing mix of unapologetic materialism, the continuous quest for celebrity status and wealth, disdain for government, braggadocio optimism, sincerely expressed but conveniently enforced morality, and total informality – captures the imagination of youth the world over. The United States is in a class by itself.

American defense politics are the most important factor in understanding international security today. US security policy surely still responds to global events – including the bluster and war-mongering of erratic foreign leaders, revolutions, failed states, and the rise of international terrorist groups – but more than ever, domestic political battles over how to interpret the threats posed by the global security environment determine American policy choices.

The lack of a peer military competitor obviously does not mean that the United States prevails in every military conflict. It does mean, however, that were its survival to be challenged in a conflict, it could bring overwhelming military power to bear. It is in a real sense undefeatable. Here the United States is in a league of its own, at least for the foreseeable future.

The United States is unique for other reasons as well. Its governmental format (constitutional framework, if you prefer) intentionally divides and constrains governmental power. Most other democracies use a parliamentary format, which concentrates power in the executive as long as the ruling party or coalition maintains a majority in the legislature. In a parliamentary system, the majority party (or coalition) always controls both the legislative and executive branches of government; the prime minister is the leader of the parliamentary majority, and almost the only job of the "backbenchers" is to vote to ratify whatever policy the prime minister chooses. As a result, parliamentary government has fewer checks and balances than the American presidential system, which is also often called the "separation of powers" system. The details of government structure vary around the world, but no other country allows its government to be as potentially divided and at odds with itself as the United States.

This unique position of power and form of governmental structure make cross-national comparisons in security policy, beyond of course the mechanical counting of tanks and ships, very difficult. We will not do much of it here. Our focus is on explaining how American security policy is made to help make sense of the exercise of American power.

Presidents are given a freer hand in foreign affairs, and especially in the conduct of military operations, than they are given in domestic policy. The federal system, which manages power between the states and the federal government, obviously has much more consequence domestically than in foreign policy. Nevertheless, there are broad constraints on the action of the executive branch that affect all the federal government does, and broad cultural biases affect many policy fields. Being a civil servant in the United States, for example, carries less status than private employment in nearly every occupation. Also, government paying the bills but contracting out to provide services is a common feature in the United States, for example in both health care and defense. So too is the search for technological solutions, which leads to generous government funding for research and development. We will point out commonalities like these among American policy fields as we work our way toward a deeper understanding of American defense politics and policy.

Enduring questions

We want this book, focused as it is on US security policy, to have broader lessons, so we begin with what we believe are the four basic questions that the American policy-making process deals with over and over again. The answers vary by policy area and with time, but it is never possible either to shake the questions entirely or to gain permanent answers. The questions are: (1) What is the appropriate division between public and private responsibility? (2) What is the appropriate balance between planning and the market? (3) What is to be centralized and what is to be decentralized? and (4) Which questions should be settled by experts and which should be settled by political means, representing the will of the people? These four questions will be central to our examination of security policy.

This list does not simply repeat the same question four different ways, although the issues overlap. And the answers to the questions need not be consistent at any particular time, though patterns surely can be discerned. In the end, essentially all defense policy reforms propose some adjustment in the American government's answer to one or more of these questions – for example, an increase in centralization to empower expert decision-makers.

Public versus private

The question about the division between the public and the private asks which responsibilities are "inherently governmental," closely linked to the reasons that political theorists use to explain why governments exist. Modern policy debates often pose the question in reverse: Which responsibilities can the private sector address better than the government, leaving the government with the minimal role of establishing the "rules of the game" and providing incentives for private actors to do certain jobs?

In defense, we will be asking about the role of private firms in providing weapons and services to the American military and how that role has grown recently. Today, companies are doing more and more: where government arsenals used to design and build weapons, today private firms do the work; where the Pentagon used to be filled with military officers and civilian government employees managing US defense effort, today many contractors sit in those chairs and contribute to important decisions; where government intelligence analysts used to process, translate, and analyze raw data collected to help understand foreign powers, today much of that work is outsourced to civilian specialists on temporary contracts who support a smaller government staff; and where soldiers used to paint ships, clean latrines, and make meals on kitchen patrol (KP), today large corporations provide logistical support to US military operations all around the world.

The question policy-makers need to ask is: What must be retained as governmental, or public, in the acquisition of weapons and the conduct of war? What tasks must the government perform directly to ensure its monopoly on the legitimate use of force, and what technical and professional knowledge do we entrust only to officials accountable to the voting public rather than to private groups, who are instead responsible to shareholders and boards of directors? What are the irreducible public functions?

The same questions can be asked about health care, education, and corrections policies (and they often are asked in those contexts). The United States has public and private hospitals, public and private schools at all levels of education, and more recently privately managed prisons as well as the traditional government-run facilities. The divisions between the public and private are not the same in all fields, but the issues are. We need to examine them in the defense politics and policy context.

The market versus planning

The question about the appropriate balance of planning and the market asks about the logic of government decision-making. A plan is an effort to determine in advance how an organization should react to contingencies, maintaining its effort to achieve its goals in light of unfolding events; it is based on the logic of hierarchy, in which participants in an effort are subservient and strive to implement the pre-determined decisions made by the planner. The market, on the other hand, offers a variety of proposals from which decision-makers can choose in due course, using their local, real-time knowledge to consider best how to achieve their goals; the logic emphasizes competition among individuals and groups, each offering their own solutions, rather than adherence to an overarching plan.

Some people naturally confuse the market with the private sector, suspecting that "markets versus planning" is just a way to restate "private versus public." The market logic can of course be applied to the private-sector economy, but it also can apply within the public sector. For example, in defense, inter-service rivalry offers an opportunity to apply market logic, as the different organizations, all within the public sphere, compete to offer the best solutions to the national security challenges facing the nation. Does the Air Force perform the air superiority mission better than the Navy? How do the services perform in their own training exercises and in the occasional head-to-head comparison? To carry out strike missions, should we buy more bombers or missiles? Is the Marine Corps better in counterinsurgency operations than the Army? In this market-like competition, the way that we know that a solution is likely to work well is by comparing it to the effectiveness of an alternative solution promoted by a different organization. Similarly, it is hard to know whether a particular weapon system costs so much because of difficult technical constraints or overly ambitious strategic goals, or if instead bad management or uninspired effort is the source of the cost escalation. One way to find out is to compare the performance of a similar product developed by a different military service.

On the other hand, planning is very important in military affairs: there are clear and powerful advantages of unified military command. The services have to cooperate to achieve national objectives; resource managers have to know what to invest in to prepare to deter and fight future enemies, and logisticians need to know where to send supplies for the main effort in a conflict; soldiers, sailors, and airmen routinely have to be able to anticipate the decisions that their counterparts will make. Everyone needs to be at least partially subservient to a plan, or no one can do his or her job.

Defense policy seeks to gain the benefits of deliberation and a diversity of judgment without sacrificing the advantages of planning when it is needed, resulting in a series of changes to the structure of the military in response to new technologies, strategic situations, and political alignments. Sometimes the military departments (the Army, the Air Force, and the Navy, which includes the Marine Corps) have had more independence, while at other times a cross-service perspective has dominated. A permanent, "best" answer is elusive.

Although policy debates on the public–private axis generally trace their roots to the goal of preserving accountability in government, advocates often frame the markets versus planning question by emphasizing another goal: efficiency. Sometimes leaders expect markets to react slowly to new information, or they worry that market failures will systematically undermine markets' ability to provide solutions to certain kinds of problems. These problems are often presumed to be especially serious in defense policy, because national security is a classic example of a public good – an area in which individuals benefit from solutions whether or not they pay their share of the cost, meaning that few people have reason to take on the responsibility, and the good may be under-provided as a result. Moreover, wars are (thankfully) relatively rare, so the market lacks feedback about the effects of various defense policies – the feedback that would provide information for continuous updates of market prices. But even in the absence of price signals, planners may be able to develop policies and use hierarchy to implement plans – planners' ability to direct rank-and-file soldiers or civil servants to follow orders – allowing quick, well-coordinated initiatives.

Outside the military environment but still in the public sphere, law enforcement agencies have overlapping missions and intense competition to make the best arrests or to develop the most favorable public image. Similarly, public universities compete with private universities, with public universities in other states, and, in a surprising number of cases, with other public universities in the same state. And non-profit, public, and private medical services compete for resources, clients, and standing within their own categories as well as against each other. Choosing to emphasize public services does not necessarily mean choosing planning over the market, because inter-organizational competition can create market-like dynamics. All too often, though, leaders decide that public services necessarily entail planning.

Centralization versus decentralization

The third question reflects our basic constitutional question: What should be the framework for government? It emphasizes who should make decisions and how many people should be involved rather than the logic on which those decisions should be made. The US Constitution favors a decentralized arrangement, dividing political power between the federal government and the states and among the branches of government at the federal level. Checks and balances prevent any particular group or interest from imposing its will, roughshod, over the rest of American society. They notably protect against "tyranny of the majority." The diversity of approaches that different jurisdictions and organizations might try out to solve similar problems also can test assumptions, limit mistakes caused by philosophical or ideological blinders, and spur innovation. Overall, the question of centralization versus decentralization most directly addresses the value of liberty in American national security.

Over time, circumstance has forced greater centralization of power in the federal government and toward the executive branch, including in defense policy. State government control of the militias (now evolved into the National Guard) – and thus of the nation's ability to fight wars – has been drastically altered, although the existence of the National Guard as an organizational competitor to the Regular military (i.e., the federal government's full-time Army, Navy, and Air Force) still influences federal budget decisions. The need for a conscious political decision to mobilize the National Guard, disrupting Americans' normal lives by calling them up for military service, also still constrains the use of American power.

The role of Congress has changed, too. National security policy does not always wait for congressional deliberations, but of course in some areas such as weapons acquisition and military personnel policy, it does. Congress still has the power to raise armies and navies and to declare war, even if it often defers to presidential authority, declines to debate the formal authorization to use military force, and engages in set-piece hearings filled with airy or ideological statements rather than detailed policy investigation and oversight.

Presidential power has increased, because mobilization has become nearly continuous, and threatened attacks, for example with nuclear weapons, can materialize instantaneously. But the president cannot manage the day-to-day affairs of national security by himself, and over time, decision-makers have tried to improve the American national security policy-making process by adjusting the organization of the executive branch. Even when procedures have been changed to increase centralization, law-makers tend to try to preserve some checks and balances in American national security decision-making. Finding the appropriate balance is a perennial goal.

The question of centralization versus decentralization also affects both the military and the civilian sides of the executive branch. On the military side, should many voices speak to the political leadership on each policy issue – for example, the leadership of each military service or of each operational command – or should the military first discuss options internally and present its single, best advice to the civilians? The former, decentralized structure offers a diverse menu of options that may avoid risks such as "strategic monoculture" or "groupthink" that are prone to mistakes; the latter, centralized structure, embodied in modern jointness, may avoid cacophony and policy incoherence. Meanwhile, the same questions can be asked about civilian defense organization: Do congressional hearings on defense matters introduce valuable perspectives, or do they undermine effective management by creating 535 "bosses" for military programs?

The division between centralization and decentralization in policy-making shifts constantly in defense as well as other policy areas. For example, the national "No Child Left Behind" standards and the so-called Common Core mobilized a powerful though not decisive backlash over whether education policy should be centralized or decentralized to state and local governments. And the executive and legislative branches have recently battled about many issues, including immigration and environmental policies. The fundamental question about the amount of centralization in government cannot be settled permanently.

Politics versus expertise

The fourth question asks how broad a spectrum of people should participate in the decision-making process. Sometimes, highly trained experts make the best decisions: rocket scientists probably should design rockets, and there's a reason to go to a brain surgeon. The technocratic decision-making model delegates power to people with specialized knowledge that makes them particularly likely to make the "right" choices. It is not always obvious, though, which experts should be in charge of making a particular decision. Government bureaucracy is famous for its baffling rigidity: sometimes no one knows who should try to solve a particular problem, so it falls through the cracks or gets decided by an expert with the wrong expertise. Other times, turf fights break out as multiple agencies get in one another's way working on the same issue.

The alternative style of decision-making uses a more open process – often, a political process in which the broader public and interest groups can participate. The great advantage of this process is the legitimacy that it provides to the eventual policy choice. When the democratic process works well, even those on the losing side of a debate "buy into" the selected option and offer its implementers time and resources to make their vision work. Politics also provide the opportunity for Americans to align government policies with their values. The people know what they believe in and what is important to them, even if they do not always understand the intricacies of how to get what they want or what goals are reasonably attainable (and what is beyond the United States' capabilities and resources). Experts, on the other hand, are a rarefied subgroup of the total population, and their very skills and professional codes of ethics give them different values from the rest of us. Because they are not elected, experts cannot claim to represent the broader population's views.

Many policy choices actually depend on values rather than on technical information. In economic policy, for example, how strenuously should the Federal Reserve Board work to ward off the risk of inflation, given that efforts to keep prices down might also lead to a higher unemployment rate? The question of which is worse – the risk of inflation or a greater number of job losses – is a values question rather than a question with a technically "correct" answer. Or in national security affairs, how much "risk" should Americans tolerate, and how should they compare the importance of one risk (say, of a terrorist attack against the United States) to another (say, a disruption of energy supplies)? Again, the answer is more subjective than scientific.

Actual decisions are usually made through some mixture of the expert and political processes. Some groups acquire disproportionate influence on policy choices because of their professional expertise, but others still get a vote based on the breadth of their membership or their appeal to core American values. Most policy reforms, though, push the decision-making institutions in one direction or the other – either increasing the role of experts (as confidence in science goes up, for example) or broadening public access (to appeal to the ideal of representation).

National defense has seen both directions of reform in recent years. Most Americans believe that Allied ingenuity (e.g., the development of radar) played a key role in the victory in World War II, and the importance of science seems self-evident in the nuclear age: new bombs, missiles, submarines, sensors, and other technologies were the West's bulwark against the communist threat. Scientists and engineers naturally gained influence in defense policy debates. And defense reformers often sought to extend the technologists' "systems approach" to the management of military problems – mapping out detailed policy alternatives based on "scientific" predictions of the future threat and the trajectory of technological progress, trying to quantify measures of military effectiveness so that different policies could easily be compared, and seeking to optimize decisions based on complicated models that only experts can manipulate.

Meanwhile, generals and admirals often asserted their unique ability to make the right decisions on defense policy based on their professional judgment – after all, they have experience leading soldiers in combat, managing the fog of war, and devising military doctrine and war plans. Civilian scientists and military officers each have real skills, so the different kinds of experts have fought a long-running battle for control of the defense policy process. Politicians often have deferred to both kinds of expertise, dodging their responsibility to make hard choices that put American lives on the line.

Ultimately, though, the American people (through their elected representatives) must accept and legitimate national security policies. Protecting the United States entails difficult choices, and periodically experts' decisions overstep the boundaries that the public will accept on issues ranging from the US role in the "collateral damage" that kills innocent civilians in war zones to how much due process suspected terrorist operatives are entitled to when they are detained and interrogated. When the public becomes aware of experts' overreach, politicians sometimes reel back the policy, as they did on so-called "enhanced interrogation techniques" in the Global War on Terror (GWOT) that bordered on torture. Even in that case, a substantial minority continued to prioritize protecting Americans at all costs, cheering loudly as several 2016 presidential candidates called for US use of waterboarding and an expansion of the detention center at Guantanamo Bay in the wake of a mass shooting attack on Americans in San Bernardino, California. Experts can debate the effectiveness of such techniques, but even their informed judgments must end up as part of the American political process: whether to even publish the results of a congressional committee's detailed investigation became a political issue, and once the "Torture Report" was actually published, rather than leading to a deliberative process, it immediately became a bludgeon in arguments and recriminations between Congress and the Intelligence Community and between Republicans and Democrats in Congress. It is not that the evidence is irrelevant – just that it does not speak for itself, and experts' views are interpreted through a political process that offers different levels of deference to expertise at different times.

Recognizing the enduring questions

Debates about the appropriate balance between the public and the private, markets and planning, centralized and decentralized authority, and the relative roles of expertise and politics guide policy-making in any given field. Participants rarely can influence the circumstances the nation confronts. This is especially the case for national security policy because the actions of other nations and non-governmental organizations are hard to control. Just as the designers of the US Constitution could not anticipate future events, so we must confront an unknowable security future. Answers to the four enduring questions set the framework for our responses to each national security challenge or opportunity. They tell us who will make the necessary decisions – or who will abdicate that essential responsibility – and on what grounds the participants will make their choices. Our experience often highlights the imperfections of our past choices, leading us to try to adjust the answers to prepare for the next security policy debate.

Questions for discussion

1   **Why is an understanding of organizations important to the study of security policy?**
2   **What roles might you (the reader) play in influencing decisions about US national security?**
3   **In what ways is the US security situation unique?**
4   **What purpose do comparisons serve in evaluating national security policy?**
5   **How many plans should the United States have as part of its national security effort, and who should make those plans?**
6   **What factors have encouraged the trend toward centralization in US national security policy-making?**
7   **Shouldn't we leave national security policy-making to the experts?**

Recommended additional reading

Paul Davis (ed.), *New Challenges for Defense Planning: Rethinking How Much Is Enough* (Santa Monica, CA: RAND, 1994). A primer on the problems and methods of defense budget analysis.
William A. Lucas and Raymond H. Dawson, *The Organizational Politics of Defense* (Pittsburgh, PA: International Studies Association, 1974). Early insight into the central questions of the field.
Peter H. Schuck and James Q. Wilson (eds.), *Understanding America: The Anatomy of an Exceptional Nation* (New York: Public Affairs, 2008). Insight from leading experts into what is special about the United States.
James Q. Wilson, *Bureaucracy* (New York: Basic Books, 1989). Still the best single source on how federal agencies seek, acquire, and exercise power.

2 America's security strategy

This chapter considers American grand strategy after the end of the Cold War – what the United States does (and what some strategists think it should do) with its commanding position in world politics. Strategy summarizes the logic and principles used to set priorities, and as Barry Posen has explained, grand strategy – distinguished from particular strategies for dealing with specific situations, problems, and opportunities – is a state's theory about how it can "cause" security for itself.[1] It offers, or purports to offer, an explanation of how the means at a state's disposal (alliances, investments, deployments of troops) will achieve the ends a state seeks. Grand strategy links economic, military, political, diplomatic, geographic, and even demographic assets.

Debates over strategy present an example of the competing influences of experts and politics, with the detailed analyses of military strategists and civilian academics struggling for influence with the instincts, judgment, and beliefs of politicians and the American people who vote for them. In American politics, leaders rarely stick to, or even attempt to formulate, a theoretically coherent, integrated grand strategy, except when threats to national security seem quite serious. Much of the time, the inherent safety that the United States enjoys allows policy entrepreneurs and organizational pressures to set the policy agenda. That is perhaps a less intellectually satisfying method of setting priorities, but it is surely a practical one. Connecting strategic decisions to domestic politics also helps supply the resources needed to implement the decisions. And political influence surely does not make American strategy ephemeral or random, because all American strategies must respond to certain long-lasting institutions, resources, and cultural characteristics of the United States that together give us an "American Way of War."

Dilemmas of American grand strategy

The United States had a coherent grand strategy during the Cold War, even if politicians and scholars often disagreed about the details. Under the strategic framework of containment and deterrence, the United States at times flirted with efforts to roll back parts of the Soviet Empire and occasionally resorted to the use of nuclear threats, but it basically sought to block further Soviet expansion, to avoid a nuclear war, and to promote economic prosperity at home and in the West generally.[2] The US spent trillions on defense, hoping to pressure the Soviets while avoiding a direct confrontation. The United States fought wars of containment in Korea and Vietnam, conducting each with restraint so as not to provoke a wider conflict with China or the Soviet Union. The deviations from the strategy, and there were many, were never great enough to force its abandonment.

Although obviously welcomed, the West's victory in the Cold War was largely a surprise. Several analysts saw the United States in the 1980s as overcommitted and vulnerable at the very time the Soviet Union was collapsing from the weight of its economic and military competition with the West. Hardly anyone predicted that the end of the long struggle would come peacefully; instead, they imagined the bloodiest of final chapters.[3] As a result, few had engaged in serious thought or planning regarding what would come afterwards. The United States in particular was unprepared for the choices that lay ahead; for decades it had organized its security policies completely and comfortably around the Cold War struggle.

The 1990s became a period of policy drift as American leaders sought another grand strategy on which to base the country's foreign relations and the size of its military forces. The vast network of study organizations, planning staffs, think tanks, university programs, laboratories, committees, consultants, and contractors that serve the American security establishment soon held countless conferences and issued reports on potential directions. There was talk of new and old threats, of dangerous regions that required close watch and possible intervention, and of important trends in warfare. Some worried about a rising China, while others saw danger in a resurgent Russia. The Middle East was described as a "powder keg" and perpetually unstable, East Asia as "ripe for rivalry," and the Balkans as on the brink of genocide that could spill across borders to threaten Central and Western Europe.[4] Other observers worried about the rise of ethnic conflict in the aftermath of the collapse of the Soviet Union and its empire of reluctant allies and captive nations. There was talk of failing states, humanitarian disasters, and the need for new international regimes to take care of them.[5] Commentary, wise and otherwise, was offered on a so-called revolution in military affairs (RMA), a product of the growing ability to identify and hit targets precisely from long ranges.[6] Others wondered whether new technologies would enable the military to fight wars with non-lethal weapons.[7]

Robert Jervis, a professor of international relations at Columbia University, believes the quest for a new grand strategy is essentially hopeless.[8] America, Jervis argues, lacks the key element for constructing a grand strategy – an enemy. During the Cold War, the Soviet Union was the enemy, and we could formulate a set of basic policies for dealing with the specific threat it posed, weighing the resources available and the likely reactions of other nations to US policies.

To be sure, al Qaeda self-selected as an American enemy after the Cold War, killing Americans around the globe, including those murdered in the homeland attacks of September 11, 2001. But from the start al Qaeda was a non-state terrorist group with diffuse and limited resources – much larger than the resources of previous terrorist groups but still much smaller than the resources of a powerful government. And then the US-led international response to 9/11 killed or captured many al Qaeda leaders, forced the organization further underground, and further undermined its ability to centrally command and organize attacks. Al Qaeda and successor terrorist groups such as the Islamic State (also called ISIS or ISIL) have never been a sufficiently large threat to force the United States to focus and prioritize its national security efforts. Even detonating a nuclear weapon in an American city, terrorists' wildest dream, would not begin to pose an existential threat of the type the United States faced in the Cold War, where thousands of Soviet nuclear weapons might have destroyed all of the major American cities at once.

Some strategists tried rhetorically to link together small threats to create an organizing principle, whether urging the United States to confront "rogue states" in the 1990s, renaming that threat in the 2000s as the "axis of evil" among Iraq, Iran, and North Korea, or grouping the entire militant Islamic terrorist threat (and throwing in non-Islamic terrorist groups, too) by naming a "Global War on Terror," or GWOT in military parlance. These efforts were unconvincing or even counter-productive, and none could provide coherence to strategy debates. The Obama administration stopped using the term GWOT, leaving the effort against al Qaeda, ISIS, and other groups without a name. There are just too many differences among militant groups' causes, ideology, and friends for the contest with terrorism, state-sponsored or not, to provide much basis for grand strategy.

The fact is that the U nited States has many foreign policy objectives, not all of which are compatible. In its foreign policy, America wants to promote democracy, free trade, and capitalism. But it also wants a stable Middle East with recognition and peace for the state of Israel; a quiet, forgotten Russia; a China that does not grow into a military threat; happy, non-warring trading partners in Asia; peaceful, multiethnic states in the Balkans; a non-nuclear North Korea and Iran; less corruption and killing in Africa so America's conscience is not bothered; cooperative European countries that seek to unite economically but remain in an American-led NATO military alliance; inter-American trade, controlled immigration, and cordial relations with Canada and Mexico; the total destruction of al Qaeda and its affiliates; and the respect and homage that the world's dominant nation is due. Each of these objectives has its own advocates, domestic and foreign. Without a clear, overwhelming security threat to help organize them, however, the United States cannot gain consensus on priorities. The key to strategic coherence remains elusive. In its stead there is only what Jervis describes as "pluralism with a vengeance."

Power is the great tempter. US administrations have been busy in the post-Cold War years managing conflicts, providing humanitarian assistance, promoting the spread of democratic institutions, and intervening in ethnic wars with or without United Nations (UN) approval. Until 9/11, some critics viewed these actions as largely beneath America's standing and contrary to its interests. The American military, too, worried that such overseas involvements would deplete its shrinking post-Cold War resources and weaken its ability to fight major wars, which it saw as its main business. And some others wondered why the charity did not begin at home. Candidate George W. Bush took up the cause in his 2000 campaign by asserting that he wanted a less arrogant foreign policy than that of President Clinton, one without the Clinton administration's nation-building inclinations.

Most people expected President Bush's first national security strategy, scheduled for the fall of 2001, to focus on potential great power threats to the United States and to invest in technology and force structure to keep the US military far stronger than any emerging competitor over the long haul. The 9/11 attacks intervened, and fear of a potential combination of weapons of mass destruction (WMD) and terrorism quickly reshaped the strategy. A second idea, not new but rarely articulated by government officials, was stapled onto the emphasis on primacy: not only would the US military far outclass all others, so that it could act against threats all around the world, but it would act preemptively, because the it did not want to wait for the awesome destruction of a nuclear attack before it addressed threats to national security.[9] The so-called preemptive strategy might more accurately have been called a strategy of preventive war. It sought to limit even latent capabilities to attack the United States with nuclear weapons rather than to undercut any particular enemy's short-term intention to blow up an American city.

The debate leading up to the 2003 invasion of Iraq followed this preventive logic. Most American policy-makers and pundits who supported the 2003 US invasion of Iraq did so for more than one reason, and their reasons often differed from one another – but essentially all advocates could agree on the rationale that the United States should prevent Saddam Hussein's possible use of WMD. When the occupation forces could find no nuclear, biological, or chemical weapons stockpiles, however, advocates shifted the emphasis of their justification for war: the spread of democracy became the dominant public rationale. A new policy consensus emphasized the importance of democracy promotion as a cornerstone of US foreign policy, allegedly to address the root causes of the 9/11 attacks, although the Bush administration's choice of means – using unilateral military force – tended to make some American liberals uncomfortable.[10] Believing that America's vast military power could transform the world, President Bush began to do many of the things he had previously criticized: in Iraq, the United States tried to manage ethnic and sectarian hatreds, offered humanitarian assistance on a large scale, and jumped very deeply into nation-building as a method to fight against insurgents. He applied the same concepts in Afghanistan, although at lower levels of effort. When President Obama was elected in 2008, he continued the same course, sending more troops and resources to Afghanistan and following the same basic theory of victory.

Building democratic institutions turns out to be difficult, especially in countries with intense ethnic or religious hatreds.[11] No one has a reliable recipe for political development, with effective ways to eliminate corruption, to shift political competition from personalistic or tribal networks to focused debates over alternative proposals to solve policy problems, and to convince the groups who lose the debate over a particular policy choice to accept peacefully their loss and to await their next electoral victory for their turn to try their policy preferences. The challenge of nation-building is to get agreement on the basic constitutional structure – on the framework within which interest groups and political parties will debate adjustments to the balance between the public and the private, between markets and planning, between centralization and decentralization, and between experts and politicians. It took very complex processes lasting hundreds of years, combining political, economic, and social changes, to achieve that end in the United States and other developed countries. No one has had much luck accelerating the process through military intervention, foreign aid, or some combination of the two. Making nation-building a tool of American grand strategy is especially fraught, because efforts to improve government from the outside often breed resistance.[12]

In Iraq, a combination of factors eventually brought the Iraqi insurgency under control at great cost, and US troops left the country at the end of 2011. For a time, people thought that Iraq was on the right nation-building track due to a "surge" deployment of larger numbers of US troops, a shift in the local balance of power among Iraqi groups in the Sunni versus Shi'a Iraqi civil war, and mass displacement of Iraqis out of intermingled communities and into ethnic and religious enclaves with fewer flashpoints.[13] But that result was more of a pause than a victory. Iraqi government and society had not really changed: Iraq's prime minister pursued policies that favored his religious group (Shi'a); corruption and disputes over the basic structure of the economy, especially the law governing oil exploration and production, held back economic development; and investment in public services languished. Disillusioned Sunni tribes and supporters of Saddam's old regime joined forces with an extremist evolution of the old al Qaeda in Iraq, and the official Iraqi army melted away, despite all of the American effort to train and equip it, allowing ISIS to seize substantial Iraqi territory.

ISIS actually split with al Qaeda, and they remain divided over both strategy and tactics. On strategy, ISIS declared a new caliphate, trying to hold territory and govern, while al Qaeda argues that the time is not yet ripe (and their power is still too weak) to form a state. On tactics, ISIS is too brutal even for al Qaeda, enforcing its medieval Islamic vision with beheadings, slavery, and routine on-the-spot executions for alleged apostates and criminals.[14] Now, ISIS and al Qaeda affiliates compete with each other around the world, sometimes directly shooting at each other (ISIS battles the al Qaeda-linked al Nusra Front in Syria) and sometimes competing for the allegiance of local groups through online rhetoric and spectacular terrorist attacks that gain publicity to attract more followers (as in a number of West African countries).[15] The old ways of politics have proven quite resilient. Consequently, the US military is back fighting ISIS, al Qaeda, and other bad actors in Iraq and elsewhere – and has never quite managed to leave Afghanistan or to stop launching strikes in Pakistan, Yemen, and various African countries.

In the mid-2010s, the strategy question for the United States was how to react to the renewed chaos and the apparent successes of radical Islamist groups willing to use terror and to kill Westerners, including Americans. The difficult Iraq and Afghanistan experiences bred distaste for nation-building and counterinsurgency among US military and political leaders. President Obama's 2012 *Strategic Guidance* seemed to caution against a foreign policy that would require future interventions, invasions, and meddling in complex, far-off conflicts, saying that the US should no longer set the size of its ground forces by the requirements for long-term stability operations. Instead, it emphasized a "rebalance to Asia" that sought to protect the liberal order – and enmesh a rising China in it.[16] But that was before ISIS dramatically seized territory in Syria and Iraq in 2014.

With no dominant adversary, events undermined even President Obama's limited effort to impose priorities on US strategy. While Obama's 2015 version of the official *National Security Strategy* still emphasized the rebalance, it also devoted many pages to new security issues such as climate change and disease outbreaks (e.g., praising the deployment of US military forces to West Africa to help control an outbreak of the Ebola virus). More strikingly, it called for multinational cooperation to try to build stable, modern institutions to resist the spread of radical fundamentalist groups – that is, for nation-building. In practice, the United States deployed airpower and Special Operations Forces (SOF) to Iraq, Syria, Libya, and elsewhere, fighting to degrade and destroy ISIS. Obama's critics argued that his efforts were too meager. They saw the need for a larger military, supported by a reformed national security apparatus suited to post-conflict stabilization and nation-building, that would more directly combat ISIS, including on the ground. Neither President Obama nor his critics showed any interest in choosing which to prioritize, fighting ISIS or paying attention to East Asia – or to other potential threats such as nuclear proliferation or renewed Russian assertiveness.

In 2014–2015, the conflicting American goals were most obvious with respect to the crisis in Syria. The United States openly backed a relatively weak group of non-ISIS Syrian rebels against President Bashar al-Assad's brutal dictatorship, but any progress weakening Assad threatened to benefit the stronger Islamist extremists (ISIS, the al Nusra Front, and others). Russia backed its traditional Syrian ally, President Assad, but seemed to bomb the US-backed rebels much more aggressively than the fundamentalists. To many, President Obama seemed paralyzed: unable to make a deal with Assad to defeat ISIS because of human rights concerns, while unable to cooperate with rebels powerful enough to potentially force Assad to the bargaining table because of terrorism. Obama's critics preferred to escalate direct US military action against ISIS at the same time that they called for the United States to establish a no-fly zone that would help the rebels against President Assad, conveniently ignoring that might mean that US fighters and air defense systems would have to shoot down Russian aircraft. In essence, the critics also declined to choose an enemy. They wanted robust action to fight all comers at once, both terrorists and great powers. Hardly a strategy.

Box 2.1   Counterinsurgency

Counterinsurgency (COIN) is a type of warfare that the US military periodically relearns. It is not that Americans are unfamiliar with this type of fighting. In the American Revolution, American forces were the insurgents, and they were ultimately successful. After the American Civil War, the US Army occupied the Southern states for a time, attempting to suppress insurgent resistance to federal political mandates – largely unsuccessfully, it turned out. Americans call this period Reconstruction. The Indian wars in the American West that followed the Civil War were essentially prolonged and ultimately successful counterinsurgency campaigns. So too were US military operations in Cuba and the Philippines that followed the brief Spanish–American War in 1898. During much of the early twentieth century, the Marine Corps engaged in counterinsurgency efforts of various intensities in the Caribbean and Central America. The Vietnam, Iraq, and Afghanistan Wars all featured counterinsurgency operations as well.

It is not the uniqueness of COIN that induces great power militaries to seem to forget how to do it, but rather its viciousness. Insurgencies involve terrorist attacks, enemies who hide among civilians and who usually do not wear uniforms, the assassination of government officials and supporters, and the resort to torture by both sides.

Insurgencies are often drawn-out affairs that dissipate public support at home. Insurgents often rely on sanctuaries outside the country they are fighting against, making it hard for counterinsurgent forces to run the insurgents down. Having security at home, the United States is more often cast as the rescuer of an ally threatened by an insurgency, a role that often carries the added burden of having to work with weak local forces. The ally that the United States is coming to rescue is often pressed to near-defeat before US forces arrive, and the allied government usually suffers from serious corruption and mismanagement (often the conditions that gave rise to the insurgency in the first place), making it hard to "win the hearts and minds" of citizens.

It is not surprising, then, that the US military has had to more than once endure a period of doctrinal denial and relearning as it entered into a counterinsurgency fight. The first inclination has usually been the use of American forces' firepower advantage to suppress opposition, but this quickly has been complicated by the fact that insurgents and the local civilian population are always comingled.

After 9/11, an extensive review of historical counterinsurgency experience produced a new US counterinsurgency manual in 2006 under the joint leadership of Army General David Petraeus and Marine Corps General James Mattis, each of whom eventually became the overall commander for the wars in Iraq and Afghanistan. The manual records best practices for separating the civilian population from the insurgents, for developing competent local government, for encouraging improvements in the prevailing economic conditions, and for discovering and tracking down the leaders in insurgent networks.

But progress in Iraq and Afghanistan seemed to come independent of the manual. In Iraq, al Qaeda provoked a civil war between Sunnis and Shi'ites that unintentionally drove the Sunnis into an alliance with US forces and convinced the Shi'ites to accept a truce, although the truce proved only temporary under the post-surge Iraqi government. In Afghanistan, challenges in governing neighboring Pakistan seemed to be the vital factor preventing the establishment of security beyond the fences of the main coalition bases. The US military tracked literally hundreds of metrics at command headquarters and in Washington, supposedly to better manage the fight, but with bureaucratic need as much as military importance driving much of that reporting.

As in most wars, the test of political wills ultimately decides the outcome. The brutality of insurgencies wears most on the most distant population, the one whose troops are far from home. The locals bear the brunt of the death and destruction, but they almost always have more at stake and so stay the course; the intervening power has less stomach for it. No wonder that the US military prefers a different kind of fight.

Post-Cold War grand strategy alternatives

Without a single, clear enemy, the United States continues to debate how important threats are and how to meet them most effectively. In the American political system, elected public of ficials and professional military commanders take lead roles in those debates, but they are joined by academic security specialists, media commentators, and various policy advocacy groups, including those who represent defense contractors. Strategic choices must combine expert and political influences.

Some strategists, especially academics, have attempted to define a grand strategy for the post-Cold War United States even if they have little expectation that their advice will gain official endorsement. But law and presidential directive mandate the periodic production of reports with titles such as *National Security Strategy* and *National Military Strategy*, so government officials (or their staffs) search for politically resonant, if vague, phrases from academic writing. They are usually led to very windy restatements of current policy that avoid specifics but that satisfy the bureaucratic and political need to have official citations for government actions. The formality of the citations pacifies only some of the many defense commentators who cannot live with strategic ambiguity and who write often about the need to develop a strategic direction for American policy. Their complaints perpetuate the strategic debate, generally among four main proposals, although two of these have dominated most of the policy discourse since the immediate post-Cold War era, and even these supposedly distinct views have begun to converge in recent years toward many shared principles.[17]

The first of the strategies is often referred to as primacy, although its advocates prefer terms such as "deep engagement."[18] Under this strategy, the United States accepts its dominance and seeks to maintain it.[19] Many advocates are political conservatives who focus heavily on the need to assert overwhelming military force to achieve foreign policy goals. They also tend to believe that shows of force will lead other countries to flock to the US side, bandwagoning with the United States rather than balancing against it.

China is most often cited as a possible challenger, given its surging economic power, and deep engagers propose that the United States maintain close political, military, and economic alliances with China's regional neighbors to contain its rise. Historically, suppressing the ambitions of rising powers has been a risky business, but they argue that China will acquiesce to American leadership if US leaders demonstrate generally beneficent US power – that is, the Chinese would understand that competing militarily would probably be fruitless, that the attempt would be expensive, and that the benefit of chasing down the US lead would be small.[20] And if China does not acquiesce, they believe, the United States would be better off undercutting its potential competitor now, rather than delaying confrontation to a day when

Figure 2.1 Primacy on display, World War II-style: US naval aircraft stage a massive flyover
above Tokyo Bay, marking the surrender of Japan, September 1945
Source: Department of Defense.

the power disparity has narrowed. Primacists also pay increasing attention these days to what
they see as a revanchist Russia poised to reclaim Soviet dominance of Eastern Europe.

Early in the post-Cold War period, primacists tended to view failed states and regional
rogues as distractions, because they could not threaten the dominance of American military
power. But many reconsidered this view after 9/11, concluding that the United States should
destroy the perceived root cause of the terrorists' strength: repressive regimes in the Middle
East. This democratization mission did not replace the goal of deterring rising powers, however. It merely added another item to the list of tasks that the dominant power had to undertake
to preserve the world order. Indeed, in practice, primacy has generated an extremely broad
conception of US interests. Almost any type of threat, anywhere in the world, can become a
reason to use military force.

Deep engagers are fundamentally optimistic about the ability of the United States to use
power in the international system to secure its goals. In this regard they have something in
common with those in another grand strategy camp: liberal internationalism. Liberal internationalists, including many Democrats who served in or advised the Clinton administration on
foreign policy matters, argue that the best way to reduce the possibility of conflict in the international system is for the United States to spread democracy and free trade, because liberal
regimes with extensive economic engagement tend not to fight each other.[21] This logic dominated President Clinton's 1996 version of the *National Security Strategy*, which was called *A
National Security Strategy of Engagement and Enlargement*, and it also underpins President
George W. Bush's second *National Security Strategy*, published in 2006, which shows the easy

Figure 2.2 Secretary of State Hillary Clinton celebrates with Libyan militia fighters – one
version of the new, post-Qaddafi government

Source: Associated Press. Reproduced with permission.

blending of the primacists' vision with the liberal internationalists'. Although many liberal internationalists rejected the rationale for the preventive use of force in Iraq, most have few qualms about using the US military to establish no-fly zones, airlift food to refugees, patrol the boundaries between warring factions, and build infrastructure in the Third World.

Liberal internationalists lack the primacists' hostility toward multilateral bodies such as the International Criminal Court and the United Nations. They often praise decades of US pressure to create institutions like the World Trade Organization and the International Monetary Fund, which they credit for the prosperity benefits of globalization, even if the connection between those economic benefits and *military* aspects of US grand strategy is only a tenuous one. In practice, though, liberal internationalists are often willing to bypass multilateral organizations. For example, the Clinton administration did not seek UN authorization of the 1999 war in Kosovo, knowing that Russia and China would not give it. Instead, the administration chose to conduct Operation Allied Force under the auspices of NATO, which became window dressing on a campaign run primarily by American generals and fought primarily by American forces. Then in 2011, when they got UN authorization for a defensive operation to protect civilians in Libya, they used it to launch a regime-change mission against Libyan dictator Muammar Qaddafi – not really wanting to be bound by the confining strictures of a UN resolution.[22] Given how slow international institutions are to take root, liberal internationalists think that the United States should be prepared to carry the burden of bringing stability, democracy, and prosperity to others, at least for a long time while they reform international organizations to make them more suitable for their grand project.[23]

The third strategy, selective engagement, draws heavily on the school of thought known as realism, which has its roots in theorizing about the balance of power among the world's major industrial and military powers. In contrast to the first two strategies, selective engagers tend to be more skeptical about the uses to which US power can be put, and they are also wary of the potential for other nations to view US power as a danger and to balance against it if this power is not used carefully.[24] Selective engagers are not reluctant about the use of force, merely aware that it often has counterproductive results and unforeseen costs. Realists also often emphasize that US popular support, critical for sustaining military operations, fades quickly when true interests are not at stake.

The phrase "selective engagement" is attractive to Washington insiders, because it sounds reasonable and wise. Many experts in academia, the officer corps, and parts of the US Foreign Service subscribe to selective engagement. But many think tank advocates also claim to advocate this strategy, even when their actual beliefs lie closer to deep engagement or liberal internationalism (or a combination of the two). Unfortunately, selective engagers struggle to articulate a clear rule by which to decide whether the United States should act. They agree that the core interest is in preventing a great power war or a nuclear war anywhere. But then they also tend to worry about a global oil or environmental crisis or perceived threats to America's long-standing allies in Europe, Japan, and Korea. They are more victim to pluralist influences in American security policy than the more intellectually coherent strategic alternatives: the reason they cannot articulate and stick to a clear rule for American intervention is that the United States does not face any major threats to discipline their thinking.

The fourth strategy, restraint, has advocates among libertarians who wish to leave others alone in all aspects of life, progressive Democrats who wish to focus America's attention on its domestic problems, and a small slice of academics (including two of your authors).[25] In the broadest sense it, too, draws on realism, the principle that a state's grand strategy should reflect its power and interests. The basic argument, however, is that the United States lacks the need, the capability, and the mandate to manage global security. With the demise of the Soviet Union, the United States is a very secure nation, because of its favorable geography, large size, and wealth. It is the world's third most populous nation and has a very capable military built on years of research and development investments and much operational experience. Beyond concern about the danger of nuclear terrorism and true cases of genocide, the United States need pay little attention to distant turmoil, be it civil war or regional conflict. Intelligence agencies should watch for the rise of a peer competitor – notably, watch China's nascent capabilities, its intentions, and its uncertain domestic stability – but the need is for strategic warning rather than near-term tactical military intelligence.

Restrainers believe that locals have more insight – and greater interest – in addressing their own problems than the far-off United States can contribute. As long as the United States leaps forward with offers of assistance, others have an incentive to free-ride on the American efforts, as most of the other capable, wealthy, industrial countries of the world have done for decades. The world ends up with less successful efforts to manage crises, and the United States ends up with an unfair burden on its finances and its soldiers. Restrainers worry that the inclination to manage global security, so much a part of the American security and foreign policy establishment, is meddling to preserve organizational and personal interests rather than national ones. Critics label such restrainers as isolationists, although proponents of restraint make it clear that they do not wish the United States to withdraw from the world, only to avoid behaving as its self-appointed global sheriff.

There are significant differences among the strategies (see Table 2.1). In practice, however, the four strategies tend to blend into two. Primacists and liberal internationalists are global interveners, seeking to use America's leadership to manage global security and promote democratic values, and the phrase "deep engagement" most accurately describes the

Table 2.1 American grand strategies

Strategy	Primacy	Liberal internationalism	Selective engagement	Restraint
Other names	Deep engagement, the Bush doctrine	Cooperative security, liberal interventionism	Balance of power realism	Neo-isolationism, Trumpism
Major problem of international politics	Rise of a peer competitor	Indivisibility of peace; need to spread liberal values to everyone for anyone to be secure	Peace among the major powers	Avoiding entanglement in the affairs of others
Preferred world order	US hegemony, with all challengers quashed	Interdependence through spread of democracy, trade, international organizations	Balance of power	Distant balance of power
View of 2003 Iraq War	Strongly in favor: important demonstration of US military power in aftermath of 9/11	Mixed: Saddam was a threatening dictator, but US lacked international/UN support and post-conflict planning	Strongly against: an unnecessary distraction likely to sap US power and provoke backlash	Strongly against: no real threat from Iraq, especially since Iraq had nothing to do with 9/11
View of intervention in Syria	Strongly in favor: US should destroy the Islamic State threat to the US; depose Assad to restore US credibility, especially after US stated a "red line" on chemical weapons; and rebuke Russian involvement in the Middle East	In favor: only the US has the power to solve the humanitarian crisis; should have intervened sooner, because the situation has grown more complex and harder to resolve over time; diplomacy and economic aid are important along with military action	Against: generally view ISIS as the bigger threat to US interests and are willing to cooperate, explicitly or implicitly, with Russia (and the Assad regime) to stamp out ISIS threat; key points are to avoid clash with Russia and to minimize prospects of extremist Islamist terrorists	Strongly against: ISIS poses limited direct threat to US; its focus on holding territory in the Middle East and North Africa threatens regional powers much more, so they should be the ones to respond

(continued)

Table 2.1 (continued)

Strategy	Primacy	Liberal internationalism	Selective engagement	Restraint
View of NATO expansion and Ukraine crisis	Favored NATO expansion as a show of power; explain Russian assertiveness as reaction to US failure to expand NATO enough/ deploy enough troops to defend Europe	Favored NATO expansion as a way to expand the community of democracies; blame Russian assertiveness on Putin's authoritarian regime, which they hope to counteract with continued democracy promotion and capacity-building aid to Ukraine	Opposed NATO expansion as likely to antagonize Russia and saw little to be gained through security commitments to new members; threatening to fight Russia for a bankrupt, weak country like Ukraine is foolhardy	Not only opposed NATO expansion as irrelevant to core US national security interests but would prefer to withdraw from NATO, because the alliance defends rich, powerful countries that don't need US help; argue that US and European pressure to democratize Ukraine caused the crisis
View of nuclear proliferation	Only the US (and perhaps close allies, e.g., Israel) should have nuclear weapons; proliferation should be stopped through preventive war if necessary	Global nuclear disarmament should be ultimate US goal; norm against proliferation very important	Nuclear weapons key to maintaining peace among great powers; further proliferation should be limited through containment and deterrence, not preventive war	Not a major concern: US has limited ability to prevent proliferation, and military efforts to do so are likely to increase adversaries' desire for the bomb
What keeps them up at night	China	Syria, Libya, and other "ungoverned space"	China, resurgent Russia, threats to the flow of oil	America's crumbling infrastructure and hollowing economy
Implications for defense policy	Current defense budget far too small	At least maintain current level of defense spending	Modest defense cuts: optimize to fight other major powers	Dramatic defense cuts: focus on homeland defense, intel
Where you may have heard these arguments	"Neocons," Bush administration, American Enterprise Institute, Project for a New American Century, academics such as Eliot Cohen and William Wohlforth	Clinton administration, some in Obama administration (Samantha Power, Anne-Marie Slaughter), Brookings Institution, Center for New American Security	Some in Obama administration (Robert Gates), academics such as Robert Art and Steve Walt. Intellectual lineage traces to Henry Kissinger, Hans Morgenthau	Cato Institute, academics such as Harvey Sapolsky, Eugene Gholz, and Barry Posen

modern mixture of these two strategies. Many selective engagers are also often tempted to meddle, though others usually find reasons to avoid advocating American military intervention in foreign disputes and end up close to the restrainers' position on many issues. The academic debate is really between restraint and deep engagement; in the policy world, the debate is usually limited to fights about various possible means of deep engagement and thus is not a true grand strategy debate at all.

Military officers may privately prefer one grand strategy to another, but their strategic pronouncements are usually limited to the promotion of operational concepts that are only marginally linked to true grand strategy. They are best viewed as doctrinal guides to justify or avoid particular programs. For example, the US Navy and the US Air Force, having found it difficult to gain much of a role in the counterinsurgency-heavy doctrinal environment of the Global War on Terror, promoted the concept of Air–Sea Battle, later renamed the Joint Concept for Access and Maneuver in the Global Commons. Their idea emphasizes the use of air and naval power to ensure US access to potential theaters of conflict, although over time they found roles for land forces in the concept, too, recognizing that it is easier to co-opt organizational adversaries rather than fight them head-on. Conveniently, Air–Sea Battle also suggests a vision of warfare that requires investment in platforms that the Air Force and the Navy have long sought, such as a longer-range stealthy manned bomber for the Air Force. But Air–Sea Battle is only a means, unlike a true grand strategy that would explain US priorities and the ways in which military, economic, and diplomatic policy tools help achieve those goals.

Constraints on American security policy

American security strategy is unlikely to be as clear and coherent as the ideal types, but all policy is not ad hoc, because American values, conditions, and the core constitutional framework change very slowly. Some security policy options are clearly more compatible with American experience than others. Alex Roland, a leading historian of technology, identified several of the constraints and explored their consequences for American security strategy.[26] With some modification, his main themes are America's labor scarcity, suspicions of a standing army, free security, civilian control of the military, and military resistance to change.

America has been a society that generally welcomes immigration. As a nation growing to fill out a continent, it has felt a perpetual labor shortage. Militarily, this condition translates into a desire to avoid casualties, a pressure to husband human resources. America's growing wealth and deepening democracy have surely reinforced this desire. Wealth allows the United States to substitute capital for labor. It is easier for the United States to buy more technology than to recruit more soldiers. America's use of force is constrained by the will and ability of its society to sustain casualties.

America's recent competitors have not been in a similar situation. For example, compared to the United States, the Soviet Union had few political constraints on its recruitment and treatment of soldiers and thus could develop military plans that expended soldiers generously. China is the same today. Labor is politically expensive in democracies, which require accountability. Soldiers' deaths have to be explained to their families and other voters. Even in the early days of the Afghanistan War, when the United States truly had its back up, fighting against a fundamentalist foe that had attacked us first, the military delayed some attacks to await combat search and rescue units that would reduce the threat of casualties. Later in that war – and in the Iraq War – casualties sapped American political support. More and more, casualties are the third rail of American security policy. It is no wonder that the American military has been known for its emphasis on firepower, its preference for airpower, and its interest in providing material support for deployed forces. The alleged gold-plating of American weapons systems may have several origins, but surely the notion that "nothing is too good for American boys" is one of them.

The Founding Fathers had English heritage and felt that they were part of the long struggle to restrict the powers of monarchy and its instruments. They were appropriately suspicious of standing armies, as they had suffered under one billeted in the colonies. Article 1 of the Constitution restricts funding of an army to two years. The Second Amendment, which is best known for pronouncing the right of citizens to bear arms, talks of the maintenance of a "well-regulated militia." The citizen-soldier protecting his home, organized by the states, was the preferred way to defend the new nation. Certainly, nations needed armies, but America's would be closely watched and small. The legacy is that, despite its global power, the United States relies in part on state-based forces: the National Guard. Although the National Guard and private gun ownership no longer provide an actual military check on the power of the national government, the federal government still periodically argues with the states and their congressional representatives about the Guard's mission and equipment. In peacetime, supporters of the Guard act as a built-in lobby to limit the size and wealth of active duty forces.

Roland's third constraint is geographic. In this sense the United States is a truly blessed nation. Unlike Poland, which lives between Germany and Russia, the United States has Canada and Mexico on its borders, hardly military giants. Unlike Israel, which is nearly surrounded by hostile nations, the United States is mostly surrounded by fish – thanks to the Atlantic and Pacific Oceans, the Gulf of Mexico, and the Great Lakes. The United States has not been invaded since 1812, and, leaving aside the Cold War's threat of nuclear attack, has not experienced a serious challenge to its survival as a nation since the Civil War. The land is rich in resources; the people are industrious. Much of America's security is free. And as a result, America is often unprepared for its international challenges, unconsciously counting on having time to mobilize before it will have to meet them. The first battles are often lost while the military recovers from the happy lull of free security that geography and fate have given the nation.

Civilian control of the military is also a fundamental premise of America's security posture. Civilian control was easy to achieve when American security depended upon militias, the citizen-soldiers of the early American experience. Officers were usually elected, and mobilization of troops, who came with much of their own equipment, required the consent of the soldiers directly or indirectly through the votes of state legislatures. But even as military activities became more professionalized, the United States did not abandon the principle. Civilian officials make major decisions, including setting priorities for both weapons acquisitions and military campaigns. Generals sometimes get fired. Domestic political interests, as crass as they may be, have a role in making national strategy, for strategy-making at its heart is about setting national priorities. It requires coalition-building, side payments, log rolling, and all the other elements of democratic politics.

The last of Roland's list of constraints, a military resistance to change, is the one that requires modification. Surely no one can claim that the US military since World War II has resisted technological change. The armed services have been the big promoters of technology, famous for their free spending and gullibility – witness such projects as the atomic-powered aircraft, the nuclear cannon, and the 20-ton tank. The services only resist changes in doctrine that threaten to weaken their standing relative to the other services or to shake up the hierarchy of communities within their service. The battleship admirals have disappeared, but carrier admirals replaced them, so the Navy came to favor the new technology. Sometimes a particular service will even invest in an innovation precisely because it promises to help the service compete against the others. Promotion opportunities and choice commands rest on the status hierarchies within and among the services. Military leaders carefully consider new technologies' implications, and they decide their preferences for potential innovations accordingly.

Roland's list also requires an important addition: the need to consider the impact defense spending will have on the American economy. As Princeton University political scientist Aaron Friedberg points out in his important work on the political economy of defense during the Cold War, the fear of destroying prosperity constrained mobilization for the Cold War.[27] Universal military training was proposed as a way to ensure the existence of an army large enough to meet the Soviet challenge. Some policy-makers also suggested a conscious effort to force American industry to relocate away from the coasts to make a surprise air attack or invasion from the sea harder. But these and other proposals were easily pushed aside because Americans were unwilling to jeopardize an economy that was recovering from World War II and the Great Depression.

Friedberg emphasizes President Eisenhower's recognition that the Cold War would be a long struggle, requiring not only a strong military but also a strong economy. Social scientists worried that the United States would come to resemble its opponent during a long struggle, a "garrison state" that ran roughshod over civil liberties. But American politicians could not easily ignore the demands of voters for consumer goods and the freedom not to wear a uniform. In the end, the constraint proved valuable, because the consumer-oriented prosperity of the West destroyed the morale of the deprived citizens of the East, undermining communism and the Soviet-led Warsaw Pact.

The American way of warfare

There is a distinctly American way of warfare. No other nation quite matches it. It is the product of the nation's wealth, geography, political system, and the other factors cited in the previous section, and it is especially clear in modern war. The phrase "The American Way of War" is actually the title of a famous book by Russell Weigley, a military historian who emphasized the formative experience of the Civil War in arguing that the United States tends to seek total victory, usually by the brutal application of firepower to annihilate opposing forces and compel unconditional surrender.[28] But that view of the American way of war has been justly criticized as too narrow and too dependent on the technology available at particular times in American history. As Eliot Cohen has pointed out, there are many continuities in American warfare that considerably predate the Civil War – for example, its goal of total victory – but at the same time, the United States has a long tradition of irregular warfare and fighting in other ways that do not rely on large land armies in climactic battles of annihilation.[29]

More important, the American Way of War really emphasizes the application of American ingenuity, which has flourished in the modern era. In another important article, Eliot Cohen discussed "the mystique of U.S. airpower," although it might be better described as the irresistible promise of airpower, an optimistic belief in a technological solution to warfare.[30] The use of aircraft in war began with World War I, which demonstrated in horrendous clarity the human cost of ground warfare in the industrial age. The United States joined the war late, but American infantry still died in the tens of thousands fighting against massed artillery and the machine gun. Airpower proponents saw the advantages of bypassing the trenches and taking the fight to the enemy's leaders and key sources of its power such as its industry and its transportation system. The proposed air attacks would be at the strategic level rather than supporting a state's military operations against enemy soldiers at the front – hence the name for the new military doctrine, "strategic bombing." The promise of wars with decisive results and without the sacrifice of a generation of the nation's young men crossing the killing fields on foot formed an irresistible temptation.[31]

Strategic bombing has proven especially appealing to the United States and Britain. After World War I, neither had any intention of returning to ground warfare on the European Continent. In 1940, the Royal Air Force, later joined by the American Army Air Force, initiated a strategic bombing campaign on a mammoth scale against Nazi Germany, Italy, and territory occupied by Axis forces. Later, the US Army Air Force initiated a similar campaign against Japan. The efforts were hardly cost-free. Well over 50,000 British and American air crew members lost their lives in the European bombing campaign, and thousands more died in the American campaign to take islands to use as bases for the strategic bombing of Japan. Building and supporting the bombers cost more than a quarter of the war's total expenditures on the Allied side. Upwards of one million Germans, Japanese, Italians, French and others, civilians as well as soldiers, were killed in the bombing raids, which included incendiary attacks against German and Japanese cities and the dropping of atomic bombs on Hiroshima and Nagasaki.

The strategic bombing raids had mixed effects at best. Despite pretensions to "precision bombing," both American and British attacks hit targets nearly at random, owing to technological limitations.[32] Efforts to assign and destroy specific targets were largely self-deceiving. Germany did devote significant resources to fighting the bombers, resources that could have been used in its multi-front ground war. The bombing, however, neither destroyed the Nazi regime nor halted German war production. Its biggest contribution was wearing down the German interceptor force, establishing the air superiority later needed for the invasion of Normandy. Meanwhile, Japan continued to resist despite the brutal conventional bombing campaign. Modern societies and economies turn out to be more resilient to foreign attacks than strategic bombing advocates had presumed.[33]

Nevertheless, strategic bombing was widely accepted as having been proven by the World War II experience. The US Air Force gained independence from the Army on the basis that strategic bombing was a separate and highly effective way to win wars.[34] Nuclear weapons were the obvious way to overcome accuracy problems, as they made near-misses irrelevant. Qualms about civilian casualties faded as the public contemplated images of conventional combat against the communist hordes from the East.

Soon, of course, there were conventional wars to fight, because the Cold War evolved into a nuclear stalemate and a competition to support allies in civil wars over the control of particular countries. Nuclear weapons were too dangerous to use in these conflicts, and few strategic targets were available anyway. The bombing of civilian targets quickly became off-limits, in part because such targeting could potentially force an escalation but also because the struggles were supposedly for the allegiance of the population in an ideological conflict. Direct attacks on the regime providing materiel support for the enemy (i.e., China or the Soviet Union) were also deterred by the threat of nuclear escalation. By the time of the Vietnam War, the restrictions on the fighting were seen by large segments of the publics in the West to indicate that the stakes were quite low, and thus the war was not worth the casualties that were being incurred by Americans and Vietnamese, soldiers and civilians, friends and foes.

Since the end of the Cold War, the American government has been hard-pressed to justify casualties of all kind.[35] The rhetoric for those advocating fighting has escalated – "the future of NATO is at risk"; "we are seeking to prevent another Holocaust"; "Saddam is another Hitler" – but not the willingness to sacrifice or to be brutal. Even the attacks of September 11th have not given license for the return of total war with its near-complete tolerance of killing and destruction.

Technology has adjusted. American wars are now largely precise affairs. The armed services use laser- and GPS-guided bombs, thermal targeting sensors, long-range conventionally armed missiles, special transmitters and digital maps to identify all friendly forces, and non-lethal weapons. The American military has to answer when innocents are killed, bombs go astray, vital infrastructure is destroyed, and American service members die, even in accidents. The strange expectation is that coercion can take place without much death and destruction. The use of drones for the targeted killing of enemy combatants even in formally neutral countries is the latest iteration. Americans want technology to identify specific "bad" people from afar and also to kill precisely those "bad" people and no others – again, from afar.[36]

Americans certainly have not given up on achieving the elusive promise of airpower. Despite the disbanding of Strategic Air Command after the end of the Cold War, the fundamental premise of strategic attack remains embedded in the American approach to war. It is evident in everything from the attempts to kill Saddam Hussein during the opening nights of Operation Iraqi Freedom to the conversion of US nuclear ballistic missile submarines into platforms for conventional missiles said to be suitable for hunting terrorists as well as for destroying air defenses. The belief is that there is still a set of targets that, if successfully attacked, will collapse the enemy's ability to resist, even if its fielded forces remain intact. There is, in military parlance, a "center of gravity," which alone holds the key to victory at low cost. It may be the other side's industrial cities, its population, its leaders, its military command structure, its tactical geniuses or nuclear scientists, or some combination of the above. The technology inflicting the destruction need not be a manned strategic bomber. It can be a ballistic missile fired from the United States or electrons launched in a cyber attack. The launch platform can be manned or not. No deaths are required, and destruction of enemy armies, populations, and infrastructure is not a goal in itself. All that is needed is for the opponent to unravel.[37]

This promise will continue to drive American military research and development investments. Precision weapons are the hallmarks of American attacks. Rather than oppose the acquisition of unmanned aerial vehicles (UAVs), the armed services compete to design and field them, because whichever service can offer the best UAV can claim the most relevance to American strategy and the most prestige. Plans call for robots to supply forward forces and to give these forces sensors and weapons with greater range and accuracy than those of their adversaries. The promise of networked, rapid, and precise warfare is seductive to a society that wants to exercise its global power without sacrificing its soldiers or losing its moral compass. The transformation of the American military has no lesser goals.

What is not clear is whether or not this form of warfare is achievable. The technology to strike identified stationary targets is at hand. Ongoing R&D projects promise to link sensors and weapons together sufficiently to allow effective attacks against mobile targets; they hope that capability is right around the corner, as they have for several decades. But acquiring the knowledge to identify precisely the vital centers of complex societies is surely a very difficult task. Except in the most hierarchical of social systems, there is not likely to be a single linchpin that can be pulled. Scientists can design the weapons, but social scientists have no idea where they should be pointed to achieve a quick and near-bloodless victory, the victory that the doctrine of strategic bombing and the broader American way of warfare promise.

Questions for discussion

1   Why is the lack of a clear enemy such a challenge to America's ability to select and implement a coherent grand strategy?

2   Are debates about the potential and costs of nation-building necessarily fundamental to debates about American grand strategy?

3   When should problems with the means become serious enough that a country should give up on certain strategic goals?

4   Why have primacy and liberal internationalism blended so easily into a common US grand strategy?

5   Would the American armed services each have a favorite grand strategy, if they were allowed to select one?

6   Which of the main historical themes of American strategy, and which aspects of the American way of war, predispose the United States to choose the role of "global policeman?" Which serve more to restrain US strategy?

7   If it is so hard to implement a coherent grand strategy, why bother concocting one?

Notes

1 Barry R. Posen, *The Sources of Military Doctrine* (Ithaca, NY: Cornell University Press, 1984), Chapter 1.
2 John Lewis Gaddis, *Strategies of Containment: A Critical Appraisal of American National Security Policy during the Cold War* (New York: Oxford University Press, rev. and expanded ed. 2005).
3 John Lewis Gaddis, "International Relations Theory and the End of the Cold War," *International Security*, 17(3) (Winter 1992–1993): 5–58.
4 For example, Geoffrey Kemp and Janice Gross Stein (eds.), *Powder Keg in the Middle East: The Struggle for Gulf Security* (Lanham, MD: Rowman & Littlefield, 1995); Aaron L. Friedberg, "Ripe for Rivalry: Prospects for Peace in a Multipolar Asia," *International Security*, 18(3) (Winter 1993–1994): 5–33; Susan L. Woodward, *Balkan Tragedy: Chaos and Dissolution after the Cold War* (Washington, DC: Brookings Institution, 1995).
5 Robert Rotberg, *When States Fail: Causes and Consequences* (Princeton, NJ: Princeton University Press, 2004); Robert D. Kaplan, "The Coming Anarchy," *The Atlantic* (February 1994).
6 Admiral William A. Owens, with Edward Offley, *Lifting the Fog of War* (New York: Farrar, Straus, Giroux, 2000).
7 John Alexander, *Future War: Non-Lethal Weapons in Twenty-First Century Warfare* (New York: St. Martin's Press, 1999).
8 Robert Jervis, "Mission Impossible: Creating a Grand Strategy," in D. J. Caraley (ed.), *The New American Interventionism* (New York: Columbia Press, 1999), pp. 205–218.
9 A government copy of the September 2002 *National Security Strategy* is available at: http://www.state.gov/documents/organization/63562.pdf (accessed September 2, 2016). For an archive of the various versions of the document over the years, see http://nssarchive.us.
10 Barry R. Posen, "The Case for Restraint," *The American Interest*, 3(2) (November–December 2007): 7–17.
11 Francis Fukuyama (ed.), *Nation-Building: Beyond Afghanistan and Iraq* (Baltimore, MD: Johns Hopkins University Press, 2006).
12 David Edelstein, *Occupational Hazards: Success and Failure in Military Occupation* (Ithaca, NY: Cornell University Press, 2008); Alexander B. Downes and Jonathan Monten, "Forced to Be Free? Why Foreign-Imposed Regime Change Rarely Leads to Democratization," *International Security*, 37(4) (Spring 2013): 90–131.
13 Stephen Biddle, Jeffrey A. Friedman, and Jacob N. Shapiro, "Testing the Surge: Why Did Violence Decline in Iraq in 2007?" *International Security*, 37(1) (Summer 2012): 7–40.
14 Graeme Wood, "What ISIS Really Wants," *The Atlantic* (March 2015).
15 Daniel Byman, "ISIS Goes Global," *Foreign Affairs*, 95(2) (March/April 2016): 76–85.

16 US Department of Defense, *Sustaining U.S. Global Leadership: Priorities for the 21st Century* (Washington, DC: US Department of Defense, 2012).
17 Barry R. Posen and Andrew Ross, "Competing Visions for US Grand Strategy," *International Security*, 21(3) (Winter 1996–1997): 5–53.
18 Stephen Brooks and William C. Wohlforth, *America Abroad: The United States' Global Role in the 21st Century* (New York: Oxford University Press, 2016).
19 For an early explanation of primacy, see "U.S. Strategy Plan Calls for Insuring No Rivals Develop: A One-Superpower World," *New York Times*, March 8, 1992.
20 Stephen G. Brooks, G. John Ikenberry, and William Wohlforth, "Don't Come Home, America: The Case Against Retrenchment," *International Security*, 37(3) (Winter 2012/13): 7–51.
21 The underlying logic is also explained in a number of policy papers, including Ashton B. Carter, William J. Perry, and John D. Steinbruner, *A New Concept of Cooperative Security*, occasional paper (Washington, DC: Brookings Institution, 1992).
22 Alan J. Kuperman, "Obama's Libya Debacle: How a Well-Meaning Intervention Ended in Failure," *Foreign Affairs*, 94(2) (March/April 2015).
23 G. John Ikenberry and Anne-Marie Slaughter, co-directors, *Forging a World of Liberty under Law: U.S. National Security in the 21st Century*, Final Report of the Princeton Project on National Security, September 27, 2006.
24 Robert J. Art, "Selective Engagement after Bush," in Michèle A. Flournoy and Shawn Brimley, eds., *Finding Our Way: Debating American Grand Strategy* (Washington, DC: Center for a New American Security, June 2008); Stephen Van Evera, "Why Europe Matters, Why the Third World Doesn't: American Grand Strategy after the Cold War," *Journal of Strategic Studies*, 13(2) (June 1990): 1–51.
25 Eugene Gholz, Daryl G. Press, and Harvey M. Sapolsky, "Come Home, America: The Strategy of Restraint in the Face of Temptation," *International Security*, 21(4) (Spring 1997): 5–48.
26 Alex Roland, "Technology, Ground Warfare, and Strategy: The Paradox of American Experience," *Journal of Military History*, 55(4) (October 1991): 447–467.
27 Aaron L. Friedberg, "Why Didn't the United States Become a Garrison State?" *International Security*, 16(4) (Spring 1994): 109–142; Aaron L. Friedberg, *In the Shadow of the Garrison State: America's Anti-Statism and Its Cold War Grand Strategy* (Princeton, NJ: Princeton University Press, 2000).
28 Russell Weigley, *The American Way of War: A History of United States Military Strategy and Policy* (New York: Macmillan, 1973).
29 Eliot A. Cohen, *Conquered into Liberty: Two Centuries of Battles along the Great Warpath That Made the American Way of War* (New York: Free Press, 2011).
30 Eliot Cohen, "The Mystique of U.S. Air Power," *Foreign Affairs*, 73(1) (January/February 1994): 109–124.
31 Tami Davis Biddle, *Rhetoric and Reality in Air Warfare: The Evolution of British and American Ideas About Strategic Bombing, 1914–1945* (Princeton, NJ: Princeton University Press, 2002).
32 Noble Frankland, *Bomber Offensive: The Devastation of Europe* (New York: Ballantine Books, 1970).
33 Robert A. Pape, *Bombing to Win: Air Power and Coercion in War* (Ithaca, NY: Cornell University Press, 1996).
34 Perry McCoy Smith, *The Air Force Plans for Peace, 1943–1945* (Baltimore, MD: Johns Hopkins University Press, 1970).
35 Harvey M. Sapolsky and Jeremy Shapiro, "Casualties, Technology and America's Future Wars," *Parameters*, 26(2) (Summer 1996): 119–127.
36 Matthew Evangelista and Henry Shue (eds.), *The American Way of Bombing: Changing Ethical and Legal Norms, from Flying Fortresses to Drones* (Ithaca, NY: Cornell University Press, 2014); John Kaag and Sarah Kreps, *Drone Warfare* (Malden, MA: Polity Press, 2014): 108–139, 175–176.
37 John A. Warden, *The Air Campaign: Planning for Combat* (Washington, DC: Pergamon-Brassey's, 1989).

Recommended additional reading

Andrew Bacevich, *America's War for the Greater Middle East* (New York: Random House, 2016). Names the war that has no name, a conflict fueled by political hubris and plagued by poor generalship.

David H. Bayley and Robert M. Perito, *The Police in War: Fighting Insurgency, Terrorism, and Violent Crime* (New York: Lynne Rienner, 2010). America discovers it needs a colonial service if it is going to provide internal security and good government to others.

Ian Bremmer, *Superpower: Three Choices for America's Role in the World* (New York: Portfolio/ Penguin, 2015). An insightful policy analyst envisions the strategy options and pleads for Americans to choose a grand strategy in the 2016 election.

Michael E. Brown, Owen R. Coté Jr., Sean M. Lynn-Jones, and Steven E. Miller (eds.), *America's Strategic Choices* (Cambridge, MA: MIT Press, rev. ed. 2000). All the grand strategic alternatives argued by their academic advocates.

Aaron L. Friedberg, *In the Shadow of the Garrison State: America's Anti-Statism and Its Cold War Strategy* (Princeton, NJ: Princeton University Press, 2000). Examines how American political and economic values shaped strategy in the nation's longest war.

John Lewis Gaddis, *Strategies of Containment: A Critical Appraisal of Postwar American National Security Policy* (New York: Oxford University Press, rev and expanded ed. 2005). The classic recounting of the ebbs and flows of America's Cold War grand strategy.

David Rieff, *At the Point of a Gun: Democratic Dreams and Armed Intervention* (New York: Simon & Schuster, 2005). Reality sets in on the hopes of interventionists.

Astri Suhrke, *When More Is Less: The International Project in Afghanistan* (London: Hurst & Co., 2012). Overwhelming Afghanistan with money and ambitious but unrealistic projects, all in the effort to save it.

3 Organizing for defense

The evolution of US civil–military relations

All four of the enduring questions of US defense policy feature in debates about how the United States should organize its national security effort. The broad boundaries are contained in the Constitution, which limits and divides powers among the branches of government and between the state and federal governments, but the relationship between the president and the military, and among the armed services within the military, is defined in laws, the most important of which is the National Security Act of 1947. It established the Department of Defense (DoD) to preside over the military after the end of World War II.

The struggles over creating the department and the first phase of reforms to it emphasized management efficiency (the question of centralization) and holding military policy accountable to elected leaders (the question of how much market-like competition among military organizations is desirable). Delimiting the circumstances when political interests should override professional military judgment – and figuring out how to get adequate military expert advice to civilian policy-makers – always hangs in the background of defense reform discussions, but it became especially salient in the second half of the Cold War and the post-Cold War era. Over time, the role of private interests also increased in developing and selling weapons and in staffing the military bureaucracy and even fighting forces, but that subject is primarily covered in later chapters.

The debates over the four enduring questions are always settled politically, reflecting the organizational interests of the participants as much as idealistic appeals to "good government." Sometimes one side wins, but other times the outcome is compromise that none of the advocates likes. The real world seems always to bring up a new set of challenges not long after a round of the debate is settled, offering an opportunity to "renegotiate" the decision.

A brief history of defense organization

Prior to World War II, the relations between the armed service departments (there were only two of them then) were quite limited. The shoreline provided a natural division of labor, with the Army responsible for defense on land and the Navy responsible for protecting the nation's interests at sea and abroad. If the Army was needed overseas, the Navy would help transport it and would maintain the logistics linkage to the United States. Coordination was achieved through a Joint Army/Navy Board. The services basically led independent lives, reporting to separate cabinet secretaries and congressional committees.

World War II forced a closer collaboration between the armed services than had existed previously, in large part because of the war's global scope and great intensity. There were invasions to coordinate, priorities to agree upon, and scarce resources to divide. There was also a need to match the top level of British military structure, which featured a general as the senior military officer, ranking above the British service chiefs. For this purpose Admiral William D. Leahy of the US Chiefs of Staff became Chief of Staff to the Commander-in-Chief, acting as a chairman of a committee that included Army General George C. Marshall, Army General Hap Arnold (on the committee as the head of the Air Force, which was part of the Army at that time), and Admiral Ernest King, the Chief of Naval Operations (CNO). Although operating at times under unified theater commanders, the armed services largely fought independent wars, with the Navy focused on the Pacific, the Army on Europe, and the Army Air Force on strategic bombing. Each service wanted to claim that it had made the greatest contribution to victory, so each had an incentive to coordinate only at arm's length; this sort of independence may have been most important to the Air Force because of its domestic political fight to break off from the Army as a third military department.[1] In the end, victory in World War II came more through a vast industrial mobilization that produced an overwhelming supply of ships, airplanes, and armored vehicles than through the clever coordination of US forces.[2]

At the end of the war, critics complained about the war's management. It was clear that the United States would need to maintain a sizable military in keeping with new global responsibilities, but the country's leaders wanted to avoid what they saw as the waste and duplication that had characterized mobilization for World War II. The main interest was in unification, the establishment of an administrative structure to link the services together and provide centralized direction to their activities.[3]

Some of the services saw opportunities to gain through the postwar reorganization; others fought for their organizational lives. The Army Air Force wanted independence, which the Army was happy to give because generals in the infantry, armor, and artillery branches feared that increasingly popular Air Force leaders would come to dominate the Army's top positions and budget priorities. In turn, the Army wanted to absorb or eliminate the Marine Corps, which it saw as a duplicative ground force. With its independence assured, the Air Force sought control of naval aviation, including Marine Corps aviation, on the argument that all aviation ought to be under central direction.

Two basic plans emerged from the discussions. The Collins Plan, which was the product of an Army task force led by Lieutenant General J. Lawton Collins, called for what many term a general staff model: a centralized structure with a clear hierarchy including a single top military leader, the Chief of the General Staff; a single top civilian, the secretary of the armed forces; and centralized supporting institutions such as a single, military-wide procurement agency, an integrated budget, and unified theater commands to oversee activities in each region of the world.

The counter was the Eberstadt Plan, named after Ferdinand Eberstadt, an aide to the Secretary of the Navy James Forrestal. This plan reflected the Navy's historic skepticism of centralization. The Navy ideal entrusted authority to the captain of each ship, so he could make quick decisions when he was on his own, over the horizon, out of touch from centralized leadership. Moreover, the Navy feared that in a general staff structure its interests would be subordinated to those of what would be the always-larger Army. The Eberstadt Plan essentially offered more of the same, a copy of the World War II structure with lots of committees, no senior military officer, no budgetary integration, and no one short of the president who could make binding decisions across the services. The Marine Corps allied with the Navy in supporting decentralization, which would preserve the Navy's own air force and army – meaning the organizational independence of the Marine Corps.

The National Security Act of 1947, still the foundation of America's global military power, implemented the Eberstadt Plan with some titles borrowed from the Collins Plan. It provided for a national military establishment – including a Department of Defense with a cabinet-ranked secretary, three armed services, a National Security Council, and a Central Intelligence Agency (CIA) – but not a general staff or a centralizing authority. Nearly everything depended upon committees with chairs rotating among the services and no central budget control. The secretary of defense was one among equals, because the secretaries of the services, including the newly created secretary of the Air Force, had independent power and cabinet seats of their own. The structure was weak and unstable. Fittingly, President Truman, a proponent of more unification, chose Secretary of the Navy Forrestal to be the first secretary of defense, and thus to have the task of coping with the bureaucratic mess that he had helped design. The strain on the secretary was apparently enormous as the Cold War was starting amid restricted budgets, the continuing occupations of Germany and Japan, and a flood of technological opportunities that had emerged from World War II. Forrestal lasted just over a year as secretary of defense, and he took his own life shortly after leaving the job.

One of the early challenges facing the secretary of defense was the competition among the services for control of America's nuclear weapons and the weapon platforms that would have the range to reach the Soviet Union. The Air Force sought funds for the giant B-36, an eight-engined long-range bomber, while the Navy planned for the construction of the supercarrier USS *United States*, a ship large enough to accommodate attack aircraft sized to deliver nuclear weapons to Soviet targets. In 1949, when Secretary of Defense Louis Johnson (Forrestal had already resigned) decided to cancel the carrier in favor of the bomber, the Navy resisted the adverse decision and took its case public.

The dispute came to be known as the "Revolt of the Admirals." A naval staff office called OP-23, headed by Captain Arleigh A. Burke, who would in less than a decade become a four-star admiral and the chief of naval operations, coordinated an effort to use friendly journalists to criticize the capabilities of the B-36, including calling its development a "wasteful blunder." Friendly sources passed around stories that Secretary of the Air Force Stuart Symington, later elected senator from Missouri, and others close to the Truman administration had financial ties to General Dynamics, the B-36 contractor. When the corruption charges were shown to be unproven and were traced back to the Navy, several admirals, including the chief of naval operations, and several Navy civilians, including the secretary of the Navy, were forced to resign; other officers had their promotion opportunities eliminated. Captain Burke, although cleared of any wrongdoing, was effectively under house arrest for a period. The incident indicated both the intensity of inter-service competition and the ill discipline that existed within the newly created Department of Defense.[4]

These early struggles led quickly to reforms to make the new department manageable, primarily changes to centralize the civilian side of American national security organization, along the lines of the Collins Plan. In 1949, amendments to the National Security Act established the position of chairman of the Joint Chiefs of Staff (JCS; then just the Chiefs of the Army, Navy, and Air Force, but expanded over the years to include the commandant of the Marine Corps and the chief of the National Guard Bureau as well as a vice chairman drawn, like the chairman, from one of the services). The amendments also created chairmen and for the several other inter-service committees and boards that were used to coordinate defense research, nuclear weapons policy, and the like. They also started to create permanent staff positions for those committees to enhance their analytical and oversight capabilities, sorely lacking under the original organization; those staffs started small in 1949, but today they have grown into the large superstructure of the Office of the Secretary of Defense, which has more than a thousand civilian employees.[5] The 1949 amendments also removed the service secretaries from the cabinet, making them subordinate to the secretary of defense, an important step in civilian centralization.

The civilian side of the Department of Defense gained even more formal power relative to the military side with another reform in 1958. The new law allowed the secretary of defense to reorganize the department at will. The services were to be only "separately organized," not "separately administered," as they previously had been, which in theory meant that the uniforms denoting separate identities could stay but not the parochial attitudes. The reforms also gave "joint" commanders operational control of the service components of unified commands – putting a single general or admiral in charge of all American forces in a particular region or performing a particular category of mission, supported of course by component commanders from each service. These joint operational commanders, initially called Commanders-in-Chief (CINCs) of unified and specified commands (President George W. Bush later changed the name to combatant commanders, COCOMs), reported to the secretary of defense rather than to the services' Chiefs of Staff, so the reform stripped the service chiefs of their role in the direct management of deployed forces. It also created several centralized defense agencies such as the Defense Nuclear Agency and the Defense Advanced Research Projects Agency that were under the direct supervision of the secretary of defense, who also controlled the agencies' budgets. That meant that the service budgets shrank as a percentage of the total spending on the national military establishment.

The net result was a tight hierarchy on the civilian side of the Department of Defense. If he chose to, the secretary of defense could control the services in their role as providers of military equipment and trainers of military personnel, the so-called "Title 10 functions" (a reference to the US Code of Laws). Given that the secretary was also in the operational chain of command that linked the president as Commander-in-Chief to field forces in the joint operational commands, the secretary of defense became a very powerful government post.

Soon thereafter, in the 1960s, Robert S. McNamara, secretary of defense under Presidents Kennedy and Johnson, would exercise these powers. McNamara antagonized the services by his willingness to overrule military judgments regarding both the design of weapons and the conduct of combat. Because the Vietnam War was such a costly disaster, it is not surprising that major friction developed between senior officers and the secretary of defense. But what set off a generation of military distrust of civilian officials was McNamara's dismissive manner, some would say arrogance, in dealing with the military. McNamara, a former automobile executive, suspected that the services' organizational and professional interests impaired military judgment. He and other critics argued that what the military called "professional advice" often really reflected "servicism," the tendency to promote the goals of one's own service at the expense of overall military effectiveness. Of course, military leaders had some experience and information that a former auto executive did not, and even the military's self-serving organizational and professional interests should not be totally ignored, as much as McNamara wished they could be. The real questions are how to achieve an appropriate balance that recognizes military interests and expertise without giving in to servicism, and how to maintain the goodwill that enables government to function well even in the face of disagreements. The destruction of goodwill was perhaps McNamara's biggest failure.[6]

Some think that American civil–military relations should have been even more strained by the long agony of the Vietnam War than they appear to have been. They chide the Joint Chiefs not for their actions but for their silence – for not standing up to the president and secretary of defense with advice that the political leaders might not have wanted to hear, especially in the war's early stages.[7] Instead, as difficult as the war was to fight, both in the field and politically, conflict between senior military leaders and the president was never a public issue. Policy disputes were played out in a contest of media leaks and counter-leaks that avoided direct confrontation. The Army sought to shift blame for failure to civilians by asking for troop increases senior officers knew would not be approved – perhaps passive-aggressive behavior, but not direct resistance to civilian control.[8]

A new set of post-McNamara critics clamored for a new set of reforms. A string of operational failures in the 1970s and early 1980s – the botched attempt to rescue seamen captured on the *Mayaguez*, a US merchant ship off Cambodia, the failed 1980 attempt to free US embassy personnel held hostage by student radicals in Iran, the 1983 terrorist bombing of the Marine barracks in Beirut, and the less-than-stellar performance of US forces that invaded Grenada in 1984 – led to the 1986 Goldwater–Nichols Act. Reformers blamed the operational mishaps on the services' inability to work together during missions and hoped to increase "jointness" in planning and training the armed forces. "Jointness" is a term widely used by defense experts to denote some form of smooth inter-service cooperation. It is not clear, however, that jointness would have changed the outcomes in any of these incidents.

Nevertheless, Congress passed the Goldwater–Nichols Act, increasing centralization of military organization. Among other things, the law made experience in a joint billet – that is, working for a central staff rather than a service-specific one – a requirement for promotion to flag rank (general or admiral) and for service as chairman of the Joint Chiefs. In other words, Goldwater–Nichols meant that any ambitious officer who wanted to rise within his own service would have to serve in more than one assignment that involved close cooperation with another service (and for a Marine, serving on a Navy staff does not count). The joint experience would give officers a better cultural understanding of their counterparts from other services, facilitating trust during operations, and also would make operations follow plans developed by joint organizations, supposedly limiting service parochialism. In a real sense, the Act brought a degree of centralization to the military side of the Defense Department that matched the centralization that had already been achieved on the civilian side.[9]

Pressure for jointness has had unintended consequences. Different types of jointness have different advantages and disadvantages. Operational jointness refers to the ability of forces from different services to fight together effectively in battle. It is often achieved by having different services train together and by equipping the services with compatible systems (especially for communications). For example, Navy and Marine aircraft provide electronic jamming for Air Force aircraft, while Air Force tankers routinely refuel Navy and Marine aircraft. Doctrinal jointness involves agreeing, formally, that certain concepts or procedures will govern service interactions – that is, striving to make the "fundamental principles by which the military forces . . . guide their actions in support of national objectives" compatible across services.[10] The services have created arrangements of this sort to cover the mission of close air support, in which aircraft drop bombs to attack enemy forces directly engaged with US ground forces. Although the benefits are at times exaggerated, it is hard to be against either of these forms of jointness, because of the claims that they reduce fratricide and improve battlefield effectiveness.

But in addition to these two forms of jointness, Goldwater–Nichols promoted a third sort of jointness, which we call managerial jointness, at the very highest levels of decision-making across the military services. It encouraged them to cooperate – some would say collude – rather than compete in meeting the nation's defense needs. In place of each service developing its own advice about the nation's strategic direction, based on its own philosophy and organizational culture, the services now collaborate to develop a single, integrated perspective to present to civilian leaders. Ideally, discussions among the Joint Chiefs will winnow ideas so that they can pass along only the very best to the president. Continuously working together on plans and investments should foment coordination, efficiency, and effectiveness. But on the other hand, managerial jointness can encourage informal agreements among service leaders, stifling competition among the services and limiting their incentives for innovative thinking. It also can allow proposals based on the "lowest common denominator" recommendation to reach the president's desk. In essence, this form of jointness leads to the cartelization of the military and works against the interests of civilians.

Although at first somewhat reluctant to embrace post-Goldwater–Nichols jointness, the services are now very committed to the new structure, because they recognize the political as well as the operational value of this cooperation. On the operational and doctrinal levels, US forces support each other more effectively in combat operations than they once did. But the services also use managerial jointness to coordinate their program preferences and present civilian officials with a united front. They avoid publicly criticizing one another's favorite programs, seeking the quiet certainty of collusion at the joint level rather than the risky life offered by open bureaucratic warfare. Despite the hopes of many of its civilian advocates, jointness appears to have weakened rather than enhanced civilian control over the military.[11]

The reforms of the late Cold War set the framework by which the US military approached the post-Cold War era. During the 1990s, American military might was unmatched by any other nation, but debate raged about the uses to which this might should be applied. At a minimum, the officially sanctioned linked-arm stance of the services has delayed the transition from the military's Cold War priorities to the security priorities of the twenty-first century, whatever they may be.

Concerns of the post-Cold War era

In a country with a military as large and powerful as America's, fears of a crisis in civil–military relations should be cause for concern. The nation's liberty and democratic character depend on having a disciplined and obedient military focused on external threats rather than domestic politics. In most of the rest of the world, studies of civil–military relations tend to focus on the threat of coups and juntas. The persistent question with regard to American civil–military relations is different – a matter of negotiating the boundaries between military expertise and civilian oversight, within an overall framework of assured civilian supremacy.

When there is direct insubordination in the United States, an outright challenge to the principle of civilian control of the military, the civilians win. The cases are rare but decisive, the classic being the confrontation between President Truman and General Douglas MacArthur early in the Korean War. General MacArthur was the highly visible World War II commander who had successfully, if somewhat strangely, run the occupation of Japan. President Truman told General MacArthur, whom he had appointed the UN Commander in Korea, not to risk a wider war by moving his forces close to the Chinese frontier, which might have been perceived as a threat to China. MacArthur disregarded the presidential directive, precipitating Chinese entry into the war. Truman then abruptly relieved MacArthur from command and forced his retirement. MacArthur returned to the United States to great acclaim, but his political stardom, including talk of his nomination for president on the Republican ticket, soon faded. Historians have almost universally agreed that in retrospect Truman's decision was correct, and this incident continues to be held up by American military leaders as precisely the kind of civil–military crisis that they will never repeat.

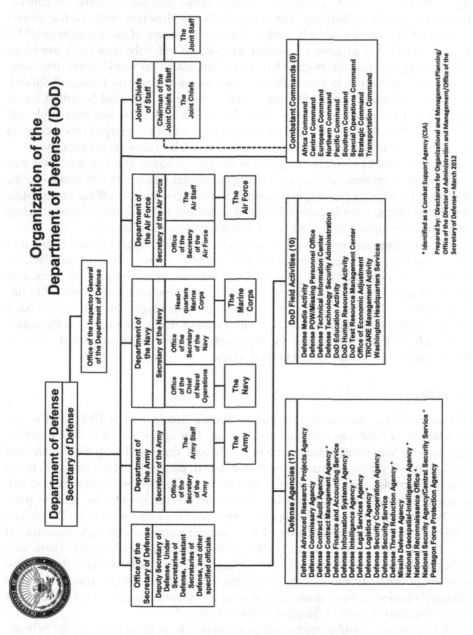

Organization of the
Department of Defense (DoD)

Department of Defense
Secretary of Defense

Office of the Inspector General
of the Department of Defense

**Office of the
Secretary of Defense**
Deputy Secretary of
Defense, Under
Secretaries of
Defense, Assistant
Secretaries of
Defense, and other
specified officials

**Department of
the Army**
Secretary of the Army

Office of the
Secretary
of the
Army

The
Army Staff

The
Army

**Department of
the Navy**
Secretary of the Navy

Office of the
Chief
of Naval
Operations

Office of the
Secretary of the
Navy

Head-
quarters
Marine
Corps

The
Navy

The
Marine
Corps

**Department of
the Air Force**
Secretary of the Air Force

Office
of the
Secretary
of the
Air Force

The
Air Staff

The
Air Force

**Joint Chiefs
of Staff**
Chairman of the
Joint Chiefs of Staff

The
Joint Chiefs

The
Joint Staff

Defense Agencies (17)
Defense Advanced Research Projects Agency
Defense Commissary Agency
Defense Contract Audit Agency
Defense Contract Management Agency *
Defense Finance and Accounting Service
Defense Information Systems Agency *
Defense Intelligence Agency *
Defense Legal Services Agency
Defense Logistics Agency *
Defense Security Cooperation Agency
Defense Security Service
Defense Threat Reduction Agency *
Missile Defense Agency
National Geospatial-Intelligence Agency *
National Reconnaissance Office *
National Security Agency/Central Security Service *
Pentagon Force Protection Agency

DoD Field Activities (10)
Defense Media Activity
Defense POW/Missing Personnel Office
Defense Technical Information Center
Defense Technology Security Administration
DoD Education Activity
DoD Human Resources Activity
DoD Test Resource Management Center
Office of Economic Adjustment
TRICARE Management Activity
Washington Headquarters Services

Combatant Commands (9)
Africa Command
Central Command
European Command
Northern Command
Pacific Command
Southern Command
Special Operations Command
Strategic Command
Transportation Command

* Identified as a Combat Support Agency (CSA)

Prepared by: Directorate for Organizational and Management Planning/
Office of the Director of Administration and Management/Office of the
Secretary of Defense – March 2012

Figure 3.1 Department of Defense organization chart
Source: Department of Defense.

Instead, most American disputes in civil–military relations are more subtle, and again history serves as a useful guide. MacArthur's successor in Korea was General Matthew Ridgway, who later became the Army Chief of Staff and had his own policy dispute with President Eisenhower over the Army's mission and budget.[12] Eisenhower's "New Look" strategy favored expanding the US nuclear deterrent rather than strengthening US conventional warfare capabilities. Ridgway, like Army chiefs to follow him, believed that ground forces remained the decisive factor in warfare, despite the advent of nuclear weapons.[13] He also believed that the US advantage in nuclear weapons on which the New Look was based might be fleeting and that the frugal Eisenhower administration would starve the Army budget. Ridgway spoke out to elite audiences such as the Council on Foreign Relations. President Eisenhower, after giving Ridgway a "day in court" at a National Security Council meeting, felt that Ridgway's continuing resistance to the New Look was intolerable and therefore forced the retirement of his old comrade in arms – a clear message to his successors that the services had to fall in line with the president's decisions about grand strategy.

So ultimate control by civilians is a given in the United States. But that leaves the perpetual challenge of creating institutions and organizational precedents that maximize the contributions of a highly educated, experienced, and professional US officer corps, while ensuring that civilians, often ignorant of military detail, are not informally forced to adopt military preferences about whether and how US military power is exercised.

Today, some observers worry that the military is potentially insubordinate, resistant to taking direction from its civilian masters. The fears take two forms. In one version, the military is seen as too partisan, favoring the positions and values of one political party over another. In the second version, the military is seen as too corporatist, too committed to furthering its own organizational interests as opposed to following legitimate political guidance from elected officials and appointed civilians. In the first version, the military is thought to listen too much to some civilians and to be improperly in league with them against others. In the second version, the military is said to heed no one.

Fears of military partisanship

Even if fear of military partisanship reached an apogee during the late 1990s, this worry, too, has a history in American civil–military relations. During the first half of the twentieth century, the American military took pride in its distance from partisan politics.[14] General George C. Marshall, the master manager of World War II, purposely did not vote so as not to allow a hint of a partisan bias. He worked closely with President Franklin Delano Roosevelt, but remained personally distant from him. The public did not know what political party General Dwight Eisenhower preferred until he announced his candidacy for the Republican presidential nomination. General Maxwell Taylor became identified with the Democrats and President John Kennedy only in the early 1960s at the end of his initial service. There were other officers with high-profile political leanings, but they were visible mostly in the National Guard, where political affiliations count, not in the Regular forces. Appointment to the service academies carried no partisan attachment, even though most students receive their slots in the incoming class through nomination by elected officials.

The 1950s saw the first real peacetime alignment between a political party and the military, when the Democrats "married" the Army, thinking the Army's dissatisfaction with President Eisenhower's New Look could help them in electoral politics. Army leaders favored maintaining the option of using nuclear weapons but also developing robust conventional forces to meet and defeat any level of Soviet or Soviet-backed aggression. Anxious to regain the presidency, the Democrats became the champions of this "Flexible Response" and the Army ground force capabilities needed to implement it, including Special Forces (Green Berets). When President Kennedy won the 1960 election, the Army welcomed its release from the nuclear weapons-dominated budgets of the Eisenhower administration, which had largely favored the Air Force. General Maxwell Taylor, the author of the Army's 1960 lament, *The Uncertain Trumpet*, was called back from retirement to become President Kennedy's military advisor and later chairman of the Joint Chiefs of Staff.[15]

Vietnam was the application of the Flexible Response strategy – and it was a complete disaster that changed partisan alignments on military issues. Although Democratic administrations initiated and accelerated this war, they quickly soured on the experience and became the main political proponents of ending it, endorsing peace candidates in the late 1960s and early 1970s. Meanwhile, the Republicans, the party of traditional isolationism that had opposed high levels of defense spending and active intervention abroad, moved in the opposite direction. Eschewing their former restraint in favor of a more aggressive US foreign policy, Republicans became the protectors of the military, large parts of which had been demoralized by the outcome in Vietnam and by Americans' criticism of the military's performance. The Republicans, in essence, "married" the military writ large, tying their political fortunes to its interests.

Republicans advocated higher defense budgets and painted a more ominous picture of the Soviet threat. In the 1970s, groups such as the Committee on the Present Danger promoted concern about America's peril in the continuing Cold War, which the Soviet Union seemed determined to win by building more missiles than the United States. The Soviets were portrayed as intent on taking advantage of the weakening of the US military caused by the strains of the Vietnam War.

The Republicans' view resonated with the American people. Although the public had wanted the end of American involvement in Vietnam, whatever the cost, ordinary citizens still feared Soviet expansionism. The Democrats' disparagement of these concerns, even if correct in hindsight, did not reassure them. Except for a four-year hiatus due to revelations about domestic crimes and their cover-up by the Nixon administration, Republicans held the presidency from the middle of the Vietnam War through the end of the Cold War. The Democrats' perceived weakness on national security significantly hampered their competitiveness in presidential elections.

Burdened by sinking morale and declining budgets in the 1970s, the American military warmed to the Republican embrace. Prominent Republicans promised to end what they called "the decade of neglect," the procurement holiday that followed Vietnam. The next Republican president, Ronald Reagan, augmented increases in defense spending that began in the late 1970s, and the spending surge became enshrined in history as the Reagan buildup. More than the growing military affiliation with Republicans, what mattered about the Reagan buildup was the extent to which it restored resources, prestige, and autonomy to a military whose self-image and public image had been badly damaged by Vietnam.

The alliance extended beyond organizational and political interests of the military to the level of individual soldiers. By the 1980s, a significant number of military personnel, enlisted as well as officers, actively self-identified as Republican. Cadets at West Point, known informally but with affection by their instructors as the "Reagan Youth," took on a decidedly Republican identity after only a few weeks of exposure to military culture. By the 1990s, political analyses routinely talked about the "Republicanization" of the military vote.[16] In the 2000 presidential election, the contest for Florida's vital electoral votes seemingly hinged on the absentee ballots of the many service personnel who voted in the state. No one doubted that those votes, if properly counted, would go heavily for George W. Bush.

Actual data on the political affiliations of the active-duty military are sparse. Researchers have only recently begun to deem it an important topic. Moreover, the services discourage such inquiries, denying easy access to officers, enlisted personnel, and families. Nevertheless, one important older study, the Foreign Policy Leadership Project (FPLP), managed to survey military officers and a comparable sector of the civilian leadership population every four years from 1976 to 1996. The FPLP found a steady Republicanization. For example, in 1976 only 33 percent of the military officers surveyed identified themselves as Republicans, but by 1996 that proportion had jumped to 67 percent. In the same period, the affiliations among comparable sectors of the civilian leadership population moved only from 25 percent to 33 percent. Moreover, within the civilian population the degree of Republican affiliation moved higher in some years and lower in others, whereas in the military population the proportion moved consistently and significantly higher every four years.[17]

In another survey in the 1990s, the Triangle Institute for Security Studies (TISS) again found that nearly two-thirds of the officers said they were Republicans, compared to less than a third of the journalists, government officials, and the like who comprise the TISS study's comparative civilian, non-veteran elite. Only 8 percent of the military officers claimed a Democratic Party affiliation, as opposed to 43 percent of the elite. Samples of Reservists looked like the active-duty military, while those of veterans and Reserve Officers' Training Corps (ROTC) members included more Democrats but were still more Republican-heavy than the general population.[18]

Note that both the FPLP and TISS surveys report data on military officers, not on the military as a whole. In 2004, a more comprehensive survey that included all but the very highest and lowest ranks of the Army showed less Republicanization, especially among junior officers and enlisted soldiers, although it confirmed that senior officers were disproportionately Republicans. Overall, the Army's identification with the Republican Party appeared to match the civilian population, contrasting with a significantly lower rate of soldiers' identification with the Democratic Party (confirming the results of the TISS survey).[19] The increasing number of enlisted women and minorities (to be discussed further in Chapter 5) is likely to resuscitate Democratic identification in the Army, as these demographic categories have strong Democratic political ties. But in terms of importance for civil–military relations, it is mostly officers, and especially senior officers, who count – the ones who surveys show are disproportionately Republican and disproportionately likely to vote.[20] They are the ones who offer military advice to civilian leaders, and the public defers to their professionalization and experience when they testify or comment on national security.

Some of this Republicanization may be normal self-selection. Political affiliations are not evenly distributed even in an evenly divided society. If the group sampled were university faculty members or black women, it is highly likely that few among them would claim a Republican affiliation. If the group sampled were Skull and Bones alumni at Yale, most would probably be Republicans (John Kerry excepted). A sample taken on the streets of Cambridge, Massachusetts, or Austin, Texas, would look quite different from one taken on the streets of Salt Lake City, Utah, or Omaha, Nebraska.

The military officer corps consists largely of white, married, male Christians under age 60, disproportionately from small towns and from the South, with above-average educations and income – a demographic group that tends to vote Republican, whether in the military or not.[21] Furthermore, military recruits also tend to come from rural areas – whether in "red" states that are politically dominated by rural voters or in "blue" states where the rural voters' Republican leanings are overwhelmed by large urban populations' Democratic tendencies.

From either sort of state, the rural upbringing might well cause both a tendency to serve and also a tendency to vote Republican.[22]

The surveys of the military's political affiliation may also be subject to cohort effects. The TISS survey sampled officers in the late Clinton years, when there was especially strong moral outrage toward the Democratic president; the 2004 survey came early in the Iraq War, and as that war dragged on, attachment to the Republican Party might have dropped. On the other hand, military disappointment with President Obama's policies might still appear to increase Republicanization: a 2009 survey shows that in recent years Democrats left the officer corps at relatively high rates after the end of their initial commitment, leaving an increasing proportion of Republicans in the active duty force and maintaining the Republicanization of the senior officers most relevant for military advice.[23] And careful follow-up analysis of the TISS results suggests that Republicans in the military have similar policy preferences to civilian Republicans (although Democrats in the military tend to be more moderate than comparable Democratic civilian elites).[24] Overall, the evidence points to some Republicanization of the post-Cold War military, whatever the cause and even if it may only be temporary.

The more important question deals not with political affiliation but rather with political consequence. How sharply are the parties divided over military policy? Would a "Republican" foreign policy differ profoundly and systematically from a "Democratic" one? Does the Republicanization of the military make adoption of a Republican security policy more likely or a Democratic security policy harder to implement?

Although the parties' policy preferences differ from time to time – so candidates often debate and criticize each other on foreign policy topics – it is hard to discern many consistent patterns. Circumstances and individual party leaders' ideas matter a lot. And the military has many professional, organizational, and otherwise non-partisan interests in American politics. So the military is unlikely to work hard to promote a Republican-only policy agenda. Indeed, after an Army Reservist appeared in uniform at a campaign rally, Army General Martin Dempsey, the chairman of the Joint Chiefs of Staff, advised military audiences to avoid "us[ing] the uniform for partisan politics."[25]

This caution particularly makes sense because the positions of the parties have changed over time on security issues. Robert Dole, Gerald Ford's running mate in the 1976 presidential election, made a famous comment about "all the Democrat wars," referring to the big American wars of the twentieth century – World War I, World War II, Korea, and Vietnam – all of which took place while the Democrats held the presidency. Of course, the major wars since then – the 1991 Gulf War, the 2001 war in Afghanistan, the 2003 Iraq War, as well as many smaller operations such as Grenada, Lebanon, and Panama, have taken place under Republican presidents. Even Senator Dole, the critic of "Democrat wars," favored a bigger American military role in Bosnia in the early 1990s than Democratic President Bill Clinton, though many Republicans criticized the senator for that position.

In general, in the post-Cold War era, Democrats have been more willing than Republicans to intervene on purely humanitarian grounds – for example, Democratic standard-bearer Hillary Clinton pushed for the intervention in Libya when she was President Barack Obama's secretary of state – but neither party has shunned the use of force.[26] Both parties generally support post-disaster humanitarian relief, including the Somalia famine relief mission that led to the infamous "Black Hawk Down" incident. The difference, rather, comes with interventions to separate warring groups or to prevent mass killings. Especially in the 1990s, Democrats tended to fear the consequences of not intervening, while the Republicans feared the consequences of sending American troops into conflicts not vital to the American national interest. But the intervention debate shifted post-9/11, as the Bush administration and many

Republicans advocated armed interventions – even preventive wars – to install democracies abroad, and especially in the Middle East, while the burdens of the long war against al Qaeda have muted interest in interventions even among Democrats. Under President Obama, the Libyan intervention had a European/Arab League face, even though there was much behind-the-scenes American involvement, and the Democrats led the US resistance to taking a direct role in the bloody Syrian civil war.

Overall, both parties agree that foreign instability often threatens the United States, replacing humanitarian arguments in intervention debates with justifications based directly on American national security. They generally cite the same problems: the proliferation of weapons of mass destruction, the dangers of ethnic conflict, the use of terrorist tactics, the competition for resources, and the rule of less-than-benevolent dictators. But the Republicans have been more likely to express confidence in the American government's unilateral judgment when badgering an international opponent fails to achieve the desired results; Democrats, on the other hand, tend to value the symbolism that endorsements from international institutions and alliances offer American action.[27]

In practice, both parties care about allies and also don't care. Republican as well as Democratic presidents recognize the need to reassure the American public that American foreign ventures are not totally crazed or totally on their bill. Before the Iraq War, the Democrats pushed for United Nations Security Council support, even though it was a futile gesture and considerably delayed military plans, but they discovered that in the endorsement game a single medium-sized country, most often Britain, is sufficient to meet the American public's test of sanity and burden-sharing. And the Democrats have had their own interventions without UN endorsement, notably the 1999 Kosovo War, the course of which also demonstrated that even the supposedly multilateral Democrats have no intention of heeding allied suggestions that conflict with American military commanders' preferences once military operations begin.[28]

Finally, on the defense budget – the issue that might be most often of interest to the military – partisanship again has limited impact. The military recognizes that it will have to work with both parties, and it knows that pork-barrel interests afflict all politicians. Even the most ardently anti-war, anti-defense leaders can succumb: for example, Bernie Sanders, the socialist, anti-war, Independent senator from Vermont, backs defense spending for Vermont firms.[29]

Fears of military corporatism

In addition to encouraging cooperation among the services, the Goldwater–Nichols Act also changed the balance of power in American civil–military relations. Its sponsors said that jointness would strengthen civilian authority within the Pentagon and improve the quality and speed of military advice provided to national command authorities, but it may not have had those effects in practice. Instead, Goldwater–Nichols may have helped contribute to the military's opportunity to "resist" civilian control by enhancing its sense of corporate identity, especially seen in the 1990s.

Goldwater–Nichols provided for a much stronger chairman of the Joint Chiefs of Staff. Prior to Goldwater–Nichols, the chairman did not have the authority to force resolution of disputes among the services or to present his own opinion of what should be done in a given situation, separate from the service positions. Indeed, despite having been intended as a forum to provide joint military advice to the president, the JCS historically served more as a collector of parochial service positions. To fix that problem, the Act gave the chairman new decision-making powers in JCS meetings. Moreover, before the reform an assignment on the

Joint Staff had been mostly a dead-end job for mid-level officers whose career tracks had mainly been dictated by their assignments in their home service; since Goldwater–Nichols, the Joint Staff has been a requirement for promotion to general or admiral. Today, the chairman's work attracts a better crop of officers, attuned to the new joint imperatives.

From the military's corporate perspective, this new centralization offers advantages. The services' leaders understand, especially given their retrospective tendency to blame the problems of the Vietnam War on civilian "micromanagement" of military decisions, that lack of consensus among the service chiefs invites civilian intervention. Even before Goldwater–Nichols, the military tried to avoid sending a "split" paper to the White House, and usually the chiefs managed to resolve their differences, albeit slowly. Still, from time to time they could not come to an agreement without civilian involvement, especially on controversial issues. For example, in the 1950s the services deadlocked on the question of whether to advise that the United States create a Single Integrated Operational Plan (SIOP) for nuclear war planning. The decision to develop it was made only after President Eisenhower examined the competing service views – rightly so, given the vast political significance of the decision. After the experiences of the 1950s, 1960s, and 1970s, in which the military saw civilians exerting increasing authority, the corporatist feelings of the Reagan buildup went hand in hand with logrolling to avoid disagreements.

Goldwater–Nichols allowed the JCS chairman to present to the president a prompt, single, unified military position on particular questions. No more would service disputes invite civilian scrutiny of competing positions on controversial topics, the style of decision-making favored by Roosevelt, Eisenhower, and Kennedy, among others. By reducing the power of the service chiefs and ingraining the habit of a "joint perspective" among promotable officers, the reform made competing service views both unpalatable and unlikely to survive the chairman's discretion.

The new system has yielded quicker advice, but it has also encouraged collusion among the services. The services still disagree about priorities, but in an era in which outright competition is frowned upon, the services choose to work out their disputes largely behind closed doors. Instead of holding out for particular service positions in slow Joint Staff deliberations, which in the past led to civilian adjudication of divergent advice on controversial topics, the military now delivers one "joint" perspective. The competitive incentive for one service to air its criticisms of another service in public or to the civilian leadership, an incentive that previously benefited civilian control, is largely gone.[30]

After the Cold War ended, the military began to assert its corporate interests more strongly. General Colin Powell, who had become the chairman of the Joint Chiefs of Staff under President George H. W. Bush, restated publicly the doctrine on the use of military force he had helped develop as aide to President Reagan's secretary of defense, Caspar Weinberger. The "Powell Doctrine," as it is known, states that the commitment of US forces requires that vital interests be at stake, that the United States be willing to use overwhelming force, that clear goals and a defined exit strategy be stated in advance, and that strong public and congressional support for the use of force be mobilized. The Army did not want more costly missions with vague political rationales. Although perfectly sensible on the face of it, the doctrine was a political as well as a strategic construct. It was an attempt by the Army to constrain the ability of political leaders to engage in limited wars, the type of war the Army told itself it had been forced to lose in Vietnam. The Powell Doctrine announced to the American people the professional military's judgment of the likely costs and benefits of limited wars. It thereby raised the political costs that leaders would face if they ordered a limited military intervention in the face of this professional military consensus.

The triumph of the Gulf War reinforced the military's self-assurance. Not only did the US military win the war, but civilians largely ceded the tasks of planning, executing, and concluding it to the military as well. Chairman of the Joint Chiefs Powell was the key figure, not Secretary of Defense Dick Cheney. Uniformed leaders, not civilians, decided when to end the war. And it was the leader of Central Command, General Norman Schwarzkopf – not Cheney or any civilian representative of the US government – who conducted the armistice negotiations with the Iraqis, largely on the basis of his own judgments rather than guidance given to him by anyone in Washington.[31]

In the aftermath of the Gulf War, when conflict broke out in the former Yugoslavia, military resistance to civilian control reached its high-water mark. With the collapse of the Soviet Union came the implosion of communist regimes throughout Eastern Europe and the Balkans. The breakup of Yugoslavia was probably both inevitable and inevitably violent. Long-suppressed ethnic hatred seemed certain to require outside, possibly American, intervention to contain. General Powell, on his own initiative, wrote an op-ed for the *New York Times* warning against any US involvement, clearly attempting to direct US policy and obviously challenging civilian authority.[32] He also prepared a military force structure reduction plan that became known as the Base Force, which was intended both to force a unified position among the services after the Cold War and to head off any interest in larger cuts by the incoming Clinton administration.[33]

The Clinton administration, even before it took office, did not help the cause of civilian control. Civilians discussed a proposal to lift the military's ban on the acceptance of acknowledged homosexuals within its ranks, but General Powell and other officers spoke out against the idea, effectively blocking the proposal. The "Don't ask, don't tell" (DADT) policy, which acknowledged that homosexuals would serve in practice but still officially condemned their service, was a face-saving compromise, but the damage was done. Because of Clinton's alleged draft dodging and his lack of foreign policy experience, it was easy for the military to push the Clinton administration around on defense-related matters, large and small, either through the power of its own professional advice or by backing Republican initiatives.

Only the most flagrant taunts drew punishment. An Air Force general was relieved of command when he spoke disparagingly of the president to an audience of military families. An admiral lost an expected promotion when sailors behaved disrespectfully toward President Clinton when he visited an aircraft carrier. But basically the Clinton administration learned to avoid policy fights with the military, leaving questions of force sizing and budget allocation to the generals and admirals, especially after the Republicans gained control of Congress in 1994.

The military's ability to resist civilian leadership continued for a time under President George W. Bush's Republican administration. It came as a surprise to many that there was any friction between the military and senior civilians, because most thought that the Republican campaign slogan directed toward the military – "help is on the way" – meant that few military interests would be neglected. But conflicts developed almost immediately with the new secretary of defense, Donald Rumsfeld, who was back for his second tour of duty, having also served as secretary of defense 25 years earlier during the Ford administration.[34] Part of the problem can be traced to the Republicans' distrust of senior military leaders who had been appointed by President Clinton. Perhaps the suspicion that the generals might remain loyal to the party that had promoted them was natural, but the distrust ran deeper. Although the Republicans had encouraged the military's assertiveness during the Clinton years, they now feared that assertiveness had become resistance to civilian control, meaning Republican control after the 2000 election.

Secretary Rumsfeld and his team of advisors had plans to change the military, and they feared that the military's pursuit of its own corporate interests would block their attempts to reset the doctrine and focus of US forces. Rumsfeld did not clearly specify the details of his plans to "transform" the military, but he seemed to call for an emphasis on space, missile defense, and a smaller Army to help pay for new technology.[35] Service leaders became nervous when Secretary Rumsfeld excluded them from a comprehensive defense review in 2001.

Rumsfeld's style, which was often described as arrogant, interfering, and impatient, also did not help maintain good relations with senior officers. The secretary especially clashed with General Eric Shinseki, the Chief of Staff of the Army, a Clinton appointee and the first Japanese-American to hold four-star rank, who was attempting to implement his own significant redesign of the Army and who was a bit of a micromanager himself.[36] By early September 2001, many thought Rumsfeld's second life as secretary of defense would meet a quick end,[37] but Rumsfeld's calm yet heroic behavior after 9/11 helped him keep his job.[38] Reinforced politically, Rumsfeld was able to remove Secretary of the Army Thomas White, a retired general, and to marginalize General Shinseki well before his term as Army Chief of Staff ended.

Rumsfeld continued to believe that the military's independence from civilian control needed to be tamed. As his broader transformation agenda fizzled (discussed in Chapter 4), the struggle for civilian control over the military shifted to the question of whether the military or civilian leadership deserved responsibility for the growing debacle in Iraq. Rumsfeld's approach was straightforward: not to admit that anyone had made mistakes in the conduct of the war. Generals on active duty in Iraq, hand-picked for their posts by Secretary Rumsfeld, mostly followed that lead, but disquiet spread through the ranks and among some military leaders in response to the costs imposed on the armed forces: deaths, debilitating wounds, and damage to recruitment and retention efforts that might harm the quality of the force over the long term. In some ways, Secretary Rumsfeld was using up the bounty that the military had enjoyed during the 1980s and 1990s.

Retired generals, what might be called the "retired officers' chorus," presented the most public face of the military's side of the debate over Iraq. They suggested that Rumsfeld's poor leadership was responsible for the insurgency, or at least that his long-time failure to acknowledge the insurgency, preventing officials from using that term, allowed it to take root and metastasize. Some even called openly for his resignation. The logical inference from their remarks was that if the military had been freed of the whims of an overbearing secretary, or if the secretary had simply listened harder to the expert military advice provided to him before the war, the war in Iraq would have turned out differently.

The debate over who is responsible for what went wrong in the Iraq War is significant in terms of civil–military relations. In assessing blame for the war's outcome, civilians bear ultimate responsibility, for it was the administration and not the Army that itched for the war in the first place. It was also the senior civilians who intentionally ignored the need for postwar planning about the occupation and rebuilding of Iraq, in the hope that the United States would be able to extricate itself quickly and pass on the responsibilities for Iraqi redevelopment to the international community and the Iraqis themselves.[39] And it was the civilian leadership's choice not to acknowledge (and correct) mistakes, including disbanding the Iraqi Army, not controlling the looting of government facilities, and not instituting counter-insurgency operations sooner. Civilians are empowered in the American system to replace generals and set new political parameters for the military's rules of engagement during an occupation, and the civilians are the ones who failed to exercise that power in Iraq. Instead, the man who commanded the coalition in Iraq during the critical years of 2004–2007, General George Casey, was made Chief of Staff of the Army. The lack of accountability for results and the reward for toeing the political leaders' line did not go unnoticed by junior officers.[40]

If retired generals have a role in reminding American citizens of these facts, then they are playing a useful role in the American system of checks and balances and in American defense policy debates. But the implication of the retired generals' chorus that civilian micromanagement lost a war the military could have won offers the military a dangerous free pass from accountability. Civilian micromanagement alone did not tell military commanders that superior firepower was the answer to the growing attacks on American forces in Iraq; field commanders made those decisions. Conversely, later field commanders' tendency to exaggerate the results of the surge of US troops and the application of the new counterinsurgency field manual, and the hagiography of General Petraeus that downplays the importance of Iraqi choices and the changing balance of power among Iraqi militias, equally contribute to the oversimplified "military good, civilians bad" storyline about the US role in Iraq.

Successfully shifting blame has troubling implications for future civil–military relations. The public needs to know when its civilian leadership makes national security mistakes, but it also needs to avoid overconfidence in military decision-making and the illusion that turning wars (or other operations, like domestic natural disaster relief) over to the military necessarily leads to better outcomes.

Defenders of Rumsfeld, both civilian and military, argue that generals who disagreed with him during the planning of the invasion should have resigned, and that because they did not, they have lost the right to protest after the fact. Many military officers have interpreted H. R. McMaster's book on the role of the JCS in the Vietnam War, *Dereliction of Duty*, to say that resignation is the preferred form of military protest against civilians, despite the author's denials on that point.[41] The problem with resignation is that it is a very awkward way to provide advice. If one or two senior officers resign, their action may not register as being important. Officers leave all the time, some happy with the president's policy and some not. If several senior officers resign, say, the entire roster of Joint Chiefs, the government would fall into a major crisis. Attention would focus as much on the military's ultimate subordination to civil authority as on any policy issue the resigning officers wanted to raise. The established norm of civilian control of the military is that senior officers are to advise civilian leaders, but civilian leaders have "the right to be wrong," and soldiers are supposed to accept their decisions and implement the civilians' strategy to the best of their ability. Growing public and military acceptance of a new norm, one that supports resignation, could pose a threat to civilian control.[42]

Furthermore, all outspoken generals are not created equal; some public comments are more hypocritical and self-serving than others. A retired general attempting to blame civilians for a decision in which his own military advice was partly to blame seems more egregious than a retired general commenting on civilian choices that did not occur on his watch. In that case, the commentary may provide a needed counterbalance to the administration's view. Either way, chatty retired generals are not going anywhere. With advances in modern health care, retired generals can live decades after the end of their military careers. It seems strange to suggest that these repositories of knowledge and experience should have no role in the public dialogue over the use of military force. The need is to recognize that retired generals, like everyone else on Sunday morning talk shows, have their own interests and organizational preferences, which may or may not be conducive to a healthy level of civilian control over the military.

President Obama seemed quite unprepared to assert control over the military when he assumed office, as he had essentially no foreign policy or military credentials and carried the burden of representing the party that had a reputation of being weak on defense. He reappointed Robert Gates, George W. Bush's last secretary of defense, and salted senior levels of the national security apparatus with retired generals and admirals, seemingly conceding control to the military. The starting point for all defense policy debate, universally acknowledged by civilian appointees in the Department of Defense, became what was best for the "warfighter," as if military requirements were somehow objectively determined without the need to strike a balance between military and civilian demands for resources.

And yet, as we shall discuss in full later, President Obama was able to temper senior officers' requests for large forces in both Iraq and Afghanistan and to begin reducing the military's budget. In part this was due to success in the fight against al Qaeda, including the killing of Osama bin Laden and the drone attacks in Pakistan. But it was also the product of the wise use of the powers inherent in the presidency to direct wars. The long wars in Iraq and Afghanistan had drained public support for those who might have opposed Obama's policies.

Civilian politicians do not always dominate their military subordinates in the normal give and take of civil–military relations, and the institutional structure created by the Goldwater–Nichols Act has increased the bargaining power of the corporate military. Nevertheless, civilian leaders still have the ultimate authority and face the ultimate blame when they choose to exercise it.

Controlling professionals

It is always difficult to get good military advice while maintaining civilian control, and, of course, some methods of ensuring allegiance are off-limits to democracies and may stifle advice, too. Nazi Germany had the Gestapo and other agencies uncover and kill those who opposed Hitler's line. The Soviet Union used periodic purges and inserted political commissars into the military hierarchy. (Both Khrushchev and Brezhnev, who rose to lead the Soviet government, made their marks as commissars in World War II.) Saddam Hussein had many Iraqi officers killed just on suspicion of plotting against him. Running parallel bureaucracies, paying informants, and holding trumped-up trials may check disloyalty, empowering the civilian government, but these practices also tend to stifle honest reporting and advice from the military.

The problem is that there are no boundaries on what is purely military and what is purely political. The military cares about the wars it fights and the budgets it receives. Whether officers are Republicans or Democrats matters very little, for in the end they share interests among themselves that will likely conflict with those of politicians, be they Republican or Democratic, American or French, elected or not. The post-World War II history of American civil–military relations is a history of these conflicts, as well as of the attempts by both officers and civilians to resolve them in ways that set institutional or political precedents favorable to their interests in the future.

Politicians cannot trust the military to buy the right equipment, pick the right targets, and say the right things to the press. Civilians may know less about military technicalities than their uniformed counterparts, but they also bring a broader strategic and political perspective that must deeply influence the actual uses of military force if they are to serve US interests.

Elected for the job, presidents need to keep control of the important decisions and cannot rely solely on their own political skills or on secretaries of defense to keep the military honest in its advice and obedient in its actions. But on the other hand, if war is too important to leave to the generals, so too must national security policy be considered too important to leave to the politicians. Good, trustworthy advice is what is needed.

Military leaders need to find the balance between professional candor and support for the administration in office. Nearly all formal power lies in the hands of the secretary of defense, acting as the president's agent. Thus, it was perfectly legal for Richard Cheney, when he was secretary of defense during President George H. W. Bush's term, to reprimand the general in charge of the Strategic Air Command when he deviated from administration policy in a public pronouncement. Secretary Cheney was also within his rights when he fired the Chief of Staff of the Air Force for talking to reporters about aspects of the plan to attack Saddam's forces in Kuwait that highlighted the Air Force's role. It was similarly proper for Secretary Rumsfeld to give the European Command to a Marine general, even though that post had traditionally been an Army assignment, and to make the chairman of the Joint Chiefs of Staff a Marine, too, even though it seemed to be the Navy's turn. Secretaries do not want their policies to be undercut or preempted by officers, and they do not want to look as if they are not in control of the department.

The secretaries also know that military bureaucracies will outlast them and that it is easy for the services to delay or to appeal negative decisions by mobilizing their many friends inside and outside of government. Leaks to the press reveal policy cleavages between the military and civilians. Publicity that portrays the secretary as an ineffective manager who is not in control of the department can reflect negatively on the president. Winning administrative battles is not enough; the secretaries must gather the department behind them in order to look effective and to win plaudits as successful in their job. It is not surprising, then, that secretaries will bargain with the military, giving officers some of what they want in exchange for gaining their acquiescence on other decisions. Governing is a political business, where politicians tend to do best.

In the end, though, civilian control over the military and effective military advice to civilians depend not on the distribution of political skills but rather on structural arrangements, the pitting of interests, and the division of power. Just as the US Constitution outlasts any given set of politicians, the laws governing the organization of the military and its relationship to civilian authority need to do more than be appropriate for one security crisis. They have to anticipate future crises by giving civilians the opportunity to see a full range of military options and the potential consequences that flow from any choice that they make. In this sense, the centralization of the military resulting from the drive toward jointness is a potential danger.

Questions for discussion

1   **What are the advantages and disadvantages of centralization and decentralization of the military and civilian sides of the Department of Defense?**

2   **Why should anyone care whether military officers favor one political party or another?**

3   **How can civilian leaders know when military advice is self-serving "corporatism" rather than the best objective professional view?**

4   **How should a secretary of defense deal with the services? Are there important organizational factors to weigh against security needs?**

5   **Should senior generals and admirals resign publicly when they disagree strongly with the security policies selected by elected officials?**

Notes

1 Perry McCoy Smith, *The Air Force Plans for Peace, 1943–1945* (Baltimore, MD: Johns Hopkins University Press, 1970).

2 Richard Overy, *Why the Allies Won* (New York: W. W. Norton, 1995), Chapter 6.
3 Douglas T. Stuart, *Creating the National Security State: A History of the Law that Transformed America* (Princeton, NJ: Princeton University Press, 2008).
4 Jeffrey D. Barlow, *Revolt of the Admirals: The Fight for Naval Aviation, 1945–1950* (Washington, DC: Brassey's, 1998).
5 Eric Katz, "Pentagon to Cut Secretary's Staff by 300 – in Four Years," *Defense One*, May 27, 2016.
6 Arnold Kanter, *Defense Politics: A Budgetary Perspective* (Chicago, IL: University of Chicago Press, 1979).
7 The most famous example is H. R. McMaster, *Dereliction of Duty: Lyndon Johnson, Robert McNamara, the Joint Chiefs of Staff, and the Lies that Led to Vietnam* (New York: HarperCollins, 1997).
8 Robert Buzzanco, "The Myth of Tet: American Failure and the Politics of War," in Marc Gilbert and William Head (eds.), *The Tet Offensive* (Westport, CT: Praeger, 1996), pp. 231–258.
9 James R. Locher, *Victory on the Potomac: The Goldwater Nichols Act Unifies the Pentagon* (College Station, TX: Texas A&M University Press, 2002).
10 US Department of Defense, *Department of Defense Dictionary of Military and Associated Terms*, Joint Publication 1-02, November 8, 2010 (as amended through February 15, 2016), p. 71, available at: http://www.dtic.mil/doctrine/new_pubs/jp1_02.pdf (accessed September 2, 2016).
11 Peter J. Roman and David W. Tarr, "The Joint Chiefs of Staff: From Service Parochialism to Jointness," *Political Science Quarterly*, 113(1) (Spring 1998): 91–111; Sharon Weiner, *Defending Congress: The Politics of Defense Organization*, PhD dissertation (Cambridge, MA: Massachusetts Institute of Technology, 1998).
12 Andrew J. Bacevich, "Generals Versus the President: Eisenhower and the Army 1953–1955," in Volker C. Franke (ed.), *Security in a Changing World* (Westport, CT: Praeger, 2002), pp. 83–100.
13 A. J. Bacevich, *The Pentomic Era: The U.S. Army between Korea and Vietnam* (Washington, DC: National Defense University Press, 1986).
14 Edward M. Coffman, *The Regulars: The American Army 1898–1941* (Cambridge, MA: Harvard University Press, 2004), pp. 245–247.
15 Bacevich, *The Pentomic Era*; Fred Kaplan, *The Wizards of Armageddon* (New York: Simon & Schuster, 1983).
16 Thomas E. Ricks, "The Widening Gap Between the Military and Society," *Atlantic Monthly*, 280(1) (July 1997): 66–78; Adam Clymer, "Sharp Divergence Found in Views of Military and Civilians," *New York Times*, September 9, 1995, p. A15. For an opposing view, see James J. Dowd, "Connected to Society: The Political Beliefs of U.S. Army Generals," *Armed Forces & Society*, 27(3) (Spring 2001): 343–372.
17 Ole R. Holsti, "A Widening Gap in the U.S. Military and Civilian Society? Some Evidence, 1976–1996," *International Security* (Winter 1998–1999): 5–42.
18 Ole R. Holsti, "Of Chasms and Convergences: Attitudes and Beliefs of Civilians and Military Elites at the Start of a New Millennium," in Peter Feaver and Richard Kohn (eds.), *Soldiers and Civilians: The Civil-Military Gap and American National Security* (Cambridge, MA: MIT Press, 2001), p. 28. For elaboration on these findings, see Peter Feaver and Richard Kohn, "The Gap: Soldiers, Civilians, and Their Mutual Misunderstanding," *The National Interest* (Fall 2000), pp. 29–37.
19 Jason K. Dempsey, *Our Army: Soldiers, Politics, and American Civil–Military Relations* (Princeton, NJ: Princeton University Press, 2010), pp. 99, 101–105, 179–181.
20 Yet another poll, conducted by YouGov in 2015, showed the same Republicanization of military officers compared to nonveteran and nonmilitary groups. Jim Goldby, Lindsay P. Cohn, and Peter D. Feaver, "Thanks for Your Service: Civilian and Veteran Attitudes after Fifteen Years of War," in Kori Schake and James Mattis, eds., *Warriors and Citizens: American Views of Our Military* (Stanford, CA: Hoover Institution Press, 2016), p. 128.
21 Michael C. Desch, "Explaining the Gap: Vietnam, the Republicanization of the South, and the End of the Mass Army," in Peter Feaver and Richard Kohn (eds.), *Soldiers and Civilians: The Civil–Military Gap and American National Security* (Cambridge, MA: MIT Press, 2001), pp. 289–324.
22 Rosa Brooks, "Civil–Military Paradoxes," in Kori Schake and James Mattis (eds.), *Warriors and Citizens: American Views of Our Military* (Stanford, CA: Hoover Institution Press, 2016), pp. 39–40.
23 Heidi A. Urben, "Civil–Military Relations in a Time of War: Party, Politics, and the Profession of Arms," unpublished PhD dissertation, Georgetown University, April 2010.

24 James T. Goldby, "Duty, Honor . . . Party? Ideology, Institutions, and the Use of Force," unpublished PhD dissertation, Stanford University, June 2011; see also Dempsey, *Our Army*, pp. 109–114, for similar analysis of the results from his 2004 survey.

25 Jim Garamone, "CJCS Army Gen. Dempsey: Political Activity Erodes Public Trust in Military," Armed Forces Press Service, August 22, 2012.

26 Conor Friedersdorf, "Hillary Defends Her Failed War in Libya," *The Atlantic*, October 14, 2015.

27 Peter Beinart, "The Rehabilitation of the Cold-War Liberal," *The New York Times Magazine*, April 30, 2006.

28 Ivo H. Daalder and Michael E. O'Hanlon, *Winning Ugly: NATO's War to Save Kosovo* (Washington, DC: Brookings Institution Press, 2000).

29 Tim Mak, "Bernie Sanders Loves This $1 Trillion War Machine," *The Daily Beast*, February 9, 2016.

30 Harvey Sapolsky, "The Interservice Competition Solution," *Breakthroughs*, 5(1) (Spring 1996): 1–3.

31 Eliot Cohen, *Supreme Command: Soldiers, Statesmen, and Leaders in Wartime* (New York: Simon & Schuster, 2002), Chapter 6.

32 Colin Powell, "Why Generals Get Nervous," *New York Times*, October 8, 1992, p. A35.

33 Sharon Weiner, "The Politics of Resource Allocation in the Post-Cold War Pentagon," *Security Studies*, 5(4) (Summer 1996): 125–142.

34 Rowan Scarborough, *Rumsfeld's War: The Untold Story of America's Anti-Terrorist Commander* (Washington, DC: Regnery Publishing, 2004), pp. 113, 121–123; Thomas E. Ricks, "Rumsfeld on High Wire of Defense: Military Brass, Conservative Lawmakers Are Among Secretive Review's Unexpected Critics," *Washington Post*, May 20, 2001, p. A01.

35 Scarborough, *Rumsfeld's War*, p. 119. On Rumsfeld's vision of the Army, see Col. Douglas A. Macgregor, "Concepts for Army Transformation," PowerPoint briefing for Transformation Task Force of the Rumsfeld/Marshall Review, March 13, 2001, available at: http://www.comw.org/qdr/01qdr.html (accessed September 2, 2016).

36 One of General Shinseki's first acts was to order the entire Army, truck drivers and clerks, as well as infantrymen, to wear black berets, an act bitterly received by the Ranger Regiment, which had previously worn the black beret as a distinctive mark.

37 Timothy Noah, "The Rumsfeld Death Watch," *Slate.com*, August 7, 2001, available at: http://www.slate.com/articles/news_and_politics/chatterbox/2001/08/the_rumsfeld_death_watch.html (accessed September 2, 2016); James Mann, *Rise of the Vulcans: The History of Bush's War Cabinet* (New York: Viking, 2004), p. 291; Al Kamen, "Donny, We Hardly Knew Ye," *Washington Post*, September 7, 2001, p. A27.

38 "Defense Secretary Earns High Marks for Handling of Crisis: Once-Embattled Rumsfeld Silences Critics," *Washington Post*, September 20, 2001, p. A23; "The Defense Secretary: For Rumsfeld, a Reputation and a Role Are Transformed," *New York Times*, October 13, 2001, p. A1; "The Best Defense: Donald Rumsfeld's Overwhelming Show of Force on the Public Relations Front," *Washington Post*, December 12, 2001, p. C1.

39 Risa Brooks, *Shaping Strategy: The Civil–Military Politics of Strategic Assessment* (Princeton, NJ: Princeton University Press, 2008), pp. 226–255.

40 Lt. Col. Paul Yingling, "A Failure in Generalship," *Armed Forces Journal* (May 2007): 16–18ff.; Thomas Ricks, *The Generals: American Military Command from World War II to Today* (New York: Penguin Press, 2012).

41 Correspondence with McMaster on this point is discussed in Feaver and Kohn, "The Gap," p. 34, fn. 14.

42 Maj. Jim Goldby, "Beyond the Resignation Debate: A New Framework for Civil–Military Dialogue," *Strategic Studies Quarterly*, 9(3) (Fall 2015): 18–46.

Recommended additional reading

Eliot Cohen, *Supreme Command: Soldiers, Statesmen, and Leadership in Wartime* (New York: Anchor Books, 2003). An influential recent challenge to Huntington by one of his most prominent students.

James E. Hewes Jr., *From Root to McNamara: Army Organization and Administration, 1900–1963* (Washington, DC: Center of Military History, 1974). The big ideas as they played out in the drawing of organizational charts.

Samuel P. Huntington, *The Soldier and the State* (Cambridge, MA: Harvard University Press, 1957). The classic and seminal work in the field.

Mackubin Thomas Owens, *US Civil–Military Relations after 9/11* (New York: Continuum, 2011). A lively discussion of civil–military relations that focuses on the conflicts that can exist between senior military officers and their civilian superiors.

Kori Schake and James Mattis (eds.), *Warriors and Citizens: American Views of Our Military* (Stanford, CA: Hoover Institution Press, 2016). Well-known experts on civil–military relations consider the most recent sample of data on military values.

Frank N. Shubert, *Other Than War: American Military Experience and Operations in the Post-Cold War Decade* (Washington, DC: Joint History Office, 2013). Over 250 operations in the decade, though the burden is a bit exaggerated as most involved few troops and were clustered in the Balkans.

4 Managing defense

Shortly after departing the Carter administration, former Secretary of Defense Harold Brown summarized the lesson of his and many other secretaries' tenure with a speech entitled "Managing the Defense Department: Why It Can't Be Done." Brown argued that the department's immense size, politically complex environment, diverse activities, and unique mission made it very different from a typical large business or other big organization, creating management challenges that were not simply more daunting but fundamentally distinct.[1] Defense policy was not just hard to manage, Brown explained; it was inherently unmanageable.

Brown's comments – echoed by other former officials from the Office of the Secretary of Defense, as well as by some close observers – seem at odds with the prevailing public image of the secretary as Pentagon overlord. But as we will see, the problem with defense management is not that the secretary lacks power over defense policy or even over the department, but rather that many others possess power, too. Like Apple, the Department of Defense is the source of many new ideas, but unlike Apple's legendary Chief Executive Officer (CEO) Steve Jobs, the secretary often has little say over which ones will be implemented. The secretary is the boss, a CEO by another name, but he doesn't have the power that a CEO usually has in the private sector.

Furthermore, the problem cannot be solved by good analytics, as some hope. Almost everyone readily acknowledges that too much political influence, denying facts and over-steering analysis, can lead to disaster, but the US defense experience also shows the limits of expertise. Although some aspects of defense policy are indeed amenable to quantitative analysis, objective technical assessments, and private-sector management techniques, many of the most important decisions are not. Experts can only rarely answer all the questions that defense policy-makers ask, or at least they can only rarely answer those questions based on "scientific" data and analysis. A lot of expert analysis in military matters relies on hidden judgment to fill in the pieces.

In this chapter, we will explore why secretaries cannot really manage the department in any detail – control the aims and actions of the department and its personnel – and we will discuss the fate of two secretaries who believed otherwise: Robert McNamara and Donald Rumsfeld. We also will learn that it pays in terms of reputation to be the secretary after an especially troubled predecessor, as Robert Gates' experience following Donald Rumsfeld demonstrates.

Management under constraints

By most measures, the DoD is the largest organization in the world. Its institutional roof covers 1.3 million soldiers, sailors, airmen, and Marines on active duty, plus nearly another 810,000 Guardsmen and Reservists and nearly 750,000 civilian employees. The DoD supports approximately two million military family dependents, many of whom must be provided housing, an education, health care services, and recreational facilities, plus another two million military paid retirees who are also eligible for some direct services. In addition, several million contractor employees come under the DoD's purview.[2] The DoD owns the world's largest fleet of ships, aircraft, and vehicles, both wheeled and tracked, and has a budget that exceeds $600 billion a year. Its operations are global, with activities under way at several hundred thousand buildings in more than 5,000 different locations spread across 30 million acres of land in more than 160 countries.[3] By contrast, Walmart, the largest private employer in the world, is still a million employees short of the DoD; the largest companies by revenue, including Walmart and oil giants such as Royal Dutch Shell, don't come close to matching the DoD's budget. Yes, China has a bigger military, in terms of numbers, and the United States spends a lot more on health care than it does on defense, but the DoD is operating on a scale that is nearly unique in every dimension.

It is not only size that makes the DoD difficult to manage, however. As James Q. Wilson has observed, what is distinct about American public agencies like the DoD is not simply that they are "big, or complex, or have rules. What is crucial is that they are government bureaucracies," operating under a series of externally imposed political constraints that do not apply in the same degree in the private sector or non-democracies.[4] It is true that running a firm is difficult. This is why many businesses fail, to be sure. But managers in the private sector are not constrained by anywhere near as many external variables as the secretary of defense. Literally hundreds, even thousands, of people and institutions outside the DoD have the ability to control its key inputs – capital and labor – and to determine what its goals should and should not be. Imagine if Walmart or Google could not set their own budgets, hire and fire personnel as they wished, decide which products to sell, make their own determinations about what consumers want, or craft their own inventory control systems.

Many of the processes that provide for democratic control of the DoD also impede its efficiency and doom the prospect that any one individual can "take control" of the organization the way a CEO can take control of a company. The DoD must cope with a president who is its often-untrained Commander-in-Chief and who has a large, ever-eager White House staff available to worry about how the DoD's actions or inactions can hurt the president politically. It faces a Congress full of second-guessing, not-always-well-informed supervisors, who always want something from the DoD, legally or not. Legions of self-appointed experts, armchair generals, know-it-all professors, and investigative reporters observe and judge its every move. It was these sorts of constraints that once led management scholar Peter Drucker to conclude, "I am not yet convinced that the job of Secretary of Defense of the United States is really possible" – or at least possible to do well.[5]

This is not to say that the DoD doesn't encourage someone to try, of course. As we discussed in Chapter 3, the secretary's formal powers have grown stronger over the years. In 1947, when the DoD was created, the secretary of defense was only one among several senior managers of the defense establishment. According to the organization chart, today he holds official authority over the services and all DoD agencies, which have themselves greatly expanded in size and number over the years. With the approval of the president, the secretary of defense hires and fires the service secretaries and nominates the nation's top military leaders. They serve at the secretary of defense's pleasure, and resign or retire when they lose the secretary's favor.

But although the secretary of defense sits atop a very high mountain, other peaks have risen in relative terms. Goldwater–Nichols overcorrected the understaffing of the Joint Chiefs of Staff, endowing the chairman with a large and capable office that now rivals the secretary's. The power of the Combatant Commanders has also increased in recent years. They are America's regional viceroys with their own political and international profiles. The secretary cannot easily ignore their opinions on foreign and defense policies.

Moreover, Congress controls the department's budget and can demand voluminous reports, frequent testimony, and specific purchases from favored suppliers. Fielding and placating these concerns is a large and time-consuming job that secretaries spend much more effort doing than CEOs devote to the mandated quarterly and annual reports to shareholders. The White House staff, too, tend to be suspicious of cabinet officers and the service bureaucracies. Defense is the receptacle of too much money and the focus of too much controversy to be turned over to the secretary as an autonomous fiefdom.

The services want the secretary to be their unhesitant champion, and they get resentful and uncooperative when he is not. Senior officers expect to be shown respect for their experience and rank from the secretary that is not always justified or offered, and they seek recognition that they are also guardians of knowledge that the secretary needs in order to do his job effectively. Each of the services has a constituency of contractors, retired officers, and fans that they know will outlast any secretary and that can be counted on to provide fanatical political support if they feel bureaucratically threatened. Although the services can be ordered to do as they are told, they do not believe themselves to be subordinates. Rather, they conceive of themselves as independent entities with proud heritages whose prosperity is vital to the nation's survival and whose support must be earned by political appointees, including the secretary of defense, whom they suspect of being as beholden to a political party at least as much as to country.

The president also requires a loyalty from the secretary of defense that can never be proven enough because nothing (beyond his own faults) hurts a president more than a secretary of defense's misstep. The secretary is always caught between the president, whose favor is his ultimate source of power, and the services, whose support he needs to run the department effectively. Wars complicate the relationship, as the secretary becomes the president's war manager and the services become absorbed in its execution. Only quick, glorious victory improves the relationship. More often, the strain of war creates fissures within the government, and certainly between the secretary and the services.

Managing to do what?

The secretary must spend much of his time worrying about the top line, not the bottom line – coping and complying with constraints on the department, especially issues related to the budget and personnel, rather than focusing on the organization's core task.[6] But what is that task, exactly? Private firms basically know what they are supposed to do and how to tell whether they are doing it correctly, even though their activities are complex and subject to much internal debate: if revenues are greater than costs, they have turned a profit; if not, they go bankrupt sooner or later. The DoD, by contrast, is supposed to provide "national security," which in itself suggests vastly different requirements to different smart, reasonable people. Ask ten different "experts" and you will likely get ten different answers. Some say it means a military must be built to fight conventional wars, while others suggest the need to focus on irregular conflicts. Others think the DoD should produce "full-spectrum forces," have a strong role in homeland security, or be competent in nation-building. WMD is the danger. No, cyber is. The list goes on.

Experts diverge greatly in their opinions about how these goals should be achieved as well. Do they require an $800 billion defense budget or a $200 billion one? More soldiers or more robots? More bases abroad or fewer? A Navy geared to the littorals or to the open ocean? Three hundred and fifty ships or 250? National security is not a science, although it obviously draws heavily from science and engineering in developing needed equipment, and some questions about the effects of certain deployment patterns or the best way to rotate forces among different missions are amenable to the scientific method. There is much room for debate about the causes of any strategic problem and the likely effects of any US action.

Suppose, for example, everyone agrees (which they do not) that the United States must improve its counterinsurgency capabilities – what policy should then be pursued? Some analysts study the historical record and argue that the United States needs a much larger army to improve its force-to-population ratio in counterinsurgencies and thus to protect locals. Others can look at different cases and argue the opposite, that smaller forces reduce the occupier's footprint and create less resentment among the people. It is hard to say who is right, because we do not know for sure the extent to which future cases will be like past ones, and it is often hard (and usually inadvisable) to conduct controlled experiments in national security. As a result, there is perfectly reasonable disagreement over which constellation of policies will produce the desired "national security" output.

National security policy debates are also usually based on limited data, and decision-makers often feel the need to make quick choices without reflecting on much data and analysis. Unlike shareholder reports, wars are infrequent, so secretaries of defense have little feedback on how the department's procedures are really working. Most of the time, day-to-day military business proceeds by following standard operating procedures, which are sometimes described in old manuals and are sometimes simply passed down informally from one soldier or DoD civilian to the next. If someone were collecting data on efficiency or effectiveness of all of the many, many military tasks, he would find it impossible to sort the important nuggets of insight from the flood. The internal analyst also would probably not be able to get the secretary's attention to change procedures anyway, given the constant, overwhelming demands on the secretary's time.

Box 4.1   Organizational traditions and rigidity

At the start of World War II, the British feared a German invasion, but they were short of coastal artillery to fortify all of their beaches. The solution was to organize truck-towed artillery batteries that would hurry to suspected landing sites and set up to repel the invaders when they received warning of a possible German assault. These units, however, did not perform well. Sector commanders believed that they took too long to set up after arriving at firing locations. Especially puzzling was the inefficiency of soldiers setting up the guns. Films of units in practice runs showed the unexplainable actions of two of the eight members of each gun crew. Upon arrival, the two would stand aside, leaving the rest of the squad to detach and orient the gun and stockpile powder and shells. No one could explain their positioning, least of all the soldiers themselves, who pointed out that they were following the official manual for manning towed guns. No one, that is, until the film was viewed by a retired colonel of artillery. They were, he said, holding the horses. The setup manual had been written when horses pulled artillery, and soldiers held the horses to prevent them from startling when the guns were fired or the battery was attacked.

Even in wars, it can take years to assess accurately whether a strategy is working or not.[7] In the absence of such feedback, there is no objective basis for deciding among the claims of various committee chairmen, NSC staffers, generals and admirals, and defense analysts about what the DoD should do, how, and for how much. It is always possible to tell a story about how closing or building a certain base, intervening or not in a certain country, procuring or canceling a certain number of new fighters, or a million other activities would harm or contribute to national security. As James Schlesinger noted even before he became secretary of defense, "The data suggest no solution in themselves. Even after the quantitative data [are] collected and organized, the pressing question still remains: what does one want to do?"[8] And the answer often depends on other goals that Congress, the president, and contractors care about as well, such as ensuring a fair bidding process, pleasing allies, keeping shipyards open, appearing politically tough on defense, adjusting defense's share of total discretionary spending, and so on.

For markets to work, firms have to be able to perceive demand. But the DoD faces many inconsistent and incompatible demand signals. And no one wants the DoD to experience the equivalent of market discipline – losing a war – if it dismisses or responds to the wrong ones. The extremely high national stakes for DoD failure mean that some "inefficiency" may be both inevitable and desirable, from the perspective of the national interest. It may be worthwhile to engage in expensive preparations to protect against very low-probability, high-consequence events, such as a terrorist nuclear attack, or to build expensive weapons that no one wants to use but which may deter America's enemies. But whether this constitutes inefficiency or just prudence depends on whom you ask and how much hindsight you have.

In short, managing the DoD is a nearly impossible task. This is why most who hold the post of secretary serve less than three years and leave little permanent impact. The wise among them select only one or two policy areas and seek to achieve what they consider to be improved outcomes. The rest of the vast department is left to run on its own with the hope that nothing too controversial or disastrous occurs. The secretaries attend the ceremonies, hand out the awards, sign the reports, greet the important visitors, take the tours of overseas bases, praise the troops and their families, and pray that they can ride out the scandals that erupt on their watch.

The presidents who appoint them want little else. Occasionally there is a specific task to accomplish – help end a war, assist the department in recovering from a scandal, improve morale after a period of unhappy foreign ventures or budget cuts – but most presidents have no higher expectations than that things are kept quiet at the Pentagon and that the department's budget requests are not too outrageous.

Often the president does not know the secretary well before appointing him. It is not a job usually given to a close political friend or a potential rival. Instead, the search is for a plausible candidate who can help the administration look competent and in control, someone who will keep the department in line without much presidential attention. Businessmen are frequently selected because the public thinks that they can manage large organizations. Democrats often select Republicans, to gain public credibility in defense and congressional support in an area of party weakness. Presidents have appointed politicians, scientists, a former White House Chief of Staff, the heads of General Motors, Ford, and Procter & Gamble, Wall Street financiers, former senators, a couple of secretaries of the Navy, and a former CIA director or two. Some are remembered fondly. Some have had ships or major military facilities named after them.

Only two, however, really tried to manage the department: Robert McNamara and Donald Rumsfeld. Neither is remembered fondly, and neither is likely ever to have a warship or a major DoD facility bearing his name.

Figure 4.1 Secretary of Defense Robert McNamara certainly knew where Vietnam was

Source: National Archives.

Robert S. McNamara

As president of the Ford Motor Company and a nominal Republican, Robert McNamara was not an unusual choice for secretary of defense when President Kennedy picked him in 1961. What was unusual was that McNamara would gain a reputation for being a highly effective public administrator while earning the everlasting animosity of the military and directing a failed and disastrously costly war. McNamara had the longest tenure of any secretary, cultivating the support of Presidents Kennedy and Johnson by demonstrating fierce loyalty to them and mastering bureaucratic politics. The military's pained endurance of his leadership, however, assured that his main legacy would be a determination to eliminate every vestige of his presence. Decades after he left office, and years after he died, one can still find editorials and articles in military and defense industry journals denouncing his actions as secretary and warning his successors against repeating them.

Disavowing precedent, McNamara envisioned what came to be called an "active management" approach to the job of secretary of defense. As he explained in 1961, "I see my position here as being that of a leader, not a judge. I'm here to originate and stimulate new ideas and programs, not just to referee arguments and harmonize interests."[9] McNamara and others recognized that although the Department of Defense was a relatively new organization, the secretary did not lack for legal authority. The Defense Reorganization Act of 1958 had recently expanded the secretary's powers. The problem, in their view, was the lack of management tools that could help the secretary actually exercise his power. McNamara wanted a Pentagon in which the secretary would have a large staff of his own to provide civilian advice, independent of service parochialism. In this way, the secretary, and only the secretary, would be able personally to assess alternatives and to make choices about how to integrate weapons and forces, defense budgets, military strategy, and foreign policy.[10] He could drive the agenda, instead of simply reacting to what the services offered.

Defense policy had played a central role in the election that brought in the Kennedy administration. During the campaign, Kennedy had attacked the Republicans not just for permitting a "bomber gap" and then a "missile gap" to develop between the United States and the Soviet Union. He also had criticized the larger Eisenhower policy known as "massive retaliation," which threatened an all-out US nuclear first strike in response to even limited, conventional Soviet aggression. Initiated because of the United States' head start in the nuclear arms race and sustained by President Eisenhower's fiscal conservatism, massive retaliation relied heavily on the Air Force and its strategic nuclear bombing capability as a one-size-fits-all solution to the Soviet threat. But in Kennedy's view, massive retaliation was not credible. In the early days of the Cold War, perhaps the United States could have launched a disarming first strike, but as the Soviet nuclear arsenal expanded, it became more and more likely that a few Soviet bombs would survive to put American cities at risk. Would the United States really initiate a nuclear holocaust in defense of Berlin or Seoul? It seemed unlikely, as well as morally abhorrent because of the number of innocent lives put in jeopardy. Yet the lack of intermediate options, and particularly the severely reduced combat capability of the Army, gave the United States a choice between what President Kennedy referred to as "inglorious retreat or unlimited retaliation."[11]

Kennedy and McNamara's objections to massive retaliation went beyond moral outrage and strategic skepticism. They believed that the Eisenhower defense posture also reflected serious shortcomings in the existing approach to defense planning and budgeting, which made it impossible to determine what the nation's defense needs and capabilities actually were. Because budgets in the 1950s were organized by service rather than mission, on short time horizons, using estimates and calculations of unclear validity, with no central coordination, there was no way to identify functional gaps or wasteful duplication.[12] Two of McNamara's protégés later wrote that:

> in 1961, for example, the airlift furnished by the Air Force and the sealift furnished by the Navy were not sufficient for the timely movement of reinforcements planned by the Army to meet an attack in Europe. The Army was counting on close air support in a non-nuclear war, but the Tactical Air Command . . . was concentrating almost exclusively on . . . theater nuclear wars.[13]

These kinds of discrepancies gave rise to serious concerns about whether the existing defense posture really had any rational basis for its allocation of resources.

During the previous 13 years, the secretary's job essentially had been to ensure that total military spending remained capped at a level determined by the administration's other fiscal priorities – not to evaluate threats and determine what level of spending was required to combat them. Kennedy wanted to change this. Presaging many of McNamara's own arguments, Kennedy noted in his first State of the Union address:

> In the past, the lack of a consistent, coherent military strategy, the absence of basic assumptions about our national requirements, and the faulty estimates and duplications arising from inter-service rivalries have all made it difficult to assess how adequate – or inadequate – our defenses really are.

Kennedy threw his weight behind McNamara in the push for change, announcing in the same speech that he had "instructed the Secretary of Defense to reappraise our entire defense strategy."[14] Kennedy promised to do what McNamara attempted – to manage defense.

With the assistance of the RAND Corporation, once solely the Air Force's think tank but now also harnessed to support the Office of the Secretary, McNamara sought to implement reforms that addressed these deficiencies. McNamara had the will and, he thought, the way.[15] The planning mechanism was the Planning, Programming, and Budgeting System (PPBS), now called the Planning, Programming, Budgeting, and Execution System (PPBES), which had its origins in the long-sought progressive goal to improve the professionalism of government via doctrines of scientific management, as explained in the Hoover Commission reports of the 1940s. PPBS was based on the creation of five-year plans (something that the Soviet Union had borrowed from the same ambitious literature) that grouped programs by military missions (strategic attack, sealift, etc.) rather than by service, so that output comparisons (targets destroyed, tons delivered) and program investment decisions could be made logically.

McNamara discovered, however, that there is a difference between DoD logic and congressional logic. Congress insisted that the department present its budget in the traditional appropriation accounts (Shipbuilding, Navy; Missiles and Aircraft Procurement, Navy; etc.), no matter how else the department wanted to analyze it internally. Congress cared a lot about particular line items and where they were made, not just the total amount of "output" devoted to certain missions. Moreover, the mission categories were hardly conducive to illuminating analysis of the budget. The strategic programs did have a lot of commonality because any nuclear-tipped ballistic missile or bomb, whatever its delivery platform, served pretty much the same purpose. But other PPBS categories such as Conventional Forces, Research and Development, or Reserve Forces were vastly too broad to be very useful for planning. There are many types of conventional ground forces (heavy, light, airborne), for example, and many uses to which they can be put (armored warfare, peacekeeping, raids, etc.). Congressional pork-barrel interests and the complexity of modern security needs made the planning process a lot less scientific than planning advocates concede.[16]

McNamara proposed to calculate defense needs using systems analysis, a technique that grew out of the operations research efforts of World War II. The general idea was to measure inputs and outputs of various processes, looking for correlations that analysts could use to optimize effort. In the fight against the Axis powers, operations research had made significant contributions to anti-submarine warfare, aircraft operations, and logistics. McNamara himself was part of these efforts as a young Army Air Force captain. After the war, RAND and other think tanks made their reputations attempting to apply systems analysis to an ever-widening circle of defense issues.[17] At the Pentagon, where rules of thumb and the authority of "experience" dominated, the attempts of McNamara and his civilian "Whiz Kids" to be both systematic and mathematical in approaching military problems were path-breaking and productive.

Like most analytical tools, however, systems analysis and the broader field of quantitative defense analysis have their limits. Operations research is excellent at determining things such as how many incoming ballistic missiles can be intercepted, with what probability of success, by a defensive system with particular characteristics. Systems analysis can even estimate the cost of each additional increment of improvement in the system's intercept probability and compare the outcomes using one type of missile or another, procured through various methods. What neither approach can do very well is estimate the effect of building such defenses on the likelihood that the enemy will alter its behavior in a particular way. Will the adversary respond by building cruise missiles, or caving in to our demands? And how do these probabilities compare to what it would do if we signed an arms control agreement instead of building the missile defense system? Systems analysis cannot say, because the answer requires too many unknown, qualitative inputs.

Even in purely quantitative analysis, however, much depends on the assumptions made in setting up problems. It is important to understand whose goals are being maximized. Budget analysts have a different perspective on military costs than do operational commanders. Although it is always good to be quantitative and systematic in approaching problems, it is not always possible to find accurate numbers or useful information when decisions have to be made. Without the key numbers and all the information, which are missing much of the time, systems analysis slides very close to being little more than applied common sense with a scientific façade.[18]

The administration's proposed strategy, Flexible Response, by itself offered no obvious ways to limit the defense budget. It was, by definition, flexible, making adjudications among competing defense priorities all the more subjective. But McNamara argued that systems analysis would provide the needed "objective" answers. He established an office staffed by a new generation of Whiz Kids, mostly with RAND connections, to apply the technique. Systems analysis provided a way for his relatively young coterie of civilians to challenge the judgments of generals. McNamara had been a non-pilot Air Corps captain; President Kennedy was just a PT boat hero. McNamara used systems analysis to challenge what would otherwise have been politically invincible military judgments.[19]

The military was caught off guard initially. Officers were familiar with the use of analysis in operational settings but not with analysis applied to defense budgets and programs. They were quick, however, to notice that the analysis was being applied selectively within the department. Programs McNamara did not like were demonstrated not to be cost-effective, while favored programs or those close to the president's political allies or needs were not subject to much analysis or criticism. Professional military judgments were dismissed as not being based on rigorous analysis, although the secretary's preferences seemed protected by layers of made-up numbers and arbitrary assumptions. The public and the press were impressed by McNamara's scientific approach to defense decision-making, but the military was not. It especially resented what one general called "the tree full of pipe-smoking owls," McNamara's young civilian analysts, telling them what was militarily viable. Soon officers were being sent to graduate schools to learn systems analysis techniques. Although the resentment toward civilian defense analysts lingers, the military can now manipulate studies with the best of them.

The other component of McNamara's agenda involved the acquisition reforms discussed further in Chapter 8. McNamara introduced the use of incentive contracts, sought total package procurement (TPP), and advocated joint systems. With incentive contracts, he hoped to avoid the temptations to escalate costs that were inherent in earlier contracts that provided a set amount of profit proportional to the estimated cost of a program. Total package procurement, which promised to set the terms for all phases of a program based on bids in a single, up-front competition, was his mechanism to avoid buy-ins where contractors would gain incumbency in specific weapon systems through early, optimistic cost and performance estimates and then escalate the costs in subsequent stages of development, procurement, and system support. Joint projects were meant to avoid duplication by combining service needs in a single project. McNamara-era jointness' most famous incarnation was the TFX Air Force–Navy tactical fighter program that became the F-111.[20]

McNamara's acquisition reforms were largely frustrated. His biggest accomplishment was redressing the budget imbalance that had previously favored the Air Force. He cut the B-58 and B-70 bombers. He also cut the Skybolt air-to-ground missile and reduced the number of Minuteman missiles to 1,200. He forced the Air Force to increase the survivability of its land-based missiles by hardening Minuteman silos, putting more bombers on airborne alert, and parking bombers in protective shelters. He also compelled the Air Force to improve early warning systems and buy more strategic airlift. And it had to invest more in its conventional mission, starting with strengthening the wings of the F-105 so the aircraft could deliver conventional ordnance.[21]

Still, the services outlast any secretary, even long-serving ones like Robert McNamara. The Navy cancelled its version of the TFX just days after McNamara left office, reining in the jointness initiative. And the Navy's resistance to jointness in this case turned out well: Navy-developed F-4s and A-7s were the star fixed-winged aircraft of the Vietnam War. The Air Force bought many hundreds of each, proving both the value of inter-service competition in the design of systems and the ability of the services to adjust to circumstances in times of war.

The ideas that the services should avoid buy-ins and misdirected incentives were good ones, but total package procurement relied on heroic assumptions about being able to predict the pace of technological progress and the cost of as-yet-undeveloped systems. Several of McNamara's signature projects using this tool, such as the C-5A transport aircraft, still paid the price for early over-optimism. The government was forced to modify contracts to pay the true costs of development and production, irrespective of the early estimates, and in the end the systems cost a fortune.

McNamara left office in disgrace, largely because of the escalation of the Vietnam War, but also for his attitude toward his generals and contractors. His image has yet to be rehabilitated.

Donald H. Rumsfeld

Donald Rumsfeld's story is stranger than McNamara's. Rumsfeld seemed like a natural when President George Bush nominated him in 2001. After all, he had been secretary of defense 25 years before for President Gerald Ford. He also had been a Navy pilot, served three terms as a congressional representative, worked in the executive branch, been a presidential envoy to the Middle East, been President Ford's Chief of Staff, chaired important national commissions, and headed a major corporation, G. D. Searle & Company. He had even been touted as a presidential candidate.[22] Rumsfeld knew politics, business, Congress, foreign policy, and defense. His appointment was greeted with predictions of success from virtually all quarters.

And yet, there is little dispute that Rumsfeld was a disaster as secretary the second time around. Like McNamara, Rumsfeld promised reform, had a war to manage, and got along poorly with senior officers. His reform effort was centered on the exceedingly vague goal of "transformation." His war was the poorly titled Global War on Terror, which, perhaps thanks to his management, has also been called the Long War. Embittering many of his aides, Rumsfeld essentially ignored or retired all senior generals and admirals who had gained their positions during the Clinton years. He was supposedly the most arrogant secretary of them all, a man who was said to be often uncivil in his relationships with subordinates.

Candidate Bush had said he would take advantage of what he termed a "revolution in the technology of war" that would enable the United States "to skip a generation" of weapons instead of incrementally improving the existing arsenal. Bush stated in a 2000 speech at The Citadel that if elected he would "begin an immediate, comprehensive review of the military – the structure of its forces, the state of its strategy, the priorities of its procurement." He said, "I will give the secretary a broad mandate – to challenge the status quo and envision a new architecture of American defense for decades to come."[23]

Figure 4.2 Secretary of Defense Donald Rumsfeld showing that the second time around isn't easier

Source: Department of Defense: Photo by Tech. Sgt. Andy Dunaway, US Air Force.

Relishing the return to government, Rumsfeld launched this comprehensive review even before Bush's inauguration on January 20, 2001. By February, he had formed a dozen or more working groups of defense experts, industry leaders, and retired officers tasked with assessing various aspects of the US defense posture and making recommendations. Rumsfeld also commissioned Andrew Marshall, the much-celebrated, long-serving director of the Pentagon's Office of Net Assessment, to "undertake a broad analysis of America's likely future adversaries, the nature of future wars, how many conflicts the United States should be prepared to fight at once and what forces it will need to do so."[24] Rumsfeld's general guidance for the process suggested that space and missile defense, information management, precision strike, rapidly deployable standing joint forces, unmanned systems, and strategic mobility would benefit from greater investment.

According to Rumsfeld, investing in some of these technologies would require reducing or eliminating some aspects of the existing defense posture. He refused to preside over a cash infusion for defense while his president was advocating a large tax cut, as Secretary of Defense Caspar Weinberger had done under President Reagan. As he assumed office again, Rumsfeld had made it clear that he wanted to rid the Pentagon of "unneeded organizations and facilities" to gain the resources required.[25]

This news came as a shock to the military leaders, who still had the phrase "help is on the way" ringing in their ears from the 2000 presidential campaign.[26] It was particularly disconcerting to the Army's leadership, who had already initiated a transformation effort to move toward lighter and more deployable forces. They had expected Secretary Rumsfeld to be their ally in defense policy-making.

Instead, Rumsfeld believed that the only way to manage the defense effort was to exclude powerful – he would say "entrenched" – bureaucratic actors from the reform process. So, he kept senior officers out of the comprehensive review, and the review's working groups floated various policy trial balloons that were anathema to the military leadership. Suggestions swirled that Secretary Rumsfeld might propose to cut two Army divisions or two carrier battle groups from America's force structure, and the transformation working groups discussed the cancellation of a high-profile system from each military service: the Army's Crusader mobile artillery system, the Marines' V-22 Osprey tilt-rotor aircraft, the Air Force's F-22 Raptor, and the Navy's DD-21 destroyer.

Not surprisingly, a reform effort that excluded powerful stakeholders and threatened important organizational and budgetary interests attracted many opponents, both inside and outside the Pentagon. Rumsfeld's approach so infuriated military officers and congressional leaders from his own party that there was considerable speculation in the late summer of 2001 that he would be the first cabinet officer in the Bush administration to leave office. This was not the record of a successful management guru, but nor is it the whole story of Rumsfeld's failure to manage national security policy.

The surprise attacks of 9/11 galvanized the nation and saved Rumsfeld's job. He offered a confident, bold presence to a shaken public, which not only revitalized his power to overcome corporate military interests (as we discussed in Chapter 3) but also offered a new opportunity to demonstrate his supposed management prowess. Soon he was leading the counter-attack, gaining quick success in Afghanistan using very unconventional tactics and warning of the dangers posed by Iraq, Iran, and North Korea, the nations President Bush labeled the "axis of evil." A year and a half later, the United States invaded Iraq. The major combat phase of the Iraq campaign was also very quick, nearly casualty-free for coalition forces, and unconventional in its tactics. Briefly, Rumsfeld held the status of military genius because it was clear that he had dictated aspects of both the Afghan and the Iraqi operations against the advice of his generals.

Only gradually did it become clear that initial military successes had degraded into dangerous insurgencies. Neither al Qaeda nor the Taliban nor the Ba'athist remnants of Saddam's regime had been totally eliminated, and the high-tech military systems that Rumsfeld had promoted, especially the emphasis on futuristic space-based equipment, did not prove very helpful in counterinsurgency warfare. Rumsfeld also seemed to ignore reality as he denied that the United States faced an insurgency and maintained that the situation was getting better all the time. As the casualties and budgetary costs mounted, Rumsfeld slipped back into character as the seemingly incompetent and roundly disliked official he was on September 10, 2001. Many Americans thought he lived in a bubble or an echo chamber, while their management heroes agilely adapted to new information.

Throughout his tenure Rumsfeld had a basic passive-aggressive style that did not serve him well. He ignored, isolated, and insulted those who displeased him by questioning his policy preferences. He only fired a few; most, he just pushed aside. General Shinseki, the Army Chief of Staff who testified that the occupation of Iraq would require more than double the number of troops being assigned, was left in office for over a year but rendered a lame duck by a very early announcement of the intent to replace him. Often Rumsfeld would delay important decisions, procrastinating rather than taking action, and frustrating the bureaucratic machine below. He shunned responsibility when trouble occurred, likely hurting his president in the process. The best example is the Abu Ghraib scandal, which involved the abuse of Iraqi prisoners by US Army Reservists and support contractors serving as guards. Though the perfect opportunity for Rumsfeld's resignation after years of escalating violence in Iraq, the lingering scandal was allowed to erode support for the war further by offering the public only one ineffective investigation after another.

Our concern here is with Rumsfeld's attempt to manage the bureaucracy through his transformation agenda, rather than his management of the wars in Iraq and Afghanistan.[27] But these topics are not unrelated. Rumsfeld's version of transformation might have been vague, but it always included using fewer, lighter, more agile forces, the mark of early operations in both Iraq and Afghanistan. The strongest criticism of his management of the wars is that he did not commit sufficient forces to either operation, allowing insurgents to cause havoc with reconstruction and democratization programs, and permitting al Qaeda's senior leaders to escape justice. The failure to achieve sufficient security delayed the training of local forces and prevented the early withdrawal of American and coalition forces. It is not hard to see the connection between Rumsfeld's reform agenda and the campaign plans he devised.

Many also criticized the support provided to the troops in the field on his watch. The Pentagon did not buy or deploy enough protective vests, armored vehicles, and interpreters. Similar criticism appeared about McNamara's management of the Vietnam War. Then, the problems were with malfunctioning rifles, rotting boots, and ammunition shortages. The United States is almost always unprepared to some degree for the wars it fights, because America's opponents have a say in the nature of the war and rarely are as accommodating as one might hope to American war plans. No imaginable investment in defense will have the right equipment in the right place for every type of warfare. Still, widespread outrage always greets a seeming lack of preparedness. Secretary Rumsfeld's plans that promised to cut back the heft of the American military walked right into the teeth of this criticism. When he needed political allies to save his floundering reform effort, he found that his imperious management style had made few close friends.[28]

Although there was talk of a Rumsfeld-inspired transformation in defense business affairs, no changes in the way the Department of Defense buys things or manages things will do away with the shortcomings of war plans. It is surprising in fact how little Rumsfeld tried to change the formal management processes within the department. Instead, he mostly ignored them or tried to co-opt them by appointing hand-picked leaders of the various organizations. But in tough political battles, those whom he had ignored were not on his side, and those whom he had appointed were sometimes viewed as "tainted" by his tightly managed selection process.

Nor did Rumsfeld use the vague concept of transformation the way McNamara used the vague tool of systems analysis to outmaneuver the military in program and budget decisions. The military and defense contractors were wiser for the McNamara experience. Within months after Rumsfeld began promoting the transformation concept, the services and their contractors were calling every program, old or new, "transformational." As a result, most of the force structure changes Rumsfeld implemented were in addition to, not instead of, existing programs.[29]

In a real sense, Rumsfeld's attempts to transform the American military were misdirected. Much of the vision behind the "revolution in military affairs" is simply unattainable. It is especially fanciful in counterinsurgencies, where the objective is to influence the hearts and minds of the people, understand local practices and conditions, and avoid collateral damage in a highly cluttered environment. The American military's interest in preparing for counterinsurgency warfare is close to non-existent. The wars the armed services prefer to fight are the big ones where technology, even in incomplete forms, gives large advantage. Counterinsurgencies are usually long, painful efforts that depend on sustaining national will, which wears away relatively quickly for distant fights such as Vietnam and Iraq. Rumsfeld's mistake was to believe that the revolution had wide applicability and that it was possible to avoid the manpower burdens of occupation that come with victory. In war, there is such a thing as being too light and too agile. Rumsfeld, of course, also did little to win hearts and minds in his own department, and he had no technological help to solve departmental problems, either.

Figure 4.3 Secretary of Defense Robert Gates: happiness is mastery of the bureaucracy

Source: Department of Defense. Photo by Mass Communication Specialist 1st Class Chad J. McNeeley, US Navy.

Robert M. Gates

Rumsfeld's successor, Robert Gates, is already considered one of the most successful secretaries of defense. Merely replacing Rumsfeld was certain to make Gates' tenure an acceptable one in many quarters, but Gates sought more than that. He cultivated the military with his attentiveness and decisiveness in dealing with their program proposals. He wooed the media and the public with his apparent toughness in holding generals and senior officials responsible for failures. He associated himself with the political golden boy of the moment, General David Petraeus, who promised a recipe for counterinsurgency (where Rumsfeld had denied that one was necessary) and was lucky enough that choices by Sunni leaders in Iraq reinforced the effectiveness of his efforts rather than undermining them. Gates also demonstrated visible concern for the welfare of the average soldier. President Bush couldn't afford to lose him after years of tolerating Rumsfeld, and President Obama wisely chose to retain him as secretary. By placing the ongoing wars in experienced hands, Republican ones at that, Obama forged a protective shield from critics on his right while offering Gates the opportunity for public service sainthood and the guaranteed absence of critics on the left. Of course, Gates' reputation was also greatly aided by his choice not to try to do a lot of "management."[30]

Gates came to the Pentagon after a career in a rival agency, having risen through the ranks to be the CIA director at the end of the Cold War. He was a Soviet analyst for the agency, earning a PhD in Russian history and appointment as the Deputy National Security Advisor for President George H. W. Bush as the Soviet Union began to collapse. Retiring from the CIA directorship when President Bush lost reelection, Gates lectured, consulted, and wrote on security issues before becoming president of Texas A&M in College Station, Texas, the home of the George H. W. Bush Presidential Library. As with other former senior officials, he was often appointed to national commissions and study groups. It was from one of these assignments, the Iraq Study Group convened to advise President George W. Bush, that he became a front-runner to succeed Rumsfeld. Yet although the Iraq Study Group recommended a phased withdrawal from Iraq, Gates would oversee the Iraq surge instead.

On Gates' watch, Iraq gradually got better and Afghanistan did not, but he found quick success at home in handling a scandal at the Army's Walter Reed Medical Center, which broke shortly after he took office. In a Pulitzer Prize-winning series, the *Washington Post* described neglect of injured soldiers at the famous Washington facility. Outpatient soldiers were supposedly housed in dilapidated buildings at the hospital and ignored in their quest for treatment and benefits. The story might have been more complicated than that – the soldiers were mostly Reservists seeking disability benefits for non-war-related injuries – but to the public it seemed like a gross dereliction on the part of the Army. Gates acted swiftly, firing a couple of generals and then the secretary of the Army for incompetence. The Army's reputation suffered, but not Gates'.

Less than a year later, another scandal broke, this time involving Air Force failures to properly handle nuclear weapons. Some units consistently failed inspections. In one instance of flagrant disregard for regulations, a bomber with a nuclear-armed cruise missile on its wing was flown to another base and parked on a taxiway unguarded overnight. Gates ended up firing the Air Force Chief of Staff and the secretary. It mattered not that he had other grievances with them, most especially their continued promotion of the costly F-22 stealth fighter. The press and the public loved that he appeared to be holding senior officials responsible for what seemed to be serious lapses. Gates soon began applying this standard to the faltering war in Afghanistan, firing three commanders in a row, including two he put there himself.

Unlike Rumsfeld, Gates made the wars, not military reform, his prime focus. Despite readily admitting that Afghanistan would never become "a central Asian Valhalla," Gates came to advocate an intensification of counterinsurgency operations, both there and especially in Iraq. Gates gained further public standing with his attempts to limit US casualties by improving protective equipment and intelligence-gathering capabilities. He was the very visible champion of both the multibillion-dollar investment in Mine Resistant Ambush Protected vehicles (MRAPs) and the dramatic increase in the use of unmanned aerial vehicles in the wars. Whereas Rumsfeld famously said in 2004 in answer to a soldier's question about the lack of vehicle protection against improvised explosive devices, "You go to war with the Army you have," Gates appeared determined to field better systems quickly.

Gates also seemed to use his popularity to cancel or limit several faltering weapons programs, including the Army's Future Combat System, the Air Force's F-22 Raptor, the Navy's new destroyer, and the Marine Corps' Expeditionary Fighting Vehicle. He also appeared interested in controlling the Pentagon's budget during the worldwide economic crisis that stressed the government's finances. But he was pursuing a more subtle game. Counterinsurgencies are difficult, time-consuming operations, requiring the securing of populations and major initiatives to improve economic conditions, as well as the cracking of militant networks and the training of local forces. That was certainly the case in Iraq and Afghanistan. The American public were tiring of the effort even before Gates took over as secretary of defense. His much-heralded actions – the firing of generals, the rapid acquisitions of MRAPs and other gear, and budget maneuvers – can be seen both as necessary and as ways to buy time.

In the end, it is the president who determines policy direction. Gates accepted military arguments for making a counterinsurgency strategy work, expanding force levels and making long-term commitments. Despite the program cuts and complaints about the acquisition process, Gates tried to protect the defense budget from significant reductions, using small, high-profile adjustments as a shield against the threat of larger cuts. But President Obama is the one who made ending the wars a priority. Gates was gone before the withdrawals in Iraq were complete and the surge in Afghanistan was reversed, replaced by another CIA director,

Leon Panetta. Gates' legacy shines in the public view thanks to his predecessor's failures and his seemingly deft political moves, but it was really quite modest: faltering interest in ongoing counterinsurgency efforts, military programs that still exceed any realistic budget expectations, and strategic confusion among the armed services. In other words, about normal for a secretary of defense.

Box 4.2 Bureaucratic strategies: the Polaris project

In American government, power is limited even within the military. Senior officers can delegate their authority, assign priorities, and command cooperation, but unless their subordinates are politically adept, they will discover the full frustration of operating within a world of recalcitrant bureaucracies. In the 1950s, Rear Admiral William Raborn was assigned responsibilities for developing the Polaris, a submarine-launched ballistic missile. The program had the highest national priority designation and the full support of Admiral Arleigh Burke, the Chief of Naval Operations. But Raborn instinctively knew that if he was to succeed, he needed to win – not command – the cooperation of many agencies inside and, more importantly, outside the Navy. To do so, he used a variety of bureaucratic strategies, including the following:

- Differentiation: There are literally hundreds of weapons development projects under way at any given time within the Department of Defense, each with its own advocates. To signal within government the unique importance of the Polaris to the Navy and the nation, Admiral Raborn had his officers and civil servants work weekends, fly first class, have their messages hand-delivered by sailors, and describe the consequences of failure in apocalyptic terms ("It is your neck, not mine . . .").
- Co-optation: Some agencies or groups hold influence over future political and budgetary support, and they must be made to believe, whether it is true or not, that the program in question is seriously taking their interests into consideration as decisions are made. Thus, Admiral Raborn funded the research suggestions of nearly every senior academic of national importance who consulted on the project – but without necessarily paying heed to the results. He still let the submarine force decide how many missiles each Polaris boat would carry (16), despite technical advice to the contrary.
- Moderation: Because even a highly successful program like Polaris, one that has resources including top-level political support, will need the cooperation of less powerful but persistent agencies in the long run, it is wise not to alienate them. Admiral Raborn had sufficient resources initially to build a modern headquarters, as did the ballistic missile agencies of the other services, but he chose not to, with the knowledge that it was better to live in inadequate facilities like the rest of the Navy acquisition agencies, rather than to flaunt Polaris's wealth. Someday, Polaris would need friends even in those agencies.
- Managerial innovation: Senior officials worry about the blame that they will receive if important, highly visible programs fail, and thus they are tempted to micromanage programs even to the point of hindering them. Intentionally or not, Admiral Raborn began to emphasize not the management skills of his staff

(continued)

(continued)

or contractors but rather the innovative management systems they created or adopted – notably, the Program Evaluation and Review Technique (PERT) and the creation of a "war" room. PERT created complex charts that purported to keep schedules aligned for all of the disparate organizations and components of the Polaris project, and the war room made near-real-time data about the overall project accessible to program leadership and to inquisitive outsiders. These innovations did not have to work but only to dazzle in order to give the program the decision space he believed it needed to succeed.

Managing the unmanageable

It is best when thinking about defense management to recall the punch line in an officer recruiting advertisement the Army used to use. After showing a young man with a briefcase contemplating his future, it showed soldiers in an exercise doing daring things. The line went, "It's not a company. It's your country!" Being in the military is surely more exciting than being in your average business. It is also very different. You might be able to manage a business, but your country is a whole other thing, and so is war. Some secretaries of defense offer the now-standard rhetoric about the value of a business-like approach to government, but most realize the difference. Robert McNamara and Donald Rumsfeld did not. They thought they could manage defense, and they failed. Even when you recognize the difference, as Robert Gates certainly did, your influence is going to be limited.

Although it is impossible to admit it, the challenge for a secretary is to attempt only a few changes, kick as many problems as possible down the road to the next administration, and attribute any major failings to the neglect of past administrations, especially those of the other party. All of this must be done without the slightest hint of cynicism. However, the Department of Defense cannot be said to be undermanaged. On the contrary, too many entities are involved in its management. The administration, Congress, the military, the media, and the contractors all have their hands on the wheel, and unavoidably so, because much depends on what happens in the department.

After their terms, both Secretary Gates and his successor, Leon Panetta, gained some notoriety by complaining in their autobiographies that the White House staff, especially the National Security Council staff, micromanaged the department. They and their successor, Ashton Carter, complained, too, about Congress' failure to allow effective budgeting and the closures of excess facilities and obsolete programs. And Gates worried publicly about the services failing to adjust to the changing battlefield: he thought they colluded with the contractors to perpetuate their preferred ways of war. As it turns out, not only do lots of people have their hands on the wheel of defense policy, they usually do not steer in the same direction.

Questions for discussion

1   **What traits should a president seek in a secretary of defense? Can personal expertise in military or business affairs help a secretary of defense?**

2   **What role can quantitative analysis play in the formulation of defense policy?**

3   **How much should a secretary of defense manage by coalition-building and accommodation, and how much should he manage by giving orders and changing personnel?**

4   **How should a secretary of defense respond to media criticism?**

Notes

1 Harold Brown, "Managing the Defense Department: Why It Can't Be Done," *Dividend*, magazine of the Graduate School of Business Administration, University of Michigan (Spring 1981): 10–14, available at: http://deepblue.lib.umich.edu/bitstream/2027.42/50728/2/1981-spring-dividend-text.pdf (accessed September 2, 2016).

2 "DOD 101: An Introductory Overview of the Department of Defense," *U.S. Department of Defense*, available at: http://www.defense.gov/About-DoD/DoD-101 (accessed September 2, 2016).

3 "Our Global Infrastructure," available at: http://www.defense.gov/About-DoD/DoD-101 (accessed September 2, 2016).

4 James Q. Wilson, *Bureaucracy: What Government Agencies Do and Why They Do It* (New York: Basic Books, 1989), p. 115.

5 Quoted in Eliot Cohen, "A Tale of Two Secretaries," *Foreign Affairs*, 81(3) (May/June 2002): 34–35.

6 Wilson, *Bureaucracy*, p. 115.

7 Stephen P. Rosen, *Winning the Next War: Innovation and the Modern Military* (Ithaca, NY: Cornell University Press, 1991).

8 James Schlesinger, "Quantitative Analysis and National Security," *World Politics*, 15(2) (January 1963): 298.

9 Quoted in William W. Kaufmann, *The McNamara Strategy* (New York: Harper & Row, 1964), p. 171.

10 Alain C. Enthoven and K. Wayne Smith, *How Much Is Enough? Shaping the Defense Program, 1961–1969* (New York: Harper & Row, 1971), p. 3.

11 Fred Kaplan, *The Wizards of Armageddon* (New York: Simon & Schuster, 1983), pp. 248–250; Christopher A. Preble, *John F. Kennedy and the Missile Gap* (DeKalb, IL: Northern Illinois University Press, 2004).

12 Lawrence J. Korb, "The Budget Process in the Department of Defense, 1947–77: The Strengths and Weaknesses of Three Systems," *Public Administration Review*, 37(4) (July–August 1977): 336.

13 Enthoven and Smith, *How Much Is Enough?*, p. 11.

14 Quoted in Kaufmann, *The McNamara Strategy*, p. 47.

15 For biographical background on McNamara, see Deborah Shapely, *Promise and Power: The Life and Times of Robert McNamara* (Boston, MA: Little Brown, 1993); Roger R. Trask and Alfred Goldberg, *The Department of Defense, 1947–1997: Organization and Leaders* (Washington, DC: Historical Office, Office of the Secretary of Defense, 1997).

16 Aaron Wildavsky, "If Planning Is Everything, Maybe It's Nothing," *Policy Sciences*, 4 (1973): 127–153.

17 Bruce Smith, *The RAND Corporation: A Case Study of a Non-Profit Advisory Corporation* (Cambridge, MA: Harvard University Press, 1966).

18 Stephen P. Rosen, "Systems Analysis and the Quest for Rational Defense," *Public Interest*, 76 (Summer 1984): 3–17; Wildavsky, "If Planning Is Everything."

19 Arnold Kanter, *Defense Politics: A Budgetary Perspective* (Chicago, IL: University of Chicago Press, 1979).

20 Robert F. Coulam, *Illusions of Choice: The F-111 and the Problem of Weapons Acquisition Reform* (Princeton, NJ: Princeton University Press, 1977).

21 Laurence E. Lynn Jr. and Richard I. Smith, "Can the Secretary of Defense Make a Difference?" *International Security*, 7(1) (Summer 1982): 56–57.

22 Rowan Scarborough, *Rumsfeld's War: The Untold Story of America's Anti-Terrorist Commander* (Washington, DC: Regnery Publishing, 2004), pp. 91–98; James Mann, *Rise of the Vulcans: The History of Bush's War Cabinet* (New York: Viking, 2004), pp. 123–125, 138–139.

23 George W. Bush, "A Period of Consequences," speech at The Citadel, Charleston, South Carolina, September 23, 1999, available at: http://www.fas.org/spp/starwars/program/news99/92399_defense.htm (accessed September 2, 2016).

24 For a favorable discussion of Andrew Marshall and the Office of Net Assessment, see Andrew F. Krepinevich and Barry Watts, *The Last Warrior: Andrew Marshall and the Shaping of Modern American Defense Strategy* (New York: Basic Books, 2015).
25 "Bush Candidate for Defense Job Sees Overhaul," *New York Times*, January 12, 2001, p. A1.
26 The line was standard in the Bush stump speech. See, for instance, "Rebuilding the Military Takes Spotlight as Bush, Gore Joust," *The San Diego Union-Tribune*, November 4, 2000, p. A-17.
27 Donald Rumsfeld, "Transforming the Military," *Foreign Affairs*, 81(3) (May/June 2002): 20–32.
28 Harvey M. Sapolsky, Benjamin H. Friedman, and Brendan Rittenhouse Green (eds.), *U.S. Military Innovation since the Cold War: Creation Without Destruction* (London: Routledge, 2009).
29 Sapolsky, Friedman, and Green, *U.S. Military Innovation since the Cold War*.
30 For a praising self-assessment, see Robert M. Gates, *Duty: Memoirs of a Secretary of War* (New York: Alfred A. Knopf, 2014).

Recommended additional reading

Alain C. Enthoven and K. Wayne Smith, *How Much Is Enough? Shaping the Defense Program, 1961–1969* (New York: Harper & Row, 1971). The classic case for McNamara-style defense planning – with the answer being, "Whatever we tell you."

Arnold Kanter, *Defense Politics: A Budgetary Perspective* (Chicago, IL: University of Chicago Press, 1979). More than its modest title claims, for it is the clearest view of the management of defense during Secretary McNamara's regime. It also includes a very useful comparison to the Eisenhower administration.

John F. Lehman, Jr., *Command of the Seas* (Annapolis, MD: Naval Institute Press, 1988). A former secretary of the Navy describes how to win the bureaucratic game for yourself and your agency.

Norman Polmar and Thomas B. Allen, *Rickover* (New York: Simon & Schuster, 1982). A good way to learn the deep story behind one of the nation's most admired bureaucratic heroes, the admiral who made life nearly impossible for many a secretary of defense.

Harvey M. Sapolsky, Benjamin H. Friedman, and Brendan R. Green (eds.), *US Military Innovation since the Cold War: Creation without Destruction* (London: Routledge, 2009). Lots of new technology but no innovation that eliminates the old or can win the wars the United States actually fights.

5 Who fights America's wars?

The basic military recruitment dilemma for the United States is that it is a free and democratic society, and as such Americans resent the unequal burdens that wars place on citizens.[1] As the world's most powerful nation, the United States needs soldiers. However, most free men and women, Americans surely included, do not want to be soldiers, because they recognize the potential sacrifices involved. Every method of recruitment burdens someone – those who go in harm's way, as military service requires. How does a democratic society allocate the risks and sustain its defense commitments when the price in freedom and lives lost has to be paid?

Historically, the United States has answered this question with three basic systems for raising armies: locally based militias, conscription, and volunteers. Although not mutually exclusive, each system of recruitment points to different methods of managing and employing forces. Behind each system is a different type of public consent for citizen service in the military, as well as a set of unique problems. This chapter will outline the systems and their implications in order to understand who fights America's wars. Whose lives are on the line when America goes to war? Is it the poor and minorities, as is often charged? What methods are used to recruit in each system, and what are their implications? How are soldiers trained to fight and socialized to obey? We want to answer these questions because they strongly shape the politics of the military.

They are also recurring questions, because the nation's strategic needs and political preferences shift with time. National strategies requiring a particular form of recruitment flounder when the nation prefers another. It is no wonder that analysts talk today about the privatization of military tasks, and the attraction of technology can only grow as the search for alternatives to placing Americans in harm's way becomes ever more pressing. "Send in the robots" may be the cry that replaces "Send in the Marines."

The different systems

In colonial times, military service in America took the form of militias, locally based units intended to protect the community. The American colonials needed to defend settlements from hostile Native Americans or intruding French. British Army forces were too few and too immobile to offer timely response to threats, so all able-bodied men in the community were required to train with arms to be ready for local action and participation in punitive expeditions. In the Revolution, these local forces formed the basis of resistance to British rule, although some national forces were created as well.

After independence, the federal (national) forces were kept small, to be supplemented when needed by the state-organized militias. The federal government's need for state consent to mobilize the militia created a clear check on federal actions. As the frontier moved westward and the urban population grew, the militia became a voluntary activity, taking on aspects of a social club conferring local status and guarding local interests. It evolved into the National Guard. Although the militia can provide for some aspects of national defense, its greatest contribution is as a reservoir of civic manpower and socialization. Today, one of the National Guard's main tasks is providing order and assistance during natural disasters and other crises.

During the Civil War, neither federal calls for volunteers nor the calling up of state militias produced a sufficient number of troops, so the federal government instituted a draft as a supplement. Conscription, of course, is compulsory service, a form of civic slavery. Big, long wars such as the American Civil War invariably need to draft soldiers to fill the ranks. And with the Civil War draft came draft riots. In New York City, for example, mobs sought out blacks on whom to vent their anger at being forced to serve in the bloody battles to end slavery. They also attacked what were known as "$300 men" – individuals who appeared wealthy enough to buy a substitute soldier to take their place in the draft. Over a hundred people were killed.[2]

Resistance and evasion are not the only challenges for the draft. Although volunteering may not generate sufficient numbers to maintain armies involved in long, difficult fights, at other times drafts can generate too many soldiers. They can also create forces too large for the task or too expensive for the Treasury to support, and they can ignore the need to maintain a viable economy, especially when call-ups disrupt the workforce in critical industries. Drafts, then, usually come with a way to temper their impact so as not to cause too much disruption or resistance. The Civil War draft used a lottery system and allowed the purchase of substitutes.

More recent drafts have had a list of deferrable conditions that temporarily exempt some otherwise eligible draftees from service. For example, in the 1940s, young men of draft age (then 18–35), mentally and physically fit for service, did not have to serve if they were fathers of dependent children. Those still in high school or working in an exempt occupation (e.g., farmer, shipyard worker) could also avoid the draft. Various groups and interests lobbied to exclude people they wished to protect from the risk of mobilization. Scientists sought protection for young researchers, their protégés. Agricultural interests certainly promoted the exemption for farmers and farm workers, not only because of their vital work, but also simply to avoid the difficulties their families would face in their absence.

Exemptions have several effects. First, they provide incentives for individuals to qualify. During the Vietnam War, being a college student was sufficient for deferment. Not surprisingly, many students worked their way slowly toward a bachelor's degree for five or six years. If being married and a father is sufficient for an exemption, expect both the marriage and birth rates to climb. An exemption policy channels people toward needed occupations and responsible social behavior, but it also may guide some people toward the commission of fraud, perhaps pretending to work in an exempt job or perhaps finding a flexible medical examiner willing to certify that they have a condition sufficient for a deferment.

Second, exemptions drain the pool of available inductees. In very large, very long wars like World War II, the nation can run out of healthy, young, non-exempt males. In 1943, the American population included about 22 million males between the ages of 18 and 37, but 7 million of them were already in the armed services, 3.2 million had job deferrals, 1 million had dependent children, and another 8 million were physically or mentally unfit. That left a pool of only 2.8 million from which the military had to find 2.5 million more soldiers and sailors – a tight squeeze.[3]

Third, exemptions create distinctions among citizens. Those with low or no risk of being called to serve have a large advantage over others. Their careers are not disrupted. Their families do not have to live in fear of terrible news. But for some to be excused, others are put at risk, and those who avoid service understand that fact. No one likes to feel unpatriotic or cowardly, and oftentimes the guilt felt by those who avoid the draft easily gives way to moral opposition to the war of the day. If people can reject the war for what seems like a plausible reason, then they can push off their guilt, and they can still feel patriotic even as they seek exemptions to avoid fighting for their country.

The Vietnam War was divisive in this way. The war was largely fought by draftees; they made up most of the infantry units and took most of the casualties. Conscripts faced a two-year term of service, one year of training, and one year in Vietnam. Vietnam was a long, medium-sized war – too large to be supported by volunteers alone, but not large enough to use the whole conscript pool.

If one wanted to get out of the draft, it could be done. Many would enlist in another branch of service or the National Guard to avoid time in the infantry. ("The Viet Cong ain't got no submarines" was a slogan often invoked by those who chose to join the Navy during this period.) And then again there was a bit of mental illness or the old football injury that many doctors were willing to certify to disqualify an 18-year-old. Others found judges who loosened the definition of what it meant to have a religious belief that prevented one's participation in war, facilitating grants of "conscientious objector" status. In World War II, only 3 out of 1,000 conscientious objector appeals were accepted. In Vietnam, it was 98 out of 1,000. In Massachusetts, admittedly an extreme case, military service was essentially voluntary. More than 350 eligible young men had to be called up to induct 100.

There were other routes out, too. Canada, America's faithful ally in World War II and the Korean War, took an anti-Vietnam War stand and welcomed Americans fleeing the draft, as did Sweden. Upwards of 100,000 potential draftees made these countries their haven. The government did little to chase those seeking to avoid service. About 150,000 males turned 18 each month during the war years. In 1966, the peak draft year, only 30,000 a month were needed. That left a lot of room for divisive debates about who should bear the cost of service.

Decisions made by neighbors were apparently more acceptable than those made by strangers far away. Conscription in the United States was administered partly through the Selective Service, a small federal agency, and primarily through a network of local draft boards, populated by state-appointed members of the local communities. Although the standards were national and the draft numbers were ordered by the armed services, apportioned to the states, and then passed to the local boards, local administration inevitably made distinctions among potential inductees. Some who sought deferments would gain approvals, while others would not. At the national level, no one could find systematic biases, yet it was difficult to call the system fair or random.

The controversies over the Vietnam War spurred the shift to the third system of recruiting troops. President Nixon formed the Gates Commission in 1969 to study and evaluate the consequences of ending the draft. The commission based its arguments for a volunteer force on the rationale that a draft is a form of hidden tax on those forced to serve. According to its report, a volunteer system would allocate labor and other resources more efficiently in society overall. But beyond these economic arguments, the All-Volunteer Force (AVF) was an idea whose time had come politically.[4] Street demonstrations by draft-eligible youths and their sympathizers during the Vietnam War had convinced politicians that there had to be another way to maintain a foreign policy, even if it meant a smaller military. The American AVF replaced conscription in 1973.

Since the AVF was established, the military itself has been unwavering in its support for a volunteer force. The services remember the early 1970s, when discipline was failing within the enlisted ranks and societal respect for a military career was at low ebb, thanks to negative images that grew out of the Vietnam experience. They associate the problems of that era with the problems of conscription. The AVF, combined with the Reagan administration's military buildup in the 1980s, gave the military expanding resources and prestige. The American military earned its self-confidence, professionalism, and societal standing when the Cold War ended with the collapse of the Soviet Empire and a convincing, quick defeat of the Soviet-style Iraqi military. Officers often credit this success to the AVF. Its improved pay and benefits, they believe, attracted a force of trainable and career-oriented soldiers, sailors, airmen, and Marines.

Some still like the draft, however, believing it to be a barrier to American overseas adventurism. By exposing people from all walks of life – the rich as well as the poor, college graduates as well as high school dropouts – to the risk of becoming cannon fodder in poorly conceived foreign wars, a draft will give politicians reason to oppose the easy use of force in American foreign policy, or so the argument goes. Indeed, this reasoning explicitly motivates post-9/11 proposals to reinstate mandatory military service for American youth.[5]

The military disagreed, however, because it favored an alternative way to check politicians' power to intervene in questionable wars. When the draft ended, the Army insisted that the active-duty forces (the "Regulars") be tied tightly to the nation's Reserves, a policy called the "Total Force." This was not just to have an assured backup to the limited number of active-duty troops; it was also to require the mobilization of Reserves for almost any serious military operation. The Regular forces did not want politicians to place the burden of war on the professionals and draftees, as was done in Vietnam. Combat support units – forces such as the military police, medical service, and truck companies needed to sustain overseas forces in the field – were stripped out of the active force and placed in the Reserves.[6] The Total Force policy meant that every time politicians committed any serious number of US ground troops, they were in fact committing themselves to calling up the National Guard and Reserves. Past experience told the Regular officers that politicians would be more reluctant to mobilize 35-year-old Reservists, married with children and civilian jobs, than 18-year-old, single high school graduates. In the post-Vietnam era, war meant calling up the locals whose service would be most noticed and therefore most carefully considered: the Guard and Reserves include the local police officer and plumber, the town nurse and doctor.

The Guard and Reserves

The Guard and Reserves (Table 5.1) together make up what is called the Reserve Component of the US military. The Reserves were designed to supplement the Regular federally controlled armed forces by replicating many of their same functions, but the Guard serves both state and federal governments and performs a broader range of activities. The Guard's exemption from the Posse Comitatus Act, which prohibits using the Regular US military to enforce laws within the United States, is a major distinction between it and the Reserves.[7] Some observers were understandably surprised, even disturbed, when Army Reservists joined Guard members in disaster relief after Hurricane Katrina in 2005. As it turned out, so many Guardsmen were deployed in the Global War on Terror that not enough were readily available to meet domestic demands.

The president, through the federal military chain of command, can mobilize the Army and Air National Guard for emergencies, including combat outside the United States. The federal

Table 5.1 Size of the National Guard and Reserve
Component

Army National Guard	348,288
Air National Guard	104,004
Army Reserve	199,403
Air Force Reserve	68,332
Navy Reserve	57,455
Marine Corps Reserve	37,918
Coast Guard Reserve	6,774

Source: Defense Manpower Data Center, April 30, 2016.

government pays for a portion of the Guard's cost when it is on standby status. When the Guard is called to federal service, domestic or otherwise, the federal government pays for all costs. State governors have the authority to mobilize the Guard in local emergencies, but then the states pay for those operations.

Although the partnership between the Regulars and the Reserve Component is central to today's system of fielding military forces, they do not get along.[8] The Regulars consider themselves to be professionals, ever more so as the United States seeks to have the best-trained and best-equipped military force in the world. To the Regulars, the Guard and Reserves are made up of amateurs who train sporadically and are more involved with their full-time civilian occupations. For their part, Reservists feel ignored and exploited. They often have outdated equipment and little access to first-class training facilities and ranges. It is the love of flying or ships or firepower that keeps the Guardsmen and Reservists moderately cooperative.

The Army and the Army National Guard have the most strained relationship. The Army resents that the Guard is politically connected and politically protected. The Guard operates in large units and is responsive to state officials, who use the Guard as a supplement to local emergency personnel but also as an opportunity to dispense patronage. In all but two states, the head of the Guard, the state adjutant general, is appointed by the governor, not elected. The various Guards run their own state-based recruitment systems, officer candidate schools, and promotion boards. Senators and representatives are notorious advocates for their home-state Guard units, earmarking federal funds for equipment purchases, blocking the transfer of missions and units, and demanding a bigger share for the Guard in military plans and budgets. All of these political pressures reduce the Army's autonomy and infringe on generals' prized professional judgment.

The Guard, of course, has its own grievances. For example, when the Guard was called to federal service in 1940, the Army systematically replaced all senior Guard commanders with Regular Army officers, an insult still remembered in Guard publications. This tension resurfaced when many Guard units were called for the 1991 Gulf War. The Army Guard wanted very much to retain a combat role, crucial for its self-image as a military force. Several Guard brigades had previously been assigned as "roundout" brigades for Regular divisions with the expectation that they would accompany the divisions into combat. Yet no Guard infantry or armor brigades were allowed to fight with their divisions in 1991. When the war actually came, these brigades were kept in training rotations in the US while the Army substituted Regular units in their place.[9] Army and Guard officers disagreed about whether or not the units were combat-ready.

The relationship between the Air Force and Air National Guard is friendlier. Amid efforts to slash its rising personnel costs, the Air Force has actually integrated Guard wings directly into the maintenance, training, and other activities of some Regular units. The Air Guard is generally regarded as a capable partner, filled with those who love to fly or be around high-performance aircraft. In addition to handling missions such as air traffic control and weather forecasting, as well as support and maintenance functions, the Air Guard owns significant combat assets, including fighters, bombers, strategic and tactical lift aircraft, special operations aircraft, and tankers. The Air Guard provided about a third of the fighter aircraft used in the initial operations in Iraq and Afghanistan, and it continues to provide the majority of the aircraft for Operation Noble Eagle, which patrols US skies to prevent another 9/11.[10] But even the Air Guard and the Air Force have their disputes, as witnessed in controversies over force reductions and base realignments in the wind-down from Iraq. The Guard sees the Air Force as always preferring to impose reductions on Guard elements, while the Air Force sees the Guard as greedy and uncooperative.

Political leaders are quite sensitive about the overseas deployment of Guard forces. The Guard now proudly notes that more than 100,000 Army and Air Guardsmen were sent to Europe in 1961 during the Berlin Crisis, but the call-up at the time was greeted with anguish by those affected, because it meant an unexpected year away from family and careers. Their complaints and recognition of the Guard's influence in Congress made President Lyndon Johnson rely instead on the draft for Vietnam. As a result, the Guard became a haven from the war: legitimate military service without the risk of combat for those like George W. Bush who had the political connections and sensibility to see the Guard for what it was.

The Global War on Terror broke the political barrier about using the Guard (and the Reserves), but heavy reliance on the Guard still causes headaches. Guard units, including combat brigades, performed well in Iraq and Afghanistan. At times they made up nearly half of the US forces in Iraq.[11] But the costs and risks of service overseas were not the same for Regular Army soldiers and Guardsmen. The Army generally rotates units in combat on a 12-month basis (extended to 15 months for the Iraq War), while the Marines use a seven-month cycle; for National Guardsmen, a tour in Iraq or Afghanistan often meant about 18 months away from home, given the needed training and processing, but less time actually in theater. Furthermore, despite laws intended to protect them, many who served in the Guard found their civilian jobs or promised promotions unavailable upon return from their tour of duty.[12] And the military struggled to keep its promise to Guardsmen to call them up for a maximum of two years, and only once within six years; as the Army National Guard ran low on soldiers to call up in the middle of the Iraq War, the Army was forced to rely on Navy and Air Force personnel to support the ground effort, driving trucks and providing base security.[13] Neither the Guard nor the active Army want to repeat the experience of the 2000s.

Long-term counterinsurgency and peacekeeping operations strain the Reserve Component, which was designed for the US military's Cold War mission, mobilizing to defend Europe. Many supporters prefer that the Guard in particular focus on its share of the increasingly important homeland defense mission. Patrolling airports, stadiums, and reservoirs while living at home is a more attractive prospect for part-time soldiers than running a gauntlet of improvised explosive devices in a sweaty convoy half a globe away.[14] President Obama's 2012 *Strategic Guidance* suggested that the official policy is to hope that long-term stabilization options won't come up in the future, but continuing operations against ISIS and the Taliban and the ongoing debate whether to intervene in Syria point to a future with either challenging remobilization of the Reserve Component or a need to expand the Regulars.

Table 5.2 Active-duty personnel by service

Year	USA	Navy	Marines	Air Force
1945	5,986,000	3,381,000	475,000	2,282,000
1950	593,000	382,000	74,000	411,000
1955	1,109,000	661,000	205,000	960,000
1960	873,000	618,000	171,000	815,000
1965	969,000	671,000	190,000	825,000
1970	1,322,000	693,000	260,000	755,000
1975	784,000	535,000	196,000	613,000
1980	777,000	527,000	188,000	558,000
1985	781,000	571,000	198,000	602,000
1990	728,345	573,737	196,353	530,865
1995	504,710	492,630	174,561	396,382
2000	479,026	367,371	172,955	351,326
2005	486,483	357,853	179,836	349,362
2010	561,979	323,139	202,612	329,640
2015	491,365	327,801	183,417	311,357

Source: Defense Manpower Data Center.

In some ways, the Regular forces support orienting the Reserves toward homeland security. They recognize that the more the armed forces depend on the Reserves, the less flexible and autonomous they are. Already the services are seeking to bring more combat support capabilities back into the active force. But this reversal of the Total Force policy comes with costs other than giving up the political check on intervention: increases in the permanent size of the military are expensive. The real lesson for the military has been that hiring private contractors can be a solution to a sudden need for logistical and other support, one that comes with less political constraint and inter-organizational competition.[15]

The high-profile reliance on the Reserve Component for the Global War on Terror also came with another political change not welcomed by the Regulars. Over the public opposition of all of the services, the Guard lobbied for and received in 2012 a full seat on the Joint Chiefs of Staff, along with additional senior posts and greater visibility for Guard members and Reservists on the Army staff. The Guard certainly still claims a role in mobilizing for America's big fights, but it also has new avenues to press its case for its unique role in homeland security and its various special claims and mobilization constraints.

Who volunteers?

The All-Volunteer Force is not representative of American society. About 15 percent female and 17 percent black, the armed services are indeed demographically different from the United States as a whole, although the invidious inferences sometimes drawn from these differences are often incorrect.

Some politicians and community leaders worry that the AVF places unfair burdens on minorities and the poor. They assume that if service is to be primarily an economic calculation – the AVF encourages enlistment with monetary bonuses and competes for volunteers with entry-level civilian jobs and educational opportunities – then those with the fewest options, in their minds,

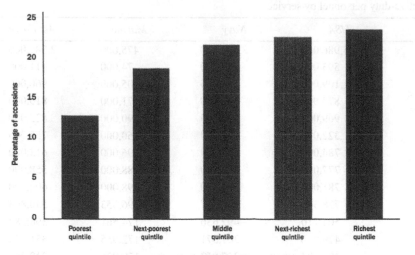

Figure 5.1 Family income levels of recruits

Source: *Air Force Magazine*, December 2010. Reproduced with permission.

primarily poor blacks, will be driven to enlist.[16] Worse, a disproportionately black military will yield disproportionately black casualties when committed to combat, and this in turn could undermine domestic support for military operations and perhaps even the legitimacy of the armed forces.

The politicians' fear stems primarily from a mistaken view of the Vietnam experience. Many believe that the rich and the well educated were able to evade the draft. We do know that relatively few from Harvard and MIT served, while many more proportionately from North Cambridge and South Boston did. But despite these sorts of discrepancies, local draft boards in relatively well-off areas had to meet their quotas, just as those from working-class areas had to meet theirs; discretion was easier to exercise within a region than across regions, and within each region, many people were willing to serve even as others looked for a way out. America overall is a big country. By tracking plausible surrogates for class, such as census income data or certain aspects of medical surveys, researchers have found that the body of individuals who served in Vietnam was largely representative of the relevant age group of males in the United States at the time.[17]

Volunteers have stayed broadly representative across the income distribution: it is a myth that the military recruits disproportionately from among the poor (see Figure 5.1). Data indicate that the family income distribution of recruits closely mirrors the family income distribution in the country overall. Most recruits come from solidly middle-class backgrounds. The proportion of recruits from higher socioeconomic strata has actually increased in recent years, and the proportion of recruits from lower socioeconomic strata has declined. Urban areas are underrepresented in the military, primarily because larger segments of the male population that come from these areas cannot meet the educational, physical, and other standards required to enter the military. Suburban and rural areas are over-represented, particularly in the South. The South produces the largest number of recruits, but it also has the largest concentration of young people of any region.[18]

Volunteers are also relatively well educated, presumably giving them relatively good options in the civilian economy, had they chosen that path. More than 99 percent of enlistees

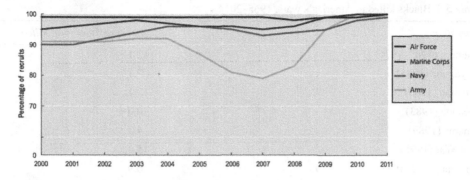

Figure 5.2 High school graduates by service

Source: *Air Force Magazine*, March 2013. Reproduced with permission.

have at least a high school diploma or its equivalent, though the percentage dropped temporarily for the Army (though not the other services) during the peak of the Iraq War (see Figure 5.2). In the general population, only 88 percent of citizens in the appropriate age range have that level of education. Meanwhile, many officers in the AVF have a master's or other advanced degree (41 percent), compared to just 32 percent of the overall US population over age 25.[19] A draft might broaden the military's base, but it would not improve its quality.

Similarly, politicians who fear racial imbalance in the military, based on their view of the Vietnam experience, are making a mistake. Casualty data show that blacks were no more likely to die in Vietnam than were whites (see Table 5.3).[20] Extending the analysis to include post-9/11 combat, as in Table 5.4, does not change the key result: the notion that minorities are disproportionately represented on the front lines is simply untrue. The percentage of fatalities suffered by black service personnel in combat since 1965 has been lower than their proportion of the US population writ large, and much lower than their proportion of the Army during most of that time.

In fact, blacks are over-represented in support military occupations such as medical technicians, engineer equipment operators, and administration, not in the infantry.[21] For example, in 2009, about half of black soldiers chose service support specialties, while only 24 percent chose the combat arms.[22] Combat occupations are a young man's game, not a place to make a 30-year career or to learn a skill marketable in the civilian world, two paths that are more common for black soldiers. Whites are actually somewhat over-represented in combat units, especially elite units such as the SEALS and Rangers, in part because many young whites tend to look to military service as a short-term adventure rather than as a long-term career.[23]

It is true that for much of the history of the AVF, the percentage of blacks in the military was more than double their percentage of the overall population and about 50 percent higher than their percentage of the relevant age group. But this may have been due less to economic necessity than to the recognition among blacks that the military had become the institution in American society most open to them. Indeed, blacks stay in the volunteer Army longer than other groups, and in the US military, blacks routinely command whites without anyone making a big deal of it, while in civilian society, black bosses directing white employees are a relatively rare exception.[24]

Since 1995, 10–15 percent of the officers in the Army have been black, while blacks made up only 8 percent of the US population of similar age and education. Notably few black colonels command combat brigades (e.g., only one out of 31 in 2016), the key jobs that serve as

Table 5.3 Blacks killed in America's wars, 1965–2014

Operation	Blacks as % of total killed
Vietnam (1965–1974)	12.1
Mayaguez (1975)	7.1
Lebanon (1983)	18.1
Grenada (1983)	0.0
Panama (1989)	4.3
Gulf War (1991)	15.4
Somalia (1992–1993)	6.9
Afghanistan (October 2001–December 2014)	8.2
Iraq (March 2003–December 2014)	10.0
Blacks as % of population as of 1990	13.1
Blacks as % of active-duty military, 1975–1995	19.1
Blacks as % of active-duty military, 2014	17.2

Note: Operations in Haiti and the Balkans are not included because overall casualties were extremely low and in almost all cases not from hostile fire.

Sources: Charles C. Moskos and John Sibley Butler, *All That We Can Be: Black Leadership and Racial Integration the Army Way* (New York: Basic Books, 1996), p. 8; "American War and Military Operations Casualties: Lists and Statistics," Congressional Research Service, January 2, 2015.

Table 5.4 Percentage killed and wounded by race, Operation Enduring Freedom and Operation Iraqi Freedom (October 2001–December 2014)

Race	Army	Navy	Marines	Air Force	Total
American Indian/Alaska Native	0.9	4.3	1.1	0.9	1.0
Asian	2.0	3.8	1.1	1.1	1.8
Black or African-American	9.7	7.6	3.8	6.7	8.1
Native Hawaiian or other Pacific Islander	0.2	0.9	0.5	0.5	0.3
White	83.0	70.3	78.1	83.9	81.5
Multiple races	1.1	3.0	0.8	1.4	1.0
Unknown	3.1	10.1	14.7	5.5	6.3

Source: "American War and Military Operations Casualties: Lists and Statistics," Congressional Research Service, January 2, 2015.

waypoints on the track for promotion to the highest ranks. Nevertheless, the Army does not try to constrain black promotions and in fact has counseling programs to expand the pool of black officers. The same goes for the other services. At the highest levels, ADM Michelle Howard became the first black female four-star in 2014, when she became the vice chief of naval operations; she joined five other black four-stars in the military at that time, including the combat commander who led US forces in the Middle East, General Lloyd Austin.[25]

The military was not always a welcoming place for minorities. Segregation of blacks from whites continued from the Civil War until President Truman ordered its formal end in 1948. Integration in combat units did not occur until manpower shortages during the Korean War forced it. And discrimination of various types caused race riots and near-mutinies through the

1960s. But firm leadership determined to overcome such problems has led to a blending of black and white social circles among enlistees and availability of opportunities in all ranks. By drawing from a large pool of enlistees and officer candidates, the military has been able to apply standards for promotion equally across races, ensuring quality at the same time that it generally maintains racial representation throughout the hierarchy. The large pool and rigorous adherence to standards avoid the hard feelings and morale problems that affirmative action sometimes generates in civilian society.[26]

In recent years, Hispanics have become the fastest-growing demographic group in the United States. This change in the eligible labor pool has resulted in some corresponding shifts in the racial composition of the military – especially since young Hispanics seem to be more likely than their black or white counterparts to want to enlist.[27] On the other hand, only a relatively small fraction of youth, regardless of race or ethnicity, meet the military's tough enlistment standards, and Hispanic youth fail more often because they are less likely to grad-uate from high school, less likely to score high enough on the Armed Forces Qualification Test, and more likely to be overweight.[28] Overall, Hispanic representation in the military has been growing, and in 2015, the representation of Hispanics in the Army caught up to Hispanics' overall population percentage in the United States (17 percent).[29] Hispanics make up an even larger percentage of the Marine Corps.[30]

Once in the military, Hispanics tend to choose career paths that more closely resemble those of whites than blacks. Rather than focusing on non-combat, support roles, as blacks do, Hispanics tend to volunteer for ground combat. Hispanics are nevertheless under-represented in the combat ground forces relative to their proportion of the overall eligible US population, likely because of the failure to meet educational requirements.

Finally, the need for more volunteers has also led in recent years to an increasing num-ber of foreign nationals joining the US military. New rules expedite the process for gaining American citizenship for anyone in the active-duty military, although foreign nationals still account for a small fraction of the total force.[31]

Despite the largely unfounded criticism of the AVF on demographic grounds, the AVF will almost certainly continue as the US recruiting system. An impressive number of vol-unteers still step forward for both the Active and Reserve force. Patriotism remains strong in America. On the other hand, the conscription alternative would create more political and social problems, especially because the pool of eligibles would be far too large, leading to exactly the sorts of unfair exemptions that prompted the abolition of conscription after the Vietnam War.

When seeking additional resources or benefits, senior military officers, retired and active, occasionally lament the burdens that are placed on "the less than 1 percent" who serve their country. Of course, service to country takes many forms. (Are the engineers working in the defense industry not serving? What about teachers, police, or Foreign Service officers?) Only in total mobilization on the scale of World War II could the percentage of the population in uniform be much higher anyway.

One unanticipated consequence of the AVF is that the US military has become a more married (and divorced) force than it was before conscription ended. In 1973, about 40 percent of military personnel were married. Today, the figure is around 55 percent, and it is much higher among active-duty officers, nearly 70 percent.[32] Forty-five percent of service members now have children to support as well.[33] Indeed, in 1990 the Marine Corps was surprised to find itself providing health care and other benefits for more dependents of Marines than for actual Marines, and it briefly considered restricting the circumstances under which younger Marines could marry.[34] Storied military traditions such as barracks life and the nights drinking

Table 5.5 Females by military branch

	Army	Navy	Marines	Air Force	Total
Women	68,696	61,336	14,619	60,284	204,935
Total	475,554	329,237	183,968	312,878	1,301,637
%	14.4	18.6	7.9	19.3	15.7

Source: Defense Manpower Data Center, April 2016.

at the club or town bars are largely gone on today's military bases; in their stead are family housing, day care centers, and base swimming pools.[35] Marriage may be losing its appeal in the broader society, but it is popular in the military, where generous benefits for dependents encourage single service members to marry and married persons to join.[36]

A more married force also means deployments are more complicated, and those who are deployed have more distractions and worries while they are away. It means personnel costs are growing because each service member may bring several other people who require support as well. This, too, is a consequence of the AVF, because family-oriented benefits are needed to attract recruits. As families live together on base, with more and more services provided on base, military families may interact less with the civilian community outside the base. Even the big box stores that used to locate just outside the base perimeter, selling to military families, are now moving inside, providing new anecdotes for those concerned that the gap between military and civilian life is growing in the United States.

With a volunteer military comes the need to improve conditions of service. The housing is better, the food is better, the equipment is better, the promises for education more substantial than in the draft-era military. Expectations are quite high. As Private Benjamin, a female, famously said in the movie of the same name, when confronting some unpleasantness of recruit training, "See, I did join the Army, but I joined . . . the one with the condos and the private rooms."[37] Her vision is increasingly coming to fruition, and because of these changes, the services are much more frugal in their use of manpower than they once were, substituting capital for labor or contractors for Reservists. There may never be a substitute for "boots on the ground," but the American military is always looking for one.

Women in the military

Women have filled the recruitment gap that otherwise would have existed with the AVF. Table 5.5 shows the percentage of women in each service in 2016; overall, they now account for more than 15 percent of the force, compared with less than 2 percent in 1973. Training is largely gender-integrated in the Army, Navy, and Air Force; male and female Marines train in separate units in boot camp but must meet the same standards to perform the same tasks once they move on in their careers.[38]

For years, female participation in the military was restricted to certain activities like administrative jobs far from the battlefield, but the restrictions dwindled over time. Long before the final step, when Secretary of Defense Ashton Carter announced that all military jobs would be open to women, the US military gave far more opportunity to women than any other comparable military – including those of Israel, Sweden, and Germany.[39] Women got to be pilots in transport aircraft, and then pilots and weapon-systems officers in strike aircraft: in a famous incident early in the Afghanistan War, an F-15 pilot commented on the radio, after his female weapon-systems officer hit a target, "You have just been killed by a girl."[40]

Figure 5.3 A female soldier, deployed and ready
Source: US Army.

Women also joined battalion-level staffs in the combat arms and the entire submarine force, where privacy is limited.

The final step came in two stages. In early 2013, Defense Secretary Leon Panetta opened combat jobs to women except for specialties for which a military service prepared a detailed justification for a waiver, and then in December 2015, his successor, Secretary Ashton Carter, decided not to accept any waivers.[41] The Marine Corps had been most reluctant, requesting an exemption for infantry and armor, and the absence of Marine General Joseph Dunford, the chairman of the Joint Chiefs of Staff, from Secretary Carter's news conference was widely noted in the press. But the DoD's civilian leaders pulled together, including Secretary of the Navy Ray Mabus, with whom Secretary Carter was simultaneously having a major public dispute over ship acquisition plans. In the American system, the civilians ultimately make the decisions, and the Marines are moving forward integrating units.[42]

In part, the new policy simply recognizes that women supporting combat already were exposed to the enemy on counterinsurgency battlefields. Over 100 women have been killed serving in Iraq and Afghanistan. Critics used to fear that the deaths of women in combat would reduce public support for war or that the combat effectiveness of military units would drop because of male reactions to female casualties. Experience has chased those fears away. It has all been rather professional.

Nevertheless, women mostly choose the combat support and medical service tasks that facilitate combat operations and keep the large service bureaucracies running, and few have expressed a strong desire to join the combat arms now that they are able to.[43] In the future, most women in the military will still serve in units other than ground combat units, because of the robust physical requirements, but the proportion of women in the military, especially the proportion of women in the Army and Marine Corps, is almost sure to increase.

This does not mean that the expansion of opportunities for women in the military has been smooth. Leaving aside the purely combat roles, the military still struggles to address the unfairness that can result from women not sharing equally the heavy lifting that is required in some military support tasks (hauling lines aboard ships, for example).

But women do not have it easy, either. Reports by female service members of sexual harassment and rape remain disturbingly common both on bases in the United States and in combat theaters.[44] In one of the most infamous episodes, 26 women reported being harassed and groped by some drunken celebrants at the Navy's 1991 Tailhook Convention (the Naval Aviation Association's annual gathering). In response, the Senate Armed Services Committee blocked the promotion and thus ended the careers of hundreds of male Navy and Marine Corps officers who had attended the sessions even though almost all were eventually cleared of any misconduct.[45] Both the secretary of the Navy and the chief of naval operations lost their jobs over the scandal.

Subsequent scandals about sexual assaults and cover-ups at the Air Force Academy, at the Air Force's enlisted basic training facility at Lackland Air Force Base, and elsewhere have been nearly as consequential, especially because of the political resonance of bad behavior at the institutions that form young people into American military personnel.[46] When the Air Force officer in charge of sexual assault prevention was himself arrested and charged with committing a sexual assault in 2013, President Obama highlighted the seriousness of the problem: "For those who are in uniform who've experienced sexual assault, I want them to hear directly from their Commander-in-Chief that I've got their backs."[47] But this was not the first time the problem had received high-level attention, and it may well persist in the future, despite earnest attempts to address it.

Neither the real nor the purely political problems of expanding women's roles in the armed services have been fully dealt with. And the military still faces more prosaic problems that also plague the civilian workforce, such as the favoritism that can result from on-the-job romances and misguided chivalry. Each year, dozens of commanders are fired for consensual relations with subordinates. The cycle of scandals, punishments, and attempted reforms will continue.

Gays and the military

The US military often outpaces other American institutions as a force for social change. This was certainly the case in race relations, where manpower needs in the Korean War led to military desegregation well before similar changes occurred in the broader society. Progress for women lagged, but it accelerated after the end of the Cold War, led by the Air Force, which had women flying combat aircraft in the early 1990s. Various ethnic groups found acceptance in the military, too, with the Army being led by a Japanese-American, Jewish officers heading the Air Force and Navy, and Hispanic-Americans, Chinese-Americans, Arab-Americans, and Greek-Americans holding flag rank and positions of prominence. But one group of Americans, homosexuals, did not find acceptance in the military until 2012. Until then, it was illegal to be openly gay or lesbian in the US military, and thousands of service personnel lost their careers and received dishonorable discharges, which involved forfeiture of all benefits, when their sexuality was discovered.

The first public attempts to change the status of gays and lesbians in the military occurred in the early days of the Clinton administration. The president sought repeal of the legislation banning gays and immediately ran into opposition from senior military leaders and

Republicans. General Colin Powell, then the chairman of the Joint Chiefs of Staff and the first black officer to hold that position, was particularly disdainful of repeal proponents' attempts to use civil rights analogies in their arguments. The compromise, conceived by Charles Moskos, the noted military sociologist, was the "Don't ask, don't tell" policy (DADT), which allowed gays to serve as long as their sexual orientation was not revealed. Nevertheless, hundreds of service members were still being dismissed from the ranks each year when their commanders in one way or another discovered their sexual orientations.[48]

The arguments against allowing gays and lesbians to serve centered on morale issues, namely the discomfort young heterosexuals supposedly feel when forced to live with homosexuals in very close quarters, a common situation in the military. There is also supposedly a danger of assault and blackmail. But changing societal acceptance of homosexuals, including the hiring of openly gay and lesbian police and teachers and the election of gay and lesbian lawmakers without notice-able consequence, undermined the argument. An Air Force officer wrote an official prize-winning essay pointing out that forcing soldiers to lie or hide their sexual orientation violated the military's claim that personal integrity is a "core military value."[49] And the military paid a cost in the public culture of American elites, for example, as many colleges and universities that had banned the presence of Reserve Officers' Training Corps units on their campuses because of the Vietnam War continued the boycott, using DADT as the justification.

With a Democratic Party coalition including significant gay and lesbian elements and an election approaching, President Obama ordered a study of the likely implications of lifting the barrier. When the study indicated that a change in policy would pose no significant issues even in wartime, Secretary Gates and Admiral Michael Mullen, the JCS chairman at the time, endorsed the repeal effort. Even retired General Powell backed off his opposition. Only the commandant of the Marine Corps voiced continuing opposition at the senior level. The Obama administration decided to push for repeal, which was achieved rather easily even though the House of Representatives was in Republican hands and surveys of the enlisted ranks in the military showed a persistent skepticism of any change. The military recognizes same-sex mar-riages, though some of the details of giving same-sex couples all of their benefits took time to work out.[50] Yet so far there seem to be none of the cohesion problems many had predicted.

Socializing the force

Militaries are what organizational theorists call "total institutions," organizations that control nearly all aspects of their members' lives. The military typically determines what time sol-diers get up, what they wear, where and what they eat, what they do and with whom they do it, what recreational opportunities they have, and when and where they sleep. Like prisoners, priests, and hospitalized patients, soldiers have to do what they are told to do. Total institu-tions are necessarily transforming in that they change the identities of their participants, making them accept the organization's values and goals as their own.

Militaries do their transforming in recruit basic training (boot camp in the Navy and Marines), basic officer training courses, plebe year in the service academies, and the like, in which recruits are stripped of their civilian identities and given military ones. The distinc-tions of civilian life – social status, education, wealth – are removed by standardized haircuts, uniforms, and personal property restrictions. In their place, new distinctions are introduced – ranks, forms of address, and codes of conduct. As Tom Ricks described in his study of Marine recruit training, the Marines learn not only basic infantry tactics and how to take care of their weapons but also Marine Corps values such as selflessness, cooperation, and unit cohesion. According to Ricks, after 13 weeks at the Parris Island recruit facility, new Marines are so acculturated to the Corps that they have near-total disdain for the civilian values that they arrived with and that their friends back home still hold.[51]

Militaries have traditionally been very hierarchical, with sharp divides between officer and enlisted, and junior and senior, ranks. The hierarchy is functional in the sense that it allows life-and-death decisions to be made with the assumption that they will be carried out without hesitation by subordinates even under the most dreadful of conditions. Allegiance is to the system, not to the particular individual holding the highest rank. But conditions are changing in ways that undermine rigid structures. The increased emphasis on technology in military operations shifts power to experts, whatever their rank. Moreover, the end of conscription has increased the need for incentives to maintain enlistments at levels sufficient to fill the ranks, and that pressure has reduced the status and pay differential between ranks. It is not just American officers who need to support a family and demand decent on-base housing, but also American enlisted personnel. Holding on to trained soldiers by treating them fairly makes sense in a military where soldiers cannot be commandeered and where those who do join can walk away when dissatisfied.

There are other hierarchies in militaries that are important besides those defined by rank. Some tasks hold higher status than others. The combat/non-combat branch distinction is a crucial one in the American military, with the former being afforded higher status than the latter. Pilots, and especially fighter pilots, dominate the US Air Force. Although less than 30 percent of the officers are rated, pilots account for nearly 90 percent of the generals in the Air Force. Most of the 12 four-star generals in the Air Force are fighter pilots.[52] In the Navy, pilots share top billing with surface warfare and submarine officers, while in the Army pilots mostly are not even commissioned officers but rather warrant officers, a category of ranks between enlisted soldiers and officers. But the services that do not hold pilots in quite such high esteem also have their informal pecking orders. In the Navy, surface combatant commands are viewed as better than amphibious warfare commands and more likely to lead to promotion. Similarly, within the submarine force, attack boat commands are seen as better than ballistic missile boat commands.[53] Rangers are considered elite light infantry soldiers, but within the Special Operations community they are considered lesser soldiers than members of Delta Force and other, still secret, commando units.[54]

As was mentioned previously, the distinction between Regulars and Reserves is important. In the days of conscription, American soldiers were drafted into the US Army Reserve rather than the Army of the United States, the preserve of the Regulars. The ROTC units situated at many colleges produce Reserve, not Regular, officers. Only "Distinguished" ROTC graduates are offered Regular commissions.

These distinctions and many more like them are not just for boasting. They are functional as well, rewarding those who take the biggest personal risks in achieving the organization's goals with organizational prestige and, sometimes, extra pay. Accountants and lawyers help to run the military's bureaucracy, crushing many in their path, but it is the fighter pilots, tank commanders, and warship captains who crush the enemy in battle and thus directly serve the military's primary purpose. Esprit de corps matters, and that is why unit emblems, uniform adornments such as barrettes, boots, and special patches or badges, and a public reputation for daring matter, too. Small distinctions stand out in a sea of conformity, but they also form the basis for the internal politics of the military.

Military professionalism

American military officers take pride in being professionals.[55] Like physicians and attorneys, military officers believe that they possess specialized knowledge, are guided by norms of public service, and should be autonomous in determining their own selection, training, and advancement. Society does allow some professions to be largely self-governing, recognizing the value gained from their knowledge and service. Thus, physicians and physicists are essentially left alone to decide the content of their work and who qualifies to perform it. But other occupations, military officers certainly among them, are afforded much less autonomy despite their claims to professional status. The reason is that the military's work is entirely governmental. Private employment as a fighter pilot or self-employment as a tank commander are discouraged; professional soldiers often look down on the few people who make their living as mercenaries, and even most mercenaries are employed by governments. But to what extent can respect for professionalism, knowledge, and experience enable soldiers to evade the state's efforts at control?

Because military officers do not operate as free, self-governed professionals and cannot easily switch employers, they are less inclined to seek rewards for themselves as individuals than they are to request resources, autonomy, and prestige for the organizations they serve. These significant organizational interests can be cloaked easily with claims of military necessity that are hard for civilians to counter. Outside control of these organizations is also made difficult by the fact that they are historic, large, wealthy, and quite popular bureaucracies that have planning horizons far longer than those of their civilian masters.

But, in practice, the military has mostly accepted civilian intrusion into its expert domain. Professionalism is important to the military, and understanding the military's professional code is important to understanding US defense policy. Continuing education is common to many professions, and the military is no exception: during the course of a military career, an officer can expect to go to several different schools, and an enlisted soldier can expect multiple trips for specialized training. These educational opportunities also inculcate the military's values into its personnel, and one of the paramount values taught over and over again is deference to civilian control. That message comes along with great pride in the institution and a strong sense that appropriate standards of conduct and performance should apply equally to everyone in the military.

Sometimes the military has been uncomfortable leading American social change, but ultimately the military has accepted civilian direction on social issues and, particularly on race, even touts its progressive role. Having already moved from resistance to acceptance on the role of women and gays in the military, perhaps the leadership will likewise soon move to pride on those issues, too, especially as these groups become ever more important to the recruitment of the All-Volunteer Force.

Questions for discussion

1   Why did the United States abandon the draft? What values did it embody?
2   Why is local influence on who gets drafted or on the National Guard helpful and important in a free society?
3   How fair is the All-Volunteer Force?
4   How should gender, marital status, parenthood, and professional education be treated in deciding who serves in the military and is subject to draft registration?
5   Did the absence of a draft affect the politics of the Global War on Terror?

Notes

1 Eliot Cohen, *Citizens and Soldiers: The Dilemmas of Military Service* (Ithaca, NY: Cornell University Press, 1985).

2 James McPherson, *Battle Cry of Freedom: The Civil War Era* (New York: Ballantine Books, 1988), pp. 609–611.

3 George Q. Flynn, *The Draft, 1940–1973* (Lawrence, KS: University of Kansas Press, 1993).

4 Bernard Rostker, *I Want You! The Evolution of the All-Volunteer Force* (Santa Monica, CA: RAND, 2006), pp. 76–81; Bernard D. Rostker, "The Gates Commission: Right for the Wrong Reasons," in Barbara A. Bicksler, Curtis L. Gilroy, and John T. Warner (eds.), *The All-Volunteer Force: Thirty Years of Service* (Washington, DC: Brassey's, 2004), pp. 25–26.

5 Thomas E. Ricks, "It's Time to Toss the All-Volunteer Military," *Washington Post*, April 19, 2012; Robin Toner, "After Many Years, It's Rangel's Turn at the Helm," *New York Times*, January 8, 2007, p. 1; "Rangel Introduces New Bill to Reinstate Military Draft," news release from the Office of Congressman Charles Rangel, January 11, 2007, available at: https://rangel.house.gov/news/press-releases/rangel-introduces-new-bill-reinstate-military-draft (accessed September 2, 2016).

6 For example, prior to 9/11 the Army National Guard contributed only 1 percent of the Army's primary combat fighters, but it contributed 17 percent of general combat support, such as military police, and 37 percent of service support for combat, such as medical and logistics work. Bradley Graham, "Uncle Sam Needs You – Not," *Washington Post*, October 27, 1997, p. 29.

7 Christine E. Wormuth, Michèle A. Flournoy, Patrick T. Henry, and Clark A. Murdoch, *The Future of the National Guard and Reserves: The Beyond Goldwater Nichols Phase III Report* (Washington, DC: Center for Strategic and International Studies, July 2006), Introduction.

8 "The National Guard in a Brave New World – Anything Useful to Do, Besides Fighting the Army?" *The Economist*, May 9, 1998, p. 25; "Budget Crunch Has a Service at War with Itself," *Congressional Quarterly*, January 3, 1998, p. 5.

9 John G. Roos, "Lingering Readiness Pains: National Guard's 'Enhanced Brigades' Suffer from All-Too-Familiar Maladies," *Armed Forces Journal International* (September 1995): 52–57; United States General Accounting Office, *Operation Desert Storm: Army Had Difficulty Providing Adequate Active and Reserve Support Forces*, March 1992, GAO/NSIAD-92-67.

10 Wormuth et al., *The Future of the National Guard and Reserves*, Introduction.

11 Bradley Graham, "Reservists May Face Longer Tours of Duty," *Washington Post*, January 7, 2005.

12 Dale McFeatters, "Reservists, Guardsmen Finding Their Jobs Gone," *San Diego Union-Tribune*, March 2, 2007.

13 Eric Schmitt and David S. Cloud, "Part-Time Forces on Active Duty Decline Steeply," *New York Times*, July 11, 2005.

14 Michael R. Gordon, "Break Point? Iraq and America's Military Forces," *Survival*, 48(4) (Winter 2005–2006): 67–82.

15 Mark Erbel and Christopher Kinsey, "Think Again – Supplying War: Reappraising Military Logistics and Its Centrality to Strategy and War," *Journal of Strategic Studies* (2015): 1–26.

16 Bill Tammeus, "The US All-Volunteer Military System Is Unjust," *National Catholic Reporter*, October 14, 2015.

17 Arnold Barnett, Timothy Stanley, and Michael Shore, "America's Vietnam Casualties: Victims of a Class War?' *Operations Research*, 40(5) (September–October 1992): 856–866; Allan Mazur, "Was Vietnam a Class War?" *Armed Forces & Society*, 21(3) (Spring 1995): 455–459. See also James Fallows, "What Did You Do in the Class War, Daddy?" *Washington Monthly*, 7(8) (1975): 5–20; and Christian Appy, *Working Class War* (Chapel Hill, NC: University of North Carolina Press, 1993).

18 "Who Is Volunteering for Today's Military? Myths Versus Facts," DOD briefing, December 2005, available at: http://www.military.com/Recruiting/Content/0,13898,062006-who-joining-marines-today-myth-fact,00.html?ESRC=recruiting.nl (accessed June 10, 2016); Jim Garamone, "Military Demographics Representative of America, Officials Say," *American Forces Information Service*, November 23, 2005.

19 US Department of Defense, *2014 Demographics: Profile of the Military Community*, http://download.militaryonesource.mil/12038/MOS/Reports/2014-Demographics-Report.pdf (accessed June 10, 2016).

20 Charles C. Moskos and John Sibley Butler, *All That We Can Be: Black Leadership and Racial Integration the Army Way* (New York: Basic Books, 1996), p. 8.

21 Thomas E. Ricks, "U.S. Infantry Surprise: It's Now Mostly White; Blacks Hold Office Jobs," *Wall Street Journal*, January 6, 1997, p. 1.

22 Gregg Zaroya, "Military Backslides on Ethnic Diversity," *USA Today*, February 17, 2014.

23 Sheila Nataraj Kirby, Margaret C. Harrell, and Jennifer Sloan, "Why Don't Minorities Join Special Forces?" *Armed Forces and Society*, 26(4) (Summer 2000): 523–545.

24 Moskos and Butler, *All That We Can Be*.

25 Tom Vanden Brook, "Black Army Officers Struggle to Climb Ranks," *USA Today*, April 14, 2015; Zarova, "Military Backslides."

26 Moskos and Butler, *All That We Can Be.*

27 Brian Gifford, "Combat Casualties and Race: What Can We Learn from the 2003–2004 Iraq Conflict?" *Armed Forces & Society*, 31(2) (Winter 2005): 202.

28 Beth J. Asch, Christopher Buck, Jacob Alex Klerman, Meredith Kleykamp, and David S. Loughran, *Military Enlistment of Hispanic Youth: Obstacles and Opportunities* (Santa Monica, CA: RAND Corporation, 2009).

29 "Hispanics in the U.S. Army," *Army.mil*, available at: https://www.army.mil/hispanics/ (accessed May 30, 2016).

30 Erika L. Sánchez, "US Military, a Growing Latino Army," *NBCLatino*, January 1, 2013.

31 Rowan Scarborough, "Foreigners Find Military Fast Track to Citizenship," *Washington Times*, August 22, 2002; Brian MacQuarrie, "Carrier Hosts Ceremony for New Citizens," *Boston Globe*, March 3, 2007, p. B1.

32 US DoD, *2014 Demographics Profile.*

33 Derek B. Stewart, *Military Personnel: Active Duty Benefits Reflect Changing Demographics, but Continued Focus Is Needed*, statement before the Subcommittee on Personnel, Armed Services Committee, U.S. Senate, April 11, 2002, available as GAO-02-557T, pp. 3–4.

34 Captain F. A. Delzompo, US Marines Corps, "The Few, the Proud, the Unwed," *Proceedings* (November 1995): 48.

35 Tony Perry, "On Base, the Comforts of Home, Minus Civilians," *Los Angeles Times*, June 13, 2015.

36 Katelyn Clark, "Soldiers Often Marry Young, and for Good Reasons," *Military Times*, January 5, 2016.

37 "Private Benjamin (1980): Quotes," *IMDb*, available at: http://www.imdb.com/title/tt0081375/quotes (accessed June 10, 2016).

38 Gina Harkins, "Marines Unveil Gender-Neutral Standards for 29 Jobs," *Marine Corps Times*, October 5, 2015.

39 As an example, see Martin Van Creveld, "Why Israel Doesn't Send Women into Combat," *Parameters*, 23(1) (Spring 1993): 5–9.

40 Mark Bowden, "The Kabul-Ki Dance," *The Atlantic* (November 2002).

41 Julian E. Barnes and Dion Nissenbaum, "Combat Ban for Women to End," *Wall Street Journal*, January 24, 2013; Matthew Rosenberg and Dave Phillips, "All Combat Roles Now Open to Women, Defense Secretary Says," *New York Times*, December 3, 2015.

42 Jeff Schogol, "Congressman: Navy Secretary's 'Social Meddling' More Dangerous to Marines than ISIS," *Marine Corps Times*, January 11, 2016.

43 Jim Michaels, "Women Not Clamoring to Enter Combat Arms Fields," *USA Today*, June 30, 2015.

44 Jennifer Steinhauer, "Sexual Assaults in Military Raise Alarm in Washington," *New York Times*, May 7, 2013.

45 John Lancaster, "Navy Pilots Feel Tarred by Tailhook," *Washington Post*, August 2, 1992, pp. 32–33; Peter J. Boyer, "Admiral Boorda's War," *The New Yorker*, September 16, 1996, pp. 68–86.

46 Sig Christensen, "Ex-Lackland Leaders Disciplined," *San Antonio News-Express*, May 1, 2013; Bradley Olson, "Admiral Hammers on Gender Equality," *Baltimore Sun*, February 27, 2006.

47 Craig Whitlock, "Obama Delivers Blunt Message on Sexual Assaults in Military," *Washington Post*, May 7, 2013. For similar cases in the Army, see Craig Whitlock, "In the War Against Sexual Assault, the Army Keeps Shooting Itself in the Foot," *Washington Post*, December 19, 2015.

48 Elizabeth Kier, "Homosexuals in the U.S. Military: Open Integration and Combat Effectiveness," *International Security*, 23(2) (Fall 1998): 5–39.

49 Om Prakash, "The Efficacy of 'Don't Ask, Don't Tell,'" *Joint Forces Quarterly*, 55 (October 2009): 88–94.

50 Steven Beardsley, "Overseas Benefits Elusive for Same-Sex Military Couples," *Stars and Stripes*, February 6, 2015.

51 Tom Ricks, *Making the Corps* (New York: Scribner, 1997).

52 Michael Worden, *Rise of the Fighter Generals: The Problem of Air Force Leadership, 1945–1982* (Maxwell AFB, AL: Air University Press, 1998); Rowan Scarborough, "Highway to the Danger Zone? Obama Picks Non-Pilot to Head Air Force in Pacific," *Washington Times*, July 17, 2014.

53 Roger Thompson, *Brown Shoes, Black Shoes, and Felt Slippers: Parochialism and the Evolution of the Post-War U.S. Navy* (Newport, RI: US Naval War College, 1995).

54 Linda Robinson, *Masters of Chaos: The Secret History of the Special Forces* (New York: Public Affairs, 2004).

55 Richard Swain, "The Obligations of Military Professionalism," National Defense University, December 2010.

Recommended additional reading

Beth Bailey, *America's Army: Making the All-Volunteer Force* (Cambridge, MA: Harvard University Press, 2009). A well-written account of the AVF with special emphasis on how it was sold to the public and potential recruits.

Donald Chisholm, *Waiting for Dead Men's Shoes: Origins and Development of the US Navy's Officer Personnel System, 1793–1941* (Stanford, CA: Stanford University Press, 2001). Congress and the bureaucracy learn to manage naval careers.

Eliot Cohen, *Citizens and Soldiers: The Dilemmas of Military Service* (Ithaca, NY: Cornell University Press, 1985). The historic tension between freedom and military service carefully discussed.

Curtis Gilroy and Cindy Williams (eds.), *Service to Country: Personnel Policies and the Transformation of Western Militaries* (Cambridge, MA: MIT Press, 2006). Leading specialists examine military personnel issues in comparative perspective.

Charles C. Moskos and John Sibley Butler, *All We Can Be: Black Leadership and Racial Integration the Army Way* (New York: Basic Books, 1997). Sets the record straight on a controversial subject.

James Wright, *Those Who Have Borne the Battle: A History of America's Wars and Those Who Fought Them* (New York: Public Affairs Press, 2012). A former president of Dartmouth College and Marine examines how service has changed in time – and changes people.

6 Service politics

Most nations have a dominant armed service whose acknowledged status as leader is the product of the nation's strategic position. In Russia, the Army dominates, as Russia is a continental power with many potential threats on its borders and only limited access to the sea. In Britain, the Royal Navy rules the roost, as Britain is an island separated from adversaries and opportunities alike by the sea. In China, which has many border disputes with its neighbors and a great fear of internal fragmentation, the People's Liberation Army (PLA) is the dominant military service and the navy is a mere subdivision of the PLA. France, living as it does between Germany and Britain, favors a strong army but can see the need for a relatively large navy, too.

The United States is somewhat isolated from its adversaries and friends and thus sometimes needs to project power far from its shores. It has four large and rivalrous armed services – the Army, Navy, Air Force, and Marine Corps – and at least two other institutions that also get involved abroad, the Coast Guard and US Special Operations Command. Normally the Coast Guard operates in conjunction with the Navy, but it has official status as the fifth armed service. Special Operations is a joint operational command with forces assigned from the Army, Navy, Air Force, and, most recently, the Marine Corps, but it also has independent budgetary authority and the ability to set requirements, which essentially make it the sixth American armed service.

Grafted on top of this pool of contentious entities are the Joint Staff; a set of unified operational commands; and the concept of jointness itself, which has gained near-religious adherence among attentive civilians and at least some officers. The pride of each of the armed services in its history and the loyalty it commands among veterans and citizens has not noticeably diminished as the belief in jointness has grown, but jointness does indeed affect the ways in which the services relate to one another.

Jointness is an example of the instinct to plan, organize, and manage. Many critics view the services' independence as contributing to operational and organizational chaos, a tendency for uncoordinated military forces to get in one another's way on the battlefield and a reflection of the services' selfish parochialism in acquiring equipment. Yet even given the powerful influence of jointness on today's military, separate service cultures persist, and they could serve as a platform for market-like competition for roles and missions in the future, under a reform that shifted America's answer to the enduring question back toward market-like solutions rather than planning. For now, jointness, when it occasionally works as intended, might improve efficiency or military effectiveness, but it more often stifles creativity. In this chapter, we examine the internal politics of the services, inter-service relations, and the contradictions and dangers posed by the rise of jointness, the religion and the reality.

The US Marine Corps

The United States Marine Corps (USMC) is unique among militaries in the world. No other nation has a marine corps anywhere near the size and capability of the USMC. Alone, it is about the size of the entire British military, one of the world's most capable combat forces. Nearly every American, and surely many others, knows its motto, "Semper Fidelis" ("Always Faithful"), and, thanks to Hollywood, they also know its reputation for heroic amphibious assaults and battlefield bravery. The Marine Corps hardly ever loses a round on Capitol Hill, misses a recruitment goal, or fails to have its wartime exploits extolled in a best-selling book. Yet it is the most insecure of America's military services, always fearing its absorption by the Army. And well it should, as the Marine Corps has prospered largely on the political missteps of the Army. If the Army were to become politically more astute, the Marine Corps would have a much less successful bureaucratic life.

The Marine Corps traces its origins to a Continental Congress vote in 1775 authorizing the creation of two battalions of Marines in anticipation of an invasion of Nova Scotia. The battalions never formed, and the operation in Nova Scotia never happened. The relatively few Marines recruited found work helping the Navy perform its mission. By World War II, however, the Marines had acquired four distinct missions, each of which the USMC clung to tenaciously, but at times precariously.[1]

First, Marines served as ship guards for the Navy, protecting officers from the crew. Life on board warships was harsh and dangerous well into the nineteenth century. Many of the men were not volunteers but rather were dragooned into service to fill out crews before the ships sailed. High percentages were immigrants unsure of the culture of naval service or their future in the United States. Outnumbered and preoccupied by their duties, officers could easily feel vulnerable. The Marines provided security. By the end of the nineteenth century, reformers sought to have the Marines removed, believing that the Navy should professionalize and instill discipline through crew training. Teddy Roosevelt, the assistant secretary of the Navy at the time, ordered the Marines beached, but Congress intervened to reverse his initiative. Marines stayed on board large warships as honor guards, crews for secondary batteries, and protectors of special weapons for the next hundred years.

The Marines' second mission, starting in the early nineteenth century, was to serve as installation guards at naval shipyards and other facilities. The Marines needed shore stations and duties when their ships returned to home ports, therefore most large naval bases acquired Marine barracks and gate guards. Eventually, the shipyards wanted to give the guard posts to disabled or retired workers and seamen, but the Marines were available and free. They stayed on at the gates of naval shore facilities until the 1990s, when they were replaced by contract civilian guards.

The third mission grew gradually as the Marines evolved into the State Department's expeditionary infantry, protecting American commerce and traders at the direction of American diplomats. As the United States acquired overseas possessions or chronic challenges, Marines were dispatched as occupiers, deployed in units as large as brigades or regiments for assignments that lasted for decades in some cases. The Marines did not leave China until 1941, having arrived on a semi-permanent basis to protect American diplomats, missionaries, and commercial interests in 1843. But the Marine Corps' relationship with the State Department did not end with World War II. It lingers to this day with the Marine's unique role as embassy guards, those spiffily dressed doorkeepers familiar to US embassy visitors worldwide, although most of the actual guard duty at most embassies is now outsourced.

The fourth mission is the very well-known amphibious assault mission, the responsibility for which the Marines have managed to enshrine in law. The concept developed in the early 1890s in response to the Navy's need for advance bases and refueling and refitting stations in any Pacific or European war. Some such bases might be pre-established or provided by allies, but others would have to be seized by assault forces. Despite the disastrous experience of the British at Gallipoli during World War I, which partially discredited amphibious efforts, the Marines kept at the task of developing appropriate forces and doctrine through the interwar period. The Marines seemed to overcome the troubled history in their invasions of Japanese-held islands during World War II, generating heroic scenes re-created in many a Hollywood movie.[2]

The World Wars also ushered in an increase in the lethality of firepower that has made amphibious assaults an extraordinarily dangerous venture ever since.[3] The United States has conducted only one opposed amphibious landing since World War II, the 1950 assault by roughly equal-sized Marine and Army units at Inchon, Korea. Nevertheless, the Marines cling to the mission, justifying the continuing investment of billions of dollars in amphibious warfare ships and training, to the puzzlement of other militaries and the US Army. Despite the doubts of others, the mission is politically and organizationally important for the Corps.

Of course, the US Army should know the reason for the Marine Corps' amazing success, because the Army itself is the primary cause. The Army's political blunders have helped generate the Marine Corps' mystique. The ground combat side of the Corps is about one-quarter the size of the Army, but it gets at least equal billing in Congress and the media. For example, the Marines' Hymn exaggerates the Corps' pre-twentieth-century role. "From the halls of Montezuma to the shores of Tripoli," it says. But it was the Army that lost over 1,000 men in combat during the Mexican War, while the Marine Corps lost 11, and the exploits of the Marines in the Barbary Campaign came after the liberation of the hostage they were seeking to free. The Marines had hardly any involvement in the Civil or Indian wars, keeping busy mainly by preventing American sailors from acting on their never-demonstrated urges to kill their officers. Thanks to the Army, it was World War I that created the Marine Corps' heroic image and World War II that sealed it.

Box 6.1   Monumental conflict

In October 2006, the United States Air Force dedicated its first memorial in Washington, DC, nearly 60 years after the Air Force split off from the Army as a separate military service and nearly 100 years after the Army first acquired airplanes. The memorial, a three-spire bomb burst modeled after the famous air show act of the Thunderbirds, the Air Force stunt team, is located on a ridge that rises behind Arlington National Cemetery, close to the Pentagon. This was not the original site for the memorial. The Air Force Association, the sponsor of the memorial, initially chose a location on the north side of Arlington Cemetery near Key Bridge and the US Marine Corps Memorial, the great statuary version of the well-known Iwo Jima flag-raising photograph.

But there was opposition to placing the Air Force Memorial in this location. Many approvals from arts commissions and the like are needed to place statues in the District of Columbia. Most permissions and endorsements for the Air Force Memorial were easily obtained. The only real opposition came from friends of the Marine Corps, who objected to placing another service's memorial near the Marine Corps', even though they acknowledged that the design for the Air Force memorial envisioned at the time would place it so far down the hill and leave it so well shielded by trees that it would not be visible from the

(continued)

(continued)

Iwo Jima statue. The opposition continued despite quietly expressed reminders of the great sacrifices airmen and women had made over the years in common cause with the Marine Corps. (In World War II the Army Air Force, the predecessor to the US Air Force, lost over 50,000 air crew members; in contrast, the Marine Corps' heroic efforts in the Pacific campaigns – Marines did not serve in Europe during World War II – cost 20,000 Marine deaths.) After several years, the Air Force Association, worried about the constant delays that Marine objections produced, proposed the alternative site.[4]

The Marine Corps' opposition is a bit strange, given the struggle it took to get a Marine Memorial in the District of Columbia after World War I. The memorial in question is a statue of a Marine now known as "Iron Mike," but today it is located at the Marine base in Quantico, Virginia, some 50 miles south of the District rather than in a prime spot in the nation's capital. Iron Mike was originally a gift of the French government to the American Expeditionary Force, which fought with France on the Western Front during World War I. Dozens of US Army brigades and two Marine brigades fought in the trenches. During the war, the Marines suffered 4,000 casualties in a battle at Belleau Woods – more than they had suffered in their entire history to that point, largely because the Marines had fought primarily on small expeditions rather than in set-piece battles before the Great War. But the Army suffered tens of thousands more casualties in other battles during the war.

At the end of the war, the French government commissioned the statue of an American soldier as a tribute to the sacrifices made by US forces. The sculptor picked a model from the many American servicemen recovering from wounds in Paris. Army General John "Black Jack" Pershing, the commanding officer of American forces, was to accept the gift at an unveiling ceremony before returning to the United States. As the drape was pulled from the statue, however, Pershing peered at it and then stomped off the stage without accepting the gift. Without realizing the implication of his choice, the sculptor had actually picked a Marine for his model, identified by the buttons and other small insignia on his uniform. Pershing noticed the difference immediately and decided on the spot not to tolerate such an affront.

In response, the Marines privately raised the money to buy the statue from the now quite unhappy French. Their plan was to bring it to a location in the District of Columbia as a tribute to their World War I sacrifices. The Army, however, controlled the Military District of Washington and refused to allow its installation. Stymied, the Marines took Iron Mike to Quantico, land that the Corps controlled, where it keeps vigil to this day.[5]

During World War II, the Marines' reputation for valor was sealed on Iwo Jima and other invasion beaches. After the war, it gave the Marines their pick of statue sites in the District – and enough political clout to make the Air Force take its memorial to another site more than 50 years after the battle.

The Army's contribution to the American Expeditionary Force in World War I was 40 divisions – over a million men – while the Marine Corps provided only two brigades. In fact, the Marines fought as part of the Army's Second Division, with one brigade up and the other in reserve and training. The Marines did fight heroically, but their relatively small piece of the war received star billing back in the United States only because of the Army's strict policy of not identifying engaged Army units. The Army insisted that combat dispatches use the generic phrase "American soldiers today . . .," while allowing the Marines to be separately identified. The result was that the hero-starved American press soon ran a disproportionately large number of stories about heroic Marines, and for the first time the nation's newspaper readers became very aware of the Marines' existence. Thanks to that public relations mistake, Americans now believed that they had two armies fighting in Europe, with one being especially valiant.

The Army was determined not to make the same mistake in World War II. It excluded the Marines almost entirely from the European theater of operations. A handful of Marines observed, but did not take part in, the Normandy landings. Another small group was sent to Iceland when the United States first entered the war, in order to help prevent a German invasion, but this unit was quickly relieved by Army forces.

The Army even performed the Marines' signature amphibious assault mission during the war at Normandy and in the other major campaigns in Europe, the Mediterranean, and the Pacific. The Army was quite skilled in managing these complex and dangerous undertakings on its own, deploying engineer assault brigades that were essentially equivalent to the first-wave Marine assault units. Despite the image of the Marines as America's amphibious assault force, the Army conducted or participated in more amphibious operations than did the Marines during the war.

Relegated to the war in the Pacific, the Marines found salvation in another Army public relations blunder. Instead of mandating the identification of individual Army units in dispatches, as was done in Europe, the Army allowed General Douglas MacArthur, the commander of the southwest Pacific theater, to cite Army actions as "MacArthur's forces today . . .," while continuing to identify Marine units separately. Although the Army had more divisions in the Pacific than did the Marines (18 to the Marines' 6), the image of the Pacific war is of island-hopping Marines defeating the Japanese. Observing the flag-raising on Iwo Jima from a nearby ship, Secretary of the Navy James Forrestal remarked that this glorious moment assured the bureaucratic survival of the Marine Corps for the next 500 years. So far, his prediction looks on target.

The Marines have been essentially untouchable since World War II. In the unification debates that followed the war, the Army sought to hobble Marine ambitions – but failed. During the Korean War, the Army tried to control the Corps' size and missions, only to have the Marines' friends on Capitol Hill pass the Douglas-Mansfield Act in 1952. This Act mandates that there be at least three active Marine divisions, plus three air wings, and it gave the Marines observational status on the Joint Chiefs of Staff. The most famous image of the Korean War is not from the Army. It is the retreat from the Chosin Reservoir, another demonstration of Marine Corps courage in the face of a numerically superior adversary and appalling physical conditions.

Vietnam brought more Army public relations blunders that helped to cement the Marines' image. After rejecting the Marines' counterinsurgency strategy, the Army relegated the Marines to static positions along the so-called Demilitarized Zone (DMZ), the combat location furthest from Saigon and most of the reporters covering the war. The Army thought that it would keep control of media relations, if not the Marines themselves. Of course, the Army was mistaken. Despite being involved in nearly all of the war's dirtiest aspects, the Marines came out of Vietnam remembered mainly for their heroic battles, especially at Khe Sahn and Hue City, and for their disparagement of the Army's attrition strategy.

By the Gulf War, the Army had given up on the media and did everything it could to hinder coverage. The Marines took the opposite stance, cultivating relations with journalists, allowing them to embed with combat units and giving medals to Marines who got their stories out. Although the Army had nearly four times the number of soldiers in theater, the Marines managed to equal or exceed the number of major newspaper articles and network TV clips focused on Army units from the initial deployments to the war's end. In the Army's view, President Truman had it right when he said that a Marine squad consisted of 10 riflemen and a public relations agent.

And the Marines used their image to protect the organization in the 1990s. When the Marines wanted more and higher-quality tanks after the Gulf War, they merely had their friends on Capitol Hill force the Army to refurbish and hand over 400 or so M-1s, the Army's first-class tank, at no cost to the Corps.[6] The Marines lost 12 percent of their end strength in the post-Cold War cuts, while the Army lost nearly 40 percent. And although the Marines claim to be offering 20 percent of the nation's combat power for about 8 percent of the total defense budget, only pliable corporate accountants would allow the Marines to ignore the fact that their requirements lie at the heart of many of America's most costly weapons projects, including the F-35B Lightning II Joint Strike Fighter, the V-22 tilt-rotor aircraft, the new amphibious assault vehicle, the new class of amphibious ships, the lightweight 155mm howitzer, and the ever-expensive LCAC air-cushioned landing craft. Moreover, the Navy pays for many a Marine need, including medical services, the crews of the amphibious ships, and, along with the Army, research and development for new military technologies. The Marines are no doubt comparatively small, but they are not cheap. In fact, they are not even that small in the post-Cold War era. Once a quarter of the Department of the Navy, they are now 40 percent. Once a quarter the size of the Army, they are now well more than a third.

The Marines do occasionally blunder. They did not object when the Navy expanded its underwater demolition teams into the SEALs (Sea, Air and Land), which have since come to epitomize the public's definition of commando, once a Marine trademark. The Marines also passed on contributing forces to the Special Operations Command (SOCOM) when it was created in 1987, while all the other services climbed on board. SOCOM has become a bureaucratic winner in the Global War on Terror, acquiring budget share, missions, and force structure. Only the forceful demands of Secretary Rumsfeld brought the Marines reluctantly into the joint special operations fold, long after the best opportunities had been claimed by special operators from the other services.

But the Marines are too politically astute to lose their most favored status in Washington and beyond. Although they tried to derail jointness, they are now among its biggest beneficiaries. They acquired full representation on the Joint Chiefs. Their general officer allocation was increased so they could take on more joint assignments. Over time, Marine officers have come to hold such coveted positions as chairman and vice chairman of the Joint Chiefs of Staff and head of the European, Strategic, Southern, and Central Commands. They keep in touch by flying Marine One, the president's helicopter; by providing the Marine Band for state occasions, national tours, and private weddings and bar mitzvahs; and by inviting favorite civilians as guests of honor to the Friday Sunset Parades at 8th and Eye, the Marine barracks in Washington, for eye-catching performances of the Marine Corps Drill Team.

Although the Marine Corps is a combined arms organization, its infantry component dominates. The Marines separate by gender their basic enlisted training, or Boot Camp as it is called. But regardless of gender, acquisition source (Annapolis or Officer Candidate School), or career intention (infantry or pilot), all officers must attend a six-month Basic Course at Quantico, Virginia, that emphasizes ground combat and binds them to the Corps. And both officers and enlisted Marines learn the "Marine Corps Rifleman's Creed" and the slogan, "Every Marine a Rifleman." Tradition, unbroken until the 2010 selection of General Amos, is that the commandant of the Marine Corps is an infantry officer, and the assistant commandant is an aviator. Amos' aviation experience was likely needed to defend the troubled acquisition of the F-35B, the Marines' expensive Short Takeoff and Vertical Landing (STOVL) version of the Joint Strike Fighter. Some say, though, that this experience, an aviator in charge, will not soon be repeated. It has not been so far.

There is division within the Marine Corps. Variations develop at times in doctrine and procedures between East Coast and West Coast Marines, the forces oriented toward the Atlantic or the Pacific. Marines tend to have careers on one coast or the other, and units sometimes interact too infrequently. More important are the struggles between Marines who want to emphasize large-scale amphibious warfare and those who want to build the Corps around low-intensity or counterinsurgency conflicts. War has pulled the Marine Corps recently in the counterinsurgency direction, but protection from jointness lies in having a unique identity, which pulls the Marines toward amphibious warfare, no matter how hard or expensive it is. As the wars in Iraq and Afghanistan were winding down amid talk of a US pivot to the Pacific, the Corps was quick to remind everyone that it had dominated the most difficult fighting in that theater in World War II and remained ready to contribute its special skill set again. It was no coincidence that the only highly visible force posture changes that accompanied announcement of the new strategic focus involved Marines being sent to Australia.

The US Army

The US Army is the beleaguered service. It has many rivals and few powerful friends. Not only is the Marine Corps another army, but so is the Army National Guard. The Army provides the bulk of the forces for the Special Operations Command but still has to compete with it for resources and missions, because it is yet another army. The Navy and Air Force have the support of many large contractors, who develop and build their equipment, but Army equipment is not as expensive and thus carries less political heft. The Marine Corps and Special Operations enjoy the prestige of being seen as commandos. The Coast Guard saves lives in dramatic rescues. But the Army is viewed as the service that takes your son or daughter to war and gives them the opportunity to be killed or maimed for not always popular and enduring causes. The hard fact is that the Army suffers the bulk of the casualties and does most of the drafting when there is drafting to be done. America is not at war unless the Army is committed, but when the Army is committed, it is very hard to turn back, and the war can get uncomfortably personal.

The Army is burdened by the need to provide lots of things to its inter-service rivals: access to its logistical system, protection, equipment, money, and its most desirable roles and missions. What the Army mostly wants is to be left alone. It is publicity-shy, seeing itself as the ever-accepting, never boastful, always dutiful servant of the nation. The Army looks inward, absorbed by its internal politics, and distrusts outsiders, even those bearing gifts. The Army is always short of something, always expecting little or no assistance from the other services and US allies, and always wanting to be out in the field and living in the mud rather than fighting in Washington – or so soldiers claim.

In the Army, nothing gets done without tedious reviews by committees and the sign-off of affected parties. The branches designated for combat operations, especially armor and infantry, are the dominant communities within the Army, but all branches have some autonomous authority and an ability to object to and delay administrative decisions. Unlike flag officers in the other services, Army generals remove their branch insignia upon reaching flag rank, but no one in the Army forgets where you came from and where your community stands in the internal pecking order.

The Army must also deal with the other services. Its relations with the Air Force are improving, but the wounds have not fully healed from the 1947 split. Prior to that year, the Air Force was part of the Army, beginning as an element of the Signal Corps in 1908 and then becoming the Army Air Corps during the interwar years and the Army Air Force during World War II. The Army was actually happy to have the Air Force become independent. It feared that World War II's glorification of airpower and the dawn of the nuclear age would lead to pilots' domination of the service's promotion lists and that the cost of aircraft would swallow the Army's procurement budget. At a meeting in Key West, Florida, in 1948, the Army and the Air Force agreed that the latter would buy and fly fixed-wing combat aircraft, while the Army would only have combat helicopters and some light aviation. The Air Force promised to devote some of its planes and missions to supporting ground troops, a promise the Air Force promptly ignored in favor of an enduring and organizationally useful focus on strategic bombing. By Vietnam, the Army realized the best way to have reliable airpower in support of ground forces was to provide it in-house, within the confines of the Key West agreements, so the Army soon developed its own air force of helicopter gunships and short-haul transport aircraft.[7]

From the Army's perspective, the Navy is just a lesser case of the Air Force: it eats up the defense budget building expensive ships, and the Army worries that the Navy will not show up when needed to help move the Army. The Army is likely right about the budget pressures that a large, blue-water, carrier-centric navy places on defense resources. It is wrong, though, on the Navy's interest in sealift. As we will describe in Chapter 9, the nations' shipyards and merchant marine interests keep the sealift spigot turned on, regardless of what the Navy believes is necessary or affordable.

The Army seems strangely resigned to being taken advantage of by its three direct rivals – the Marine Corps, the Army National Guard, and the Special Operations Command – apparently believing that the others will always enjoy better public and congressional support than the play-by-the-rules Army. No one is shocked anymore when the Guard retains missions it is ill-suited for, when the Marines get to acquire equipment at the Army's expense, or when the Special Operations Command takes over billets previously assigned to the Army. Instead, there is just the self-congratulatory feeling that comes with believing that by not stooping to their level of political groveling for material gain, the Army has held to its values of stoicism and loyal service.

Some things the Army will fight to get or keep. It is very numbers-oriented. For a long time, it was end strength that mattered most to the Army. Through much of the latter half of the Cold War, the Army insisted on staying at roughly the 780,000-soldier mark. When the Cold War ended, it was ten active-duty divisions that mattered most. Secretary Rumsfeld's modularity reforms shifted the units from divisions to Brigade Combat Teams (BCTs), and then as the budget cuts started in earnest in 2013, the Army reshuffled again, shedding some BCTs but increasing the number of soldiers in each one. So even as the number of BCTs drops, the number of soldiers does not drop proportionately. The Army struggles to preserve its size.

It has dawned on the Army that maintaining a higher end strength actually leads to greater political vulnerability, because on the downside of budget cycles it is easier to cut manpower than weapons systems. Manpower expenditures are mostly current expenditures, leading to visible and immediate savings when they are cut, while equipment expenditures are spread out over years in the future. Many of the savings from acquisition cuts are therefore on paper only. The Army's budget is the source civilians tap to keep the shipyards and aircraft factories working when peace returns.

The Army faces a difficult future. For the first time in its history, the Army's longer-term relevance can be questioned. During most of America's history, and certainly during the Cold War, the Army's mission was unassailable. It defended the nation *in extremis* and defeated the nation's enemies, preferably on their soil, not ours. But the Army offers the hard way to fight, taking ground meter by meter, with the potential for heavy losses and great destruction. Western society frowns on both.[8] The war that technology sometimes allows and the public much prefers is precise and relatively cost-free, neither of which comes easily to an Army moving through populated areas, whether for conquest, occupation, or counterinsurgency.

Although nuanced, the internal Army debate over the last 15 years has basically been between those who want to return to an Army built around its conventional-war, big-battle capabilities (on the belief that such capabilities are the essence of any professional army and enable all other missions) and those who see a likely future in continuing stability operations and counterinsurgencies (and little possibility of engaging in combat with another serious conventional force). Russia's recently expanded footprint in Eastern Europe has strengthened the hand of those inside and outside the service arguing for the return to conventional warfare. They had a hard case to make only a few years ago, when the United States was still fighting two big insurgencies and the only looming peer competitor was China, unlikely to pose a land warfare challenge to the United States. Even though the Army was largely left out of the pivot to Asia (notwithstanding the creation of a Strategic Landpower Office, intended to avoid just such a fate), Russia's renewed threat to Ukraine and the Baltics gave the Army a good reason to leave behind its unpopular foray into counterinsurgency. All the better, since stability operations offer few opportunities for large acquisition projects, and shifting the Army's focus to them might touch off an unwanted direct competition with a crisis-oriented Marine Corps and a growing, ever-busy Special Operations Command.

The US Navy

The Navy is a second Department of Defense. It has its own air force, its own army, its own strategic weapons, its own language (CINCLANTFLT, COMSUBPAC, and SPAWAR) and its own strange set of ranks (commodore, master chief petty officer, and rear admiral, lower half). It is huge compared to the next biggest navy, having more than ten times the tonnage of Britain's Royal Navy, and being equal in size to virtually all the other navies in the world combined;[9] most are happy to exercise with the US Navy whenever it is in the neighborhood. The Navy also has a very loyal little brother, the Coast Guard, which itself is the world's seventh largest fleet. Despite its name, the Coast Guard loves to tag along on the Navy's adventures far from US shores, including its big and little wars, from Korea to Iraq.

The Navy even has its own enemies. During the first half of the twentieth century, the Navy was preoccupied with its relationship to the Royal Navy. It never got over the World War I slights of being assigned to convoy duty and having to pay patent royalties on Royal Navy equipment needed for mobilization.[10] In the naval disarmament treaties of the 1920s, the US Navy insisted that it be allocated a fleet size equal to the Royal Navy. During World War II, its late arrival finally gave the US Navy the upper hand, and it insisted that the Royal Navy (along with the Canadians) handle the less glamorous mission of convoy protection in the Atlantic. It enforced that priority by withholding ships being built to replace British losses.

The US Navy was clearly dominant at the war's end, with a fleet five times bigger than the Royal Navy, but it still insisted on a public acknowledgement. During negotiations for the

NATO Treaty in 1948, it was obvious that a US Army general would be assigned Supreme Allied Commander Europe (SACEUR), the all-important NATO post. The British assumed that a Royal Navy admiral would get the Supreme Allied Commander Atlantic (SACLANT) spot as the consolation prize. So, too, did the American negotiators. But not the US Navy. It refused its consent to the NATO Treaty, politically essential to ensure Senate ratification, until the SACLANT post was reserved for the US Navy. All the Royal Navy got was a newly created and totally subordinate Channel Command, a post with a purview approximately 12 miles wide and 100 miles long.[11]

The Navy has challenged not only allies but presidents. In the early days of World War II, President Franklin D. Roosevelt declared that Europe was to be the priority theater, with the big push in the Pacific to await the defeat of the Nazis. But the Navy, embittered by the surprise destruction of the fleet at Pearl Harbor, never quite signed on for his prioritization, although Roosevelt was once an assistant secretary of the Navy and certainly was a Navy loyalist. The Navy shifted its main surviving resources to the Pacific for what would have to be described as more than a holding action. Within six months of the Pearl Harbor attack, the Navy had begun the rollback by defeating the Japanese fleet at the Battle of Midway. It had also initiated a vigorous submarine campaign against Japanese shipping; once this campaign overcame some torpedo design and training problems, it nearly won the war in the Pacific by itself. Today the Japanese Navy is the sailing buddy of the US Navy – never mind the fact that for years the US Navy had the USS *Midway* as its Japan-based aircraft carrier.

In the Cold War, the US Navy had to embellish the Soviet Navy's capabilities in order to gain an equivalent opponent. The Soviet Navy never enjoyed much prestige among the civilian and military leaders of the Soviet Union. Its air arm was commanded by a ground forces general, and its "Marine Corps" was a brigade-sized unit of naval infantry. The Soviet Navy's 400 submarines included many nearly useless coastal diesel boats and several classes of very noisy and accident-prone nuclear submarines (noisy submarines being easy to find and destroy in wartime). On the basis of this threat, the US Navy built a fleet of nearly 600 warships that included 15 large aircraft carriers, 100 nuclear attack submarines, 60 amphibious warfare ships, and an aggressive naval strategy that had the Soviet Navy locked behind several natural choke points and under close surveillance.

Box 6.2   Jim Webb and the 594-ship Navy

The Navy counts funny. Sometimes the Navy includes in its ship totals combatant auxiliaries – oilers, ammunition ships, and the like – and sometimes it doesn't. Sometimes the Navy includes patrol craft and minesweepers, and sometimes it doesn't. Ships can be put on the inactive list, kept in reserve, retired early, or overhauled to extend their lives. The Coast Guard has armed, frigate-sized ships and often deploys them overseas with the Navy's battle groups, but none of its ships get counted in the Navy totals. The Military Sealift Command (MSC) has 110 ships, many of which were recently in commission and all of which provide support for military operations, including tracking submarines, hauling combat vehicles, monitoring foreign missile tests, and replenishing supplies to combat ships under way, just as auxiliaries do. The MSC is even headed by an admiral and is the Navy's component of US Transportation Command, one of the joint operational commands, yet none of the MSC's ships is included in the Navy's numbers.

Until the Cold War, fleet sizes were measured mostly in tonnage rather than in ship numbers. The 1920s naval arms control treaties were based on tonnage, and set ratios between the US Navy and Royal Navy totals in an ultimately vain attempt to prevent arms-racing among naval powers. The naval course of World War II was measured in tonnage as well – tonnage produced and tonnage sunk, with the US Navy dominating both by the end.

But the Navy's Cold War opponent, the Soviet Union, had a small fleet, at least in terms of tonnage. It turns out that the Soviets never threw away a ship, and built a lot of them, even though they were light in weight and therefore combat power and sustainability at sea. The Soviet Navy, organized in four isolated fleets, comprised numerous coastal submarines, patrol craft, and missile boats. Not surprisingly, the US Navy created a rationale to base comparisons on ship numbers rather than tonnage, the fact that warships were packing more electronics into smaller vessels making tonnage less important. Soon the Soviet Navy didn't look that puny, having hundreds more submarines and almost as many surface combatants as the US Navy.

Of course, the US Navy remained a formidable force, no matter the metric. It had well over a thousand ships in the early 1970s as the Vietnam War wound down and the useful life of combatants built during World War II came to an end. Rebuilding of the fleet was slow, with the number of active ships during the Cold War bottoming out at 479 in 1980. The Reagan administration, with John Lehman as secretary of the Navy, set a goal of a 600-ship fleet by the end of the decade. They downplayed the fact that the new warships were substantially bigger, heavier, and more powerful than the ones being decommissioned. A World War II destroyer was 2,500 tons at best. The *Spruance*-class replacement was 6,000 tons heavier and 200 feet longer. The 1950s carriers were around 45,000 tons. The nuclear-powered *Nimitz* carriers of the 1980s were more than twice as heavy. Though it had fewer ships in the late 1980s than in the early 1970s, the US Navy had not lost a pound.

Numbers may not be a good indicator of naval capabilities, but they certainly are a good measure of political prowess. The "600-ship Navy" became a political rallying cry for those unhappy with the supposedly anti-military Democrats who dominated Congress after Vietnam. James Webb – a Vietnam war hero, novelist, Lehman's successor as secretary of the Navy, and, ironically, later an anti-war Democratic senator from Virginia – resigned in protest in 1988 when the 600-ship Navy seemed destined to top out at 580 (or 700, depending on what was counted).

In the 2000s and 2010s, the Reagan-era ships are being retired, sometimes early, to save operating costs. The Navy is struggling to get back to 313 ships, its post-9/11 goal. The ships, like many Americans, continue to gain weight. The carriers are now described as 110,000 tons. The *Virginia*-class replacement for the *Los Angeles*-class attack submarine is a little heavier and a lot more expensive. The problem is that the Navy has no peer competitor naval enemy and no way to calculate precise needs. The 313 number sounds more calculated than 300 or 333, but it isn't.

The Navy carries with it the advantage that much of the nation's maritime industry depends on it. Without exception, the large US shipyards have long shed the competitive commercial ship market for the more reliable fortunes in warship construction. Rarely can an American combatant be built for less than a billion dollars a copy. Even that price is becoming a fond memory. The DDG-1000 *Zumwalt* class of destroyers under construction in the 2010s cost around $3.5 billion each – so much that the Navy adjusted its plans to buy only three of this class, replacing them with additional ships of the "cheaper" DDG-51 *Arleigh Burke* class at nearly $2 billion each. This is actually a good deal for the shipyards, because the DDG-1000 experience has somehow made the DDG-51 seem like a bargain. Meanwhile, a nuclear submarine is more than $2 billion a copy. Aircraft carriers, which once cost $4–$5 billion, have been redesigned and now cost around $12–$14 billion apiece. It is not surprising that the Navy's shipbuilding budget has friends inside and outside the Navy. Similar dependencies exist for the US Merchant Marine and a good chunk of the aircraft and missile industries. The unity of maritime interests on the need for a big, modern navy is unshakable.

Strangely, within the Navy itself there is more ambivalence over the shipbuilding budget. That is because the Navy is internally divided into platform communities that engender their own loyalties. The main communities are surface, aviation, and submarine, but each has its own subdivisions. For example, surface breaks down into large and small combatants, while aviation is divided many ways, including fighter versus support, patrol versus carrier, and fixed-wing versus helicopter. The Department of the Navy also includes a large shore establishment, many civilians, the Marines, and the Naval Special Warfare community, among others. Some in the Navy are happy to see more destroyers built, but others might prefer amphibious warfare ships, carriers, or fewer ships altogether and more of something else.[12]

It is no wonder, then, that the Navy takes pains to maintain unity, or at least avoid disunity. For example, it allows few variations in uniforms. Officers wear a single emblem that designates their platform community (wings, dolphins, etc.) above their ribbons. Sailors are nearly indistinguishable except for small ship-name ribbons on their shoulders and rank insignia variations that include skill designations. Nearly all four-star admirals are Naval Academy graduates; only one chief of naval operations was not, and he committed suicide, apparently in part because of an attack on him in a speech to midshipmen at the Academy by a retired officer graduate.[13] For a while, it seemed the Navy even had its own religion, Episcopalianism, with the main chapel at the Academy remaining so even after Catholicism supplanted Episcopalianism as the midshipmen's dominant religion. Admiral Rickover, supposedly discriminated against when he came up for promotion to flag rank because he was Jewish, had actually converted to Episcopalianism when he was a young lieutenant, recognizing where the power was within the Navy.[14]

Traditions count in the Navy, and indeed it is the most tradition-bound of all the services.[15] But politics counts even more. The Navy long held to a set of rules for naming ships based on both tradition and politics. Battleships were named after states, cruisers after cities, destroyers and frigates after deceased national heroes, submarines after fish, and so on. But as battleships disappeared, so did the Navy's ship-naming traditions. Ballistic missile submarines, nuclear cruisers, and attack submarines have recently been christened after states. Carriers used to be named after historic ships, most recently in the early 1960s, but since then the honor has gone to presidents, sometimes living, or members of Congress, particularly those who did the Navy a good turn. And heroes have been both redefined and ignored when the name (and funding) search is on for a new surface combatant. The US Navy's ships are more and more like pyramids: impressive, hard-to-build, religiously endowed symbols of the country's wealth and power.

The Navy was the outsider in America's most recent wars. The terrorists did not have a navy, and the struggle against them was focused on one landlocked country, Afghanistan, and another country, Iraq, that was nearly so. Naval aviation did play a role, but a relatively minor one. Sailors served in various support units – construction, development assistance, medical – and as SEALs and counter-improvised explosive device (IED) experts, but not in great numbers. It was not surprising, then, that the Navy's choice for a new recruiting motto in 2010 emphasized humanitarian activities rather than warfighting: "America's Navy, a Global Force for Good." Critics began calling it the Salvation Navy.

With the counterinsurgency wars winding down, however, the Navy has begun to find again its warrior spirit. The Obama administration's pivot to the Pacific seemed made for the Navy. After all, the Navy has long had the Pacific as its main domain. The Air–Sea Battle operational concept that pits technology against a possible attempt by some very large, unnamed Pacific power to deny American access to the region fits well with calls for naval resurgence. It may be telling that the two most recent Chiefs of Naval Operations (Admirals Richardson and Greenert) are submariners. Submariners were the dominant platform community in the Navy during the height of the Cold War, and submarines are the Navy's most technologically advanced platform.

The US Air Force

There is little mystery about what has made the US Air Force tick: strategic attack. Pilots can fly many types of mission, nearly all of which were identified quite early in the history of military aviation. Aircraft can be used for observation and reconnaissance, the transport of supplies and troops, the interdiction of enemy supply lines, the close support of ground operations, the interception of attacking enemy aircraft, the suppression of enemy air defenses, and strategic bombing – that is, attacks intended not merely to reduce the enemy's forces but to coerce it into capitulating short of the full physical destruction of its means of waging war.[16] Airpower can be centralized or decentralized, employed under one command or under many. From World War I on, the US Air Force in its several organizational guises has been dominated by the belief in the use of centralized airpower directed toward strategic attack. Despite the limitations of technology and major changes in warfare, the US Air Force's faith in this mission has been unshakeable.

The Air Force's theology both reflects and enables a broader American commitment to low-casualty, standoff attacks. The appeal is obvious. Strategic bombing promises to bypass the long, hard slog across the battlefield by substituting capital for labor. As technology improves, fewer and fewer airmen can inflict ever-more-precise destruction upon the enemy. The question then becomes what targets to hit, but targeting has never been the Air Force's prime preoccupation. Instead, it is the other tenet of the theology that has absorbed most of the Air Force's attention, the need to centralize the command of air assets and the application of airpower.

It took the Air Force more than three decades to free itself from the control of the Army. During that time, the other services found ways to accommodate their airmen so that they would resist the lure of an independent air force. The Navy gave its airmen their own flag officers, their own materiel development bureau, and their own ships. Naval aviators could and did rise to the Navy's top ranks, and several served as chief of naval operations soon after the establishment of the Air Force. After World War II, the Marine Corps fixed a 1:1 ratio between its divisions and air wings and guaranteed that an aviator would always serve at least as the assistant commandant, the Corps' second-highest ranking officer. Airpower escaped from the Army, but the other services co-opted their aviators, winning the battle to retain significant airpower capabilities outside the control of the Air Force.

In the decades that followed its independence, the Air Force had to deal with a series of jurisdictional challenges over the control of emerging aerospace technologies, most of which it lost. The Air Force had to share ballistic missiles with the Army and the Navy;

communications and reconnaissance satellites with civilians, the Navy, and defense agencies; and unmanned aerial vehicles with everyone, even the CIA and US Customs and Border Protection. The Air Force was hardly out of the Army's organizational tent when the Army began building a large air force of its own, mostly helicopter-based but increasingly lethal.[17] And even when the Air Force gained some exclusivity in areas such as long-range airlift or satellite management, it ended up having to use its capabilities to support others, under conditions of less than total control. One natural result is that those parts of the Air Force associated with these less unique missions, the thousands of airmen and officers that handle everything from strategic missiles to special operations and combat search and rescue helicopters, are lower in the service's internal pecking order.

Box 6.3   The Air Force tries to retire the A-10

The A-10 Thunderbolt II is a twin-jet engine aircraft designed specifically to provide close air support (CAS) for engaged ground forces. With its titanium-armored cockpit, uncommon ability to fly low and slow, long loiter time, unique cigar-shaped fuselage, seven-barrel rotary cannon that rapidly fires 30mm armor-piercing rounds, and 11 hardpoints for carrying up to 16,000 pounds of precision and non-precision bombs, rockets, and missiles, the A-10 is a very welcome sight for US and allied troops as it takes a run at opposing forces. A bit ugly by fighter-plane standards, the A-10 is often referred to with affection by ground forces and its own pilots as the "warthog" or "hog."

The knock against the Air Force is that it does not value the CAS mission. Certainly, in the run up to its independence, it emphasized its strategic bombing capabilities. At the end of World War II, as it was leaving the Army, the leaders of the Air Force pledged not to neglect CAS, a pledge that was soon forgotten with the start of the Cold War and the rise to dominance of the bomber-focused Strategic Air Command. When Fairchild Republic, the A-10's designer, pushed hard in the 1970s to expand procurement of the A-10, the Air Force resisted, caving only when the Army sought to revive the Cheyenne, a heavily armed helicopter, as a battlefield alternative. Fairchild Republic paid a price: the Air Force never bought another combat aircraft from the firm, and it eventually folded. Although capable of chewing up Soviet tank formations, the A-10 found its home on the battlefields of post-Cold War conflicts: Kuwait, the Balkans, Iraq, and Afghanistan.

Thus when the Air Force proposed in 2013 to retire its roughly 275 A-10s (715 were built), more than half of which reside in the Air National Guard and Reserves, it met quick resistance, especially in Congress. The Air Force's reasoning was that it needed multi-purpose aircraft in the future, namely the Joint Strike Fighter, now called the F-35 Lightning II. In 2013, it cost nearly a billion dollars a year to retain the A-10s, and the Air Force needed that money for new aircraft. Moreover, it wanted to retrain 800 A-10 maintainers to work on the F-35. CAS was not going to be neglected because the mission was already tasked to other aircraft – F-16s, F-15Es, B-1s, and B-52s. CAS itself was also changing due to precision and standoff weapons.

Congressional opposes to the A-10 retirement for all the expected reasons. Some representatives and senators are from states destined to lose aircraft and jobs if the Air Force shifts resources among platforms and bases. Others have a personal interest. Senator John McCain from Arizona, once a Navy attack pilot, cares a lot about

Davis-Monthan Air Force Base, home of 355th Fighter Wing, an active-duty A-10 unit. So does Congresswoman Martha McSally who represents Tucson, where Davis-Monthan is located, but she has other reasons as well. She is a retired Air Force pilot, the first woman to fly a combat mission, hers over Iraq in an A-10. She later commanded the 354th Fighter Squadron, a component of the 355th Fighter Wing. Senator Kelly Ayotte of New Hampshire does not have a base to defend, but she is both a close political ally of Senator McCain and married to a former A-10 pilot. Some people love the plane and some the pilots.

A-10 pilots and Air Force ground combat air controllers believe themselves to be the guardians of the CAS mission in the Air Force. They recognize that it is training and commitment that makes the mission, not a platform, but they worry that without a dedicated CAS platform, really a community formed around a platform, there will be less training and little commitment for CAS. They know that the F-35 development lags and that the aircraft will not have the right software and weapons capability for the full mission until the mid-2020s. With new wings and sensor and display updates, the A-10 could be flying CAS for decades to come.

But the Air Force sees a different world. It is focused on the F-35, hoping to reduce the support costs that a multi-aircraft inventory requires to survive in the defended airspace of a peer competitor. The F-35, it expects, with its stealth and its sensor/network capabilities, will make an effective CAS platform, or at least it will be the platform that enables less capable aircraft to survive against advanced air defense systems. The Marine Corps and the Navy, one more willing than the other, are flying in the same formation. In this vision, the A-10 is collateral damage, Congress permitting.

Does effective CAS require a platform community? The Marine Corps is good at CAS without a dedicated CAS platform; it now relies on a multi-role aircraft, the AV-8B, and in the future it will use the F-35B. Declining attention to CAS could present a problem when the Air Force has a strategic option that draws its attention, but joint air operations may actually present a solution: the Air Operations Center now can assign any capable and available platform to support troops on the ground, regardless of its service affiliation.

The goal of centralizing airpower proved elusive, but the Air Force has persistently fought for its defining ambitions. The joint arena provided additional opportunities for the Air Force to assert control over US airpower capabilities. The Air Force has the highest officer-to-enlisted ratio, even excluding pilots, of any of the services, and thus it has a larger pool from which to draw officers for joint assignments. Unlike the other services, the Air Force was quick to adopt a policy of sending many of its most talented officers to joint staffs. It lobbied hard for the key positions, especially in regional commands. More important, it realized that as the United States engaged in various regional conflicts, the really crucial position was the theater air component commander. This commander controlled all the air assets used in a given conflict, and assigned combat roles and missions to aviation units from all of the services, as well as allies.

The mechanism through which the air component commander exercises his authority is the Air Operations Center, now usually called the Combined Air Operations Center (CAOC). This center seeks to control manned and unmanned aircraft activities and all fires from all sources, including missile launches and long-range artillery. The goal is to coordinate attacks and avoid friendly-fire incidents. The Air Force has invested heavily in CAOC technology and training and calls the CAOC a weapon system in its own right. What was once movable, if not mobile, now resides in expensive, dedicated facilities capable of operating thousands of miles from the conflict, too big to be used aboard ships.

The Air Force is willing to share the attack and support missions. Jointness is everywhere in the skies, with Marine attack and jammer aircraft flying missions with Air Force fighters and bombers, protected by Navy fighters and surveillance aircraft and refueled by US or Royal Air Force tankers. But almost always the overall effort is under the command of an Air Force general acting as the air component commander, supported by a largely Air Force-dominated CAOC. It is this officer who decides the overall allocation of airpower assets and prioritizes targets. The dream is being realized. Navy admirals and Marine Corps generals are working for Air Force generals.

Internally, pilots dominate the Air Force, in a hierarchy ordered by aircraft missions. From the 1930s through the 1960s, the bomber pilots sat atop this hierarchy. They received the bulk of the service's resources and the promotions. Indeed, as the provider of America's first platform for delivering nuclear weapons, Strategic Air Command (SAC) dominated not only the Air Force but the entire US military for much of this period. Tactical Air Command (TAC) was considered a necessary but largely unimportant sideshow, with its emphasis on missions such as airlift and close air support. Even TAC's offensive counter-air mission – flying fighter escorts to protect bomber aircraft – received short shrift during the first half of the Cold War. TAC was not the place for ambitious officers. And of course internally within SAC, the ballistic missile crews had low status, even if their weapons promised the truest kind of long-range standoff strike. During the period 1947–1982, not a single fighter pilot or missileer became Air Force Chief of Staff. And well into the 1960s, the service's senior leadership consisted entirely of bomber pilots with backgrounds in SAC.

The Vietnam War punctured SAC's aura of political invincibility, though it took over a decade for it to deflate fully. The war, and the Kennedy-era Flexible Response strategy that had provided its justification, showed that America needed more than strategic bombing capabilities from its Air Force. It turned out that in limited land wars, the ability to nuke the enemy out of existence was not especially helpful. Tactical missions such as close air support and lift were important, and the strategic air war did not consist of daring one-shot gambles. Aircraft had to live to fight another day in a long, graduated campaign. Slow, vulnerable B-52s and the SAC culture whence they came were poorly suited to these demands. Versatile TAC fighter-bombers were better at evading North Vietnamese ground-based air defenses and aerial interceptors while still delivering ordnance. They quickly replaced expensive bombers as the service's workhorses, even though the war saw three full-blown strategic bombing campaigns against targets in the North. (Navy fighter-bombers were also integral to this effort, and indeed, lacking the preexisting organizational attachment to bombers, the Navy's fighter-bomber performance was superior in many ways to TAC's performance.[18])

With the mission goes the prize. Their combat contribution in Vietnam gave fighter pilots the status to compete for Air Force promotions that previously had eluded them. Civilians took notice, too, and were no longer willing to support SAC's intra-service hegemony. Funding for new bombers dried up. Fighter pilots soon rose into the service's senior leadership ranks, culminating in 1982 when Charles Gabriel became the first fighter pilot Air Force Chief of Staff. Until the 2008 appointment of General Norton Schwartz, a C-130 Special Operations pilot, fighter pilots locked up this top leadership role, and they continue to dominate the other important Air Force leadership posts.[19]

After the Cold War ended, SAC and TAC were disbanded in favor of two new commands, Air Combat Command and Air Mobility Command. As the names suggest, the Air Force recognized that "attack/support" had become a more useful distinction than "strategic/tactical." After all, airlift can be strategic, and bombing a target still requires the assistance of "tactical" counter-air missions to defeat enemy fighters. Roles such as developing and operating space and missile systems went elsewhere, to Air Force Space Command and Global Strike Command.

But despite the rise of fighter pilots and major post-Cold War structural changes, the service's fundamental commitment to strategic attack is as strong as ever. For all the service's emphasis on counter-air platforms such as the new F-22 Raptor, the air-to-air capabilities of these aircraft are touted not as ends in themselves but rather as the key enablers of strategic attack. Fighter pilots, as much as their bomber pilot predecessors, continue to stake the service's organizational fortunes on strategic bombing campaigns such as those used in the Gulf War and Kosovo.[20] The dream of a new hypersonic bomber is alive and well. The F-22 was even briefly renamed a "fighter/attack" aircraft, because even the top-of-the-line air-to-air fighter wants to claim precision strike capabilities.

The notion that hitting the right targets will collapse the enemy, sparing the United States a hard fight on the ground, retains its appeal. This theory has had its latest incarnations in the attempted attacks on enemy leaders, aiming to "decapitate" the enemy, as in the Dora Farms strike in the opening phase of Operation Iraqi Freedom and the shots against al Qaeda leaders since 9/11.

But the Air Force has had to adjust to changing threats and changing times. Two of its 12 four-star generals in 2012 were not even pilots, and two more were airlifters. It has had to relax its early requirement that only experienced officer pilots would "fly" its remotely piloted aircraft (what others refer to as unmanned aerial vehicles or drones) in order to keep more than 60 flying intelligence, surveillance, reconnaissance, and weaponized missions in Afghanistan and elsewhere at all times. One senior pilot disparagingly remarked that this effort was the Air Force's equivalent to running a puppy mill. And Air Force bombers, B-1s and B-52s, have used precision-guided munitions in close air support missions alongside Air Force and coalition fighters.

Secretary of Defense Robert Gates nevertheless accused the Air Force of shortchanging the counterinsurgency fight, of being too focused on the goal of coercion through airpower. Some in the Air Force believe that Gates' selection of General Schwartz, the non-fighter pilot and at the time head of US Transportation Command, as Chief of Staff of the Air Force was payback for the Air Force senior leadership's well and often publicly expressed desire to continue the F-22 program when Secretary Gates had decided to curtail F-22 procurement in 2011 at just 187 operational aircraft, a much smaller number than the originally planned production run.[21] Suspicious of the Air Force's motives, Gates also blocked its attempt to control the development of all UAVs.

The Air Force cannot help itself. It pushes technology in search of the American answer to warfare, and it seeks to be in charge of everything that flies. It wants to have the capability to win wars by itself via a standoff strike and not just serve targets in support of ground operations. Counterinsurgency under modern constraints, with an enemy that hides among the civilians, making discriminating precision strikes from afar next to impossible, is never the Air Force's preference. In 2015, the return of Russia and the rise of China helped the Air Force make the case to launch an acquisition program for a very expensive long-range stealthy bomber.

The US Coast Guard

The US Coast Guard is America's fifth armed service, assigned to the Department of Navy during formal wars and always ready to stand by its big brother, the US Navy, in anything else. In peacetime it has been housed in other cabinet departments, first Treasury, then

Transportation, and now Homeland Security. It evolved from the Revenue Cutter Service, amalgamated with the Life Saving Service in 1915, and later the US Lighthouse Service in 1939. During the World Wars, the Coast Guard patrolled the beaches and the coast, managed ports, and helped the Navy with convoying and amphibious operations. The relationship with the Navy is a relatively easy one, but in peacetime the Coast Guard has a difficult time fitting into departments with a domestic policy focus, as it combines law enforcement powers from its Revenue Service days and life-saving aid to navigation from the Lighthouse Service with military responsibilities, an agglomeration of ill-aligned talents.[22]

The service's post-Vietnam years were spent honing two missions, each with a coast of its own. On the East Coast of the US and down into the Caribbean, the Coast Guard became a drug and illegal immigrant interdiction service, competing with other federal agencies in making the biggest drug busts while trying to prevent Haitians from gaining refugee status by touching American soil. On the West Coast, and especially in Alaskan waters, the Coast Guard sought to protect the American fishing fleet from being overwhelmed by Asian factory fishing. And all the while, the Coast Guard was making little progress in renewing its roster of aging aircraft and ships, locked as it was in the Transportation Department, primarily concerned with passing federal grants to eager state and local agencies bent on maintaining transportation infrastructure.

Reaching senior command in the 1990s, Coast Guard Admiral Thad Allen recalled some advice of an old carpooling friend from his commander rank days. The friend worked in the Naval Sea Systems Command at the same time that then-Commander Allen was in charge of an ever-failing Coast Guard buoy tender project. His friend said success in acquisition requires a big project with a big defense contractor pulling it through the political maze of Washington. As an Admiral, Allen followed that advice, deciding to pile all of the Coast Guard's main acquisition needs into one big project. Thus was born the Deepwater Program, a multibillion-dollar attempt to develop and procure the Coast Guard fleet of the future, complete with integrated communications, aircraft, sensors, high-endurance cutters (now known as National Security Cutters), and patrol boats. A consortium led by Lockheed Martin and Northrop Grumman won the contract to manage the effort in 2002, outsourcing program leadership to the big defense contractors. The very name Deepwater tells you much about the internal politics of the Coast Guard, for that is the designation of the part of the force that can keep up with the Navy. Apparently, saving drunken boaters on weekend outings does not hold that much prestige.

Although Deepwater had acquisition problems almost from the start, Admiral Allen went on to be the commandant of the Coast Guard and the senior federal representative for both the Katrina relief effort and the clean-up of the Deepwater Horizon oil spill in the Gulf of Mexico. The real troubles kicked in later: in a major reorganization in 2007, the Coast Guard took program management back in-house and split up the mega-project into separate acquisition offices. But it turned out that internal program management at that point was no more able to push through the project than the old system that had frustrated Admiral Allen a decade before. In 2012, the name Deepwater was replaced by "recapitalization" in Coast Guard procurement, and the Coast Guard sued some of its major Deepwater suppliers. The Coast Guard was still the Coast Guard, after all – an organization with split identities, complex needs, and limited technology management capabilities. The problem just seems to get worse, with the Coast Guard finding new missions: the Arctic and the requirement for ice breakers now beckons.[23]

But some good things happened to the Coast Guard in the 2000s, too. After the 9/11 attacks, the Coast Guard, as a bridge between civilian law enforcement and the military, was given center stage in the early efforts at assuring the security of the homeland. It became a key component of the Department of Homeland Security when it formed in 2003, in large part because its officers have experience in crisis management and the creative wonders of military-style PowerPoint presentations. Its prize was a new headquarters building in the evolving campus of Homeland Security in the Anacostia section of Washington, DC (see Chapter 12).

The link with the Department of Homeland Security has brought benefits but also costs. The Coast Guard does have an important homeland security mission and has stood up a variety of port security, anti-terror, anti-piracy, and special weapons teams. But it is now locked into another domestic cabinet department where the focus is passing out grants to state and local agencies eager to have their own federally funded armored vehicles and counter-IED capabilities. The Coast Guard's hopes for a thorough modernization of its equipment often get pushed aside by Congress' need to keep constituents happy and the president's desire to reward domestic allies.[24] Only those drunk weekend boaters and Alaskan fishermen seem grateful for the Coast Guard.

The US Special Operations Command

Special Operations Command is America's unacknowledged sixth armed service. SOCOM draws all of its personnel from the other services: the US Army's Special Forces, psychological operations and civil affairs units, the 75th Ranger Regiment, and the 160th Special Operations Aviation Regiment (SOAR); the US Navy's SEALs; the US Air Force's various Special Operations Forces aviation units and combat controllers, pararescue, and weather support; and, more recently, the US Marine Corps' Special Operations battalions, now called Marine Raiders. Formally, SOCOM is one of the nine unified regional and functional commands that control America's operationally deployed forces under the National Command Structure.

Some of SOCOM's components can trace their lineage back to the Revolutionary War, but the command was created only in 1987. Unlike the regular services, which each have their own civilian secretaries, SOCOM's top civilian leader is an Assistant Secretary of Defense for Special Operations and Low-Intensity Conflict (ASD-SOLIC). Not only is this civilian lower-ranking than the civilians at the helms of the other services, but he or she lacks control over SOCOM's budget, which is instead determined by the four-star officer given the SOCOM billet, an important difference from the other services.

The services, but especially the Army and Marine Corps, see SOCOM as both a drain and a rival. Some of their brightest, most physically fit, and most committed officers and enlisted personnel are attracted to special operations units, and they move to SOCOM after the services have recruited and trained them. The regular services lose the combat return on their investment but must still pay the personnel costs. SOCOM then uses these people to compete with the regular services for budget dollars and missions, fostering some unsurprising resentment.

Of course, it is this attitude that led to the creation of SOCOM in the first place. Special Operations Forces were always the oppressed minorities of their respective services. The blue-water Navy has long referred derisively to SEALs as "surfers with guns." The Army especially dislikes elite units, though the Army itself established many of them and even retains some. Such elite units not only take the best soldiers away from regular units, where they would lead by example, but they are also seen as offering useless diversions from the Army's main mission, which is destroying the enemy's large-scale combat forces' capacity to resist. From Big Army's perspective, commando units are agile enough to get into trouble but too light to get out of it and too small to defeat a meaningful enemy on their own. Their actions complicate military campaigns rather than help win them. The conventional Army sees the 1993 battle in Mogadishu, the famous "Black Hawk Down" incident, as an example of what results from commando operations.[25]

Despite the Army's disdain, the post-9/11 search for al Qaeda, and the subsequent wars in both Afghanistan and Iraq, led to a significant expansion in the forces assigned to SOCOM.[26] The command itself was given the lead as the "supported command" in the hunt for al Qaeda and affiliated terrorist groups globally.

However, the increased activity revealed a growing split within the command itself, a split that mirrors the original split between Big Army and SOCOM. Historically, Army Special Forces took on at least nine primary missions: direct action, unconventional warfare, special reconnaissance, foreign internal defense, counterterrorism, counterproliferation, civil affairs, psychological operations, and information operations. The Army was particularly well known for its Green Berets, as the Special Forces were called, highly trained soldiers culturally knowledgeable about particular regions of the world and proficient in the language(s) spoken there.[27] Although they possess significant combat capabilities, the Green Berets specialize in unconventional warfare and foreign internal defense. Much of this work does not involve traditional fighting but rather training indigenous security forces (police, army) so as to engender local stability, a departure from the larger Army's priorities.

Today, however, SOCOM increasingly emphasizes direct action and counterterrorism, the "door-kicking" activities such as commando raids, special reconnaissance, hostage rescue, and terrorist hunting.[28] Not only have officially unacknowledged "black" SOF units enjoyed greatly expanded latitude to conduct these missions, but publicly known "white" SOF units have gravitated toward them as well, away from unconventional warfare and foreign internal defense. Although there is little evidence that these latter missions are growing less important to US security, there is much evidence that they are not the organizationally rewarded activities within SOCOM. The top positions and most of the equipment purchases go to the door-kickers, concentrated in the Joint Special Operations Command (JSOC), the operational arm of SOCOM.

SOCOM's external supporters – legions of them, as politicians and commentators brand SOF the key asset in the Global War on Terror – laud the operators' heroic profile, hope they can work in troubled foreign lands, and call for broad expansion of the command.[29] Even with the winding down of the counterinsurgency- and counterterrorism-heavy missions in Iraq and Afghanistan, and the announced grand strategic pivot to Asia, Special Operations Forces are slated to grow to over 70,000. The killing of Osama bin Laden in a daring raid deep inside Pakistan was SOCOM's Iwo Jima moment.[30]

Jointness

Differences among the services help make the organizations what they are, contribute to their unique capabilities, and build emotional and political support for them among American servicemen, veterans, and civilians. But critics worry that separate service identities promote needless conflict that disrupts American defense planning and military operations, so reformers call for jointness.

Jointness promises all the good things that citizens want from the military: efficiency, effectiveness, and coordination. Specifically, it promises that coordination leads to efficiency (the frugal use of resources) and effectiveness (improved performance in wars). But there are various types of coordination, and not all lead to improved military performance. The advocates of jointness who created the Goldwater–Nichols Act were suspicious of the DoD's civilian leadership of the time and wanted a structure that would give senior military officers more power to coordinate military operations. They assumed that the Act's structure and educational and promotional requirements would harmonize military doctrine. And they blamed all operational failures on the parochialism of the services, their unwillingness to work together and to support each other.[31]

But the key question to ask when considering government coordination proposals is: Coordination in whose interest? Whose goals are being pursued?[32] If the coordination is to take place at the Joint Staff and combatant commander level, as mandated by Goldwater–Nichols, then one should not be surprised that military rather than civilian goals are the focus of the coordination effort.

The services have potentially conflicting goals, the products of their internal politics. The Air Force wants the most advanced aircraft and believes that airpower can win wars on its own. The Army thinks that in the end there is no victory without the physical control of territory. And the Navy wants America's power projected from the seas.

The only harmonization that they can easily agree upon is not to undermine one another's position. They do indeed want harmonization, achieved by ensuring a fair and stable share of budgets, missions, and commands for each of them. What they can also agree upon is not to give civilians, in Congress or the DoD, a wedge to divide them, so they all recognize the need to avoid publicly criticizing one another's plans and programs. Harmonization under Goldwater–Nichols comes at a big price for civilians: the cartelization of defense policy.

Coordination need not take this form. The services' ideas for US doctrine and weapons acquisition emphasis could be pitted against one another. Inter-service competition can break the military cartel, just as competition among firms and universities breaks private cartels. Rather than suppressing inter-service competition, the supposed evil of bureaucratic rivalry, civilians could harness it to give them leverage in discerning the strengths and weaknesses of service ideas. Indeed, prior to Goldwater–Nichols, DoD restructuring had centralized civilian power in the hands of the secretary of defense. A skilled secretary could play one service off against another to gain options and discover the chinks in the competitors' proposals. The coordination would be the secretary's and ultimately the president's choice among the policies, be it a compromise among several services or a strong embrace of one service over the others. Given that the secretary is an appointee of an elected Commander-in-Chief, this form of coordination is basically democratic.

Competition has other benefits. It encourages innovation by forcing the services to focus on national objectives rather than their own. Services potentially displaced by advances in technology or shifts in national strategy will have incentives to find alternatives to put them back in contention for civilian favor, the key to organizational success under a system that encourages inter-service competition. But an environment in which the services are essentially safe from inter-service criticism gives little impetus to improve doctrine absent a catastrophic failure on the battlefield. In a careful study of the technology and military doctrine of America's strategic nuclear deterrent, Owen Coté compared the Polaris submarine-launched ballistic missile system, deployed in the early 1960s through relatively competitive institutions, to its Trident missile successor, deployed under a more collusive system in the 1980s. With Polaris, inter-service rivalry spurred real innovation from the Navy that significantly changed the course of subsequent investment in Air Force bombers. With Trident, bureaucratic political maneuvering inoculated the Air Force's competing MX missile program, giving both services a set-aside in the defense budget and roles and missions debates. The latter situation may preserve service preferences, but it is surely suboptimal for the country.[33]

The current lack of inter-service competition also explains the near-irrelevance of efforts such as the Quadrennial Defense Review (QDR), the congressionally required report on US strategy and programs. The documents produced every four years are dull, because the services avoid surfacing issues that would put one or more of them at a disadvantage. No service wants to trigger a competition in which each reveals the others' weaknesses. It is better to collude. As such, these strategy documents use tremendous energy and resources to produce prose that is often sharply at odds with the DoD's priorities as actually reflected in the budget. Despite filling dozens of pages, defense reviews have a mysterious tendency to avoid recommending substantial shifts in force structure. To be sure, the QDR is occasionally useful to roll out particular initiatives, but the notion that it is a truly objective "review" matching capabilities to needs is simply wrong. It is best understood as an opportunity for the services to work out many of their differences behind closed doors and to present the favored compromises.

Not surprisingly, the services have become champions of jointness. This is the system that assures them of being able to obtain the $3.5 billion destroyers and $200 million aircraft that are high on their individual wish lists. Bad operational ideas go unchallenged, as do bad acquisition ideas. Those outside the cartel with knowledge of alternatives – e.g. the CIA and even the US Agency for International Development in the era of counterinsurgency and nation-building – could threaten to bring it down, thus the push to include non-DoD agencies and coalition partners in the system. Still, the services, with their greater resources and established procedures and training facilities, are certain to remain the system's senior partners. And civilian leaders have learned that appeals to the religion of jointness can be the excuse they need for not asking the hard questions or seeking better advice. Civilian politicians actually sometimes prefer a system that does not force them to make the hard choices about strategy and investments; especially in recent years, they gratefully abdicate their role as elected leaders, passing the buck to the military cartel.

The downward side of the defense budget cycle threatens the cartelization of the military in two ways. Civilians will push for ever more consolidation, as is already evident in weapons acquisition (e.g. the Joint Strike Fighter), base management, and medical services. At a certain point, civilians may care about cost savings enough to disrupt the cartel's comfortable allocation. Alternatively, the stress of cutbacks could lead to a reversion to type and some healthy bureaucratic rivalry. Rather than suppressing overlap, the services could compete for one another's missions. The wise policy analyst might think the latter more likely than the former.

Questions for discussion

1   **Why do the services have such distinctive organizational cultures? Why do the services' leaders cultivate those cultures?**

2   **What technologies may have an impact on the services similar to that which aviation had in the twentieth century?**

3   **Do the relationships that have existed among the services hold lessons for the internal governance of the Army? What about the Air Force?**

4   **How has jointness affected the relationships among the services and overall defense policy?**

Notes

1 Allan R. Millett, *Semper Fidelis: A History of the United States Marine Corps* (New York: Free Press, 1991).

2 See *Sands of Iwo Jima* (1949), *Heartbreak Ridge* (1986), *Full Metal Jacket* (1987), *A Few Good Men* (1992), and *Flags of Our Fathers* (2006).
3 On the difficulty of amphibious assault, see Michael O'Hanlon, "Why China Cannot Conquer Taiwan," *International Security* 25(2) (Fall 2000): 51–86.
4 "Wild Blue Wonder: The New Air Force Memorial Is at Its Best When Reaching for the Sky," *Washington Post*, October 12, 2006, p. C1.
5 Dick Culver, "Floyd Gibbons' Legacy to the Marines," available at: http://www.bobrohrer.com/sea_stories/legacy_to_the_marines.pdf (accessed September 2, 2016).
6 Allan R. Millett, "Why the Army and the Marine Corps Should Be Friends," *Parameters* 24(4) (Winter 1994–1995): 30–40.
7 Frederic A. Bergerson, *The Army Gets an Air Force: Tactics of Insurgent Bureaucratic Politics* (Baltimore, MD: Johns Hopkins University Press, 1980).
8 John Mueller, *The Remnants of War* (Ithaca, NY: Cornell University Press, 2004); John Mueller, *Retreat from Doomsday: The Obsolescence of Major War* (New York: Basic Books, 1989).
9 David Burbach, Marc Devore, Harvey M. Sapolsky, and Stephen Van Evera, "Weighing the U.S. Navy," *Defense and Security Analysis*, 17(3) (December 2001): 259–265; Edward Rhodes, ". . . From the Sea – and Back Again: Naval Power in the Second American Century," *Naval War College Review* 52(2) (Spring 1999): 13–54.
10 Harvey M. Sapolsky, *Science and the Navy: The History of the Office of Naval Research* (Princeton, NJ: Princeton University Press, 1990).
11 Joel Sokolsky, *Seapower in the Nuclear Age: The United States Navy and NATO, 1949–1980* (London: Routledge, 1991).
12 Roger Thompson, *Brown Shoes, Black Shoes, and Felt Slippers: Parochialism and the Evolution of the Post-War U.S. Navy* (Newport, RI: US Naval War College, 1995).
13 Peter J. Boyer, "Admiral Boorda's War," *The New Yorker*, September 16, 1996, pp. 68–86.
14 Norman Polmar and Thomas B. Allen, *Rickover* (New York: Simon & Schuster, 1982).
15 Carl Builder, *The Masks of War: American Military Styles in Strategy and Analysis* (Baltimore, MD: Johns Hopkins University Press, 1989).
16 Robert A. Pape, *Bombing to Win: Air Power and Coercion in War* (Ithaca, NY: Cornell University Press, 1996).
17 Bergerson, *The Army Gets an Air Force*.
18 Marshall Michel, *Clashes: Air Combat over North Vietnam, 1965–1972* (Annapolis, MD: Naval Institute Press, 1997); Marshall Michel, *The Eleven Days of Christmas: America's Last Vietnam Battle* (San Francisco, CA: Encounter Books, 2002); Robert Pape, "Coercive Airpower in the Vietnam War," *International Security*, 15(2) (Autumn 1990): 103–146.
19 John Worden, *Rise of the Fighter Generals: The Problem of Air Force Leadership, 1945–1982* (Maxwell, AL: Air University Press, 1998).
20 Daryl Press, "The Myth of Air Power in the Persian Gulf War and the Future of Warfare," *International Security*, 26(2) (Fall 2001): 5–44; Andrew Stigler, "A Clear Victory for Air Power: NATO's Empty Threat to Invade Kosovo," *International Security*, 27(3) (Winter 2002/3): 124–157; Daniel Byman and Matthew Waxman, "Kosovo and the Great Air Power Debate," *International Security*, 24(4) (Spring 2000): 5–38.
21 John A. Tirpak, "Gates Versus the Air Force," *Air Force* (February 2014).
22 Louis K. Bragaw, *Managing a Federal Agency: The Hidden Stimulus* (Baltimore, MD: Johns Hopkins University Press, 1980).
23 Yasmin Tadjdeh, "Coast Guard Refocusing Missions Toward Western Hemisphere, Arctic," *National Defense* (March 2015), pp. 29–31.
24 John C. Marcario, "Budget Ax Falls on Coast Guard," *Seapower* (June 2013): 18–19.
25 Mark Bowden, *Black Hawk Down: A Story of Modern War* (New York: Atlantic Monthly Press, 1999).
26 Sean Naylor, *Not a Good Day to Die: The Untold Story of Operation Anaconda* (New York: Berkeley Books, 2005); Richard B. Andres, Craig Willis, and Thomas E. Griffith, "Winning with Allies: the Strategic Value of the Afghan Model," *International Security*, 30(3) (Winter 2005/6): 124–160; Stephen Biddle, "Allies, Airpower, and Modern Warfare: The Afghan Model in Afghanistan and Iraq," *International Security*, 30(3) (Winter 2005/6): 161–176.
27 Linda Robinson, *Masters of Chaos: The Secret History of the Special Forces* (New York: Public Affairs, 2004).

28 Linda Robinson, *The Future of Special Operations Forces* (New York: Council on Foreign Relations Press, 2013).
29 Michael Fumento, "The Democrats' Special Forces Fetish," *The Weekly Standard*, 12(4) (March 5, 2007).
30 There are now many SEALs movies. Note *Zero Dark Thirty* (2012), *Captain Phillips* (2013), *Lone Survivor* (2013), and *American Sniper* (2014).
31 James R. Locher, *Victory on the Potomac: The Goldwater Nichols Act Unifies the Pentagon* (College Station, TX: Texas A&M University Press, 2002); Samuel Huntington, "Defense Organization and Military Strategy," *The Public Interest* 75 (Spring 1984): 20–46.
32 James Q. Wilson, *Bureaucracy: What Government Agencies Do and Why They Do It* (New York: Basic Books, 1989).
33 Owen R. Coté Jr., "The Politics of Innovative Military Doctrine: The U.S. Navy and Fleet Ballistic Missiles," PhD dissertation (Cambridge, MA: Massachusetts Institute of Technology, 1995).

Recommended additional reading

Louis K. Bragaw, *Managing a Federal Agency: The Hidden Stimulus* (Baltimore, MD: Johns Hopkins University Press, 1980). The Agency is the Coast Guard and the stimulus is fear of competition and merger.
Carl H. Builder, *The Masks of War* (Baltimore, MD: Johns Hopkins University Press, 1989). A classic analysis of how the services see themselves and one another.
James R. Locher, III, *Victory on the Potomac* (College Station, TX: Texas A&M Press, 2002). A congressional staffer happily seeks the credit for the drafting and passage of Goldwater–Nichols, the path to jointness.
Marshall L. Michel III, *Clashes: Air Combat over North Vietnam, 1965–1972* (Annapolis, MD: Naval Institute Press, 1998). A fighter pilot shows how rivalries among US air forces improved their performance.
Allan R. Millett, *Semper Fidelis: The History of the United States Marine Corps* (New York: Free Press, 1991). A model of candor and concision in telling the history of the Marines, by a former Marine.
Sean Naylor, *Relentless Strike: The Secret History of Joint Special Operations Command* (New York: St. Martin's Press, 2015). How the network-tracing and killing came about, with good war stories and a fair assessment of limits.

7 The political economy of defense

It is impossible to understand the politics of defense in the United States without understanding the political economy of defense. Defense policy depends on the resources allocated to the defense budget, and the various categories of defense spending give life (and profits) to a set of interests, notably including the defense industry, that actively participate in the American political process. Indeed, their lobbying efforts help explain both the level of the defense budget and how it is spent.

The defense industry – the combination of the military aircraft, space, shipbuilding, armored vehicles, and defense electronics and information technology sectors – is at the same time international in scope and totally parochial. For example, Lockheed Martin sells its F-16 fighter mostly to non-US customers these days, but if the company does not get along with the US Air Force, it will not sell any F-16s for long. Then again, if the US Air Force does not pay attention to the needs of the major defense contractors, Lockheed Martin included, it will not get the kinds of aircraft with next-generation technology that it thinks it needs. Military buyers and their suppliers are interdependent. Defense is truly an area of policy that blends the public and the private; the emphasis shifts somewhat over time, and the private sector is more influential today than in the past, but neither element can be permanently banished.

Military aircraft, warships, armored vehicles, and other systems are made of metal, electronics, pork, the hopes and dreams of the armed services, national perceptions of threats to America's security, and the promises of the contractors and weapons designers. All of those ingredients are mixed (or jumbled) together through a process that is very variable – the push and pull of politics, innovation, and military analysis rather than a carefully planned agenda. That means that neither a greedy and allegedly nefarious military-industrial complex nor the logical results of a crafty national security strategy determine defense investment. The United States is proof by example that intense national security threats (as during the Cold War) do not necessarily produce a "strong state" with high levels of centralization, planning, and deference to expertise. All of those tendencies were counterbalanced by other interests, with results varying over time and issue area.

In modern America, defense is a cyclical business, with years of booms and years of busts. The cycles shape industry behavior and frustrate procurement reforms. The efforts at reform, though, leave defense a much-regulated business, with volumes of rules on how the contractors shall interact with their overseers, and how the accountants and budget managers should calculate costs and profits. Even so, the defense industry is expected to be very innovative, agile, and responsive, characteristics that few people routinely associate with regulated businesses. And finally, defense is a business that caters to a single customer, what economists call a monopsonist, that contractors and other close observers know to be a very, very strange and fickle buyer: arbitrary, powerful, and a bit insane.

The defense budget

The nation is not always at war. Fears rise and fade. Since the Cold War began, US defense outlays have ranged from about $400 billion to $750 billion each year (adjusted for inflation into constant 2016 dollars).[1] The peaks are the wars that have been the focus of recent history – 1953 for Korea, 1968 for Vietnam, 1989 for the Reagan buildup, and 2010 for Iraq. After each peak came a drawdown, and each drawdown was followed by a flattening, a bottom, a turn and a sustained increase – that is, by another cycle. Most people might hope to see the end of war for all time when one ends, allowing them to beat swords into plowshares. Sadly experience shows that they will only live to see another turn in the budget cycle. America is permanently mobilized: it maintains a large defense establishment (standing forces, bases, laboratories, depots, and contractors) that can expand further to meet particular crises.

As Figure 7.1 shows, the downturns generally grew gentler over time. After Korea, outlays dropped about 10.4 percent per year for three years – less steep than the 50 percent-plus per year drop after World War II, but still a fairly sharp contraction. The Vietnam drawdown stretched over eight years and was only about 6.1 percent per year. After the Reagan buildup, the post-Cold War decline was the gentlest of all, about 3.8 percent per year for nine years. The downturn after the Iraq War was a bit steeper (4.8 percent per year for five years), but it flattened out at a level higher than the peak of the Reagan buildup, far above the peaks of the Vietnam and Korea cycles. In principle, if politicians stuck to the targets set out in the Budget Control Act (BCA) of 2011, the defense budget would resume its decline in the future after a two-year hiatus agreed in a bipartisan budget deal in 2015. However, the debate over the fiscal 2017 budget was about whether to violate the bipartisan 2015 budget deal by *raising* the defense budget, not about returning to the deeper cuts promised in the BCA.[2]

Even the supposedly draconian austerity of the BCA, decried by leaders (military and civilian, appointed and elected), mostly promised cuts relative to planned increases, not relative to historic spending. What the BCA established was an automatic cutting mechanism: unless Congress and the president agree to a different spending level by passing some form of defense appropriations bill, "sequestration" forces the defense budget back onto the downward path agreed in 2011. Congress only allowed that to happen once in this down cycle, in 2013, leading to a real 8.1 percent drop in outlays that year and to much complaining about how sequestration cuts are not strategic, because all DoD functions are hit equally. Because Congress created the sequestration rule, of course it can exempt itself from it at any time – unless the president is willing to veto the exemption bill that Congress passes, at great political cost. So, even when Congress cannot agree on a complete, detailed appropriation bill, as it often has not in recent years, it can agree on a "continuing resolution" that keeps the DoD funded at the same level as the previous year (or the previous year's level plus a percentage, or the previous year's level tweaked by a few widely supported additions). A continuing resolution does not allow the DoD to start any new programs, which frustrates the leadership because of its inflexibility, and if Congress does not include an explicit provision exempting the continuing resolution from the BCA's caps, then the sequestration mechanism will kick in. Of course, Congress can include whatever language it wants in the continuing resolution, and to save itself the political pain of automatic cuts, it usually will, thereby keeping American military effort quite high.

In public debates, several different figures are often cited for the amount of spending on defense. Figure 7.1 shows defense outlays rather than authorizations, reflecting the actual amount spent in each year. In some budget categories, such as procurement of many major systems, actual spending of funds authorized in a single year extends across several fiscal years, although Congress can later change its mind with a "rescission," which cuts back an

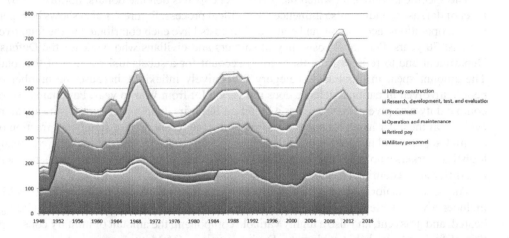

Figure 7.1 Defense outlays in billions of 2016 dollars (by category of spending)

Source: *National Defense Budget Estimates for FY 2017*, Office of the Under Secretary of Defense (Comptroller), March 2016, available at: http://comptroller.defense.gov/Portals/45/Documents/defbudget/fy2017/FY17_Green_Book.pdf (accessed September 2, 2016).

ongoing program's authority. The American economy feels the actual impact of the defense spending at the time of the defense outlays, when taxpayer dollars are transferred to military personnel or defense contractors for work that they have performed.

The difference between outlays and authorizations generally has less political resonance than the difference between the absolute value of defense spending and the value of defense spending measured as a percentage of American gross domestic product. Gross domestic product measures the total size of the economy in a given year – how much "stuff" there is to go around to all consumers, public and private. Defense spending takes a share of GDP: the Defense Department receives goods and services that otherwise could have been purchased by civilians or used for investment. Defense spending as a percentage of GDP measures the real cost of the defense burden to society, presumably a cost worth bearing because American citizens are willing to pay for national security. As economic growth has increased American GDP over the years, the amount of defense spending that the United States can "afford" has increased, just as the United States can afford more of anything else. Today, Americans can get more defense for the same "burden" by increasing the defense budget in parallel with economic growth, or Americans can get the same level of defense outlays year after year and have more economic activity left over for other consumption and investment.

Politicians, especially those who hope to increase defense spending, sometimes point out that the United States allocated a much greater economic effort to defense in the past. Although that statement is true, it does not imply that the government is shirking its responsibilities today. Just because the United States can afford to spend more on defense because the country is richer does not mean that the United States should spend more. To most people, the right amount of defense spending depends on how usefully the outlays can respond to threats and opportunities facing the United States. But, in practice, threats and opportunities are subjective, difficult to measure, and determined through the pushing and hauling of politics.

The specific activities on which the government spends defense dollars, not just the total level of defense spending, also influence the political process. Figure 7.1 also shows how personnel, operations, acquisition, and construction costs have each contributed to the total over the past 70 years. Personnel costs (pay to soldiers and civilians who work for the Defense Department and to retirees from those jobs) account for a substantial fraction of the total. The amount spent in this budget category is relatively inflexible, because the number of people involved in national defense does not vary a lot from year to year. Pay increases for combat duty also give personnel costs a bump during wars, helping account for the apparent cycles. On the other hand, for some wars, including the recent ones, a significant fraction of additional personnel needed for the fight comes in the form of private contractors (e.g. many logistics workers who transport supplies and maintain equipment); the military pays for them in a different accounting category.

The second major category of defense spending, operations and maintenance (O&M), includes a very stable component, the fixed overhead cost of keeping bases open, buildings heated, and grass cut, and also a highly variable component, the amount of military consumption of fuel and perishable equipment. During wartime, O&M costs soar, and in peacetime they return to a baseline level that includes a budget for training exercises and spare parts. The bulk of the cuts after the Iraq War came in O&M accounts, including those designated for Overseas Contingency Operations (OCO). Much of the political controversy over recent defense budgets has come in the form of fights about whether to use OCO funds to buy new equipment such as ground vehicles: some argue that the spending replaces equipment worn out in the war, covering purchases that would not have been required if the United States had not fought that contingency; others argue that spending OCO on investment in vehicles that could stay in the inventory for many years is a budget gimmick. Over the years, funds flowed back and forth between OCO and the "base budget," to O&M and other accounts, depending on short-term expediency.[3]

When Congress is in a budget-cutting mood and wants to show quick results linking a new authorization bill to reduced outlays and a smaller budget deficit, it tends to cut O&M funding. The implicit assumption is that war is unlikely in the short term, so, as long as the core manpower (personnel budget) and basic equipment (acquisition budget) are provided for, there will be time to make up training and repairs later.[4] O&M cuts are constrained, however, by a "readiness religion" prevalent among some politicians. The military services regularly rate their units' readiness status on the basis of their recent performance in training exercises, the mission-capable rates of their equipment (i.e., how many airplanes and tanks are in need of repair before they can operate according to specifications), and the subjective judgment of the units' commanders. The ratings are often tainted by the desires of the incumbent administration. Since the days of the "hollow force" in the 1970s, when the military was unpopular and reeling from its Vietnam War experience, the accusation that a politician's actions might contribute to a return to a situation like that difficult time has been very telling, so politicians have tried to limit O&M cuts (at least compared to cuts in the size of the force).[5]

The acquisition component of the defense budget includes spending for procurement, which outfits today's force, and for the research and development that prepares the systems needed for the future. More so than the rest of the defense budget, acquisition spending is supported by interest groups outside of the military – by private companies that make equipment for the military in factories all across the United States. Some acquisition spending is for truly routine products, from toilet paper to aviation fuel, where commercial markets offer readily accessible products at competitive prices. The government strives to buy these products efficiently, often exempting them from the special regulations that apply to defense-unique products such as fighter aircraft and submarines. The amount spent on these basic products is also essentially part of the DoD's overhead cost, like the baseline level of O&M spending needed to keep military bases open.

The marquee items – the cutting-edge equipment that gives the American military its technological advantage – take up most of the debate about defense acquisition. These items cost billions of dollars in research and development investment before the fighting forces see any benefit at all in terms of combat effectiveness, and major acquisition programs last for many years. An initial commitment to a system creates a "bow wave" of future expenditures that make outlays in future years difficult to adjust without making it seem that past investment in a program was in vain. To an economist, past expenditure is a sunk cost: regardless of the choice made this year, the government cannot get back the money that it spent in past years, so that past spending should not influence economic calculations about today's investments. But in political practice, the American government and the DoD in particular are highly sensitive to sunk costs, partly because the previous investment has created a constituency that seeks to sustain the program and partly because voters hope that by spending more money they can at least get some value out of the past expenditure. This acquisition momentum sometimes makes the defense budget difficult to manage, or at least to fine-tune. Major acquisition spending is the most important part of the political economy of defense.

Economists and policy analysts debate the effect of defense spending, particularly acquisition spending, on the overall economy. Traditionally increases in government spending on shipbuilding and aircraft production were viewed as valuable economic stimuli that could help manage the business cycle.[6] Government purchases of course are income for defense companies, and from that income the firms pay workers' salaries and investors' profits, and then those people spend their income on other products. This is all an example of the standard "multiplier effect" from introductory macroeconomics, where government spending can fuel the economy, especially if the money that the government spends does not simultaneously come out of private citizens' pockets, thereby reducing their spending. Nowadays, the marginal dollar of federal spending is borrowed from foreign countries (e.g., China), and unless Americans stuff an equal amount of money in their mattresses to prepare to pay back that debt – which they do not – the government's spending borrowed money temporarily stimulates the economy.

However, the value of defense stimulus depends on a second, crucial question: whether the defense spending multiplier is larger or smaller than the effect of other ways the government could spend that borrowed money, whether on tax cuts, direct government payments such as unemployment benefits, or building roads.[7] Some argue that capital-intensive defense products are particularly expensive ways to stimulate the economy.[8] Nevertheless, the siren call of increasing defense buying for political purposes is hard for politicians to resist at election times: the Obama administration found ways to bring forward planned spending on weapons contracts so that the money would go out the door before the 2012 election, juicing the economy a little bit.[9]

Finally, the defense budget includes several small categories that relate to construction. These categories pay for building and maintaining structures, roads, and the like on bases. The military construction budget also includes what are called civil works activities of the Army Corps of Engineers, which manages much of America's large-scale infrastructure projects such as flood control and inland water transportation. Because the projects in this expenditure category are less directly linked to the combat effectiveness of the American military, Congress has felt free to use military construction to achieve pork-barrel ends.[10] Scandals have been frequent, whether over allocating contracts for political patronage or for shoddy construction of poor-quality designs that do not respond to the needs of communities.[11] As we will discuss in Chapter 8, though, such problems in large construction projects are not unique to the defense business: all projects have problems. But within the defense budget, military construction is more likely to be politicized in a pernicious way than the other components of spending.

Replacing public arsenals with private firms

Once, defense was not a good business. The United States was not often at war, and when the United States did fight, the wars were not very demanding, the Civil War being the major exception. A network of government-owned, government-run arsenals, depots, and shipyards met most of the military's needs for materiel and kept military technologies alive between wars. Even percolating slowly between wars, the arsenals were not totally uncreative. They are credited, for example, with developing the idea of interchangeable parts, the system that is crucial for modern manufacturing. But there were few resources to spread around to the defense industry: few Americans, least of all leading politicians, favored spending money to buy weapons from a private defense industry when the need seemed small.

To be sure, the United States fought big wars on occasion, and in those times, private contractors were called in to help meet the emergency spike in military demand. The private firms built weapons following standard designs created by the arsenal system or designs imported from abroad.[12] The sudden surge in acquisition was never efficient; in the rush to equip the military in time, efficiency simply was not the government's main goal. And the contracting officers would have been fired or punished during the war had they failed to take initiative while the war's outcome hung in the balance.

But after the war's end, Congress naturally asked where all the money went. Congressional hearings followed, where representatives criticized the inefficiencies of wartime production and decried the high profits accumulated by the contractors.[13] The defense industry's reputation for corruption was sealed – for example, the pejorative phrase "merchants of death" was coined after World War I, the precursor of the Cold War's "military-industrial complex" – even if only a small minority actually bribed their way to contracts, charged extortionate prices, or willfully sold shoddy merchandise.

But the defense business changed after World War II, as the United States stayed mobilized, maintained significant military capabilities, and remained engaged in world affairs. No other nation invests more in the development and procurement of military hardware, and the United States routinely spends more just on research and development than all but a couple of other countries spend on their entire defense budgets. So, what used to be an episodic business, hardly worth the continuing attention of major industrial enterprises, has become a significant and ongoing economic activity. Many of the firms called to help the war effort in World War II saw the change and wanted to remain involved in defense after the war.

The attraction of the defense market was not only its scale. British Prime Minister Winston Churchill had called World War II "the Wizard War" to emphasize how vital scientists and engineers were to the war's successful outcome.[14] The war certainly included an unparalleled mobilization of scientific talent on both sides of the Atlantic and brought forth technologies that would come to dominate the Cold War that followed: nuclear weapons, missiles, radar, advanced submarine systems, and operations research. Aviation progressed rapidly, showing its global reach and its capacity to wreak devastation. And the American military's continuing Cold War focus on gaining a technological edge over potential opponents, most importantly the Soviet Union, attracted the interest of cutting-edge researchers and lent style and prestige to the defense business.

The government arsenals were less prepared for the new technology-intensive defense business, presenting an opening to private contractors. The United States had government-owned facilities for the old technologies but not for the new ones. To be sure, both the Air Force and the Navy had in-house capability to design aircraft, and the Navy even ran a factory in the Philadelphia area to build some of its own planes.[15] But the vast majority of aircraft for both services were designed and produced by contractors. Similarly, the design and production of nuclear weapons and missiles depended on contractors. The more the military sought to exploit these technologies during the Cold War, the more it came to rely on the skills of private industry.

Cold War defense spending still had ups and downs, even though the budget was always higher than it had been before World War II. With each downturn, the military preferred to close arsenals and shipyards and to preserve support for private contractors. There were waves of closures in the early 1960s and the mid-1970s. And after the end of the Cold War, the privatization continued. Congress established the Base Realignment and Closure (BRAC) Act process to overcome traditional political resistance to closing unneeded military facilities. In general, individual representatives fight tooth and nail to keep open the military bases located in their districts; even representatives who favor shrinking the military's overall footprint prefer the specific cuts to fall on someone else. So, the BRAC process intentionally limits the ability of representatives to single out individual bases in their deliberations. Instead, Congress must vote to accept or reject an entire list of bases recommended by a military-advised independent commission. The idea is to constrain legislators' political instincts through a technocratic advising process.[16] The five BRAC rounds since the first began in 1988 have closed dozens of installations, including several arsenals and three government shipyards. Contractor facilities were left untouched by this process.

Box 7.1 Military bases and facilities in New England

New England has very few remaining military installations. Gone are the Boston Naval Shipyard and its famous rope walk (1974); the Watertown Arsenal near Boston, where the atomic cannon was developed (phased out in 1967; finally closed in 1988); the Springfield Armory of Springfield rifle fame (1968); Fort Devens, once home of a Special Forces Group and the Army Intelligence School (BRAC 2; closed in 1995); Weymouth Naval Air Station (BRAC 4; closed in 1997); Loring Air Force Base in Maine (BRAC 2; closed in 1994); Brunswick Naval Air Station in Maine (BRAC 5; closed in 2011); Pease Air Force Base in New Hampshire (BRAC 1; closed in 1991); and the Quonset Point Naval Air Station in Rhode Island (1974). BRAC 5 also recommended the closure of Otis Air National Guard Base on Cape Cod, but it was saved when one of its units was redesignated as an intelligence unit. Even though Air Guard F-15s flew from Otis to try to intercept the 9/11 airplanes before they reached New York – perhaps the sort of mission that might have political resonance – the BRAC removed all combat aircraft from the base; the Coast Guard handles remaining flights.

A handful of other bases were saved by the politicization of BRAC 5: the New London Naval Base in Connecticut where submarines are homeported and the Portsmouth, New Hampshire, Naval Shipyard which does submarine overhauls. Besides them, all that is left in New England are the Naval War College and related facilities in Newport, Rhode Island; the Natick, Massachusetts Army Laboratory, now called

(continued)

(continued)

the Soldier Systems Center, where uniforms and rations including the famous MREs (Meals Ready to Eat) are developed; a Reserve air base at Westover, Massachusetts, an Air Guard base in Burlington, Vermont, and Hanscom Air Force Base in Bedford, Massachusetts, the home of the Air Force Electronic Systems Center (which has no assigned aircraft). The completion of BRAC 5 means there will be no Navy aircraft, Air Force aircraft, Army or Marine active-duty units, or surface warfare ships stationed in New England – except for the USS *Constitution*, a three-master from the eighteenth century that is officially still part of the fleet but is really a crewed museum.

How private arsenals work

When private firms sought to stay in the defense business in the early days of the Cold War, they had several advantages beyond technical prowess. The defense industry over time developed its own style of business–government relations that built on a few key attributes of American culture and the American political process. Private arsenals learned that the advantages that would allow them to flourish were their responsiveness to the particular desires of the military customers and their ability to operate in a complex environment that blended technological skill, economic investments, and political aptitude.

One of the factors favoring the bias toward private facilities over public ones is inherent in American society. Americans do not think public service is the highest calling. The French might, the British might, the Japanese might, but not Americans. Being an American civil servant affords one little prestige, especially compared to the prestige of a private entrepreneur or a private doctor. So, in the United States it is hard to attract the most talented, most ambitious people to government employment. Military service is an exception, but largely because it is portrayed as being something different from the civil service. A military recruit is considered selfless, while joining the civil service is viewed as asking to live off of private-sector taxpayers. The stereotype of civil servants caricatures them as lazy, lacking initiative and interest in their work, rule-bound, and nearly impossible to fire. Increasing the pay for civil servants does not do much to close the prestige gap, and it is highly unlikely that public-sector salaries will ever match those in the private sector, especially for senior management. It is no wonder that military officers, who see themselves as dedicated to their mission and as responsible for failures, lean heavily toward the private sector when it comes to allocating tasks.

Military officers preparing to fight future wars want responsive suppliers, those that will take up the challenge to build advanced weapons, no matter the obstacles. Government agencies – the arsenals, shipyards, depots, and laboratories – have their own hierarchy, and even those led by military flag officers are generally led by a different breed of officer with their own chain of command separate from the warfighting commands. The arsenals' leaders stand as independent judges of what can and should be done in their areas of responsibility. They often have separate budgets and report to different congressional overseers from the warfighting parts of the military. So, many military leaders suspect, often with basis in fact, that the arsenals will not leap into action when asked to develop and produce a new system.

In contrast, contractors, if they are wise, respond to the wishes of their government sponsors, as technologically ill-informed as they may be. If the customer says that he believes in a new set of buzzwords such as "transformation," "systems of systems," and/or "Network-Centric Warfare," so should the contractor. The big defense firms got to their top rankings in revenue terms precisely because they are wise in this way. For example, Boeing gained a favored spot in the early Cold War competition to build Air Force bombers because it was the most willing to sign up for the always-out-of-reach requirements for range, speed, and payload that the Air Force set.[17]

Figure 7.2 B-24 Liberators being assembled in 1943 at Army Air Force Plant #4, Fort Worth, Texas, operated by the Convair Corporation

Source: Lockheed Martin archives. Reproduced with permission.

Responsiveness also means that if the customer wants a favor, the contractor should be ready to offer one. For example, in the late 1970s, Pratt & Whitney thought that the Air Force should wait until the next contract to ask the company to fix the reliability problem that developed with Pratt's jet engine for the F-16 fighter. The Air Force kept asking – until it decided to fund General Electric (GE) to build a rival engine. By the time the contract was up for renewal, the Air Force found that GE was the right supplier. It took congressional intervention, requiring that all contracts be divided on a 60/40 basis, to keep Pratt in the F-16 engine business at all.[18]

In fact, the successful firms became very good at adapting to their military customers' requirements – to the point that they always seemed to have a product on offer that the military wanted to buy. Some analysts of the Cold War defense budget, picking up on President Eisenhower's warning that the military-industrial complex might gain too much influence, got the feeling that the contractors were able to force the military to buy their products, whether the military needed them or not. The top ten lists of defense contractors with the highest revenue did not change much from year to year or decade to decade during the Cold War.[19] But that is because the firms that got into the top ten were the responsive firms, the ones that understood their relationship to the military (and to politics).

The other side of the success of responsive firms is that those that were less ready to cooperate with the military's requirements were punished: the Cold War was taken seriously in the United States; unresponsive contractors could be fired. Some significant contractor facilities closed even as the overall scale of the private-sector defense effort generally expanded throughout the Cold War (see Table 7.1). The lesson is that what the military services appreciate, some would say too much, is the responsiveness of the private sector.

Figure 7.3 F-35 Lightning IIs being assembled in 2009 at Air Force Plant #4, Fort Worth, Texas, now operated by the Lockheed Martin Corporation

Source: Lockheed Martin. Photo by Neal Chapman. Reproduced with permission.

Table 7.1 Partial list of closed prime contractor production lines

Company	Plant	Last project	Year
Curtiss Aircraft	Columbus, OH	F-87, SB2C	1951
Westinghouse	Kansas City, MO	J-40 engine	1955
Wright Aeronautical	Woodridge, NJ	J-65 engine	1957
Martin	Baltimore, MD	P5M-2	1960
Convair	San Diego, CA	F-106	1960
Chance-Vought	Dallas, TX	F8U-2N	1961
Republic	Farmingdale, NY	F-105	1965
New York Ship	Camden, NJ	Nuclear-powered ships	1967
LTV	Fort Worth, TX	A-7	1983
Fairchild	Hagerstown, MD	A-10	1983
GD Quincy Shipyard	Quincy, MA	Navy auxiliary ships	1986
Todd Shipyards	Seattle, WA	FFG-7	1987
Fairchild	Farmingdale, NY	T-46	1987
Todd Shipyards	San Pedro, CA	FFG-7	1988
Rockwell	California	B-1B	1988
Grumman	Bethpage, NY	F-14	1992

Source: Eugene Gholz and Harvey M. Sapolsky, "Restructuring the U.S. Defense Industry," *International Security*, 24(3) (Winter 1999–2000): 5–51.

Box 7.2   Know your customer: the lesson of Curtiss-Wright

What firm was the second largest manufacturer in America in 1945? General Motors was number one, to be sure. But which was number two? Was it General Electric? Ford? Chrysler? No. It was Curtiss-Wright, the bearer of two great names in the history of American aviation, a manufacturer of fighter aircraft, propellers, and aircraft engines. It had factories scattered across the nation and had grown large producing for World War II.

Curtiss-Wright still exists, but as a shadow of its former self. It makes aircraft components, not aircraft, and its 2015 sales were less than one-twentieth those of the largest defense contractor, Lockheed Martin. It essentially fell off the charts in the 1950s, when America was mobilizing again for war and seemingly needed all of its defense production capacity. The corporation nearly went out of business because it forgot who its customer was.

Dependent then on military contracts, Curtiss-Wright had only two customers: the US Air Force and the US Navy. During the late 1940s, when defense budgets were tight, both services came to Curtiss-Wright asking for some R&D work to further important projects. There was no money for this work, but the services expected Curtiss-Wright's cooperation, given the profits that the firm had earned during the war. Curtiss-Wright management told the services to come back when they had funded contracts. No contract, no work.

This was a near-fatal mistake. Soon the services had lots of money and lots of contracts to award. Curtiss-Wright competed for the contracts but always came in third or fourth. The services had a good memory, even if Curtiss-Wright did not. Forgetting who your customer is hurts business in every market, but most especially when that market is a monopsony, or nearly one.[20]

Of course, the military likes to work with the private-sector defense industry not only for its technical responsiveness but also for its political support. Firms help the services lobby for their favorite projects. The services can only lobby discreetly, constrained by the law that prohibits agencies from directly trying to influence legislation and by the need to defer to their civilian masters in the executive branch on policy matters. Contractors are not so confined. They can hire lobbyists, contribute resources to political campaigns, and have their executives lose gracefully to congressional representatives and senators in golf tournaments at comfortable resorts. They can remind locals and their representatives in Washington about the jobs at risk if projects go unfunded. Weapons acquisition is a political process that successful contractors master. The services have favorite projects and the contractors help make them happen.

It is the big players – the prime contractors – that contribute the political heft to defense systems. Prime contractors do not make entire defense systems by themselves; they usually design the overall system, make some parts, and assemble the final product for delivery to the customer. They hire networks of subcontractors to make components, and many people naturally think that the network of subcontractors helps distribute the money across many congressional districts, adding political clout to the program. Although subcontracting does add geographical breadth to defense acquisitions, it only adds a small increment of political strength.[21] Political impact comes from the size of a plant's workforce, its local economic impact. Every congressional district encompasses countless small and medium-sized businesses, but each has only a handful of firms large enough that the district is widely identified with them. Everyone knows that Detroit is Motor City; that some smaller Detroit factories also make some components for the military does not turn many heads. Legislators are generally interested in the prosperity of their districts, and they want all the small businesses to thrive, but they take direct action to protect only the few businesses that employ a substantial percentage of their constituents or whose products have important symbolic value for the community.

So, on a big defense program only a few of the countless subcontracts, those for major subsystems such as engines and radars, involve enough work in particular congressional districts to tip their representatives' votes in favor of the overall program; only the representatives of the prime and the biggest subcontractors are "forced" to vote for it. But those key representatives essentially become lobbyists for the program in their own right, cajoling their colleagues in the legislature and agreeing to trade votes with them. The system gets funded not because it is built in 320 congressional districts but because it really matters in a half-dozen districts, whose representatives make it a priority to protect.

Working with the contractors in their post-World War II quest for technologically advanced weapons systems, the armed services created what Don K. Price, the noted observer of American public administration, called "the Contract State." They blurred the distinction between the public and the private in the American economy.[22] On the one hand, the tasks of the old public arsenals migrated to the defense industry, but on the other, government funding of private-sector research and capital investment took some of the "privateness" away from defense companies compared to their commercial counterparts. The government became the entrepreneur, in that it assumed the risks of developing new technology. The contractors that managed these projects in turn took over what had been governmental functions of project administration and technology integration. The government and the contractors are now very dependent upon one another.[23]

What are Lockheed Martin, Northrop Grumman, General Dynamics, and Raytheon? Private firms? You can indeed buy their stock. But would they exist without government contracts, and could the government design and build warships, military aircraft, ballistic missiles, and spy satellites without them? Aren't they, in fact, *private arsenals*? The defense business involves private firms that have largely displaced government arsenals to design and build the nation's weapons with government money. Those firms now exercise some governmental authority in the process.

A cyclical business

The defense budget has its ups and downs, as does the acquisition component of the budget that flows to private contractors. The participants in the weapons acquisition process have adjusted to the periodic nature of the budget cycle. They realize that an upturn will last only a few years, and projects that are not well along before the budgetary peak will feel the squeeze much more than those that are locked in early.

Because much of the political support for a project comes from visible activity in manufacturing plants – manufacturing is the stage that employs thousands of workers rather than hundreds of engineers – contractors (and the military's acquisition officials) push to forge ahead even when testing is not entirely finished and the design is not completely settled. The premature commitment to production is known as "concurrency" because the project proceeds with research and development and manufacturing at the same time. The idea is that manufacturing employment and weapons coming off the assembly line will protect the program when hard choices about defense priorities and budgets have to be made. But concurrency often leads to costly reworking of systems as the initial tools in the plant sometimes have to be thrown away and components of partially completed products have to be remade. Even though concurrent programs get an early start, the rush often causes delays in fielding operationally useful weapons because out-of-order production snarls the assembly line, and remanufacturing takes longer than getting things right the first time.[24]

The Air Force in particular has been notorious for moving aircraft into production before completing the R&D that defines them. Thanks to concurrency, the B-1 bomber's defensive subsystems could not operate when its offensive subsystems were being used, even though the most likely time the aircraft would come under attack was precisely when it flew over its target. But for the Air Force and its contractors, getting the bomber into production meant more than getting it right. Once the first aircraft is built, it is easier to get the funds to fix it than it is to get the money to start production on the wrong side of the budget cycle.[25]

Worse still is the incentive to exaggerate the threat and thereby increase the scale of the buildup and/or prolong its length. Because the cycle's intensity depends so much upon strategic assessments offered by the military and its contractors, enhancement is both easy and a major temptation. A bit of creative imagination is hardly a big stretch for those describing security threats in the competitive world of budget politics. Not surprisingly, the Soviet Navy turned out to be less capable than the US Navy said it was, and the Red Army was less robust than the US Army imagined during the Cold War. We may well discover that the terrorist threat of the twenty-first century is smaller than interested contractors and affected agencies describe.[26] And how much of a concern is China's new stealth fighter or their aircraft carrier, a refurbished hand-me-down from the Soviet Union?

A regulated industry, not a managed one

Defense is a government-regulated industry, not a government-managed one. Government auditors carefully monitor the costs, purchases, and profits of defense contractors. Congressional investigations following the procurement scandals of the past have led the legislature to pass literally volumes of binding regulations that contractors must follow if they are to remain eligible to work on defense projects. In fact, contractors' deep knowledge of government procurement regulations is one of their key competitive advantages, for this knowledge acts essentially as a barrier to entry for other firms that might be interested in supplying the defense market.[27]

On and off, there are calls for the United States to adopt an even more interventionist economic policy, along the lines of that said to be common among its industrial competitors in Europe and Japan. This interventionist policy, often labeled "industrial policy," would have the government direct an industry's restructuring and technological investments so as to enhance its competitiveness internationally – even to the point of favoring some firms over others.[28] Banking and the automobile industry received big, high-profile government assistance in the 2008 financial crisis, and agriculture has received support year-in, year-out for decades. But these are basically examples of failing industries picking the government as a source of subsidies rather than the government picking winners in viable industries.

Early on, Bill Clinton's administration was enthralled by industrial policy, but, ironically, it failed to manage the restructuring of the industry where it seems most appropriate – the defense industry. At the end of the Cold War, most politicians and military leaders understood that the United States would not need to build as many weapons in the future as it had in the past, because it no longer faced a superpower adversary in international politics. But the defense industry was prepared to crank out Cold War-sized production runs of military systems, meaning that its factories had vast overcapacity. Clinton's deputy secretary of defense, William Perry, spoke at a famous "Last Supper" dinner, where he told defense industry executives that the budget would not be able to sustain all their companies, but instead of announcing a restructuring plan for the industry, he said that the firms were on their own. What soon followed was the largest merger and acquisition wave in the industry's history. Wall Street financiers prospered as they arranged transaction after transaction, and the number of surviving firms declined significantly.[29]

The firms made different choices. Nearly all of the Fortune 500 conglomerates that had defense subsidiaries – including IBM, Ford, General Motors, Westinghouse, and Goodyear – sold them off; those subsidiaries each accounted for only a small percentage of the parent firms' total sales, and the firms' leadership assumed, incorrectly, that the defense business lacked potential for growth. Lockheed and a few of the other major contractors were net buyers, expanding their portfolios across the subcategories of the defense business. Boeing, which had drifted toward the commercial airliner business and away from defense since the 1960s, bought back in by acquiring McDonnell Douglas, a major military aircraft maker, and Rockwell, a defense aerospace supplier.

Some, such as Raytheon, tried to diversify beyond the defense business by moving into the commercial construction industry and other non-defense fields. This proved to be an expensive mistake, because defense is like no other business in its forgiveness of cost overruns and time slippages: Raytheon could not manage construction and environmental cleanup projects, even for government customers, the way it was used to managing defense projects. Raytheon later retrenched, focusing on defense electronics, where it is still a major player.

Some firms, McDonnell Douglas and Grumman being examples, just gave up. Their management sold the companies to others who wanted to fight for continuing business. Meanwhile, others, such as United Technologies and Textron, did essentially nothing besides pursue business as they always had. And still others, General Dynamics being a shining example, did some of everything, selling some defense divisions while buying others.

Despite all of this merger and acquisition activity, essentially no military platform assembly lines closed. Corporate names and logos changed, and some subcontractor networks blended, squeezing some parts makers and closing some plant space. But the basic structure of the defense industry, dictated by the big factories in which the final products are assembled for delivery to the military customer, stayed the same. The Cold War ended with six privately owned shipyards building warships, with each yard owned by a separate company. Today, *seven* yards build ships for the Navy – five of the original six plus two additions. One firm owns three facilities, another owns two, and each of the two (smaller) yards that are new to Navy business is partnered with a major, established defense company. The one Cold War yard that is no longer in business did not close until 2015, long after the merger wave. And the same pattern followed in other segments of the defense business. In 1991, workers in 13 plants built military aircraft, and 11 plants built armored vehicles for the Army and Marine Corps. Twenty-five years later, fewer companies are in these businesses, but more new plants have opened than old plants have closed, and the few closures waited decades after the end of the Cold War.

Normally, a merger wave reduces both production capacity and the number of competitors, but not so in defense. In the United States after the Cold War, it has grown increasingly difficult to fire anyone – whether a worker or a prime contractor. The defense industry, unlike most others, can lobby its only customer for work. Every platform facility – every shipyard, military aircraft plant, helicopter plant, armored vehicle assembly line – needs a project to stay alive, and if asked, Congress nearly always gives in to the temptation to provide it. With no peer competitor threatening American security, the military only needs a limited number of high-end systems. Because politics keep the production lines open, the few platforms actually produced are spread around too many facilities, causing all weapons projects to be burdened by unnecessarily high overhead costs.

Barry Posen has explained that strategic decisions are made through both rational strategic thinking and also domestic bureaucratic and pork-barrel politics; which process dominates depends on the level of strategic threat at the time.[30] Applied to the United States, his argument is that when military threats are relatively serious and generally acknowledged by all Americans, politicians, especially in Congress, tend to defer to professional military advice.[31] The military services have their own organizational interests, but part of their interest is that they generally value weapons' performance quite highly; warfighters are willing to fire unresponsive firms when they need to. But when military threats are less salient or less widely agreed across society, Congress pays less attention to military requirements and more attention to domestic politics. Even at times of high threat, lobbying and pork-barrel politics play a role in the political economy of defense, but today that role is more important than ever before. Defense in the United States has become a jobs program – much as it was in Europe during as well as after the Cold War.

The result has further tilted the balance of public and private interests in defense acquisition. As Table 7.2 shows, employment in defense dropped after the Cold War. Over 700,000 military personnel and more than 300,000 civil servants were removed from the rolls. Defense contractors cut back as well, with well over a million employees losing their jobs after the Soviet Empire collapsed. But the cuts never took defense contracting or reserve forces to levels below their Cold War lows. And with the Global War on Terror, contractor employment roared back.

The contrast to the numbers of soldiers and civil servants is stark. During the Iraq and Afghanistan Wars, politicians temporarily increased the size of the military by tens of thousands of soldiers, but even at the peak, the numbers did not approach the Cold War figures. Meanwhile, Secretary of Defense Robert Gates' insourcing initiative to bring "inherently governmental" program management activities back under civil service control largely stumbled due to public attitudes about expanding government employment and contractor resistance. Outsourcing is more popular than industrial policy in the defense business.

The "Last Supper" could have been the time to initiate a government-directed restructuring of the defense industry by buying out excess capacity, paying off the corporations, the workers, and the communities for a job well done, and rewarding their contributions to winning the Cold War. Instead, the government treated its private arsenals as if they were typical free-enterprise firms and told them to fend for themselves. The mistake is taking a long time to correct, because to defense firms, fending for themselves means lobbying for a line in the defense budget. Each firm's successful lobbying wins a 20- to 30-year weapons project, plus options for upgrades and follow-ons.

The 2010s are another crucial period in defense industry history, because some of the projects started in the 1990s reached the end of their planned production just as the defense budget cycle turned down. Take, for example, the Avondale Shipyard in New Orleans, which built amphibious ships. Over some 15 years, Avondale alienated the Navy, especially by messing up the lead ship of the LPD-17 class, an amphibious ship that joined the fleet in the early 2000s. Northrop Grumman, Avondale's owner, understood both the

Table 7.2 Defense employment by fiscal year (in thousands of employees)

	1966	1976	1986	1998	2003	2008	2013	2015
Active Duty Military	3,094	2,082	2,169	1,407	1,434	1,402	1,383	1,314
DoD Civilian	1,138	1,010	1,068	693	636	670	729	729
Defense-Related Contractor	2,640	1,690	3,315	1,902	2,721	3,339	3,760	3,023

Source: Active Duty Military figures from Defense Manpower Data Center. DoD Civilian figures from US Office of Personnel Management. Defense-Related Contractor figures, 1966-1986, from Harlan K. Ullman, In Irons: *U.S. Military Might in the New Century* (Washington, DC: NDU Press, 1995), pp. 169–170; 1998-2015 from US Department of Defense Office of Cost Assessment and Program Evaluation, *Projected Defense Purchases: Detail by Industry and State*, various years.

Navy's unhappiness with the yard and the awkward politics when the defense budget was under pressure. So Northrop Grumman slated Avondale for closure, assured that much of the work done there would go to another of Northrop's shipyards, Ingalls in Mississippi. Northrop Grumman also spun off its shipbuilding business to a new company, Huntington Ingalls Industries (HII), saving Northrop from having to expend any of its (bountiful) lobbying resources on such a challenging task as trying to save Avondale. HII considered several options to keep Avondale open, such as converting it to manufacture equipment for the energy industry, but it could not mount a major political effort to arrange a bailout. Sometimes, the burden of customer unhappiness is too great to overcome, even for the powerful defense lobby. And as Avondale closed in 2015, Congress and the shipbuilding industry reinvigorated their political coalition: Congress awarded HII a contract for an extra LPD that the Navy did not request, to be built in the Ingalls yard for a cool $2 billion, and Congress compensated HII's rival, General Dynamics, by giving its yard in Bath, Maine, a contract for an extra destroyer.[32]

Meanwhile, in 2011 Boeing, after a big fight with the Air Force, won the contract for the next refueling aircraft, and it has since been making amends by closing facilities that the Air Force saw as surplus. Through the 1990s and 2010s, Boeing built C-17 transport aircraft in a facility in Long Beach, California, but the Air Force said it did not need more. Instead, the Air Force's top priority was to defend its mammoth F-35 fighter program from investigative reporters and congressional gadflies who want to brand its cost overruns and performance shortfalls a major scandal. The political coalition between the industry, the Air Force, and Congress that kept Long Beach alive for so long was frayed. The last C-17 took off from the factory in November 2015; recognizing the end, Boeing had started selling off the factory's tooling the previous summer.[33] Closing the plant was hardly a victory for careful strategic planning, though. It was a political decision that starts to realign the industry, 25 years after the major shift in the international security environment.

The big industrial issue for Boeing's military aircraft business, after Long Beach, is how to handle the future of its fighter factory in St. Louis, Missouri, where it makes the F-15 and the F/A-18: the F-15 was once the Air Force's premier air superiority fighter and advanced attack plane, but now the factory hangs on through export sales; the F/A-18 is the Navy's sole tactical aircraft design and is also used by the Marine Corps, but the arrival of the F-35 versions for the Navy and the Marines are supposed to end F/A-18 production, too. Boeing must find a deft political strategy to encourage more F/A-18 purchases, perhaps by convincing the Navy that the F-35 program's troubles and delays suggest a prudent strategy of buying more of the known, effective planes, without upsetting the broader coalition with the Air Force that is crucial to the tanker and other programs.[34] That kind of political judgment is one of the defense industry's core competencies.

Similarly, in the early 2010s, the Army had far more M-1 tanks (over 6,000) than it fielded in its operational units, and Army priorities called for using every scrap of budget and political capital to defend the service's relevance to whatever politicians decide are America's strategic priorities. So the Army's public budget proposal actually called for a "hiatus" in tank production. The locals in Lima, Ohio, where General Dynamics Land Systems operates the government-owned tank plant, saw the Army's need differently. In 2012, both General Dynamics and congressional leaders got nervous that the pause might be a backdoor way to permanently close the big facility, and with Ohio an important swing state in the presidential election, they had the leverage to block the Army's plan. The immediate outcome reduced funding for M-1 production but included language to direct spending towards "advanced procurement" of critical items, anticipating a later production ramp-up in the facility once the budget cycle turned back upward.[35] Even at a high-water mark for national concern about deficits, pork-barrel politics still mattered, and another one of the big Cold War weapons factories survived with very limited restructuring, at significant long-term cost to taxpayers.

Box 7.3   Crusader: gone but not forgotten

The US Army names its tanks after generals – for example, the Sherman, the Patton, and the Abrams – and its artillery after religious figures – for example, the Priest, the Paladin, and the Crusader. The latter was the unfortunate name chosen for the mobile howitzer that the Army was developing during the 1990s and expected to field in the first decade of the new millennium. Secretary of Defense Donald Rumsfeld abruptly cancelled the project in 2002. The cancellation cost the secretary of the Army, a retired general, his job, because he was caught attempting to go around the secretary of defense to get Congress to save the project.

The howitzer's name was never cited officially as a liability, but surely the XM2001 Crusader must have seemed an especially awkward program to be pursuing as the United States began to fight Islamic militants in Afghanistan and Iraq. What was coming next, the Rabbi or the Imam?

Officially, the problem lay in the Crusader's size (too big and heavy) and lagging progress. Rumsfeld wanted a lighter, more agile force. The Crusader was actually two vehicles: a tracked, automatic-loading 155mm howitzer and a tracked ammunition carrier that trailed behind to resupply Crusader in the field via a connecting conveyer. Together they weighed nearly 70 tons, making them difficult to transport in an airplane and certain to wreck any country's roads and bridges. Attempts to cut the weight by switching to wheels, jettisoning the ammunition carrier, and redesigning the loader only delayed the program and increased costs.

Moreover, the Crusader seemed like an easy target politically because it was to be assembled in a yet-to-be-built factory near Fort Sill, Oklahoma, the home base of the artillery branch. Cancellation thus would not actually lay off any workers.

The Army wanted the Crusader because the self-propelled howitzer it was to supplant, the M109 Paladin, which was fielded initially in the early 1960s, had not been replaced in the 1980s, as had the armor branch's tank, the infantry branch's armored

(continued)

(continued)

fighting vehicle, and the aviation branch's attack and transport helicopters. It was the artillery branch's turn, according to the rules that govern the Army's internal politics. The end of the Cold War, budget deficits, changing military requirements, and a bullying secretary of defense only complicated what seemed necessary and inevitable in the Army: the Paladin was next in line to be replaced.

Despite the cancellation, the Army did not give up on the Crusader. Complaints that it was awkward to deploy due to the weight of its equipment led the Army on a quest for armored vehicles that would be light enough to fly in a C-130 transport airplane, which meant that they had to weigh less than 20 tons. The Army also was told that the future was digital and networked, and that bigger projects led by aerospace contractors fared better than isolated, little ones. So the Army created the Future Combat Systems (FCS) project, a system of a dozen-and-a-half manned and unmanned air and ground vehicles, all built around a digital communications network. And the Army hired a team of Boeing and SAIC, two large, successful prime contractors previously associated with aerospace, to manage the project. Lo and behold, included among the FCS ground vehicles was to be a mobile artillery system that used the same gun system as the Crusader, that looked a lot like the wheeled version of the Crusader, and that was to be made by the Crusader contactor at a new plant located near Fort Sill.

Although some called it the Son of Crusader, the official Army designation was the XM1203 Non-Line of Sight Cannon (NLOS-C). The Army even got Congress to mandate that NLOS-C would be the first vehicle built as part of FCS. But then complications with the network and problems with the vehicles led Secretary of Defense Robert Gates to cancel the entire FCS project, including the NLOS-C.

Down again, but not out. The Army hatched a new plan to redo the Paladin, putting the old howitzer's gun on a new chassis with the engine, transmission, and tracks of the M2/3 Bradley Fighting Vehicle and adding the Crusader/NLOS-C's automatic loader and electric gun drive. It will travel with a companion Field Artillery Ammunition Support Vehicle that carries 90 shells to supply the gun. Low-rate initial production started in 2015. The work is being done by Anniston Army Depot and BAE Systems (the Crusader's original contractor) at facilities in Aiken, South Carolina; York, Pennsylvania; and Elgin, Oklahoma – which turns out to be just outside of Fort Sill. All that is missing is the religious connection. The howitzer is officially designated the M109A6 PIM. PIM stands for Paladin Integrated Management.

The strangest of customers

The defense industry should be described as a structural monopsony, the rare market arrangement in which there are several suppliers but only one buyer. More familiar are the cases of monopoly, with one seller and many buyers. In a monopolized market, the seller has enormous power; the seller cannot unilaterally set prices, because customers' willingness to pay still matters, but the seller can often arrange to earn unusually high profits and can sometimes inhibit the pace and change the direction of innovation to suit its own ends. Anti-trust laws have been enacted to protect buyers from that power. The tables are turned, supposedly, in a monopsony market, with the sellers subject to the total power of their lone buyer. But the buyer in the defense market is the strangest customer of all. None of the buyer's decisions are truly final, project goals are neither stable nor clear, appeals are constant, and appearances count more than substantive success because of a prevailing fear of scandal. And on top of all that, the anti-trust laws do not apply because the government's market actions are statutorily exempt.

The defense monopsony is unusually complex, because the government is both a single customer and also a small clique of customers at the same time. All of the money for all the projects comes from Congress, generally in a single vote on the defense budget, and the budget is proposed by the centralized Office of the Secretary of Defense in one fell swoop. But the budget is put together from proposals from each of the military services, and each service has a key role in buying its own equipment. When the services have influence, the defense market looks more like an "oligopsony" – a small number of buyers, whose behavior deviates from perfect competition along the lines that an oligopoly, a small number of sellers, also distorts the market. Whether oligopsony or monopsony, the buyer in the defense business is unusually powerful compared to the sellers: at most, they work with a very few customers, and if the contractors do not please those few customers, they have little recourse to find alternative consumers for their wares. In fact, the government generally makes it illegal to sell weapons to anyone else.

Defense contractors must know their customers' whims in detail because they have so few customers. So, it is obvious why defense contractors are so willing to hire retired military officers: the practice is a search for insight into the government's decision-making process. The firms are desperate to know the buyer's true priorities, who within government holds the most influence, and what is likely to survive the next budget review. To be sure, influence-trading is another possible result of military officers' second careers (and of the "revolving door" through which some civilian defense experts alternate between government service and contractor employment). Hiring the right person might give one contractor an unfair advantage in a competition, if that person brings insider knowledge to the firm. So Congress has passed laws to restrict such hiring, taking advantage of the fact that influence with former subordinates in the military is fleeting: transfers and command changes constantly shuffle the personnel in program offices. The legal restrictions impose a waiting period on former government employees, including officers, who generally have to wait at least a year before they can work for contractors directly on the topics and projects they managed for the government. The idea is that any insider knowledge will become stale before companies can take advantage of it. So what the companies really gain by hiring military officers is knowledge about priorities and preferences – things that the officers learned through long careers as tankers, fighter pilots, or submariners.

The limited number of buyers also makes it clear why there are costs to establishing joint acquisition projects or otherwise encouraging greater centralization. Efforts such as the modern Joint Strike Fighter (the Air Force, Navy, and Marine Corps are all buying versions of the same F-35 aircraft) or the TFX of the 1960s (which eventually became the Air Force's F-111 fighter/bomber) reduce the number of government buyers to one for an entire category of equipment. In such cases, sellers, no matter how numerous, will not stray at all from the preferences of the single buyer, no matter how inappropriate strategically or misdirected technologically.[36] That pattern puts all of the military's eggs in one basket, stifles creativity, and threatens the future for firms.

When each service runs its own project, the total cost of the effort may increase, as each project has to develop similar technology or tool up its own factory that will garner fewer economies of scale than a combined factory might have achieved. But the two projects are never exactly the same, so combining them would sacrifice some performance in the hope of gaining some efficiency: each separate product might perform somewhat better for the service that sponsored it, because it would be tailored to that service's particular needs. Moreover, if one project did not work out, whether because of unexpected engineering problems or bad luck, the other program could serve as a fallback. Or when the strategic environment turns out differently from what defense planners had expected, having more equipment options helps the armed services to adapt relatively quickly and cheaply. The skies over North Vietnam provide a good example of the advantages of such "redundancy": the F-4, originally designed for the Navy, replaced the Air Force's F-105 fighter/bomber when the F-105, originally intended for nuclear bombing missions, turned out not to be well suited to dropping conventional bombs or mixing with MiGs.[37] And, finally, all the projected savings that a joint project promises tend to evaporate in the face of a reality full of technical and political twists and turns.

In addition, resisting monopsony as much as possible improves opportunities for innovation. For example, when the Air Force and the Navy buy aircraft separately, each worries that the other service will buy a better aircraft, and that drives each service to think creatively about its own requirements.[38] Without the Army's interest in buying the Cheyenne attack helicopter, the Air Force would never have bought the A-10 ground attack aircraft, considered to be the best aircraft for flying many close air support missions.[39] And it was the Navy's fear that the Air Force would dominate the American military's strategic nuclear forces during the Cold War that brought forth the Polaris submarine-launched ballistic missile, the military innovation that made the expensive, vulnerable bomber force obsolete as part of the US second-strike nuclear deterrent.[40]

But even if decentralization prevails, the defense buyer is quite peculiar. The hierarchy within the services almost always places "warfighters" at the top. There are indeed engineering duty flag officers, in some cases even in larger numbers than their prevalence within the officer corps would seem to justify, but they lack influence. For example, in the Navy a three-star vice admiral engineer formally outranks a one- or two-star rear admiral, but the engineering vice admirals who head the systems commands end up having to defer to the two-stars on the Navy staff who direct aircraft or ship requirements. The Navy conveniently even has different-colored flags for the different categories of flag officers, so savvy visitors to their offices know with whom they are dealing – a real warfighter or just a high-ranking engineer. This dominance of the non-engineers helps the services to value system performance and operational availability over cost in the acquisition process. And if the technical specialists within the services warn of over-optimism, they are branded as obstructionists seeking to enhance their authority.

Agreements to buy defense systems are also built from strange coalitions. Paying off potential opponents and winning new friends with government-funded rewards is the way legislative coalitions are built. Without pork-barrel politics, the defense budget would be smaller than it is: national defense is a classic "public good," meaning that all citizens benefit from the military's protection whether or not they personally contribute to paying the military's costs. As a result, individual legislators hope to "free-ride" on the efforts of their colleagues, and each would vote to underfund the defense budget unless pork-barrel benefits were also available to strengthen his or her interest. Some legislators are persuaded by appeals to the national interest, but others join the coalition because of local interests. The Air Force would have fewer planes and the Navy fewer ships were it not for the seemingly dirty business of politics.[41]

The buyer is also naïve about the working of the defense market. Many officers persist in believing that defense functions like a normal market, where competition among suppliers can be invoked to reduce costs. The Navy's attempt to use smaller shipyards that build commercial ships to design and produce its new class of Littoral Combat Ships (LCS) is a good example of the naïveté. By letting new players into the defense business, the Navy gained more yards to feed, and neither old nor new suppliers can be easily shed. In 2009, just as the first couple of LCSs were delivered to the fleet, then-Undersecretary of Defense for Acquisition, Technology, and Logistics Ashton Carter rejected proposed contracts with the two LCS shipyards, saying that they were based on "directed buys rather than real competition," an acquisition strategy effectively intended to keep both yards in business.[42] Three months later, though, he said he was so pleased with the new round of bids that he signed multiyear contracts to buy ten LCSs from each shipyard, keeping them both in business after all. When, in December 2015, as secretary of defense, he pointedly cut back the program in what was widely perceived as a slap at the Navy, he did not announce that an existing contract would immediately be cancelled. Instead, the total purchase would end up being 42 instead of 50 LCSs, meaning that production would stop sooner than planned but actually far in the future. He also announced that several years in the future, the Pentagon will "downselect" to a single shipyard producing LCSs – that is, he deferred the real political cost of trying to close a Navy-dependent shipyard until someone else's term as secretary of defense.[43]

The contractors may not really be private entities anymore, given the mutual dependence between the buyer and the sellers in the defense business, but they do have the advantage of having the veneer of being private: a corporate form, stockholders, and high salaries for executives. The veneer is valuable because it helps paper over their dependence on government work, and it carries with it the societal bias, shared by most military officers, that the private sector is more efficient, harder-working, and more technologically capable than the public sector. Despite the difficulties in their relations with the contractors, the services have outsourced more and more of the support function to them. The military cannot go to war without contractors, and the contractors have no business without the military. Both find it best to proclaim the half-truth that private enterprises compete with each other for military business. Even after the end of the Cold War, the military keeps the not-very-realistic threat that the incompetent and the unresponsive among the contractors can and will be punished, and the contractors keep the status and salary benefits of not being part of government. The only missing element is an industrial policy that recognizes the unique problems of a business in which there is only one buyer and the suppliers can lobby for additional work.

Questions for discussion

1 In what ways does defense differ from a normal market?
2 Does the United States spend more than it can afford on defense?
3 How did the end of the Cold War affect the defense industry in the United States?
4 Could public arsenals do more in twenty-first-century defense production?
5 Should retired officers be barred from working for defense contractors?

Notes

1 Office of the Undersecretary of Defense (Comptroller), *National Defense Budget Estimates for FY2017* (March 2016), Table 6-11.
2 Kristina Wong, "Pentagon Chief Fears Going Back to Sequestration," *The Hill*, May 25, 2016.
3 "BRAC, OCO, and Truth in Budgeting," *Defense News*, April 26, 2016.
4 Jacques Gansler, *Affording Defense* (Cambridge, MA: MIT Press, 1989), pp. 104–106.
5 Richard K. Betts, *Military Readiness: Concepts, Choices, Consequences* (Washington, DC: Brookings Institution, 1995); Michael O'Hanlon, "A Look at the Readiness Debate," *Washington Post*, October 27, 2000, p. B3. For an example of the political use of threats to readiness, see Tyrone

C. Marshall Jr., "Official Describes Sequestration's 'Devastating' Impact," *Armed Forces Press Service*, November 5, 2012.

6 Martin Feldstein, "Defense Spending Would Be Great Stimulus," *Wall Street Journal*, December 24, 2008.

7 Benjamin Zycher, "Economic Effects of Reductions in Defense Outlays," *Cato Policy Analysis*, 706 (August 8, 2012); Robert Barro and Veronique de Rugy, "Defense Spending and the Economy," *Mercatus Research*, May 7, 2013.

8 Michael Shank and Elizabeth Kucinich, "Military Spending Is Not Right Way to Boost America's Economic Security," *FoxNews.com*, May 15, 2013.

9 "The Little Dipper," *The Economist*, February 2, 2013, p. 22; "Why Defense Spending Plunged 22% Last Quarter – and Killed GDP," *Washington Post*, January 30, 2013.

10 Bruce A. Ray, "Military Committee Membership in the House of Representatives and the Allocation of Defense Department Outlays," *Western Political Quarterly*, 34(2) (June 1981): 222–234.

11 John A. Ferejohn, *Pork Barrel Politics: Rivers and Harbors Legislation, 1947–1968* (Stanford, CA: Stanford University Press, 1974). The failure of the levees in New Orleans during Hurricane Katrina in 2005 provides a very visible example of some of the Corps of Engineers' management problems: American Society of Civil Engineers Hurricane Katrina External Review Panel, *New Orleans Hurricane Protection System: What Went Wrong and Why* (Reston, VA: American Society of Civil Engineers, 2007).

12 Merritt Roe Smith, "Military Arsenals and Industry before World War I," in Benjamin Franklin Cooling (ed.), *War Business and American Society: Historical Perspectives on the Military-Industrial Complex* (Port Washington, NY: Kennikort Press, 1977).

13 Mathew Ware Coulter, *The Senate Munitions Inquiry of the 1930s: Beyond the Merchants of Death* (Westport, CT: Greenwood Press, 1997); John E. Wiltz, *In Search of Peace: The Senate Munitions Inquiry, 1934–1936* (Baton Rouge, LA: Louisiana State University Press, 1963).

14 R. V. Jones, *The Wizard War: British Scientific Intelligence, 1939–1945* (New York: Coward, McCann, and Geoghegan, 1978).

15 William F. Trimble, *Wings for the Navy: A History of the Naval Aircraft Factory, 1917–1956* (Annapolis, MD: Naval Institute Press, 1990).

16 Kenneth R. Mayer, "The Limits of Delegation: The Rise and Fall of BRAC," *Regulation*, 22(3) (Fall 1999): 32–38.

17 Michael E. Brown, *Flying Blind: Politics of the U.S. Strategic Bomber Program* (Ithaca, NY: Cornell University Press, 1992).

18 Robert W. Drewes, *The Air Force and the Great Engine War* (Washington, DC: National Defense University Press, 1987).

19 James R. Kurth, "The Political Economy of Weapons Procurement: The Follow-On Imperative," *American Economic Review*, 62(2) (May 1972): 304–311. The article is updated in James R. Kurth, "The Military-Industrial Complex Revisited," in Joseph Kruzel (ed.), *American Defense Annual, 1989–1990* (Lexington, MA: Lexington Books, 1989), and James R. Kurth, "The Follow-On Imperative in American Weapons Procurement, 1960–90," in Jürgen Brauer and Manas Chatterji (eds.), *Economic Issues of Disarmament* (New York: New York University Press, 1993), pp. 304–321.

20 Eugene Gholz, "The Curtiss-Wright Corporation and Cold War-Era Defense Procurement: A Challenge to Military-Industrial Complex Theory," *Journal of Cold War Studies*, 2(1) (Winter 2000): 35–75.

21 Kenneth Mayer, *The Political Economy of Defense Contracting* (New Haven, CT: Yale University Press, 1991).

22 Don K. Price, *Government and Science* (New York: New York University Press, 1954); Don K. Price, *The Scientific Estate* (Cambridge, MA: Harvard University Press, 1965).

23 Harvey M. Sapolsky, *The Polaris System Development* (Cambridge, MA: Harvard University Press, 1972).

24 Thomas L. McNaugher, *New Weapons, Old Politics: America's Military Procurement Muddle* (Washington, DC: Brookings Institution, 1989).

25 Nick Kotz, *Wild Blue Yonder: Money, Politics, and the B-1 Bomber* (New York: Pantheon Books, 1988); contrast with Brown, *Flying Blind*.

26 Ben Friedman and Harvey Sapolsky, "You Never Knowism," *Breakthroughs*, 15(1) (Spring 2006): 3–11; John Mueller, "Is There Still a Terrorist Threat? The Myth of the Omnipresent Enemy," *Foreign Affairs*, 85(5) (September/October 2006): 2–8.

27 Peter J. Dombrowski and Eugene Gholz, *Buying Military Transformation: Technological Innovation and the Defense Industry* (New York: Columbia University Press, 2006).
28 Laura Tyson, *Who's Bashing Whom? Trade Conflict in High-Technology Industries* (Washington, DC: Institute for International Economics, 1992).
29 Eugene Gholz and Harvey M. Sapolsky, "Restructuring the U.S. Defense Industry," *International Security*, 24(3) (Winter 1999–2000): 5–51.
30 Barry R. Posen, *The Sources of Military Doctrine* (Ithaca, NY: Cornell University Press, 1984).
31 Gholz, "The Curtiss-Wright Corporation and Cold War-Era Defense Procurement."
32 Christopher P. Cavas, "New Amphibious Ship Ordered for Navy, Destroyer to Come," *Defense News*, December 4, 2015.
33 Dan Weikel, "Last C-17 Built in Long Beach Takes Flight," *Los Angeles Times*, November 29, 2015.
34 James Drew, "US Navy Seeks 16 More F/A-18 Super Hornets," *Flight Global*, February 11, 2016.
35 Brian Bull, "Plant Pleads to Stay Afloat, but Army Says 'No Tanks,'" *NPR's Morning Edition*, July 25, 2012; Tyrel Linkhorn, "Lima Tank Plant to Gain with Budget by Obama," *The Toledo Blade*, February 18, 2016.
36 Clayton M. Christensen, *The Innovator's Dilemma: When New Technologies Cause Great Firms to Fail* (Boston, MA: Harvard Business School Press, 1997), describes the crucial role non-dominant buyers play in the innovation process and how dominant suppliers are unwilling to move far from the profitable preferences of their best buyers.
37 Marshall L. Michel III, *Clashes: Air Combat over North Vietnam, 1965–1972* (Annapolis, MD: Naval Institute Press, 1997).
38 Richard P. Hallion, "A Troubling Past: Air Force Fighter Acquisition since 1945," *Airpower Journal*, 4(4) (March 1990): 4–23.
39 Douglas Campbell, *The Warthog and the Close Air Support Debate* (Annapolis, MD: Naval Institute Press, 2003).
40 Sapolsky, "Polaris;" see also Harvey M. Sapolsky, Eugene Gholz, and Allen Kaufman, "Security Lessons from the Cold War," *Foreign Affairs*, 78(4) (July/August, 1999): 77–89.
41 Dwight R. Lee, "Public Goods, Politics, and Two Cheers for the Military-Industrial Complex," in Robert Higgs (ed.), *Arms, Politics, and the Economy: Historical and Contemporary Perspectives* (New York: Holmes & Meier, 1990), pp. 22–36.
42 Hon. Ashton Carter, *Memorandum for Acquisition Professionals: Better Buying Power* (Washington, DC: Office of the Undersecretary of Defense, 2010), p. 9.
43 Belva M. Martin, *Navy's Proposed Dual Award Acquisition Strategy for the Littoral Combat Ship Program*, GAO-11-249R, December 8, 2010; Christopher P. Cavas, "Pentagon Cuts LCS to 40 Ships, 1 Shipbuilder," *Defense News*, December 17, 2015.

Recommended additional reading

Peter Dombrowski and Eugene Gholz, *Buying Military Transformation: Technological Innovation and the Defense Industry* (New York: Columbia University Press, 2006). Politics, technology, military analysis, and corporate profits combine in the acquisition process.

Jeffery M. Dorwart, *The Philadelphia Navy Yard: From the Birth of the U.S. Navy to the Nuclear Age* (Philadelphia, PA: University of Pennsylvania Press, 2001). The private yards on the river did them in.

Ann R. Markusen and Sean S. Costigan (eds.), *Arming the Future: A Defense Industry for the 21st Century* (New York: Council on Foreign Relations, 1999). Various perspectives on the economics of defense as the Clinton years were coming to a close.

Vernon W. Ruttan, *Is War Necessary for Economic Growth?* (New York: Oxford University Press, 2006). Yes and no.

Harvey M. Sapolsky, *Science and the Navy: The History of the Office of Naval Research* (Princeton, NJ: Princeton University Press, 1991). The engine for rapid growth in post-World War II academic science turns out to be a bureaucratic accident, a lesson for would-be planners.

8 The weapons acquisition process

The claims are familiar: the $435 hammer, the $640 toilet seat, the $91 screw, the $2,917 wrench, and the $7,000 coffee pot. Oh, sometimes we get the amounts mixed up and say the $600 hammer and $2,000 toilet seat, but we all know these are outrageous examples of apparent contractor fraud and abuse and incompetent government management that draw attention to the Department of Defense's weapons acquisition process. What we usually do not know is the real story, the boring bureaucratic explanations that would, if widely known, temper the late-night TV talk show hosts' jokes and calm to some extent the moral outrage of taxpayers contemplating their annual bill.

In this chapter, we explain the performance of the defense acquisition system and review efforts to reform it. Many reforms have been tried in the past, but the trade-offs inherent in the defense acquisition process stymie easy answers – the problems of trying to buy super-high-performance equipment on a very rapid schedule without breaking the bank. In fact, all things considered, the defense acquisition process does quite well.

A closer look at those "egregious" examples helps clarify the situation. Accounting rules that allocate overhead charges by transaction rather than in proportion to cost explain much of the apparently excessive charges.[1] The rest can usually be explained by the complex requirements caused by military operations. The toilet seat, for example, actually was an entire toilet assembly for the Navy's P-3 patrol aircraft. Hounded by unfavorable press, Lockheed, the plane's maker, offered to give the task of providing the assembly to any of those claiming that they could pick up the part at Sears or Walmart for $15, but found no takers who could meet the Navy's actual specifications for a price less than its own $640. The wrench was one of a kind, designed to be used in a very confined space during aircraft engine repair. The screw was made out of titanium, a metal that is very difficult to machine, and it was purchased in a small lot as a special order. And the coffee pot was more than just a pot. It was a galley insert for the C-5A transport – and the apparent victim of excessive Air Force crash survivability standards.[2]

In a more recent example, in a frustrated speech in 2016, the Chief of Staff of the Army, General Mark Milley, asked for a credit card to go to Cabela's to buy new pistols for the Army – the classic "I can buy a better, cheaper product at a commercial store" response. Of course, he couldn't, really.[3]

But the complaints about waste and mismanagement are not really about components; components are just evocative examples of products with which most Americans are relatively familiar. The true source of unease is the multibillion-dollar cost of complete systems. The entire weapons acquisition process is beset with cost overruns, schedule slips, and weapon performance deficiencies, at least compared to the ambitious targets set when programs are announced. It is not hard to find examples from any era, with any type of technology, for any

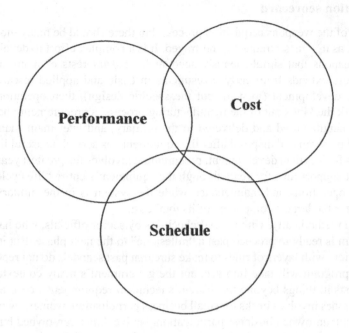

The acquisition process involves inherent trade-offs among weapon performance, cost, and schedule. It is virtually impossible to deliver the most technologically advanced weapon, on time, at a bargain-basement price. More often, the process manages to do well on two of its three goals: to deliver high-performance weapons on time, but with significant cost overruns; to meet schedule and cost targets, but only by forgoing the most cutting-edge technology; or to produce high-performance weapons at a reasonable cost, but only after many years of slow and steady work. Rather than actually solving this dilemma, acquisition reforms simply shift which of these goals – performance, cost, or schedule – receives priority. In times of crisis, like World War II, people tend to care about producing lots of weapons, fast; in the Cold War, performance came to matter more than cost or schedule; and in times of relative safety, expectations about performance tend to relax, while oversight of cost and schedule increases.

Figure 8.1 Acquisition trade-offs

service customer. The Marine Corps' Expeditionary Fighting Vehicle was way over budget and years late when it was finally cancelled in 2011. The first MILSTAR communications satellite went into orbit in 1994 with sand as ballast in some of its equipment bays because the planned electronic systems were not ready on time. The waters off the Atlantic Missile Test Range launch site were called "Snark-infested waters" in the 1960s because of the number of failed Snark cruise missiles that crashed there. The Joint Tactical Radio System, JTRS to its friends, was at the $17 billion mark and counting when it was finally terminated in 2012 without a fielded product. And the Bradley Fighting Vehicle was ridiculed in a *60 Minutes* exposé and a feature film because it carries only 9 instead of the intended 11 soldiers, stands a tempting 2 feet taller on the battlefield than its Russian rival (the BMP), does not swim as well as it was supposed to (making river crossings problematic), and costs eight times as much as the M113, the vehicle it partially replaced.

The process to develop and produce advanced weapons systems is genuinely expensive. It has serious, systematic flaws, but most of those flaws involve trade-offs among various goals: there is no way to fix every problem at the same time (see Figure 8.1).

The weapons acquisition scorecard

There are few defenders of the weapons acquisition process, but there should be many more. It is not an utter disaster, as it   is so frequently portrayed. It is a complex effort to develop technically advanced weapons that simultaneously account for the interests of many different groups. The process extends from early investments in basic and applied research, through product-specific development (to work out the specific design), then operational testing and efforts to work the kinks out of the manufacturing process, a procurement phase when the equipment is manufactured and delivered to the military, and later maintenance support, finally followed by scrap and disposal after the equipment has served its useful life. In general, research costs far less than development, procurement involves the greatest yearly expenditure, and product support runs for years through the equipment's entire "life cycle." The cumulative bill for operations and maintenance while the system is in the military's inventory often contributes the largest component of its total cost.

The idea is to proceed methodically, with regular check-ins by senior officials, who have to certify that the program is ready to proceed past a "milestone" to the next phase. But it is still government acquisition, with layers of rules to make sure that past scandals do not repeat and to confirm that the program will take into account the government's many contextual interests – that is, interests in things beyond the system's technical requirements, cost, and delivery date.[4] The milestones involve checks for small business participation, women-owned business participation, veteran-owned business participation, Native American-owned business participation, veterans' employment in the program, employment of disabled people in the program, employment of disabled veterans in the program, contractors' payment of appropriate wages, contractors' attention to energy efficiency, contractors' use of good cyber security protections, contractors' use of the right government-specific accounting systems, contractors' filing of the right documentation, in the right format, for all deliveries and for receipt of all payments, and many other things. The list is both endless and, for the most part, reasonable, at least in the sense that it is a list of things that Americans might legitimately care about. But the list dramatically expands the number of participants in the milestone decision process and the complexity of each decision. Government program managers and decision-makers never have enough information to understand all of the intricacies that they hope to monitor, so the reporting requirements as part of the process expand to a flood of information that is both expensive to produce and impossible to fully review. Moreover, the information can never be free from the appearance of bias, because much of it must necessarily be provided by the contractors, who are the only ones in a position to know. To try to protect programs from that appearance of bias, the government imposes extra, sometimes adversarial, investigation by auditors who work for the government, whether in the Defense Contract Management Agency or the Defense Contract Auditing Agency or the Government Accountability Office or another organization. Sometimes the various auditors have overlapping jurisdiction or even require data on the same topics in different formats, for different purposes. No wonder people think the defense acquisition process is Byzantine and likely subject to waste, fraud, and abuse.

For a number of years, the Defense Acquisition University (DAU) published a helpful reference flowchart of the "Integrated Defense Acquisition, Technology, and Logistics Life Cycle Management System" that attempted to capture the system's "simple," linear approach. But it was extremely complicated, and over time, it embarrassed leaders who were trying to streamline the system, for example through the series of Better Buying Power initiatives in the 2010s. Those leaders could only make a small dent through their efforts to reduce the number of people involved or the number of decision gates in the acquisition process, each contributing its own huge paperwork burden. In 2014, the DAU published a simplified chart that abstracts away from much of the complexity, but the complexity actually remains. Many acquisition professionals continue to refer to the older chart, which is too detailed to print legibly in a normal-sized book but is still available at many places on the Web, though not at the DAU's official website.[5]

Overall, despite the complexity and constraints, the American defense acquisition process does a pretty good job of delivering what Americans ask for. During the Cold War, the United States needed to offset the Soviet Union's edge in sheer numbers (the West had more people, but was unwilling to put millions more in uniform). Indeed, the United States did not simply want to substitute capital for labor, racing against the Soviets to buy industrial-age equipment. The US military sought a technological edge, beginning with strategic systems to deliver nuclear attacks and to defend against them (intercontinental ballistic missiles, advanced submarines, and continental air defense) and later pressing the electronics revolution for information-age conventional forces (the ability to see and operate at night and in fog, tanks that could fire accurately while still moving, accurate bombs that could devastate enemy formations and supply lines). The systems that the defense industry delivered rarely matched all of their extreme performance goals – called "requirements" but often more like wish lists – and almost always cost more than expected and took longer to deploy. But the systems were good enough to make the technological offset strategy work, defeating America's Cold War adversaries without an actual combat test – and leaving a highly effective, high-tech, post-Cold War military.[6]

So before we criticize defense acquisition's "poor" performance, we always should ask: Compared to what? The problems are well known – cost overruns, schedule slippages, and performance disappointments – but the technological challenges posed by military requirements are enormous. The US military seeks the fastest, stealthiest aircraft, the most lethal, robust ships, and the toughest, most networked vehicles. And when you compare the outcomes of defense acquisition efforts with civilian projects of much lesser technological challenge, in both the private and the public sectors, the military projects fare quite well.

Consider Boston's "Big Dig," the federally subsidized project to move underground the old elevated interstate highway that ran north–south through the heart of the city and to connect the tunnel system to the airport across Boston harbor and with the main east–west highway. The original estimate was in the $2–3 billion range. The result was a project that was five years late, with costs of more than $17 billion. Some of the 17 miles of tunnels leaked, and the project faced multiple lawsuits over the tunnels' falling ceiling tiles, which crushed one user and scared millions of others. Yes, it is a public-sector project in a state notorious for its creative forms of corruption. Not surprisingly, the project's workers called it the "Gold Mine" rather than the Big Dig.[7]

But commercial and non-profit projects hardly fare any better. Boston is also home to the 60-story John Hancock Tower, which gained fame for its unpredictable falling windows that made entry and exit to the building – or even walking along the adjacent sidewalk – a very sporty event. America has built a lot of tall buildings, most with windows, but it took two total window replacements for the Hancock before it was safe to go near it.

Universities, even those with schools of engineering and architecture, also have trouble managing big projects. MIT commissioned Frank Gehry, the much-acclaimed Canadian architect, to design its Stata Center for Computer, Information, and Intelligence Sciences, which became a campus landmark because of its odd shapes, materials, and colors. Unfortunately, the building came in at double its construction cost estimate, and its occupants are distressed to discover that sloping walls do not accommodate bookshelves well and that long, odd-angled, and narrow corridors do not encourage much collaboration. Faculty members in other departments were even less happy to learn that their cost-of-living pay increases would be forfeited for a year to help cover the cost overrun. MIT, Gehry, and the construction firms involved ended up settling after more than two years of litigation to affix blame for design flaws that led to mold, cracks in the masonry, and drainage problems.

Building odd buildings is likely not as much of a challenge as creating a fifth-generation fighter or a survivable, air-transportable combat vehicle, so difficulties with civilian construction contracts make the US defense acquisition effort seem more successful. Comparing US weapons projects with those of other nations also offers useful insight. Foreign aircraft, armored vehicles, and ships of equivalent military capability either do not exist or are much more expensive than equivalent American ones. Attaché files brim with reports of problematic ventures such as Australia's *Collins*-class submarines, Britain's Nimrod patrol plane, France's *Charles de Gaulle* aircraft carrier, and India's new tank.[8] Japan has built American designs, but for at least twice the cost.[9] Russia sells lots of cheap weapons, but they are just that – inexpensive and disposable. If you had some other choice, would you want to buy a Russian nuclear submarine? There is no magic in the way others acquire weapons, thus there is little to learn from their experience.

America has indeed tried to improve defense acquisition. Nearly every administration and every Congress since World War II have studied the process. Reform has followed reform. To be sure, it is difficult to measure progress in the acquisition outcomes because that requires comparing the degree of technological difficulty in weapons projects across time. Can you really compare the challenge of building a jet aircraft in the 1950s with that of building one today? It was the dawn of the jet age, so even things that seem obvious to current designers were difficult then, but on the other hand, the planes that they produced were much simpler, pushed less aggressively at the physical limits, and had fewer problems of integrating advanced materials and electronics. Despite the difficulties drawing direct comparisons, experts believe that things have gotten better in acquisitions, that weapons development projects have smaller overruns, that delays are less severe, and that weapons system performance has improved.[10]

Why, then, has the criticism of the weapons acquisition process not abated? As Daniel Wirls has discussed, the complaints provide both political cover and advantage.[11] Democrats do not want to be viewed as opposed to defense spending itself, so they attack it indirectly by attacking the waste, fraud, and abuse that they say characterizes the Republicans' mismanagement of defense procurement. The Republican representatives and senators do not want to be portrayed as lackeys of the so-called military-industrial complex, so they become champions of both defense spending and efficiency. They, too, complain about mismanagement.

Republican or Democratic, new administrations find it convenient to blame problems on past administrations. "Yes, there are overruns and slippages in defense projects, but that is the fault of the previous leadership, who didn't address the real problems," they might say. "Our administration, however, has a set of reforms that will at last make the acquisition process efficient." The results are a constant barrage of criticisms and constant changes in the organization of and the rules for weapons acquisition.

Two types of uncertainty

Weapons projects have to cope with two types of uncertainty: political and technological.[12] First, proponents have to persuade politicians to want the weapon. Politicians have to agree about the strategic situation and that the project will produce something that will address a strategic threat or opportunity. The politics of deciding what the international environment is like usually blends with politicians' understanding of existing American defense capabilities and equipment;

advocates of new systems usually have to make the case that potential adversaries are threatening enough to overcome the already awesome American arsenal. So, efforts to invest in new weapons are complicated by the fact that America already has similar weapons.

For example, in the 2000s, the United States debated whether to buy the F-22 air superiority fighter (and if so, how many?). The F-22 is a stealthy, fast, highly maneuverable airplane with very advanced electronics; it was originally imagined in the context of a conflict in Central Europe between NATO and the Soviet Union. But in the 2000s, American leaders had to ask what the F-22 would be used for in the coming decades. Many people trying to imagine the future naturally focused on the terrorist threat from al Qaeda or the chance that the US would have to execute more missions like those to stabilize Afghanistan and Iraq. Would the F-22 help? Would it be important if the United States had to fight against China, and, if so, in what sort of scenario – with the United States on the offense or the defense? And would the F-22 be substantially better than what the US armed forces already have? The F-15 is a very capable Air Force interceptor with an advanced radar (though not as advanced as the one in the F-22). The F/A-18E and F, a bigger and very revised version of the Navy's standard fighter, was also already at hand. And the US similarly could have bought the Block 60 F-16, just upgraded with very advanced electronics for an export sale to the United Arab Emirates. Finally, the stealthy F-35 was scheduled soon to join the Air Force, Navy, and Marine Corps. Each aircraft in this cornucopia of fighters undermined the case for buying the rest, even though politicians tend to accept the need to spend a lot on national defense and the preference for advanced, high-tech equipment. For a particular project like the F-22 fighter, the chance that it might lose political support during its long gestation period is political uncertainty.

Meanwhile, assuming that strong support for the fighter could be mobilized and maintained, the project's engineers and manufacturing workforce still had to resolve a second uncertainty: how to make what the military requested. Would the F-22 be able to cruise efficiently at supersonic speed? Would the radar and other electronic gear work as designed? Could the fighter be manufactured at a reasonable price? Would its pilots have sufficient oxygen in all aspects of the flight envelope? And would it have acceptable mission availability and not become a hangar queen because maintenance was too difficult? The chance that a project may not be able to fulfill its technical promises – especially on schedule and at a reasonable cost – is technological uncertainty. For the F-22, the price turned out to be quite high, and years after its initial deployment, engineers were still working on problems with the pilot's oxygen system. Technological uncertainty is very real for advanced projects.

Overall, projects have to overcome both types of uncertainty. An acquisition project only "succeeds" if politicians fund it long enough to deliver an operational capability and if the technology develops as the engineers hoped it would, enabling adequate performance.

Unfortunately, efforts to address the uncertainties tend to fall victim to trade-offs. Political uncertainty gives project proponents an irresistible urge either to exaggerate the capabilities that the system will deploy or underestimate its costs or both. The tendency (it may actually be a necessity) to exaggerate the benefits and underestimate the expense makes weapons acquisition projects very, very difficult to manage. The promises are so great that disappointment in some degree is almost inevitable, and most of the promises actually compound the project's technological uncertainty by forcing designers to try yet another impossible technical feat. Engineers and scientists, meanwhile, can achieve a great deal, if you give them time and resources to try a variety of solutions and to push the state of the art – that is, if you accept delays and high costs. But the longer a program takes to reach fruition, the more time there is for its coalition of political supporters to come apart, whether because the international strategic situation changed or because of a chance event such as the death or electoral defeat of a system's key congressional advocate (say, in a tidal wave of voter anger over immigration policy). The tried and true ways to reduce political uncertainty are to over-promise and to rush the program into production, but both increase technological uncertainty. The tried and true ways to reduce technological uncertainty are to invest heavily and to slow the program down, but both increase political uncertainty. There is no perfect solution for program managers.

All the imperfect contract types

During the Cold War, the federal government learned that its traditional purchasing practices were inadequate to the task of buying modern weapons, although the efforts to fix problems in the acquisition system often just revealed a different facet of the challenging job of defense acquisition.[13] In traditional contracting, government agencies state their desires and ask for fixed-price bids. The bids are opened on a specified date, and the contract goes to the firm that offers the lowest price that meets the specifications – for example, the government might ask for 15 3,000-pound vehicles that seat five, are painted white, and include air conditioning, automatic transmission, and six cylinders, delivered in four months for no more than $21,299 each. If the cars actually cost more than specified in the winning company's bid, then the firm absorbs the loss. If the firm gets lucky, receives an order from Avis for 50,000 cars of the same model, and discovers that it can make the government's vehicles for less than its bid, it gets to keep the extra profits. All the risks fall on the contractor, but they are usually not large for most items that the government might want to buy.

Unfortunately, modern weapons development involves much more risk than potential contractors can absorb. Military requirements rarely demand a product based on already developed technologies; the military hopes that its requirements will anticipate what will be the state of the art five years hence, assuming that the defense R&D effort aggressively pushes the state of the art. Moreover, defense contractors can be confident that Avis will never place an order for 50,000 of the same product that they are promising to develop for the military, so the contractors can be relatively sure that they will not benefit from a cost-reducing surprise.

Finally, because of political uncertainty, the government buyer cannot promise that its requirements will not "evolve" during the development process, leading to a renegotiation of the terms of the contract that would make some of the contractor's initial investment in designing the product and tooling up a production line totally wasted. In such an uncertain environment, contractors cannot raise working capital for product development based on the promise of a fixed-price contract, at least not at a reasonable cost of capital. Although fixed-price contracts are still used for some defense acquisition – sometimes appropriately, because the desired product is relatively straightforward, and sometimes inappropriately, because past problems managing uncertainty have been forgotten – this contracting method no longer dominates in the world of defense. Nevertheless, some prominent politicians, led by Senator John McCain, for years a leading Republican voice on defense policy and the chairman of the Senate Armed Services Committee, continue to push the Department of Defense to use fixed-price contracts, even for extremely technologically ambitious programs such as the development of the Long-Range Strike Bomber (the B-21).[14]

The alternative is to let defense contractors invest with the buyer's money rather than with money from normal capital markets – the blending of the public and the private discussed in Chapter 7. Acquisition regulations adapted to provide a way to do that. Initially, the military used an exemption to contracting regulations granted during World War II that permitted cost plus a percentage of the cost (CPPC) contracts instead of the traditional fixed-price ones. Intended to reward quick deliveries of needed equipment, CPPC turned out to be a school for scandal, because the contractors earned more profit by making their products more expensive. CPPC rewards never-ending delays and refinements of the design. Congress passed laws to bar the military from using CPPC contracts.

After World War II, during the early Cold War, the defense acquisition model shifted to the cost plus fixed fee (CPFF) contract. Because the government buyer promised to cover all of the contractor's costs, a firm would not stand to lose money if the project encountered insurmountable technological obstacles or was canceled due to politicians' (or military leaders') changing preferences. Yet the fixed fee aspect of the contract would supposedly temper the contractor's urge to run up the bill because the bill's total was irrelevant to the amount of profit that the firm would make. Also, because cost escalation might increase the chance that politicians would cancel the project, which would generally lead to the contractor forfeiting a part of its fee proportional to the amount of effort not yet completed, the contractor might even try to control costs.

But in practice, the risk that a CPFF contract might be canceled was a weak sanction, especially since cost increases could often be explained away. It is not always clear what is a necessary cost and what is a wasteful or misapplied charge. A lot of sins can be hidden in overhead and contractor-provided services. Government auditors examine contractors' cost reimbursement requests carefully, trying to reimburse only "reasonable" and "responsible" costs rather than contractor profligacy. Defense suppliers have to agree, as part of a CPFF contract, to allow incredibly intrusive oversight of their business decisions, which itself increases overhead costs in the defense business, as every decision must be exhaustively documented and as decisions are delayed while they are reviewed. But even the exhaustive reviews only get the auditors so far, because the rules are so complicated and because the experts in the rules are rarely also expert in the technology, so they cannot really understand everything that the contractor is billing for. As a result, Cold War CPFF contracting did not control rising weapons system costs very well.[15]

Searching for a stronger incentive to control costs, Secretary of Defense Robert McNamara pushed the cost plus incentive fee (CPIF) contracting form in the 1960s. He was lionized at the time as the great management expert who would reform the broken Defense Department system for buying weapons.[16] CPIF contracting rewards contractors for meeting or exceeding agreed-upon targets for cost, scheduling, and performance: the more the project exceeds the targets, the bigger the fee paid. It also punishes contractors when they fail to meet targets: under CPIF contracts, cost overruns are shared between the government and contractors in an agreed-upon formula; contractors usually bear an increasing proportion of the costs as the amount of the overrun increases.

CPIF contracts turn out to work less well in practice than they do in theory. The weapons development organizations crafting and managing the incentive contracts have priority rankings that value system performance and scheduling goals over cost-control goals, reflecting military interests. Moreover, contractors facing a cost overrun on their projects have, after a point in the work, great incentive to run up the bill. A contractor that might be able to absorb a $200 million overrun probably cannot absorb a $2–3 billion one. Seeing that costs are rising, the contractor might be tempted to make a moderate problem into a $2 billion disaster, which would threaten the survival of the contractor and thus jeopardize delivery of a weapon system that the military needs. In that scenario, a government bailout is a more likely solution than a forced bankruptcy. One of McNamara's signature projects, the C-5 cargo airplane produced by Lockheed, ran into precisely this situation in the early 1970s.[17]

The general problem persists today: programs whose costs are truly soaring are often "rebaselined," meaning that after a painful process in which individual program managers may be fired and executives likely sit through some uncomfortable hearings, the program's cost targets are reset to higher numbers and everyone starts to report that it is back on budget (the new budget, that is). For example, in the early 2000s, the Air Force's F-22, the Army's Stryker vehicle, and the Navy's DD(X) destroyer were all rebaselined, after which each program reported that it was doing well on its budget targets – despite being billions of dollars over its original target. The mammoth F-35 fighter program was rebaselined in 2011 (not for the first time). But the military, civilian DoD leadership, and Congress all agreed that these were essential programs, and so the government paid the higher costs.[18] In the end, the military buyer cannot escape the public nature of the defense business, and the government must pay the bill.[19]

Reformers have also tried another way to reduce costs, changing the scope of contracts rather than their payment terms. Specifically, they have included more and more within the scope of a single "systems" contract. Secretary McNamara endorsed this idea in the 1960s, but similar efforts have recurred through the history of acquisition reform, including the late 1990s and early 2000s trend toward Lead Systems Integrator (LSI) contracts. By incorporating the entire system into a single competition, the government ideally forces companies to think everything through.

The germ of the idea for these megacontracts is sensible, but they face practical problems. Military project managers thought (perhaps correctly) that the military's in-house arsenals and laboratories lacked the technical sophistication to understand all the interdependencies in the systems contracts. First the Air Force and then the other services began hiring aircraft manufacturers as "prime contractors," giving them the responsibility to oversee the work of subsystem contractors. What was once coordinated by bargaining among various offices within the services became coordinated through networks of firms. The desire for organizational primacy, a common pathology of government agencies, is less prevalent in a contractor network built on the desire for profits. In many cases, though, the definition of a single "system" became so comprehensive that systems management organizations acquired their own internal coordination problems. And even if shifting technical leadership to private firms helps resolve some managerial problems, it introduces other problems for the systems development mega-projects. Industry's profit motive offers the government a lever to ensure responsiveness, but it also leads industry sometimes to make choices that government program managers would not.

Moreover, industry's vaunted management skill actually has limits in complex networks of subcontractors: because each firm closely guards its proprietary data and competitive advantage – fearing that if the prime contractor really understood the component technology, the prime would just make the subcomponent itself instead of outsourcing it – even a technically sophisticated prime contractor cannot fully comprehend all of the technological and managerial risks in a system. The prime also cannot readily make trade-offs across the modules delivered by subcontractors: if a modification to one component would increase its cost only slightly but would dramatically reduce the cost of a neighboring component in the overall system, the prime may not know or may be unable to adjust the legally binding subcontracts. Sometimes, the government's ability to act as a relatively impartial arbiter among different companies can actually give the government an important advantage in system planning and management.

Seeking reform

Technological and political uncertainties are inherent in the weapons acquisition process. No reform can ever resolve them. Buyers (politicians and military officers) rarely know whether particular systems are needed, and they do not know whether the technological objectives can be met in a reasonable time and at a reasonable price. They promise a lot, and when the promises do not work out, politicians and policy entrepreneurs promise reform.

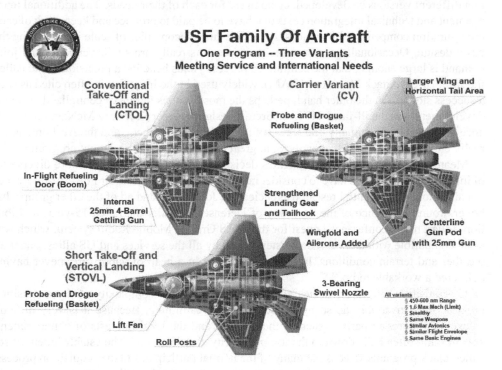

JSF Family Of Aircraft
One Program -- Three Variants
Meeting Service and International Needs

Figure 8.2 The F-35 program tries to produce Joint Strike Fighters for the Air Force (CTOL), Navy (CV), and Marine Corps (STOVL), while maximizing commonality among the aircraft

Source: Department of Defense.

There have been literally dozens of special commissions and official studies over the years promising to improve the weapons acquisition process. To the close observer, the reports rarely offer new ideas.[20] Basically, the reforms produce or recycle failed and ineffective proposals. They often address the problem revealed in the most recent acquisition scandal, conveniently forgetting that the proposed reform looks like an earlier acquisition system that led to a different scandal, the solution to which was the very system that led to the latest crisis. In the end, the usual effect of reform proposals is to hide or shift the risks in developing and fielding exotic weapons. Admitting that uncertainties are inherent in the process and impossible to eliminate apparently is not an option for officials who believe that they are politically required to claim that they have answers.

One standard approach is to advocate increased centralization, taking decisions away from the supposedly parochial interests of the services and giving them to the civilian leadership working for the Office of the Secretary of Defense. The idea is that projects can be consolidated to reflect joint needs (making systems more multi-purpose), thereby taking advantage of economies of scale to drive down unit costs. Powerful centralized decision-makers might also be able to force projects to incorporate cheaper, more advanced commercial technologies in place of the services' supposed preference for allowing friendly defense contractors to develop expensive, military-unique components.

But acquisition centralization does not tend to work out as its advocates hope. The promised economies of scale rarely materialize, as the warfighters in the various services insist that different versions be developed, customized for each of their needs. The additional management and technical integration costs that have to be paid to produce and keep track of each configuration compensate for any cost reduction due to economies of scale in producing the basic design. Occasionally, the services' requirements really are similar enough, and joint demand is large enough, that the centralized process yields benefits: a precision bomb called the Joint Direct Attack Munition (JDAM), widely used in the Iraq War, is often cited as such a success story.[21] On the other hand, perhaps the most famous failure of centralized weapons development was the ill-fated TFX, an aircraft designed under Secretary McNamara's guidance in the 1960s. Eventually, the Navy refused to buy any of them, and the Air Force never really embraced the F-111 that evolved, at great cost, from the development program.[22]

Meanwhile, centralization complicates decision-making by involving a more diverse set of interests. Joint projects have to consider not only the Navy's or the Air Force's preferences but also those of the central research agencies, the Joint Staff, and all of the other groups that hover around the Office of the Secretary of Defense. Consider the failed 15-year, multibillion-dollar, many-conferenced quest for the JTRS Ground Mobile Radio system, which was to be compatible with tactical radio systems used by all the services and US allies, under all weather and terrain conditions. Instead, it collapsed in a heap of vaporware, never having delivered a workable radio.[23]

If acquisition reform advocates attempt to deal with the complexity of the acquisition process, they invariably do so by advocating its streamlining. Because it is very difficult to exclude interested parties (such as the services and the local interests of congressmen), streamlining often boils down to the use of security classifications. The establishment of so-called black programs screens out many of the normal participants in the acquisition process, because they lack the necessary clearances; compartmentalization helps keep out even people who hold clearances for other purposes. Tens of billions of dollars of weapons developments have been hidden from public knowledge and full congressional review, but at the cost of democratic control, increased opportunity for corruption, and the risk of the mistakes that small groups sometimes make when they do not have to explain their reasoning in public.

On the other hand, sometimes acquisition streamlining can have a salutary effect, because there are times when standard procedures are not only expensive but also endanger lives. For the wars in Iraq and Afghanistan, the Army established the Rapid Equipping Force (REF) in 2002, the other services established similar offices, and the Office of the Secretary of Defense created its own Joint Rapid Acquisition Cell. These organizations allowed deploying units either to seek out commercial equipment that fit special needs or to reach out to industry and universities for prototypes that had the potential to solve anticipated problems. The units were allowed to test such new equipment in the field, with the REF acting as a broker between users and developers. Little of what the REF did could be accommodated within the existing procurement regulations, which add years and dollars to the effort, largely to avoid the hint of favoritism. In time of war, the political interest in appearing responsive to the troops' needs trumps the normal American emphasis on slow, methodical, competitive procurement that gives all bidders a fair chance. The evolving threat and feedback from the troops kept the REF honest in a way that worked during the wars but may not in peacetime. Praise for the rapid acquisition organizations' responsiveness kept them alive after the wars – it is hard to actually eliminate anything in government – but they face smaller budgets and more restrictions as acquisition tilts back to its normal procedures. The REF, for example, no longer reports directly to the Army's senior leadership.[24]

Another favorite reform – one that often pushes the acquisition process in the opposite direction from streamlining – is to propose to increase competition among defense contractors for the opportunity to manage, design, and build defense systems. These proposals cope with the financial and technological disappointments that are the inevitable result of overpromising by trying to shift more risk to the contractors. As private enterprises, they are presumed to be efficient, especially when competition holds their feet to the fire. Incentive contracts seek to harness competition like this.

These proposals follow a certain logic, sensible in its own way, though it unfortunately ignores important realities of the defense business. One of the recurring problems in defense acquisition is called "buy-in." Firms offer very low bids in projects' initial phases – offering to do the research and development at very reasonable rates. The winner of that early contract, though, will have enormous advantages in any later competition for contracts to manufacture the system, to provide spare parts, or to service and repair the products. So even if the firm loses money on the development contract, it can "get well" – and more – by exploiting its near-monopoly in the procurement phase of the project. The reform proposal, then, is to bind all of the work into a single competition. Secretary McNamara called one iteration of this idea "total package procurement"; later efforts emphasized contracts that considered a product's "lifecycle cost." In theory, bidders will need to offer a price that will cover development, procurement, and after-market costs, and that offer will have to be reasonable, because competition will prevent overcharging. For example, if all costs are involved in the competition, then the contractor cannot propose a technological solution to meet a performance requirement that will be phenomenally expensive to keep operational ten years down the road. If everyone has enough information – if strategic conditions do not change too much, if inflation does not throw off projections of future costs, and so on – this form of contracting should lead to a good deal.[25]

Unfortunately, the more phases of a project that are wrapped into an up-front bid, the less information the contractor has about the eventual technical difficulties and real costs of the product. Competition indeed forces contractors to bid low for the total package, so the low bids rely on optimistic assumptions about the challenges to be faced while executing the contract. The most optimistic contractor generally wins the bid – a version of the "winner's curse." Under normal circumstances, complications inevitably arise in military systems development; under these hypercompetitive contracting forms, the impact of those complications is magnified. The trouble is that intense competition makes it more likely that the most optimistic firm will win rather than the most likely to be able to really execute the project at the lowest cost or closest to the promised schedule. After the competition is over, the government is generally stuck paying for whatever turns out to be that optimistic firm's best effort, as in the C-5A case, discussed earlier.

Note the Navy's experience when it sought a low price by placing a bulk order for 13 nuclear submarines. Electric Boat won the competition, promising to meet the Navy's requirements for delivery dates and product capabilities while offering a volume discount. When government inspectors found costly welding errors relatively early in the effort, Electric Boat could not afford the rework needed, so it threatened to abandon the project. Many harsh words were exchanged, but the outcome was predictable. The Navy really wanted the submarines, which had outstanding anti-submarine warfare capabilities (as long as the welds held). It wanted them more than it wanted to hold down costs.[26]

Reformers also frequently recommend improved education and professional standing for acquisition officials so that they can stand up to the warfighters' sometimes unreasonable or excessive demands for capability and to the contractors' lawyers trying to avoid responsibility for failures. The Department of Defense has followed through by establishing the Defense Acquisition University (which must have one terrific football team), better promotion opportunities for officers who designate an acquisition career (including opening the possibility of promotion to flag rank), and additional professional training (including stints at the nation's best business schools). Nevertheless, it has been essentially impossible to improve the status of acquisition within the military and of the civil service within the society. The private sector gets more money, and the warfighter gets more deference. Diplomas do not make the man (or woman) or change the balance of power.

Certainly it is sensible to propose, as the acquisition reform reports often do, that more systems get trial runs as prototypes before the government commits to paying for full-scale production. Prototyping would allow the development and comparisons of alternative weapon designs before the bulk of the systems' costs kick in. Many costly mistakes could be avoided. But the politics of prototyping are difficult. It is powerfully seductive to argue, as Secretary Ashton Carter did more than once, that the truly important acquisition reform would be for the Department of Defense not to start any program that it cannot afford to procure in full.[27] But of course the point of prototypes is to start more projects than you know that you can complete; you will decide which ones are most promising after seeing how the prototypes work. But that means that many prototype programs will be cancelled, giving the appearance of wasted effort. As pointed out in Chapter 7, politicians do not let sunk costs go easily; they are always tempted to keep paying more, keeping the project alive in hopes of a miracle to make it functional and useful.

It is the politics of budget cycles – not simple mistakes or misunderstandings – that encourage early commitments to large-quantity purchases and overly optimistic cost and performance projections.[28] The manufacturers know that money is to be made in production and after-market support to fielded systems, and the military services believe that once production starts, their favored weapons gain near-irreversible momentum. So the services rush through the development phase or even finish it concurrently with full-rate manufacturing. From the perspective of both the military and the contractors, all mistakes are correctable except the decision to study options some more. Security panics can subside, and defense budgets can peak, and if the favored program has not started by that time, then it might never get going.

Making it worse

It may be difficult to improve the weapons acquisition process, but it sure isn't difficult to make it worse. The round of acquisition reform in the 2000s is a good example. Tempted by the politics, the services (and other acquisition organizations) chose to make their projects overly complex, to reduce their ability to monitor contractors, and to increase the likelihood of project failures and cost overruns. These are the consequences of using Lead Systems Integrator contractors, often not one contractor but an ad hoc alliance of two firms in a joint venture for the project.

Politically weak agencies, such as the Army and the Coast Guard, believe that there are advantages in organizing very large-scale projects, those that are likely to make the government's list of the ten biggest in terms of total costs. They also seek political clout by handing the project's direction over to an aerospace firm to be its integrating contractor or system development manager. Big projects, it is assumed, have a momentum of their own. And the big aerospace contractors are thought to be wise in the ways of Washington and thus able to use their lobbying muscle to protect a project through the vagaries of Capitol Hill and Pentagon politics.[29]

The aerospace giants – Lockheed Martin, Boeing, Northrop Grumman, General Dynamics, and the like – have an undeniable expertise in acquisition politics as well as in the

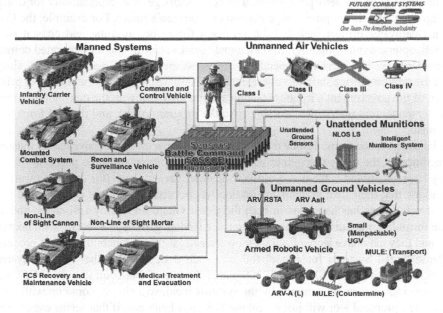

Figure 8.3 Future Combat Systems

Source: "System of Systems Analysis of Future Combat Systems Sustainment Requirements," presentation by Ivan W. Wolnek at the *8th Annual NDIA Systems Engineering Conference*, October 2005.

management of large-scale projects.[30] And some agencies certainly do better than others in the competition for resources, not only because they have projects and programs that are appealing, but also because they pick their congressional friends and contractors wisely. A lot depends on where large parts of the project are likely to be built and who can persuade the committee staffers that all of their important suggestions and concerns have been carefully addressed.

But working the system by hiring an LSI contractor is a bit too calculating. One of the reasons for handing over most of the agency's future work to a big aerospace firm is a belief that the agency's traditional contractors are ineffective in both gaining and using resources. The switch to an aerospace firm is meant to replace them with a politically savvy, technologically effective alternative. The old contractors, however, do not go away. Mustering their own political skills, they get their congressional representatives to include them in the big project. Expanding the political coalition is much easier than the mortal combat that would drive a company out of the defense industry. Instead of the intended substitution of one set of contractors for another, the LSI contract becomes one gigantic program employing them all. For example, the Army's Future Combat Systems project had Boeing and SAIC as co-LSIs and planned to deliver a set of new, all-networked robot and manned combat vehicles that was to replace most of the Army's major items of equipment (tanks, artillery pieces, infantry fighting vehicles, and scout vehicles). But the contract mandated that BAE Systems and General Dynamics, the prime contractors for the Army's older tanks, howitzers, and armored vehicles – the very ones the Army hoped to shed with the FCS – end up on tap to make some of the vehicles. And when the FCS project was canceled, the traditional suppliers got contracts for the next try.

LSI projects tend to be very broad, to gain the heft to climb into the top ten list and to attract the interest of the aerospace giants. The contractors get the responsibility for designing, integrating, and developing a large portion of a service's future. For example, the Coast Guard's Deepwater Project included the service's future ocean-going and coastal patrol ships, helicopters, fixed-wing aircraft, unmanned aerial vehicles, and an integrated communications network. The service's dependency grows as the scope of work increases, simply because the program office staff gets overextended. Couple this with the inclination to privatize much of the government's in-house technical capability and with the constant rotation of service personnel that undermines continuity in the program office, and the LSI firms work largely unsupervised.

The large aerospace firms, despite their broad range of specialization, have hardly mastered the integration of the many disciplines and capabilities represented in the portfolio of firms that they have assembled in the post-Cold War defense merger wave. It is only in PowerPoint presentations that their own systems integration has occurred. Combine two of these firms in a joint venture, as has happened in both the Coast Guard and Army LSI cases, and you have the formula for acquisition chaos. The service leaders gambled too easily with taxpayer dollars, and they may have jeopardized their own services' future capabilities in the process.[31] The phrase "Lead Systems Integrator" fell into such disrepute that the Weapon Systems Acquisition Reform Act (WSARA) of 2009 ended the use of that contract type.[32] Of course future acquisition reformers, tempted by the systems ideal, will simply come up with a new name for their proposal – or will just repeal the WSARA language, if that seems expedient.

Making it work

Success is indeed elusive but not impossible to achieve in the weapons acquisition process. There are many veto points, opportunities to highlight program problems and criticize management decisions. Yet American forces are equipped with the most advanced weapons and perform effectively in combat. And the regulatory hurdles cannot be too onerous, because foreign-based defense firms are eager to enter the US defense market, even if American firms that sell in commercial markets tend to keep their distance.

Success should be defined not just as the achievement of program goals but rather as minimizing or overcoming criticism. Public projects have many legitimate goals. The sponsoring organization has its goals: for example, the part of the Air Force that flies attack missions may want an aircraft that flies faster and farther than the enemy's. But there are other goals to consider, those of the service as a whole, the Department of Defense, the president, and Congress. Some will want the aircraft to cost no more than X dollars per copy. Others will want the aircraft to be in service within a decade. Still others will want it built in their district or sold to certain allies (but not others), or made using their favorite jet engine. And then there are the contextual goals of government – affirmative action, the attempt to create jobs in areas of high unemployment, the preference for hiring small businesses, and so on. There are lots of people to satisfy in American defense politics.

There are also lots of places to express dissatisfaction with a particular project or project team. Congress holds hearings. The Government Accountability Office writes reports. The Department of Defense holds reviews and must file reports to Congress certifying compliance with all sorts of rules. Trade publications devoted to the defense business follow progress closely. And nearly every reporter is looking for a whistle-blower to make his or her journalism career skyrocket. For defense acquisition efforts, success is relative, avoiding more of these minefields than the next project.

Following James D. Thompson's work in organization theory, the road to acquisition success has three requirements.[33] It first needs convergence between a policy consensus and a technological opportunity. We might all agree that we should end poverty (a policy consensus) but still find ourselves in wide disagreement about the efficacy of particular approaches. Should we start job training programs or mail money to poor people or give employers incentives to hire the poor? Do poor people need more day care for their children, more mentors to build their skills, or just a strong push? The equivalent issue in defense acquisition is the question we asked before: Do we need a new tank when we have the M1A2 already? Do we need a new interceptor when we have the F-15? And can we agree that we need them both? Can the new tank be made to weigh only 20 tons, and can the new fighter be stealthy, agile, and cost no more than your average airliner?

But as Thompson noted, success requires more than an agreement on need and feasibility. It also requires assembling and maintaining a powerful political coalition. The project's proponents need to find ways of winning friends and diverting potential enemies. Those who care about thwarting international threats and those who care about contracts to buck up employment in their districts must see the acquisition project as serving both of their interests. The effort needs to offer something for the technologists and something for the equal-opportunity advocates. Policy entrepreneurs find many ways to shape projects to meet these needs, but the purpose is always building and sustaining support. Those looking to ridicule government spending or to find dollars for their pet projects must be made to look somewhere else. The project must be both intimidating and appealing. The support for the program has to last years while it works its way through research, design, development, testing, production, and deployment. For much of the time it is just a brochure or some PowerPoint slides, making it a big target for budget cutters. It is not safe until the aircraft is on the ramp or the ship is tied to a pier. To get to that point requires a winning skill in bureaucratic politics, the real test of a project manager, whether or not he or she is also a military officer.

Of course, success also requires a good product. At the end of the day, it is the quality of the weapon that determines its reputation, and no project is fully judged until it delivers. The Abrams tank was much criticized, even within the Army, when it first appeared. But after its use in Operation Desert Storm, the drive to oust Saddam Hussain from Kuwait, it became known as a terrific system.[34] Similarly, the F-4 fighter proved its worth in Vietnam. On the other hand, the Space Shuttle soaked up National Aeronautics and Space Administration (NASA) dollars for decades, but it is not warmly regarded as a successful enterprise. It never met the promises of rapid turnaround and safe flight. Unlike the systems whose less-than-initial-requirements performance turns out to be very good, the Shuttle's poor performance threatened NASA's ability to perform its critical tasks.

Projects require more to succeed than desire for an object to be built and friends who agree to support the effort. The process cannot be only about politics. No matter how many congressmen feel that their districts got a big share of the work, they, too, will abandon the project if it cannot serve its assigned missions.

Questions for discussion

1   **Why does the government need to bear most of the risk in weapons development?**
2   **Why is privatization a bipartisan policy in defense?**
3   **What are the sources of uncertainty in peacetime defense policy-making?**
4   **Why are proposals for reform so frequently offered?**
5   **Is the US defense acquisition process really scandalous?**

Notes

1 Steven Kelman, "The Grace Commission: How Much Waste in Government?" *The Public Interest*, 78 (Winter 1985): 63–65, 77–82.
2 James Fairhall, "The Case for the $435 Hammer," *Washington Monthly* (January 1987); Gregg Easterbrook, "Sack Weinberger, Bankrupt General Dynamics, and other Procurement Reforms," *Washington Monthly* (January 1987): 33ff.
3 Kyle Jahner, Army Chief: You Want a New Pistol? Send Me to Cabela's with $17 Million," *Army Times*, March 29, 2016.
4 James Q. Wilson, *Bureaucracy: What Government Agencies Do and Why They Do It* (New York: Basic Books, 1989), pp. 315–332.
5 For convenience, we have made a PDF of the chart available at http://www.strausscenter.org/images/pdf/gholz-figure.pdf (accessed September 2, 2016).
6 Michael O'Hanlon, *Technological Change and the Future of Warfare* (Washington, DC: Brookings Institution, 2000); Kenneth P. Werrell, *Chasing the Silver Bullet: U.S. Air Force Weapon Development from Vietnam to Desert Storm* (Washington, DC: Smithsonian Books, 2003); Michael Russell Rip and James M. Hasik, *The Precision Revolution: GPS and the Future of Aerial Warfare* (Annapolis, MD: US Naval Institute Press, 2002); Richard G. Davis, *On Target: Organizing and Executing the Strategic Air Campaign Against Iraq* (Washington DC: Air Force History and Museums Program, 2002); Paul G. Gillespie, *Weapons of Choice: The Development of Precision Guided Munitions* (Tuscaloosa, AL: University of Alabama Press, 2006); Harvey M. Sapolsky, Brendan Green, and Benjamin Friedman (eds.), *U.S. Military Innovation Since the Cold War: Creation Without Destruction* (London: Routledge, 2009).
7 Thomas Hughes, *Rescuing Prometheus* (New York: Vintage Books, 2000). See also an excellent series of articles by Raphael Lewis and Sean P. Murphy that ran in the *Boston Globe*, starting on February 9, 2003.
8 Almost every issue of *Defense News*, a defense industry weekly, describes the common problem of overrun projects and failed weapons system tests both in the United States and abroad.
9 Richard J. Samuels, *"Rich Nation, Strong Army": National Security and Ideology in Japan's Technological Transformation* (Ithaca, NY: Cornell University Press, 1994).
10 Christopher Hanks, Elliot Axelband, Shuna Lindsay, Rehan Malik, and Brett Steele, *Reexamining Military Acquisition Reform: Are We There Yet?* (Santa Monica, CA: RAND Corporation, 2005).
11 Daniel Wirls, *Buildup: The Politics of Defense in the Reagan Era* (Ithaca, NY: Cornell University Press, 1992).
12 Harvey M. Sapolsky, "Equipping the Armed Forces," *Armed Forces and Society*, 14(1) (Fall 1987): 113–128; Thomas L. McNaugher, "Weapons Procurement: The Futility of Reform," in M. Mandelbaum (ed.), *America's Defense* (New York: Holmes & Meier, 1989), pp. 68–112.
13 There are a number of excellent reviews of the various types of acquisition contracts. See, for example, Thomas McNaugher, *New Weapons Old Politics: America's Military Procurement Muddle* (Washington, DC: Brookings Institution, 1989).
14 Joe Gould and Lara Seligman, "McCain Threatens to Block New Air Force Bomber," *Defense News*, February 25, 2016.
15 Jacques Gansler, *Affording Defense* (Cambridge, MA: MIT Press, 1989).
16 Charles J. Hitch, *Decision-Making for Defense* (Berkeley, CA: University of California Press, 1965).
17 Richard A. Stubbing, *The Defense Game* (New York: Harper & Row, 1986), pp. 179–182; Walter J. Boyne, *Beyond the Horizons: The Lockheed Story* (New York: St. Martin's Press, 1998).
18 Robert E. Levin, *Defense Acquisition: Information for Congress on Performance of Major Programs Can Be More Complete, Timely, and Accessible*, GAO-05-182, March 2005; Aaron Mehta, "Bogdan: F-35 Costs Down, Despite Worries," *Defense News*, March 25, 2015.
19 William P. Rogerson, "Economic Incentives and the Defense Procurement Process," *Journal of Economic Perspectives*, 8(4) (Fall 1994): 65–90.
20 William E. Kovacic, "Blue Ribbon Defense Commissions: The Acquisition of Major Weapons Systems," in Robert Higgs (ed.), *Arms, Politics, and the Economy Historical and Contemporary Perspectives* (New York: Holmes & Meier, 1990).
21 Jacques Gansler, *Democracy's Arsenal: Creating a Twenty-First Century Defense Industry* (Cambridge, MA: MIT Press, 2011); Valerie Grasso, *Defense Acquisition Reform: Status and Current Issues*, Congressional Research Service Issue Brief, September 7, 2000, p. CRS-8.

22 Robert J. Art, *The TFX Decision: McNamara and the Military* (Boston, MA: Little, Brown, 1968); Robert F. Coulam, *Illusions of Choice: The F-111 and the Problem of Weapons Acquisition Reform* (Princeton, NJ: Princeton University Press, 1977).
23 Dan Ward, "Tactical Radios: Military Procurement Gone Awry," *National Defense* (July 2012): 18–20.
24 Joe Gould, "Rapid-Equipping, Asymmetric Groups to Remain," *Defense News*, March 31, 2015.
25 David I. Cleland and William R. King, *Systems Analysis and Project Management* (New York: McGraw-Hill, 1968); Andrea Prencipe, Andrew Davies, and Mike Hobday (eds.), *The Business of Systems Integration* (New York: Oxford University Press, 2003).
26 Patrick Tyler, *Running Critical: The Silent War, Rickover, and General Dynamics* (New York: Harper & Row, 1986).
27 Even Secretary Carter's Undersecretary for Acquisition, Technology, and Logistics, Frank Kendall, a big promoter of prototyping, fell into the trap in congressional testimony: US Senate Committee on Armed Services, "Department of Defense Authorization of Appropriations for Fiscal Year 2015 and the Future Years Defense Program," *Hearing*, April 30, 2014, p. 13.
28 David L. McNicol and Linda Wu, *Evidence on the Effect of DoD Acquisition Policy and Process on Cost Growth of Major Defense Acquisition Programs* (Alexandria, VA: Institute for Defense Analyses, September 2014); Michael Brown, *Flying Blind: The Politics of the U.S. Strategic Bomber Program* (Ithaca, NY: Cornell University Press, 1992).
29 Vikram Mansharamani, "The Deepwater Program: A Case Study in Organizational Transformation Inspired by the Parallel Interaction of Internal and External Core Groups," SM thesis, Massachusetts Institute of Technology, 2004.
30 Peter Dombrowski and Eugene Gholz, *Buying Military Transformation: Technological Innovation and the Defense Industry* (New York: Columbia University Press, 2006).
31 *Challenges Affecting Deepwater Asset Deployment and Management and Efforts to Address Them*, report of the Government Accountability Office to the Subcommittees on Homeland Security, House and Senate Committees on Appropriations, GAO-07-874, Washington, DC, June 2007; *Role of Lead Systems Integrator on Future Combat Systems Program Poses Oversight Challenges*, report of the Government Accountability Office to Congressional Committees, GAO-07-380, Washington, DC, June 2007.
32 Kathlyn Hopkins Loudin, "Lead Systems Integrators: A Post-Acquisition Reform Retrospective," *Defense Acquisition Review Journal*, 53 (January 2010): 27–44.
33 Harvey M. Sapolsky, *The Polaris System Development: Bureaucratic and Programmatic Success in Government* (Cambridge, MA: Harvard University Press, 1972).
34 Chris C. Demchak, *Military Organizations, Complex Machines: Modernization in the U.S. Armed Services* (Ithaca, NY: Cornell University Press, 1991).

Recommended additional reading

Thomas L. McNaugher, *New Weapons, Old Politics: America's Procurement Muddle* (Washington, DC: Brookings Institution, 1989). Still the best single source for understanding why things rarely go right in buying modern weapons.

Andrea Prencipe, Andrew Davies, and Mike Hobday (eds.), *The Business of Systems Integration* (Oxford: Oxford University Press, 2003). The way big projects get done.

Harvey M. Sapolsky, *The Polaris Systems Development* (Cambridge, MA: Harvard University Press, 1972). How a Navy development agency fought to get its way and changed the strategic dynamics of the Cold War. One of us thinks of it as a classic.

Richard Whittle, *The Dream Machine: The Untold History of the Notorious V-22 Osprey* (New York: Simon & Shuster, 2010). A crazy idea overcomes all obstacles, including horrible crashes and a scandal over fraudulent data, with the help of a determined and politically popular USMC.

Daniel Wirls, *Buildup: The Politics of Defense in the Reagan Years* (Ithaca, NY: Cornell University Press, 1992). An education for us all on the way the Reagan buildup came and went.

9   Congress and special interests

Being a member of Congress is a great job, better than any job most people will ever hold. It pays well, offers a good pension, gives you a big staff, provides several well-furnished offices, ensures invitations to lots of interesting trips and events, attracts a pile of instant friends who just want to lose a golf game to you while talking a bit about pending legislation, and generally ensures a great deal of incumbent job security. Representatives often think about running for the Senate, while at least several senators each election cycle believe that they are presidential material. Mostly, though, the members work on keeping their seats. Fighting with colleagues over the merits of programs they hold dear is not usually a good way to do this. Neither is becoming a management expert on some aspect of government. But gaining a reputation for gathering up federal funds for projects in your district/state is an often-tried and proven way to secure more time in Congress.[1]

But Congress actually has important work to do, according to the Constitution. Congress, not the president, has the power to declare war, raise an army, and fund military operations. The Senate must consent to appointments to high office, including the most senior ranks of the military. Every year, the "defense policy bill," called the National Defense Authorization Act (though frequently with an influential individual's name added as reward for long service in Congress, such as 2011's Ike Skelton National Defense Authorization Act), extends to hundreds of pages of dense legislative language. It tweaks the organization and activities of the Department of Defense, calls for studies, and imposes rules to remedy apparent deficiencies and repair scandal-prone regulations. It also provides a platform to implement many an interest group's wishes.

Even though Congress shirks many of its responsibilities for national defense, as when it passes the "continuing resolution" budgets discussed in Chapter 7, it pretty much always manages to logroll its way to a policy bill. For most policy issues, most participants in the political process care little about which policy option is chosen, and so they reserve their resources for other political battles. But on each issue at least some people care passionately about their particular goals, substantive or procedural. Somehow, they must work together. While decisions are occasionally unanimous, more often, cooperation requires bargaining, and the path to policy coordination is rarely smooth. It usually involves compromises on principles and legislative trades that are essentially legal bribes. No one is more favored or more offended by this process than the American military.

Here we consider the ways interests, foreign and domestic, try to use the defense budget and US policy for their own ends. Congress sometimes holds hearings to investigate the crisis du jour, generally after the crisis is over, when it's time for political recriminations. But it mostly works on long-term issues such as budgets, force structure, personnel policy, and confirmation debates that discuss the strategic preferences of high-level appointees. Congress turns out not to be very brave, for it is reluctant to oversee a president's national security policies, surely fearing the consequences of being held responsible for military operations it cannot possibly control. When it comes down to it, Congress reacts to the pressures of political interests, especially focused by its members' steady concern about reelection.

Little interest in oversight

As a collective entity, Congress finds it extremely difficult to take responsibility for ongoing military operations. So much of what influences results in the field requires deeper involvement and more timely decision-making than a legislature can muster. Members of the president's party do not want to undermine the president's opportunities to succeed. Members of the opposing party do not want to be held accountable for failures, especially given that implementation is necessarily out of their hands. Public criticism of presidential actions is easier to offer and much more politically acceptable than attempts to hamper military strategy and operations directly through laws and budget cuts.[2]

But it is not just oversight of ongoing military operations where Congress hesitates. Reformers believe in the value of congressional oversight of administration, seeing it as a way to reveal and correct governmental failures. Legislators, however, see it differently. They view program oversight as a difficult and unrewarding task, and representatives prefer to spend their time in many other ways.[3] It is no wonder, then, that the word "oversight" has two meanings. Oversight is "close monitoring," but it also means "unintentional neglect." With Congress, the neglect is often intentional.

To begin with, governing is hard. For effective program monitoring, the members and their staffs would have to know the problems affecting the programs at a level of detail similar to that understood by the program administrators. Even if the auditors could dig that deeply, their efforts would often just reveal the complexity of the situation, the inherent murkiness in program management decisions that must balance the varying and conflicting goals that burden government programs.

Consider the procurement of armored trucks for the Army and Marine Corps during the insurgency in Iraq. Roadside bombs used against patrols and supply convoys caused the greatest number of American casualties, but the services seemed slow to react to the need for vehicles with more protection than the ones that they initially sent. As portrayed in media reports, the situation looks like an obvious case of mismanagement, and surely there was some of that.[4]

But the real cause was more than mismanagement. The situation was genuinely complicated.[5] No one knew whether the insurgency would persist, and consequently whether protection against roadside bombs was a long-term requirement for military vehicles. Before the war, the Army had developed elaborate plans to create a lighter, more mobile force. Shifting the vehicle fleet in the opposite direction would have been a bureaucratically wrenching decision.[6] Moreover, buying heavy armored vehicles that button up American soldiers would have pushed American counterinsurgency operations in the opposite direction from the much-heralded joint doctrine agreed by the Army and Marine Corps in 2006, which called for more rather than less emphasis on interaction with the local population and less rather than more emphasis on force protection.[7]

Indeed, the real question is how fair it is to criticize the military for reacting slowly to the roadside bomb threat. The enemy steadily adapted to American countermeasures. The Americans' first move was to seek protection through adding armor plating to vehicles – something that could be accomplished relatively quickly. Even though the soldiers' attempts to add armor in the field by simply welding on steel plate generally failed, the more organized acquisition process did deploy some "up-armored" vehicles that had been designed to resist landmines and other attacks. Some people argue with the benefit of hindsight that everyone should have known that the up-armored vehicles would not solve the roadside bomb problem, and a few people probably knew it at the time. The roadside bombers improved their devices to penetrate the additional armor, and meanwhile the heavier armor plating imposed dangerous wear and tear on the vehicles' transmissions. But how soon could sufficient numbers of the alternative – the MRAP – really have reached the field? Designing and producing a new vehicle takes time.

Even more time-consuming is the contracting path required by procurement regulations, which include the need to notify the public and to solicit bids for each new product. Many of the regulations require acquisition officers to "go slow" for good reasons: in the short term, the best designs are sometimes offered by companies that either are too small to produce vehicles in large numbers quickly or are prone to promise more military production than they can handle, and acquisition officers need to ferret out bidders' true capabilities.

At the same time, procurement laws require acquisition officers to give special favors to small businesses and to minority- and women-owned businesses, advantages for constituencies that are very important to influential lawmakers. Even though the regulations include emergency procurement procedures that can be invoked to speed contract awards, Congress often complains when they are used. Those rules exist because legislators value them. And every losing contender for a contract lives in a congressional district and thus has a congressional champion just a letter or a phone call away. A contract allotted under emergency terms may look to some like favoritism that circumvented regulatory safeguards. Even if an investigation ultimately determines that the protest was unfounded, the accelerated contracting procedure almost guarantees a delay for investigation.

A few congressmen pursued the roadside bomb issue, because the deaths of American soldiers in Iraq had such strong resonance on the national political scene. For example, Senator Joseph Biden hoped to gain traction for his presidential campaign by associating the "slow" response with the Bush administration's broader difficulties managing the Iraq War. But even this high-profile oversight effort ran into real-world complexity and political costs. It shows why Congress ignores the day-to-day decisions on countless other programs and military operations.

In addition to technical difficulties, incompatible goals, and institutional prerogatives, potential watchdogs in Congress face other opposition to oversight efforts. Behind every program are interests and people who favor its goals and/or benefit from it. Those interests do not react favorably to threats to the program. Take the revolutionary V-22 tilt-rotor aircraft, which takes off, hovers, and lands like a helicopter but flies like a turboprop airplane at higher speed and with greater range than a pure helicopter. The V-22's development extended for 20 expensive years, including several crashes during test flights and a scandal in which contract managers covered up unfavorable test results to help keep the contract on track.[8] The product was deployed for the first time in 2007 – to Iraq – and criticism continued despite the platform's operational advantages, because it is vulnerable to enemy fire, weather, or other mishaps.[9]

What if you object to continuing the V-22 program? You will discover how passionate the Marines are for the V-22; how many more elements of the military want it as well (Special Operations, for example); how well connected its makers, Boeing and Bell Helicopter, are; how strongly committed the firms that expect to make its engines and radars are; how unforgiving the congressmen from the districts where it is being made can be; and how many other interests support its production in order to expand the use of rotary-wing aircraft, even if they

Figure 9.1 MV-22 Osprey takes off from the amphibious assault ship USS *Bonhomme Richard*
Source: United States Navy. Photo by Mass Communication Specialist 2nd Class Jerome D. Johnson.

think the V-22 is likely to be semi-worthless in real-world military operations. In the mix of supporters will be union leaders, technologists, businessmen, politicians, former Marines, and a half-dozen of your long-lost friends who have been mobilized to persuade you to leave the program alone. You wanted to oppose waste, and suddenly you realize that you might be antagonizing people who might now find reason to object to some other program that you very much want to see supported.

Worse, hardly anyone cares whether the V-22 program deserves termination or curtailment. To be sure, some people oppose defense spending on principle, and others care deeply about government waste and inefficiency. There just are not many of them. Most people, most of the time, have other things to worry about: illness in the family, their company's possible move to another state, how the New England Patriots are faring, and the very latest news about Lindsay Lohan. Unless something threatens the viability of the president, the fate of the nation, or something equivalent in historical importance, few people will value the preparation and effort required for good administrative oversight.

The avoidance extends to policy oversight, too. In the Defense Authorization Acts, Congress requests a torrent of information and analyses from the Department of Defense, often with tight deadlines for the DoD's reply. Sometimes it requests an annual report on an issue that seems to have recurring importance, such as the Department of Defense Suicide Event Report or the report on Military and Security Developments Involving the People's Republic of China. Many other reports are one-off affairs, including a 2016 mandate to investigate "how the government can evaluate and emulate how companies in the private sector assure the purchase of foreign-produced trusted microelectronics semiconductors and components." The DoD must also submit a strategy for trusted microelectronics within a year.[10] The demands can be both incredibly broad and incredibly detailed.

These reporting requirements produce a lot of paperwork, but it is often not clear whether anyone in Congress even reads the results, let alone follows up with a policy reform or pressure on the DoD to comply with an existing policy. Many of the required reports are delivered late, perhaps because their deadlines were unrealistic; others request data that is impossible to obtain or provide, perhaps because the reporting requirement was meant to make a point and no one bothered to ask if the mandate could be fulfilled. Of course, sometimes it may be the DoD that drops the ball or that slow-rolls the investigation, but it can often get away with that because Congress usually does not really pay attention. Congress' professional staffers may be genuinely interested, may actually read some of what they receive, and may legitimately try to formulate constructive reform initiatives, but they have many tasks and meetings to attend, and even smart, hardworking people have trouble following up – and getting their principals, the congressional representatives, to pay attention to the details.

Congress also tries to give itself opportunities to use feedback from experience with defense policies to improve them over time. While some legislation carelessly makes new rules and initiatives permanent, other bills include sunset provisions so that after a few years, Congress needs to pass a reauthorization if wants the policy to continue. Perhaps some good policies fall through the cracks and are not reauthorized when the time comes, but good policies usually have advocates – or people who want to claim credit for them – who will make sure that the language gets included in the massive authorization bill. The bigger problem is that Congress rarely has the interest and stamina to pay attention to bad policies or the willingness to engage publicly with a controversial issue. For example, many controversial parts of the PATRIOT Act, which provided for expanded surveillance to try to prevent terrorist attacks, had sunset provisions, because even in the immediate aftermath of 9/11 representatives worried that they were too willing to infringe on civil liberties because of their temporary panic. It was easier to pass the bill if Congress could promise itself that it would revisit the issues in a few years, in a calmer state of mind.

But when the time came to look at the experience, hold hearings, and perhaps rein in the law, Congress declined – repeatedly, as it reauthorized the Act for years until the 2015 USA Freedom Act finally made important changes. Specifically, as two astute observers of congressional oversight reported, "Congress mostly ignored the information and debated reauthorization on the basis of demonstrably false factual premises." Many representatives failed to attend the classified briefings where they were supposed to learn about PATRIOT Act implementation or declined to visit the classified reading room where reports were made available. They are, after all, very busy people, and many of them didn't have the background to make sense of the complex technical reports. Of course the reality was that the National Security Agency (NSA) was collecting data that the Act did not authorize, but representatives just did not want to know; they were afraid of the controversial subject. And perhaps worst of all, before the 2010 reauthorization, the Republican leadership was suspicious of the libertarian leanings of the newly elected Tea Party members of their caucus, so they opted not to circulate the letter that the Obama administration provided to Congress with information on the surveillance programs, instead rushing through the reauthorization without hearings and markup and with limited floor debate. As in other cases, the program's small number of advocates controlled the agenda, and other representatives simply went along without asking many questions.[11]

Granted, some oversight hearings have been sensational, conferring real political rewards. Senator Harry Truman gained national prominence and a place on the 1944 presidential ticket with FDR by conducting investigations into contractor failures during World War II. Senator McCarthy's hearings into Communist infiltration of the government crashed spectacularly in

Figure 9.2 Time to testify: Defense Secretary Gates and Chairman of the Joint Chiefs Admiral
Mullen testify before the Senate Armed Services Committee

Source: Department of Defense.

a confrontation with the Army. Senator Church's investigations of the CIA's behavior during
the Vietnam War led to important changes in that agency. The Watergate and Iran-Contra
hearings each tested a presidency. But these are rare events at best, and their ability to grab
and hold the public's attention is likely fading as people turn to the Web and social media
for their news and entertainment. Moreover, their legislative impact is sometimes troubling.
The McCarthy hearings were part of an effort to rid government of "subversives" but often
swept up innocents as well. They complicated government employment procedures. The
Church hearings led to temerity in the Intelligence Community, including reluctance to share
information that some say harmed US security in later years.

Usually the oversight Congress exercises is much more program/agency-friendly. The
committee members seek their slots on particular committees because of their district's
interests. Massachusetts members of Congress rarely request a seat on the Agriculture
Committee, but those from Iowa and Nebraska often do. Because the big shipyards that sell
to the Navy are located in Maine, Virginia, and Mississippi, senators from Maine, Virginia,
and Mississippi usually want seats on the Armed Services or Appropriations subcommittees that deal with naval ship construction. And senators and representatives from Alaska
and Hawaii often appear on military-relevant committees not only because their states feel
especially vulnerable owing to their separation from the mainland, but also because past
representation and circumstance have given these states very big stakes in the fortunes of the
defense budget. Few committee members would benefit from a crusade to disrupt the familiar, routine distribution of national security tasks.[12]

Members of Congress prefer to celebrate programs rather than condemn them. Hearings
are planned to show the need for programs: members hope that the testimony will describe

the virtues of particular weapons and the threats that they are designed to counter. The committees often ask the military's congressional liaison officers to provide the members with smart-sounding questions, and of course the officers oblige with questions that are hardly likely to challenge military priorities. If there is an inkling that the administration might refuse a request from a program office or military service for a favorite system, Congress will grill political appointees in public hearings about the reasons for trying to force such "unacceptable risks" upon the nation. Critics rarely receive invitations to speak. The sessions are more bipartisan than not, with members united in asserting their intent to ensure that American servicemen and women are the best paid and equipped in the world. Everyone thanks everyone else for their service to the nation.

"Normal" interest group politics

Congress' friendly process helps to ensure a steady flow of resources to the interests most concerned with defense issues. The defense budget is an excellent source of funds for home districts. It is the largest portion of federal discretionary expenditures – that is, funds requiring annual appropriations and periodic reauthorization. The defense effort employs more civilians than any other federal government function: over 800,000 direct employees, supplemented by millions of defense contractor employees. Getting many of these jobs located in your home district becomes a common obsession for members of Congress. Some have bases to fill, while others have contractor facilities to keep busy. A big defense budget hides all the pork. There is always room for an additional engineering research grant for the local university and an extra accounting office in a town where the mill closed. Those are the small-scale earmarks. The big dollars go with bases and the defense contracts, discussed in Chapter 7. They all give congressional representatives an opportunity to claim credit for helping the district's economy.

Congressmen do not have to figure out the opportunities all by themselves. They have help from interest groups, people who organize around a shared preference for government policy. In American democracy, voting is only one way to express citizens' political desires. Citizens of course have the right to state their ideas and to try to persuade others to go along (free speech), but individuals on their own would have a tough time contacting enough people to matter in such a large country. Most amplify their free speech through participation in organized interest groups in which like-minded people contribute time, effort, and especially money to promote their cause. The groups often hire professional staff to express their views, to research and analyze the topic to build persuasive expertise, and to know the right people to contact to get things done in government. And the staff constantly looks for opportunities to achieve their group's interests, and then they tell the right members of Congress about them. Interest groups' activities are quite entrepreneurial, even though the stereotypical American entrepreneur has little to do with government.[13]

However, all interest groups face a collective action problem. If the interest group gets what it wants, all of the like-minded people get what *they* wanted, whether they contributed resources to the interest group or not. Interest group success has the characteristics of a public good (just as defense has the characteristics of a public good for everyone in the United States), and consequently, most people who share a group's goals free-ride on the efforts of their compatriots – that is, they don't contribute, hoping that others' efforts will be sufficient to achieve the group's goals. Moreover, each potential group member knows that it is extremely unlikely that his contribution will be the pivotal contribution that pushes the group over the edge to success, and that fact further attenuates willingness to contribute.[14]

The best-known interest in defense politics, the defense industry, solves the collective action problem through industry's normal organization: companies' management is a small group tasked with investing the company's resources to earn profit, and executives naturally consider investment in politics along with investment in research and development, machines and factories, and advertising. The company can also mobilize its workers, who not only have a shared interest in the company's profitability but also work together every day, get to know each other, exert peer pressure on each other to participate, and are easy to contact with suggestions about public policy. Finally, everyone can readily measure the stakes involved, at least for the big question of whether the firm wins a contract or not (though not necessarily for the regulations that dictate the processes through which that contract will be executed): the defense industry's interest is a pecuniary interest, measured in dollars and cents.

Different defense companies may have trouble working together – an inter-firm collective action problem – and sometimes various companies oppose each other, for example when competitors vie against each other to win a major contract. On industry-wide issues, they partially solve their collective action problem by joining together in industry associations such as the Aerospace Industries Association (AIA) and the National Defense Industrial Association (NDIA). The opportunity to repeat their interaction, because the roster of the major defense companies does not change very frequently, helps each company to contribute even on issues where another company cares more, because they each expect their turn to come around soon enough, where the industry organization will lobby on an issue that they especially care about. The industry organizations also enjoy "convening power," organizing committees and conferences through which various companies' representatives meet to discuss, in general terms, important defense issues of the day – sometimes policy issues, and sometimes technical or manufacturing challenges faced across the industry. Industry organizations can provide an important forum for positive-sum discussions that improve industrial performance and national defense, but they may also increase the political power of the defense industry, diverting a greater share of the national economic pie to the special interest's benefit.

A few interest groups work to counterbalance the power of the defense industry, but not very many, and none is very powerful. Some groups such as the Project on Government Oversight and the Center for Defense Information try to organize around the ideal of "good government," opposing waste, fraud, and abuse, and trying to limit egregious increases in the defense budget. All taxpayers of course have an interest in these groups' stated goals, but the collective action problem of getting those taxpayers to contribute to the groups' activities is nearly insurmountable: the bill for defense programs is spread across millions of Americans, few of whom know each other and none of whom pays enough for any particular defense project to make it worthwhile to understand the ins and outs of that project – the same apathy that prevents people from encouraging their members of Congress to engage in oversight. Only a few gadflies who care deeply about government accounting support these organizations, the same few who push for aggressive congressional oversight.

They are joined by perhaps a slightly bigger pool of Americans who are motivated to oppose the defense industry not by pecuniary interest but instead by a dislike for hawkish defense policy – that is, Americans who fear arms races, dislike weapons and war for moral reasons, or believe the United States, in the words of John Quincy Adams, should "not [go] abroad in search of monsters to destroy," among other reasons. These interests are really advocacy interests rather than pecuniary interests. Including the softline advocacy groups such as the Council for a Livable World and Greenpeace adds a few more organizations to the coalition that regularly tries to check the influence of the defense industry. But pure advocacy groups face especially severe collective action problems: their interests are very diffuse, and their goals are often abstract, like those of the government agencies given the missions to "improve diplomatic relations" or "protect America."

The inherent advantage in organization and political effectiveness that the defense industry lobby enjoys compared to the peace and good government lobbies was an important reason that President Eisenhower warned of the potential "unwarranted influence" of the military-industrial complex in his famous Farewell Address.[15] The military-industrial complex may create a tendency for profligate defense spending without being a conspiracy executing a nefarious plan. It is just the result of normal interest group politics, American citizens expressing their political preferences, a fundamental tenet of our democracy. The mechanisms and results have certain positive characteristics – liberty, some technical improvements to defense industry practices, and a robust investment in defense on those occasions that the United States needs it – but they also come with an important trade-off. And as we discussed in Chapter 7, the key check on the military-industrial complex need not come in the interest group environment; the military's own desire for top-quality equipment that supports its organizational needs limits the influence of the defense industry pork barrel, at least when the United States faces a national security threat.

The anti-militarist advocacy groups on the Left are far from the only advocacy groups active in American defense politics; indeed, they are not even the only such groups on the Left. There is also a human rights lobby (e.g., Amnesty International) and a humanitarian relief lobby (which often crosses over to include non-governmental organizations such as Mercy Corps and Save the Children that directly distribute aid). Some advocacy groups are surprisingly powerful. A few domestic policy groups are known for their immense influence, including the National Rifle Association and the AARP (which for a long time was known as the American Association of Retired People and is actually in large part a pecuniary interest, defending entitlement spending for aged Americans), but one foreign policy group often is listed among groups that hold great influence: the American Israel Public Affairs Committee (AIPAC). AIPAC is the most important component of the broader Israel lobby. Although it turns out to be hard to measure the Israel lobby's power or to observe it directly in action, few doubt it affects defense policy touching on Israel or its neighbors.[16] The Israel lobby is not alone historically – there was once a strong China lobby that tried to protect Nationalist China – or in contemporary politics – the UK, Canadian, Korean, Saudi, and Japanese governments, companies, and their domestic friends all seek to influence US defense policy. The intensity of pressure applied and resources generated for the cause likely relates to the intensity of fear of both the consequences of potential changes in American policy and the possibility that change might actually occur.

Intensity of interest is one source of lobbying power, but not the only one. Some groups have an easier time than others because their preferences are closer to the general values embodied in American political culture or to the ideological predilections of policy-makers or the general public. Some analysts think these latter factors were especially important in the debates leading up to the Iraq War, where neoconservative groups such as the Project for a New American Century seemed especially influential.[17]

Although many people suspect that interest groups directly "buy votes" by exchanging campaign contributions for politicians' agreement to support the interest's preferences, that mechanism of gaining influence seems to be the exception rather than the rule.[18] It is true that interest groups make campaign contributions, and that likely buys them some influence. But it is also true that they mostly contribute to representatives who already strongly agree with the interests' perspective. They "buy" the votes of people who do not need to be bought, rather than contributing to the marginal representative who does not feel strongly about an issue and might be swayed to vote either way by a contribution.

Moreover, the bulk of most interest groups' spending does not go for campaign contributions. Instead, it goes for lobbying: providing information and rhetoric that an ally might use to justify a vote or to convince other representatives to join a logroll. Interest groups sometimes even provide legislative language that a congressman (or his staff) can use in drafting a bill. It is the lobbying that explains why interest groups mostly work with known allies rather than with fence-sitters: the known allies are too busy and do not have enough person-hours of legislative staff support to do everything that they would like to do in Congress; the interest groups help subsidize their legislative effort, allowing them to accomplish things that they would like to do anyway. Naturally, those things benefit both the interest group and also the congressman with whom it cooperates.

The information-providing model of interest group behavior also clarifies the role of "think tanks" in the defense policy community. Think tanks are organizations that specialize in research and analysis. Many of them are formally non-partisan, but most have well-known ideological predispositions. The Heritage Foundation and the American Enterprise Institute are hawkish, the Cato Institute is libertarian, and the Center for American Progress is liberal. They produce studies and send experts to testify at Congress' set-piece hearings. They compete for influence, touting with press releases and tweets whenever a representative repeats one of their comments or whenever one of their suggestions is picked up in legislation.

Because they do not have individual members, think tanks are not exactly interest groups, yet they surely have an interest in influencing political decisions. And their funding comes from somewhere, usually a combination of wealthy donors and businesses with a stake in public policy. The businesses also receive private briefings from the experts who hang their hats at the think tanks, another part of the Washington echo chamber of insiders talking to insiders. There was even a mini-scandal when the *New York Times* ran a story about the extensive foreign government funding of influential think tanks such as the Center for Strategic and International Studies, the Brookings Institution, and the Atlantic Council.[19] The think tanks all released statements justifying their funding models, proclaiming their impartiality and reminding the policy world that someone has to pay their experts' salaries and the cost of their research projects. No one in the Washington policy elite had much incentive to follow up on the criticism, which soon died out. Think tank expertise is often valuable, both to specific politicians and to the country as a whole, if you remember that it is probably not really impartial – just like pretty much all other advice in defense policy. Fortunately, no single think tank or interest group can guarantee a lasting monopoly of influence, although they all dream about that possibility. A few of them might come close.

Super special interests as "cargo cults"

The federal budget can be divided into entitlement programs and discretionary programs. Entitlements refer to expenditures that are mandated, in the sense that Congress has established benefits that must be paid to all who qualify. For example, wounded veterans are eligible for medical treatment at Department of Veterans Affairs hospitals whenever they need it. It is a benefit to which they are "entitled" for life, because they were injured while on active duty. By contrast, discretionary expenditures require annual or biannual authorization and appropriations. If Congress does not vote to authorize and fund new ships every year, the fleet will begin to shrink: construction in US shipyards that build for the Navy will stop once the approved appropriation runs out, even as retirements of older ships continue.

In this section, we examine attempts to convert discretionary expenditures into the equivalent of entitlements, if not actual entitlements. Most special interests lobby year in, year out, for the programs that they favor. "Cargo cultist" is a good name for those who seek to entrench parts of the defense budget as virtual entitlements, reducing the future lobbying burden by establishing a regular pattern of resource allocation. Anthropologists first coined the term "cargo cult" in seeking to describe the behavior of native islanders in the South Pacific who tried to make sense of their encounters with outsiders.[20] They often believed that the mysterious foreigners – missionaries in the nineteenth century, but later European, Japanese, Australian, and American military detachments – were deities or ancestors. The islanders developed rituals that they believed caused these figures to return again and again and to bring great material gifts with them: food, technology, and of course military equipment.

One example, the John Frum cult, gained notoriety after World War II when American soldiers withdrawing from Pacific islands after the defeat of the Japanese abandoned all sorts of items (food, tents, containers, etc.) valuable for the natives. The cultists adopted makeshift American military uniforms and ritually marched around with bamboo rifles in the hopes that the American ships and planes would return. Another cult later sought to adopt President Lyndon Johnson as its leader because the cult's members were convinced that he was the key to American largesse – not a bad first approximation for those not trained at the graduate level in political science.

Often the term "cargo cult" refers to a group with beliefs that do not work. In discussing defense politics, we take a more positive view. If you believe hard enough, if you play the angles well enough – in short, if you develop the right rituals – you can succeed in getting the American military to keep bringing the gifts. You may not want to follow the cult by putting your faith in President Johnson; Senate Majority Leader Lyndon Johnson might have been a better bet.

The American defense budget is quite big. There is a lot of room in it for cults to thrive, especially with the aid of well-paid lobbyists and some locals who will write letters or make phone calls to further the quest. Powerful members of Congress earmark all sorts of gifts in the defense budget, and presidents usually only complain about the practice rather than actually stopping it. The South Sea islanders are not alone in expecting to be taken care of by defense expenditures. They just may have given up a little too soon.[21]

A few examples tell the story. Hard coal fell on hard times when Americans stopped using it to heat their homes. A little hard thinking resulted in a congressional mandate that US troops in Europe be kept warm with coal imported from the United States, even though Europe has plenty of coal of its own to sell on-site. The cargo cult worked in this case by explaining that the alternative was to heat American soldiers in Europe with natural gas imported from the Soviet Union, the enemy in the Cold War. The US coal industry, its lobbyists, and their supporters in Congress – the cargo cultists in this example – taunted the few politicians who complained about the inefficiency of the American coal subsidy by suggesting that they assure Americans that the Soviets would "not attack Western Europe during the winter months when our bases would be dependent on their natural gas."[22] The requirement to use US coal endured until 2015, long after its initial sponsors had left Congress – a "zombie earmark" supported by a handful of lobbyists.[23]

Other industries also benefit from Pentagon largesse when they suffer economic downturns. In contrast to what its foreign rivals claim, the American commercial aircraft industry normally does not seek assistance from the federal government. The aircraft makers are cynical cultists, because they only "convert" to the religion occasionally and temporarily. Their business is usually strong enough to attract private capital and/or to generate sufficient sales to support aircraft development. When bad times hit, however, the firms remember Washington and the defense budget, and they perform the tried and true rituals.

For example, after the 9/11 attacks, when air travel faltered, Boeing's 767 was espe-cially hard hit, losing sales to newer designs. Strangely, it was at this moment that the Air Force felt the urge, with a little congressional prodding, to buy 100 KC-767s to renew its air refueling fleet. Boeing, of course, explained that the tanker contract was not a bailout but a vital contribution to American national security – the essence of cargo cult ritual because it put the request in a form that mimicked the routine national security spending process. Unfortunately for the cultists, though, the contract was caught up in a procurement scandal: an Air Force procurement official and a Boeing executive each went to jail, and the contract for the KC-767 tankers was cancelled. But in this case, the Air Force's alleged need for new tanker aircraft had indeed become an entitlement: even though the commercial aircraft indus-try downturn had passed, the Air Force's in-house supporters of tanker acquisition continued the ritual appeal and convinced Congress that new tankers were an important priority. The result was a new competition for a multibillion-dollar tanker contract.[24] When a European competitor, Airbus, won the contract to supply the tankers, the Air Force was required to rethink its decision until the service found the right answer. Boeing offered a highly optimis-tic bid in the last round of the competition, and the Air Force accepted its nominally fixed price terms, providing cover for the shift to the American supplier. Of course, Boeing had good reason to suspect that it would get many opportunities to renegotiate that deal, once the contract was no longer subject to competition from Airbus. By early 2013, within two years of the contract award, changes in the defense budget already started to offer Boeing such opportunities.[25] And not surprisingly, Boeing acknowledged in 2016 that it would not be able to meet the optimistic schedule it promised in order to win the contract.[26] Optimism is, of course, a key part of the ritual.

Allies, too, are in this game. Israel never asks for US troops to help ease its security bur-den, but it does steadily receive $3 billion a year via the US defense budget to buy weapons and keep its defense industry operating. Egypt, Jordan, and Taiwan have found the same religion. All of these countries argue that the US military aid that they receive really helps protect the United States. Their task is relatively easy, because allies feature prominently in the official *National Security Strategy* and *National Defense Strategy*, which in some iterations have openly declared that protecting allies is a vital interest of the United States, regardless of what specific help those allies do or do not provide to American forces in the field or to the defense of the American homeland.[27] America's allies are surely useful from time to time, but that declaration – protecting them indefinitely, under all circumstances – is just as surely the result of a successful cargo cult. Allies benefit from an entitlement rather than discretionary foreign policy.

Scientists also follow a cargo cult, intoning the rituals linking scientific research to national security over and over again. In weak moments, scientists will assert their belief that governments should support basic research because new knowledge is inherently good. Scientists, though, are more politically sophisticated than they like to let on. They know that politicians support research in the belief that it can help solve current problems and allevi-ate the public's fears. That is why the various institutes at the National Institutes of Health feature diseases in their names (cancer, heart, stroke, etc.), even though the research being supported is mostly fundamental work organized by discipline rather than by the immediate demands of patients.[28] By making the right argument, performing the right ritual, they ensure that the dollars keep coming.

In defense, scientific investment actually flows much more toward applied research and weapons development work, because military officers control most of the funds and know what they want: faster aircraft and better ships.[29] Moreover, most of the money goes to industrial contractors, whose interest in basic research is negligible because it is work that by definition is useful to all, such that no single firm can use it to its competitive advantage.

But in some fields, most notably high-energy physics, the government research funds flow freely. Working as applied scientists, physicists converted theoretical speculations into an atomic bomb during World War II. Ever since, most of the ambitions of high-energy physicists have been fulfilled, even though their work requires expensive machines such as the billion-dollar National Ignition Facility. The scientists want to work openly with international partners, including Chinese and Russians along with French, German, British, and Indian scientists. Hardly any of their big experiments have the least connection with weapons or military matters. But to build their machines and conduct these experiments, American physicists perform a ritualistic dance. They do not promise that their work has direct application to weapons development, but they remind Congress that physicists have developed weapons in the past. They imply that they could develop weapons much faster in the future, if called upon, because pure science projects in the present would help them "keep sharp." They also recite the history of nuclear physics and lasers, where important weapons were produced, and hint vaguely that more may be in the offing. And they ominously caution Congress that failure to fund their research might cede leadership at the cutting edge to strategic competitors such as Russia or France, which, according to the cargo cultists, would surely continue the experiments without American participation and largesse. Somehow, their logic seems to work, year after year, with relatively little overt lobbying.[30]

The South Sea Islanders never got much for their efforts, but the physicists have, along with the oceanographers and computer scientists. Not every discipline or profession can have a successful cargo cult. Do not expect the political scientists to be believed when they say that with just a few billion defense dollars they will be able to bring world peace. The plausibility standard, however, is not especially high – witness the millions that are poured into keeping the American merchant marine alive on the false assumption that the military services lack sufficient government-owned sealift and that America's allies and the international cargo industry will forgo wartime opportunities to make money.[31] The US, in fact, has a huge military cargo fleet of roll-on/roll-off ships, crane ships, and the like that helps sustain forces globally. Furthermore, while our allies might not show up for America's wars, their merchant fleets do. Many interests, domestic and foreign, want to lock on to a share of the US defense budget. Others disparagingly call these seekers special interests – that is, until they themselves feel the need to believe in a cargo cult.

Non-believers

As James Q. Wilson noted, pork is kosher in American politics.[32] Those who want their politics to be principled and who think that purity can be achieved resist this truth. Two groups stand out among them. The Tea Party is a political reaction, mostly but not entirely within the Republican Party, to the spiraling public budget deficit. Tea Party supporters were especially appalled by the earmarking that had become prevalent in Congress by well-placed members of both parties, especially in the midst of the huge spending increases in the 2000s for the Global War on Terror and for economic stimulus to try to end the Great Recession. Mid-level military officers are another group unhappy with the practice of requiring parts of programs that they carefully craft on a Pentagon staff to be directed to a particular firm or university in a particular congressional district. Both groups think that congressmen are being selfish and unpatriotic by grabbing a chunk of the federal budget for their constituents, even though earmarking is a natural, timeworn step to support reelection bids and perhaps is even an appropriate step, in the American constitutional system, to represent constituents' interests.

The success of Tea Party-endorsed candidates in the 2010 congressional elections produced a strange twist in congressional behaviors. The Republicans regained control of the House but at the demand of Tea Party freshmen sought to eliminate the use of earmarks, one of the great perks of congressional power and seniority. Most earmarks are relatively small, but the principle of limiting set-asides for favored constituents has extended to some large defense contract decisions, too. The highest-profile case of the new restraint is the cancellation of the second engine for the Joint Strike Fighter, the F-35. Some aircraft programs include two efforts to develop high-performance engines when the performance targets are especially risky. This happened initially with the F-35, but relatively early on the Pentagon chose a Pratt & Whitney engine for the program that derived from the engine already in use for the F-22. For a while, the Pentagon continued to support GE's competitor as a backup, but when costs for the overall F-35 program began to spiral upward, the DoD sought to cut the second engine, only to be continually rebuffed by its congressional supporters, both Democrats and Republicans. In the new Tea Party-influenced Congress, seated in January 2011, both the Speaker of the House and the Majority Leader had GE engine plants in their districts. It surely was a unique moment in congressional history when one of that Congress' first important decisions denied funding to the GE engine, a deliberate rejection of a congressional opportunity to direct dollars to districts.

Nevertheless, the Air Force, which is the lead service for jet engine research, soon saw the need for a big research contract to help sustain GE's work on advanced engine concepts. The military clearly wants to be certain that Pratt is never totally comfortable in its F-35 engine monopoly. Some among the senior Air Force leaders also undoubtedly wanted to keep the House Speaker, the House Majority Leader, and the chairmen of several key committees – all of whom supported the second engine over the objections of Tea Party colleagues – happy and interested in military aeronautics. And just to be certain Pratt would not try to block the effort by having its supporters claim it was just a work-around for the cancelled second engine, Pratt, too, was awarded its own advanced engine technology development contract, and the Air Force promised that the new engine development was only for future aircraft, not for a future re-competition of the F-35 engine.[33]

Military officers often express horror that politics in any way affects the defense budget, sacred vessel that they claim it is. When officers describe their ideal world, they often suggest that defense spending should flow directly from military analyses of the strategic environment. When politicians sense a serious threat to national security, they are more likely to defer to the military's wishes, but even then, their political interests will channel the ways in which they implement the military's strategic advice. And in the real world, knowing this pattern, the military services maintain large congressional liaison offices, treat congressmen visiting bases as royalty, and find a ship to name after a particularly deserving, some might say generous, committee chairman. Without reelection-driven pork, the defense budget would include fewer airplanes and ships. With more careful congressional oversight on security issues, there might be fewer still. Deep inside the Pentagon, military leaders are quite willing to play along with American politics.

Ultimately, neither principle nor strategy is a complete guide to defense policy. Principles often conflict and strategies are rarely sharply defined. Americans want to avoid deficits but also have a robust defense. Official strategy documents proclaim broad ideas such as "rebalancing" American forces toward the Pacific – concepts that provide only vague and ambiguous direction to policy. To build majority legislative support, advocates combine people who believe in the policy (as they understand it) with those who are indifferent to it but are looking for a personal benefit wherever they can find one. Tea Party members and idealistic military officers are bound to be disappointed by the policy-making process, which is never more than temporarily devoid of political favors.

Death and taxes

There is, supposedly, no greater certainty than death and taxes, but not if the US Congress is involved. It is very popular for Congress to fight against the prospect of illness and death by both extending health care subsidies and appropriating money for medical research. Entitlements, the promises that the federal government makes to benefit recipients that their claims will be honored if they meet the benefit criteria, are a growing share of the federal budget, and health care entitlements are a growing share of overall entitlements. And Congress has not met a disease upon which it will not declare war. In contrast, taxes are not so popular. The reluctance of Congress to increase taxes to pay for America's expanding entitlement programs and never-ending wars, either in the lab or overseas, is the source of the growing federal budget deficit and the ballooning national debt.

In turn, the national debt becomes the ultimate security threat – the true peer competitor – that can wipe out most of America's defense spending, if not America itself. Unless the United States contemplates bankruptcy, interest on the debt is a priority claimant on the federal budget. If interest rates ever return to historically normal levels – after a decade of extremely low rates intended to spur the recovery from the 2008 financial crisis – the costs of the national debt will skyrocket.

Right behind interest on the debt in budgetary priority are entitlements, money for the elderly, the disabled, and the poor. Entitlement opponents hope at best for the containment, not the rollback, of these costs. In fact, with an aging population, costs of entitlements are certain to grow even without politically tempting votes to expand benefits. Both parties are guilty. George W. Bush offered an expensive expansion of Medicare's drug benefit as apparent amends for the Iraq invasion. Barack Obama gave us subsidized health insurance for all, the full cost for which has yet to be felt.

On the expenditure side of the budget, once preference is given to the servicing of the debt and entitlements, there is nothing left to fight about but defense expenditures and non-defense discretionary expenditures, which is essentially the money for the rest of government, including the regulatory agencies, the national weather service, the national parks, the FBI, Veterans Affairs, and so on. Each side has its congressional supporters and its advocates of various kinds: employees, contractors, clients. As we have pointed out, defense spending is on a war/non-war cycle. The up slopes involve security panics with little opposition to the increased expenditures for war or its preparation. The down slopes are when the budgetary fights intensify, with the congressional advocates for non-defense spending seeing the decline in war costs as "found money" for their favorite causes, while the advocates of defense seek to prevent raids on what they see as the new base level of spending for the military that the most recent security panic provided.

Spending makes friends; taxing rarely does. It used to be that wars brought increases in taxes, if only temporarily, as the way both to pay for the new spending and to share the burden of the fighting more widely, beyond the young men facing combat and possible death.[34] Taxes are the citizen's stake in war. But as conscription fades in memory, so do war taxes. The Gulf War's costs were paid for by allies, particularly Japan, Germany, and Kuwait. The funds for Iraq and Afghanistan were mainly borrowed from China and elsewhere in Asia. It is some subsequent generation, far removed from the fighting, who will vote for an entirely new crop of politicians that will have to deal with the big bill.

Questions for discussion

1 Why might a congressman seek to close a local military base?
2 Could anything make Congress take its oversight role more seriously?
3 What is the difference between a campaign contribution and a bribe?
4 Can interest groups improve the quality of US defense policy?
5 Pork may be kosher in American politics, but is it necessary?

Notes

1 David Mayhew, *Congress: The Electoral Connection* (New Haven, CT: Yale University Press, 1974).
2 Louis Fisher, *Congressional Abdication on War and Spending* (College Station, TX: Texas A&M Press, 2000).
3 Terry M. Moe, "The Politics of Structural Choice: Toward a Theory of Public Bureaucracy," in Oliver E. Williamson (ed.), *Organization Theory: From Chester Barnard to the Present and Beyond* (New York: Oxford University Press, 1990), pp. 139–140.
4 Tom Vanden Brook, "Corps Refused 2005 Plea for MRAP Vehicles," *USA Today*, May 23, 2007.
5 Andrew F. Krepinevich and Dakota L. Wood, *Of IEDs and MRAPs: Force Protection in Complex Irregular Operations* (Washington, DC: Center for Strategic and Budgetary Assessments, 2007).
6 Sharon K. Weiner, "Organizational Interests versus Battlefield Needs: The U.S. Military and Mine-Resistant, Ambush Protected Vehicles in Iraq," *Polity* 42(4) (October 2010): 461–482.
7 Gordon Lubold, "Will MRAPs Become White Elephants?" *Christian Science Monitor*, October 17, 2007, p. 3.
8 Robert Wall, "V-22 Support Fades Amid Accidents, Accusations, Probes," *Aviation Week and Space Technology*, January 29, 2001, p. 28.
9 Mark Thompson, "V-22 Osprey: A Flying Shame," *Time*, September 26, 2007; Giovanni di Briganti, "V-22 'Reputation Remake' Falls Flat," *Defense-Aerospace.com*, May 13, 2013, available at: http://www.defense-aerospace.com/articles-view/feature/5/144961/v_22-'reputation-remake'-falls-flat.html (accessed June 9, 2016).
10 Richard A. McCormack, "DoD, NSA Enter a New World Order: U.S. Is Now Dependent on Foreign Companies for its Most Sensitive Electronics," *Manufacturing and Technology News*, May 31, 2016.
11 William Bendix and Paul J. Quirk, "Secrecy and Negligence: How Congress Lost Control of Domestic Surveillance," *Brookings Institution, Issues in Governance Studies* (March 2015); quote from p. 1.
12 James M. Lindsay, "Congress and the Defense Budget: Parochialism or Policy?" in Robert Higgs (ed.), *Arms, Politics, and the Economy: Historical and Contemporary Perspectives* (New York: Holmes & Meier, 1990), pp. 174–201; Kenneth R. Mayer, *The Political Economy of Defense Contracting* (New Haven, CT: Yale University Press, 1991), pp. 133–179.
13 Terry Moe, *The Organization of Interests: Incentives and the Internal Dynamics of Political Interest Groups* (Chicago, IL: University of Chicago Press, 1980).
14 James E. Alt and Michael Gilligan, "The Political Economy of Trading States: Collective Action Problems and Domestic Political Institutions," *Journal of Political Philosophy*, 2(2) (June 1994): 165–192.
15 James Ledbetter, *Unwarranted Influence: Dwight D. Eisenhower and the Military-Industrial Complex* (New Haven, CT: Yale University Press, 2011).
16 Jerome Slater, "Two Books of Mearsheimer and Walt," *Security Studies*, 18(1) (January–March 2009): 4–57.
17 Brian C. Schmidt and Michael C. Williams, "The Bush Doctrine and the Iraq War: Neoconservatives versus Realists," *Security Studies*, 17(2) (April–June 2008): 191–220.
18 Richard L. Hall and Alan V. Deardorff, "Lobbying as Legislative Subsidy," *American Political Science Review*, 100(1) (February 2006): 69–81.
19 Eric Lipton, Brooke Williams, and Nicholas Confessore, "Foreign Powers Buy Influence at Think Tanks," *New York Times*, September 6, 2014.

174 Congress and special interests

20 Lamont Lindstrom, *Cargo Cult: Strange Stories of Desire from Melanesia and Beyond* (Christchurch, New Zealand: South Seas Books, 1993).
21 C. V. Glines, "The Cargo Cults," *Air Force Magazine*, 74(1) (January 1991): 84–87; Paul Raffaele, "In John They Trust," *Smithsonian* (February 2006): 70–77.
22 Representative Paul E. Kanjorski, "Coal – in the National Interest," *Washington Post*, June 10, 1988, p. A22.
23 Ari Natter, "House Kills Earmark Requiring Defense Department to Purchase Pennsylvania Coal," Taxpayers for Common Sense press release, June 11, 2015.
24 Sam Hananel, "Politics Seeping into Tanker Contract Decision," *Associated Press News Wire*, October 26, 2007.
25 Aaron Mehta, "Experts: Budget Woes Could Affect AF's KC-46," *Air Force Times*, January 15, 2013.
26 Lara Seligman, "Boeing's KC-46 Tanker Will Miss Major Deadline," *Defense News*, May 27, 2016.
27 *The National Defense Strategy of the United States of America* (Washington, DC: US Department of Defense, March 2005).
28 Harvey M. Sapolsky, "The Truly Endless Frontier," *Technology Review* (November/z 1995): 37–43.
29 Harvey M. Sapolsky, *Science and the Navy: The History of the Office of Naval Research* (Princeton, NJ: Princeton University Press, 1990).
30 Sybil Francis, "Save the Labs?" *Breakthroughs*, 4(1) (Spring 1995): 18–22.
31 Rob Quartel, "America's Welfare Queen Fleet," *Regulation* (Summer 1991): 58–67.
32 James Q. Wilson, "Pork Is Kosher under Our Constitution," *Wall Street Journal*, February 15, 2000, p. A26.
33 Graham Warwick, "The Third Way: Pratt in, Rolls out, GE Stays on as U.S. Air Force Advances Adaptive-Engine Technology," *Aviation Week & Space Technology*, September 24, 2012, p. 31; Rebecca Grant, "Adaptive Engines," *Air Force Magazine* (September 2012): 62–65; see also Jim Hodges, "Better Bridges: U.S. Earmark Ban Leaves Aircraft Carrier Upgrades in Precarious Place," *C4ISR Journal* (July 2012): 26.
34 Gustavo A. Flores-Macías and Sarah E. Kreps, "Political Parties at War: A Study of American War Finance, 1789–2010," *American Political Science Review*, 107(4) (November 2013): 833–848.

Recommended additional reading

Gordon Adams, *The Politics of Defense Contracting: The Iron Triangle* (New Brunswick, NJ: Transaction Publishers, 1981). The classic study of the ties between Congress and interest groups in defense contracting.

Colton C. Campbell and David P. Auerswald (eds.), *Congress and Civil–Military Relations* (Washington, DC: Georgetown University Press, 2015). Essays on Congress' various roles, generally looking for good news to report but finding at best modest positives.

James Ledbetter, *Unwarranted Influence: Dwight D. Eisenhower and the Military-Industrial Complex* (New Haven, CT: Yale University Press, 2011). Ike originally wanted to call it the "military-industrial-congressional complex," and Congress is a main target of the "unwarranted influence" that he warned about.

Daniel Wirls, *Irrational Security: The Politics of Defense from Reagan to Obama* (Baltimore, MD: Johns Hopkins University Press, 2010). Vividly explains the broad logroll that supports US defense effort.

10 Presidents and the National Security Council

You might think being elected president would be sufficient. You are famous, perhaps the most well-known person in the world. You are certain to be in the history books, to have your name memorized by schoolchildren for ages to come. Many things will be named after you – buildings, streets, towns. George Washington, the nation's first president, has among other things Washington, DC, the Washington Monument, and George Washington University, where one of us teaches, named after him.

But the true measure of national honor lies in the Navy's fleet, in the naming of a warship and the importance of its type. The pinnacle these days is a nuclear-powered aircraft carrier. There are carriers named USS *George Washington, Abraham Lincoln, Theodore Roosevelt, Harry S. Truman, Dwight D. Eisenhower,* and *George H. W. Bush.* There is a new class of carriers being built, the *Ford* class, named after President Gerald R. Ford – Ford being a congressional favorite for his years of House service. The second ship in that class is the USS *John F. Kennedy.* There is a USS *Jimmy Carter,* but it's a submarine, not a carrier; Carter was a Naval Academy graduate and a submariner himself, creating a natural reason to name a sub for him, even if his presidency is not widely called a great success. Soon there is to be a USS *Lyndon B. Johnson,* a destroyer, not a carrier. But don't hold your breath waiting for a carrier or even a frigate to be named USS *Richard Nixon, Bill Clinton,* or *George W. Bush.* Getting elected is one thing. Being remembered as a success is another.

A named warship is an appropriate honor for a president, as Article II, Section 2 of the Constitution makes the president the Commander-in-Chief of the US armed forces. With that title goes great responsibility and much power. The United States has used force abroad more than 300 times since its founding, dozens of these actions occurring since the end of the Cold War. But Congress has declared war officially only five times; the last was World War II.[1] It is the president who gets to choose most of the fights, pick the generals and the admirals, decide the strategy, and approve the rules of engagement. And the requirements of modern warfare – the need for unity in command, secrecy in planning, and speed in decision-making – limit the opportunity for the other branches of government to have much say.

Really it is the responsibility that tames the other branches. Congress and the courts give much leeway. For example, neither the Supreme Court in Lincoln's day nor the current one wanted to rule on whether the government's detention policies were consistent with the Constitution, at least not while the bullets were flying.[2] Because the president has the formal authority, he gains credit for the successes in America's international use of force but also the blame for the failures. Each time a president sends a carrier in harm's way, he gambles both the ship and his reputation.

Consequently, presidents have an incentive to centralize national security decision-making, even in the context of the decentralized American system. Leaders naturally want to control every decision for which they will be blamed.[3] Legislation and practice may have created centralized civilian and military hierarchies within the Department of Defense, as explained in Chapter 3, but both parts of the department have yielded influence, at least on strategy and foreign policy decisions, to the president's White House staff. The expansion of the National Security Council's role sets up a potential clash between political advisors who are more likely to share the president's ideological inclinations – or who may simply want to protect the president's standing in the polls – and the defense policy experts in the Pentagon. The latter may complain about White House micromanagement, but ultimately they defer to persons elected by the American people to make national security decisions.

Even with a growing, centralized staff in the White House, though, the president rarely imposes his stamp on national security just the way he wants when he takes office, because he has to react to unforeseen crises and foreign policy opportunities. Election campaigns focus on candidates' general attributes and inclinations more than on detailed strategy and plans, because the candidate does not yet have access to all of the details that will influence decisions once the presidency is won. The public, too, lacks much detailed knowledge of foreign policy, and while voters want to see that candidates seem "presidential," so they expect some comments about strategy and national security investment, they usually vote mainly on domestic issues, especially the state of the economy.[4] The upshot is that new presidents generally don't have extensive national security plans that they really care to implement. At most, they have a general approach in mind.

After the election, a hurried transition gives the new president a flood of new information and the need to choose not just a handful of trusted advisors but literally thousands of people to appoint to leadership posts in the executive branch (from secretaries to deputy assistant secretaries, directors, etc.).[5] Meanwhile, the need to react to events every day and to the piles of requests in every inbox distracts from the ability to think or implement a strategic vision.[6] It is those events that end up driving high-level national security policy choices.

Here we examine four presidents' experiences with security policy, mindful of Seyom Brown's wonderful title for his book on US foreign policy after the Cold War, *The Illusion of Control*.[7] No matter how great the staff and how sharp the president, success in managing global security is illusive. Good things may happen, but more likely through reaction than planning. The large and growing effort at policy planning, interagency coordination, and program monitoring that takes place in the White House may be both comforting and politically necessary, but it is mostly the illusion of control.

The top of the pyramid

The modern presidency is very complex. The government takes a large role in domestic life, and that commands much of the president's attention. Internationally, the United States claims interests in countless places and events, and those interests are complicated. It not only fights many distant wars for limited purposes but attempts to influence friends and foes with troop deployments and the movement of ships. Today, high-level US officials and even senior military officers believe it is their assignment to "shape" the global security environment. Effective national security policy, in their view, involves not just having a strategy to protect America but also using US resources, including the military, to avoid the outbreak or temper the heat of regional conflicts. They assert that those conflicts might ultimately affect US security. Presidents act as if they are being held accountable by the American and other Western publics for managing nearly every security crisis around the world, and it is they who push for plans and programs to control international problems. The collapse of the Soviet counterweight strengthened this trend, and then the 9/11 attacks amplified it some more.[8]

Presidents have sought help in managing it all. Mainly the help has been assembled in the White House by the national security advisor to the president, a position that evolved to direct the staff of the National Security Council (NSC), which itself was created by the National Security Act of 1947 to advise and assist the president. Much depends on the personality and preparation of the president and the abilities of the persons presidents select to be their national security advisor.

Statutorily the NSC is composed of the president, the vice president and the secretaries of state and defense, with the director of national intelligence (initially it was the director of the CIA) and the chairman of the Joint Chiefs of Staff as attendees and designated advisors. The hope was the NSC meetings would bring order and coordination to security policy-making, correcting the chaotic informally and subterfuge that marked Franklin Roosevelt's wartime years.[9] Having the principal officers for foreign and defense policy in the same room for decisions made it possible to believe that the key agencies dealing with national security would have the same understanding of and commitment to the president's policies.

But presidents have different decision-making styles and different levels of trust in their senior officials. The heads of State and Defense are often rivals, driven by bureaucratic interest and personal ambitions. Presidents sometimes appoint trusted and able friends to high office and other times pick political opponents or near incompetents for those same jobs. And over time, presidents have found that the key issues in foreign affairs involved others, such as the Treasury secretary and the president's chief of staff, so more executives were invited to attend NSC meetings on a regular basis. It all depends on the needs of the day. President Truman, a politician and former senator, did not like using the NSC for decisions, but President Eisenhower, a career military officer, was quite comfortable in a staff meeting setting.[10]

Gradually the NSC acquired staff. The national security advisor's effort was initially to build an orderly interagency process for vetting decisions.[11] But the failure of the Bay of Pigs invasion, the April 1961 attempt to overthrow the Castro regime in Cuba, changed the NSC. President Kennedy felt misled by the CIA and the military, and the national security advisor's main job became protecting the president's equities in the making of security policy.[12] That job required an NSC of trusted political advisors rather than the formal heads of powerful executive branch departments: even if the president appoints and can fire the departments' leadership, those appointees develop organizational interests of their own, and the president wants White House staffers who represent only the president's interests. Consequently, the NSC staff is less a clearinghouse for agency advice than an appendage of presidential power.

Most presidents convene few formal NSC sessions, which have grown to be large, set-piece affairs for media consumption. For actual policy-making, presidents usually prefer to use informal mechanisms.[13] Policy planning, coordination, and monitoring are the tasks of NSC subcommittees, the most prominent of which is the Deputies Committee, the number twos of the departments and agencies represented on the NSC itself. Those committees operate with lots of staff input and agenda control, and on some issues, the NSC staffers reach out directly to the departments to inform line managers of the president's desires and policies. President Obama's NSC was especially criticized for young White House staffers' micromanagement of the departments.[14] The administration's defenders pointed out similar history

Figure 10.1 President Reagan and his NSC team meet in the oval office with Nicaraguan Contra
rebel leaders, March 3, 1986. The gang's all there: White House Chief of Staff
Don Regan, Secretary of Defense Caspar Weinberger, National Security Advisor
Admiral John Poindexter, Deputy National Security Advisor Don Fortier, and NSC
staffer Oliver North

Source: Reagan Library Archives.

in other presidential administrations, mostly arguing that the centralization is normal rather
than that it is desirable, though they also noted that the strong NSC role protected the president from criticism that the administration had "tak[en] its eye off the ball and abdicat[ed]
leadership."[15]

Some national security advisors are good at furthering the president's goals while others
are near disasters. Henry Kissinger, a master of both bureaucratic maneuver and grand theorizing, helped Richard Nixon open the door to China and get out of the Vietnam War, while
Zbigniew Brzezinski, also a politically connected, ambitious academic, brought only interne-
cine warfare to Jimmy Carter's cabinet. Ronald Reagan's team, especially National Security
Advisor John Poindexter and NSC staffer Ollie North, brought near impeachment with their
elaborate and bizarre scheme to trade arms for hostages and circumvent a law prohibiting US
support to rebels in Nicaragua; Iran-Contra was a clear case of the risks of allowing a small
group of committed White House advisors to run field operations without the line agencies'
normal rules, checks, and balances.[16] Many think that Brent Scowcroft in his role as George
H. W. Bush's national security advisor was crucial in guiding the Cold War to a peaceful end.
Certainly, he is admired for his ability to generate trust among colleagues and for his insist-
ence on following a deliberative process in making policy decisions.[17]

The president takes the hit when things go wrong. It is no wonder that the apparatus set up
to protect the president's policy interests keeps growing and that decisions affecting national
security move ever closer to the Oval Office. The NSC staff has ballooned from 50 in Ronald

Reagan's time to 200 in the George W. Bush era to about 400 under Barack Obama. The counsel to the president and the assistant to the president for economic policy regularly attend, and the attorney general, the secretary for homeland security, and the director of the Office of Management and Budget are frequently invited, too. There are now several deputy national security advisors. The vice president has his own security advisor and staff.

The complaints keep rolling in. Cabinet members worry that their jobs are being usurped by presidential assistants staffing the NSC. Certainly, cabinet officials, the secretary of defense among them, have to clear many of their decisions with the NSC staff. Subcabinet officials and cabinet members complain about the number and length of meetings, especially those called by NSC staff. Senior military officers grumble about how long it takes to get decisions out of the White House but also fear that decisions will not stick, because other parts of the sprawling NSC constantly initiate policy reviews. Critics fear that the strong political focus of the White House hinders the ability to recruit and train the right people for the NSC. And everyone fears that both crisis management and the day-to-day flood of information rushing into the NSC will drive out strategic thinking and long-range policy planning.[18]

It is ironic. The desire to be in control of the bureaucratic system that in the name of protecting American security seeks to control global security creates another bureaucratic layer, one that is itself difficult to control. But at the top of all the bureaucratic layers there is still only one person, the president. Many scholars study how presidents interact with the national security enterprise – how they select and use advisors, pick and manage their generals, and choose and implement policies – but they have discovered no laws.

Presidents react to opportunities

The problem is that each president has a unique personality and set of experiences. Some try to follow an ideology, "a coherent set of ideas, arguments, and conclusions from experience."[19] Others hope to make good decisions based on input from advisors or gut instinct, especially on issues that do not especially interest them and about which they have not thought very deeply. And events can change which advisors seem most relevant and which ones the president particularly trusts – or change the president's attentiveness or even worldview. Ultimately, different presidents' approaches to national security have important impacts, not because they implement detailed strategies but because their general ideas about how the world works influence the choices that they make.[20]

About the only thing that presidents have in common is that they are politicians, and very successful ones at that. They may act as though they are managing world events, but surely they know better. The politics that they know best are American domestic politics. They worry about reelection, their political party's support in the nation and Congress, and perhaps their legacy during their second term, if they have one. They are aware that their freedom of action internationally depends greatly on their popularity at home. And they know from their own political experience how unpredictable politics can be. Their success comes mostly from their reactions to unexpected events. Like a good fielder in baseball, a president needs opportunities to make a difference. His influence depends on how he deals with the few bad hops that come his way – the non-routine plays that make or break a team's chances for victory.

President Eisenhower and the Sputnik *satellite*

In the late 1950s, the United States and the Soviet Union seemed to be racing to build ballistic missiles. Both countries were also working on satellites for the International Geophysical

Year (IGY), a global scientific initiative. The Eisenhower administration was generally aware of the Soviet IGY effort but dismissed its likely impact on the missile race as unimportant. At the president's direction, the United States had kept the American IGY satellite program separate from its four parallel and highly classified ballistic missile development programs; the United States assigned the IGY task to the weakest of the several rocket development teams that were available. The launch of the Soviet satellite, *Sputnik 1*, on October 4, 1957, caught the administration by surprise, as did the domestic and international reaction to the Soviets' achievement. The press and the public took *Sputnik* as a clear indication of a Soviet lead in the missile race, a view that was significantly reinforced when the much bigger *Sputnik 2* went into orbit on November 3, followed by the failure of America's first launch attempt in a spectacular fireball on December 6.[21]

Eisenhower believed that the United States held the lead in the missile race, and said so publicly, but he was unwilling on security grounds to reveal the extent of the US military's progress in ballistic missiles or the Soviet Union's disadvantages, which were significant. Eisenhower's political critics were quick to brush aside his attempts at reassurance and blamed the administration's allegedly irresponsible and ideologically driven reluctance to expand government spending for a dangerous "gap" between Soviet and American strategic capabilities.

The president sought to regain his political footing by accepting claims that the United States was falling behind the Soviet Union in basic research. He appointed James Killian of MIT as his science advisor and promised to increase investments in science and engineering. These moves, though largely irrelevant to the problem at hand, were enthusiastically received by academic researchers, who believed that they deserved an independent voice at the highest levels of government and that the government never invested enough money in their work. The budget for the National Science Foundation, which until then had been a barely visible presence on America's campuses, surged. Soon, reorganizations established the National Aeronautics and Space Administration (NASA) and the Defense Advance Research Projects Agency (DARPA) and added a few billion dollars to the preexisting federal allocations for space and defense research. The argument was that the renewal of science in America would win the missile race with the Soviets. *Time* magazine picked American scientists collectively as the "Man of the Year" for 1960. The article said they would save the Republic.

In one sense, this sudden reverence for science was nonsense. Investments in science at best take decades to pay off. If America lagged behind the Soviet Union in missiles, science funding could not save it. But America was not behind. As the Kennedy administration would later acknowledge, the American lead was large and expanding.

In another sense – the one that counts – President Eisenhower chose a very effective strategy. For a few billion dollars, he co-opted scientists whom the public trusted as an authority on security issues, and he avoided unneeded and much larger investments in space and defense. The Democrats narrowly won the 1960 election, largely because of some uncontested voting fraud by the political machine of Chicago's Mayor Richard Daley and the apparently intentional distortion by John F. Kennedy of the actual state of the missile competition with the Soviet Union.[22] Sometimes campaigns are like that.

President Reagan and the Strategic Defense Initiative

The ballistic missile issue did not go away. The Soviet Union accelerated its deployment of ballistic missiles in the early 1970s. Toward the end of the decade, the Committee on the Present Danger and other Republican-oriented groups began to talk about a "Window of Vulnerability," the potential that the growing number of Soviet missiles could fire a disarming first strike at American land-based missiles. Few questioned why the Soviets would want to launch a nuclear war to disarm the US land-based missiles, given the existence of the fleet of American ballistic missile submarines, which would surely survive to destroy the Soviet Union in retaliation. Nevertheless, the Republicans brought the issue forward and argued for a compensating buildup of US forces. America's unpreparedness became a major feature of the 1980 presidential campaign. The Iranian hostage crisis and failed rescue attempt reinforced the nuclear fears, supposedly showing the decline of American military power during the 1970s at the hands of President Jimmy Carter and the Democratic Congress.

Ronald Reagan won the presidency and with him came the "Reagan buildup," a significant increase in defense spending intended to repair the damage of the so-called "decade of neglect." The buildup included a plan to renew US strategic forces by reviving the B-1 bomber program, purchasing Trident submarines with highly accurate D-5 ballistic missiles, and deploying the land-based MX Inter-Continental Ballistic Missiles (ICBMs). The program intentionally omitted an increase in spending for ballistic missile defense (BMD), though the president and many of his supporters were on record as favoring BMD. The controversial Anti-Ballistic Missile Treaty of 1972 had limited such defenses to a single complex, and in 1975 the United States had decommissioned its North Dakota site unilaterally. Reagan's political advisors rejected a BMD initiative because of its highly controversial nature and because the military could not point to any significant technical progress in missile defense research, despite a few billion dollars a year of investment.

The Reagan buildup, especially its strategic weapons component, drew determined opposition from arms control advocates. Instead of challenging specific projects as they had in the past, this time the arms controllers sought to limit all US nuclear weapons programs. They established the Nuclear Freeze Movement to find public support for their idea. In the spring of 1982, the Freeze began to gain traction through referenda declaring nuclear-free zones, often at the local level even though no mayors had control over nuclear arsenals. In June, the movement held a large rally in New York City that supposedly drew a million attendees. At the same time, the Catholic Bishops' Conference was drafting a statement drawing on the Just War tradition that would declare the mere possession, not just the use, of nuclear weapons to be immoral. Such an action was particularly troubling to the administration because Catholics made up a third of the population, and several key members of the administration were prominent Catholic laymen.

Real trouble for the administration started in the fall, when the Senate began to consider deployment schemes for the MX missiles. Analysts were certain that the MX missiles would be key targets for a Soviet first strike, if one were to be attempted, so the Senate debated several basing schemes to deal with that possible threat. One would have placed the missiles on mobile carriers that would try to confuse attackers by moving around a network of protective shelters. Another would have placed the missiles on rail cars that would constantly move. And a third, called appropriately if disparagingly "Dense Pack," would have jammed a number of MXs tightly together, most likely causing attacking missiles to get in each other's way during a Soviet strike. In the end, no plan satisfied, and the Senate rejected funding for the MX, the first time Congress had ever refused to support a strategic nuclear weapons program. This outcome was not quite what the Nuclear Freeze called for, but it was a big step, and one that caused great alarm in Reagan's National Security Council. Members feared that this defeat would mark the end not only of the strategic weapons modernization plan but also of the entire Reagan buildup.[23]

The Deputy National Security Advisor, Bud McFarlane, led the effort to counter this outcome by reviving the missile defense program. If the Democrats rejected offense, then the administration would promote defense. There had been no technical breakthrough. On the contrary, a routine although secret review of missile defense technology conducted by the administration's science advisors found the same old obstacles to effective missile defense: detection, tracking, targeting, and non-nuclear destruction. Nevertheless, the McFarlane team quietly prepared the way for an announcement of a program to develop and build defenses. The secretary of defense and other key officials were not informed of President Reagan's plan to announce a Strategic Defense Initiative (SDI) until just before its insertion in a March 23, 1983, televised speech on the defense budget. As one of its supporters, Admiral James Watkins, the Chief of Naval Operations, would later say in defense of SDI, "Isn't it better to save lives rather than avenge them?"

Not everyone agreed. Many Democrats immediately attacked SDI as wasteful and dangerous. Others wanted it banned because it might undermine the doctrine of mutual assured destruction (MAD), the prevailing view that Admiral Watkins attacked. Senator Ted Kennedy attempted to ridicule SDI by calling it "Star Wars" after the popular science fiction movie. Although academic specialists, many self-designated, joined in the ridicule of missile defense, the public seemed to love the idea of defending America from missile attack. In fact, many members of the public believed that effective defenses already existed.

Advocates never told a coherent story in support of SDI. SDI was just research; no, it was to be deployed – and soon. It was to be nuclear, non-nuclear, and anti-nuclear. The United States would share the technology with the Soviets, but we would never give up an advantage in missile defense. The program would be cheap, but it also had to be bought no matter the expense. And some saw SDI as a boon for space technology. Most important, though, its advocates were passionate, making SDI a key part of the Republican creed. There was religious fervor on both sides.

Meanwhile, the services seemed to hide from it, preferring offense to defense and fearing that SDI would take a big share of their acquisition budgets. For their part, the Soviets tended to treat missile defense as a reality, apparently having more faith in the prowess of American technology than did most American academics. Books and conferences poured forth, exploring the soul and soundness of SDI.

The administration, as some advocates noticed, did not actually seem to be particularly interested in acquiring missile defenses. Its leaders gave many speeches promoting SDI, but they took little action to establish a viable program or allocate significant resources. The budget for missile defense increased not much more than did the overall defense budget. It was a priority only in rhetoric. By keeping SDI in the news, however, the Reagan administration took attention away from its strategic systems renewal efforts. It managed to acquire most of what it had sought in terms of offensive forces: Trident submarines with D-5 missiles, more secure communications, improved warning systems, and even 50 MXs, which replaced older Minuteman ICBMs in existing silos. If its purpose was to defend the Reagan buildup, SDI was very successful. Getting the programs the administration really wanted took precedence over getting missile defense.[24]

President Bush, Iraq, and WMD

Sometimes, apparently successful responses to trouble lead to even worse trouble. The George W. Bush administration got off to a bad start. The disputed 2000 election soured relations with the Democrat-controlled Senate, which led to delays in confirmation hearings for some defense officials. President Bush seemed to mishandle an early crisis with China that erupted when a Chinese fighter collided in mid-air with a sophisticated US surveillance aircraft and did enough damage to force the US airplane to land on a Chinese-controlled island. Secretary of Defense Donald Rumsfeld – despite being a former congressman, a White House chief of staff, and on his second tour as secretary of defense – somehow managed to alienate many of the senior military officers and most of the key Republican leaders in Congress. Then al Qaeda struck the World Trade Center in New York City and the Pentagon in Washington, DC, on 9/11. Initially stunned, the Bush administration regrouped and rallied the nation behind what it came to call the Global War on Terror. The war in Afghanistan to kill or capture al Qaeda members and oust the Taliban from power began almost immediately, but it was clear that the Bush administration had a wider war in mind, one that would include deposing Saddam Hussein and confronting the deeper causes of Islamic radicalization.[25]

The case for the attack on Iraq was publicly built narrowly around the issue of weapons of mass destruction, in part because the reasoning seemed so convincing, given Iraq's clear past use of chemical weapons and its refusal to allow full inspections of possible nuclear weapons research sites, but also because the WMD case was the only one that might gain United Nations approval, a requirement for persuading several allies, particularly the British, who were crucial for US domestic support, to join an American-led military operation. International opposition to an attack was surprisingly strong, but domestic support held. Some may have been misled by confusing half-claims that Saddam had 9/11 ties, but the administration's defenders said that they only believed that the 9/11 surprise attack demonstrated how terrible it would be if an unreliable and despotic leader such as Saddam had nuclear weapons, perhaps reason enough to go to war. In March 2003, US forces invaded Iraq, heading for Baghdad to overthrow Saddam and his Ba'athist regime. Victory was quick.

And it unraveled almost as fast. The Iraqi people refused to accept a government led by the exiles that the administration had assembled. Looting and the collapse of civil order swept away feelings of liberation. Iraq's infrastructure was devastated by years of wars, sanctions, corruption, and ineptitude. The administration's plans to draw down US forces rapidly fell victim to the chaos caused by a growing insurgency. Both local Iraqis and foreign fighters answering al Qaeda's call resisted the American occupation. No WMD were found, not even a warehouse or two full of chemical shells, which nearly every intelligence agency around the world had believed existed. Saddam had been bluffing, more concerned about deterring his neighbors than about warding off a potential US counter-proliferation attack.

Using 9/11 to gain the initiative domestically and in the Middle East was a bold gamble that carried the Bush administration through the 2004 presidential election but no further. Al Qaeda survived the initial onslaught. The call for reform and democracy did not quickly sweep through Islam or Middle Eastern governments. And failure to find WMD gave the appearance that the administration had lied to get into a long, bloody war with no benefits.

The war cost the Republicans the political initiative that had carried them to power, and it undercut the post-Vietnam feeling that the Republicans were the capable party on foreign policy issues. They lost control of Congress in 2006. The war also strained America's relationships with its allies, and it exhausted the All-Volunteer Force, which had seemed so well suited to the post-Cold War security environment.

Presidents try to turn unexpected events into national security policy advantages. They do not always succeed. The 9/11 attacks gave the Bush administration an opportunity for redemption. Security fears were high and malleable. However, what was a good recovery soon became a disaster and a burden – or maybe an opportunity for the next president.

President Obama and the expanded Afghan surge

President Obama almost mishandled the gift from his predecessor. As a candidate, Barack Obama condemned the war in Iraq, arguing that America's interest lay in victory in

Figure 10.2 Secretary of State Colin Powell briefs the UN Security Council on evidence of
WMD in Iraq. He showed a small vial that, had it contained dry anthrax, would
have been enough to wreak havoc, just like Saddam could have wreaked havoc, if
he had had dry anthrax and a means to deliver it

Source: UN Photo/Mark Garten. Reproduced with permission.

Afghanistan. George W. Bush, he claimed, neglected a war of necessity in Afghanistan to
pursue one of choice in Iraq. By the time President Obama took office, troops were leaving
Iraq, and the first wave of reinforcements was heading toward Afghanistan on orders from
George W. Bush. Obama soon replaced commanders in Afghanistan and sought a review
of options there. Military leaders and Secretary of Defense Robert Gates vigorously pushed
a plan that called for a significant surge of US troops and a sustained effort to enhance

the capabilities and sway of the Afghan government. The idea was to defeat the Taliban, eliminate al Qaeda footholds, and stabilize Afghanistan, as close to victory as Afghanistan would seemingly permit. They based their recommendations in part on the experience of the surge in Iraq, which had seemed to work (at least at the time; ISIS did not unravel Iraq until several years later). General Stanley McChrystal, who had led Joint Special Operations Command and was associated with important parts of the apparent Iraq success, would lead the Afghanistan surge. Obama appeared to be getting what he wished.[26]

But then came Obama's bad hop: the plan did not work as expected. American and coalition casualties, already on the rise as Obama took office, skyrocketed as the surge forces pursued the Taliban. The Afghan government made little progress in eliminating corruption. The US military wanted more resources committed on a longer-term basis. There was grumbling everywhere about Obama's mishandling of the war.

General McChrystal, the field commander in Afghanistan who was persistently asking for troop increases, became embroiled in a scandal and resigned when his staff insulted civilian leaders to the press. General David Petraeus, another hero of the Iraq surge and proponent of the same policy for Afghanistan, replaced McChrystal, but he did not seem able to make progress in the grinding fight against the Taliban either.

Fortune brightened for the administration when the long manhunt for Osama bin Laden paid off in a spectacular raid in Pakistan that killed al Qaeda's leader. The administration also increased the use of drone strikes in Pakistan and elsewhere, which eliminated most of the other senior figures in al Qaeda. Americans were briefly proud, but mainly they stopped following news of the war.

President Obama's surge is little remembered, and few people paid much attention to the debate over the size of the detachment of American forces to leave behind after the main withdrawal of combat troops.[27] National security debates turned to new events. ISIS took control of large swaths of Syria and Iraq, and terrorists attacked in Europe and the United States in 2015. The president's Afghanistan policies actually may have had only limited effect on his legacy. Many debates that seem extremely consequential at the time, even on US strategy in war, turn out not to matter so much in the public's overall evaluation of a presidency.

The politics of national security policy-making

The politics that often count the most in setting US national security policy are domestic politics. Elections loom large in most policy discussions because individual politicians and parties seek to gain advantage with voters by shaping public perception of the issues. Crises have to be addressed, and they offer opportunities to make a political reputation, but crises can destroy reputations, too. The nation's geographic separation from other major powers, its huge economy, and large population protect the United States against bad security policies chosen for good domestic reasons and allow most Americans to forget about national security, at least most of the time. Mostly, politics is about seeing opportunities to further one's interests and attempting to grab those opportunities when you can. Sometimes it works, and sometimes it doesn't.

Questions for discussion

1   If power is centralized in the White House, why would anyone want to be secretary of defense or secretary of state?

2   **Given the high stakes, why would a president want to emphasize political trustworthiness rather than national security expertise in choosing staffers for the NSC?**

3   **Can a coherent ideology help a president make national security decisions? What about a carefully thought out national security strategy?**

4   **Would the discovery of warehouses full of WMD in Iraq after the US invasion have made President Bush a hero?**

5   **Which hampers effective US national security policy more, the decentralization of having so many voices involved in congressional defense politics or the centralization of having so much decision-making power concentrated with the president?**

Notes

 1 Seth Lipsky, *The Citizen's Constitution: An Annotated Guide* (New York: Basic Books, 2009). p. 134.
 2 Robert M. Chesney, "Disaggregating Deference: The Judicial Power and Executive Treaty Interpretations," *Iowa Law Review*, 92 (2007): 1,723–1,782; Robert M. Chesney, "National Security Fact Deference," *Virginia Law Review*, 95(6) (2009).
 3 James Q. Wilson, *Bureaucracy: What Government Agencies Do and Why They Do It* (New York: Basic Books, 1989), p. 133.
 4 John Sides and Jake Haselswerdt, "Campaigns and Elections," in Adam Berinsky (ed.), *New Directions in Public Opinion* (New York: Routledge, 2011), pp. 241–257.
 5 Charles S. Clark, "Must Presidential Transitions End with Sabotaged White House Keyboards?" *Government Executive*, February 19, 2016.
 6 Kurt M. Campbell and James B. Steinberg, *Difficult Transitions: Foreign Policy Troubles at the Outset of Presidential Power* (Washington, DC: Brookings Institution, 2008).
 7 Seyom Brown, *The Illusion of Control* (Washington, DC: Brookings Institution, 2006).
 8 William C. Banks and Jeffrey D. Straussman, "A New Imperial Presidency? Insights from U.S. Involvement in Bosnia," *Political Science Quarterly*, 114(2) (Summer 1999): 195–217.
 9 Ivo H. Daalder and I. M. Destler, *In the Shadow of the Oval Office* (New York: Simon & Schuster, 2011), pp. 4–5.
10 Daalder and Destler, *In the Shadow of the Oval Office*.
11 Bruce Auerswald, "The Evolution of the NSC Process," in Roger Z. George and Harvey Rishkof (eds.), *The National Security Enterprise: Navigating the Labyrinth* (Washington DC: Georgetown University Press, 2011), p. 32.
12 Daalder and Destler, *In the Shadow of the Oval Office*, pp. 8–10.
13 Auerswald, "The Evolution of the NSC Process," p. 35.
14 Karen DeYoung, "How the Obama White House Runs Foreign Policy," *Washington Post*, August 4, 2015.
15 Derek Chollet, "What's Wrong with Obama's National Security Council?" *Defense One*, April 26, 2016.
16 Theodore Draper, *A Very Thin Line: The Iran-Contra Affairs* (New York: Hill & Wang, 1991). Good description, analysis, and many documents about the scandal are available at: *Understanding the Iran-Contra Affairs*, https://www.brown.edu/Research/Understanding_the_Iran_Contra_Affair/index.php (accessed September 2, 2016).
17 Bartholomew Sparrow, *The Strategist: Brent Scowcroft and the Call of National Security* (New York: Public Affairs, 2014).
18 Shawn Brimley, Julianne Smith, Jacob Stokes, and Dafan H. Rand, *Enabling Decision: Shaping the National Security Council for the Next President* (Washington DC: Center for a New American Security, 2015).
19 Francis Fukuyama, *America at the Crossroads: Democracy, Power, and the Neoconservative Legacy* (New Haven, CT: Yale University Press, 2006), p. 13.
20 Elizabeth N. Saunders, "Transformative Choices: Leaders and the Origins of Intervention Strategy," *International Security*, 34(2) (Fall 2009), pp. 119–161.

21 Robert A. Divine, *The Sputnik Challenge* (New York: Oxford University Press, 1993).
22 Christopher A. Preble, *John F. Kennedy and the Missile Gap* (DeKalb, IL: Northern Illinois University Press, 2004).
23 Daniel Wirls, *Buildup: The Politics of Defense in the Reagan Era* (Ithaca, NY: Cornell University Press, 1992), pp. 133–168.
24 Frances Fitzgerald, *Way Out There in the Blue* (New York: Simon & Schuster, 2000); Donald S. Baucom, *The Origins of SDI, 1944–1983* (Lawrence, KS: University of Kansas Press, 1992); Robert C. McFarlane with Zofia Smardz, *Special Trust* (New York: Cadell and Davies, 1994).
25 James Mann, *The Rise of the Vulcans: The History of Bush's War Cabinet* (New York: Viking, 2004).
26 Peter Baker, "How Obama Came to Plan for 'Surge' in Afghanistan," *New York Times*, December 5, 2009.
27 Greg Jaffe and Missy Ryan, "The U.S. Was Supposed to Leave Afghanistan by 2017. Now It Might Take Decades," *Washington Post*, January 26, 2016.

Recommended additional reading

Ivo Daalder and I. M. Destler, *In the Shadow of the Oval Office* (New York: Simon & Schuster, 2009). Insightful profiles of the National Security Advisors and the issues they dealt with, from John F. Kennedy to George W. Bush.

Robert Divine, *The Sputnik Challenge* (New York: Oxford University Press, 1993). The dramatic story of Eisenhower diverting attention while keeping his eye on the ball during a crucial moment in the very serious competition for global dominance between the United States and the Soviet Union.

Roger Z. George and Harvey Rishikof (eds.), *The National Security Enterprise: Navigating the Labyrinth* (Washington DC: Georgetown University Press, 2011). Excellent collection of essays on the major institutions, with most especially good ones on the interagency process, NSC, and the State Department.

Frank P. Harvey, *Explaining the Iraq War: Counterfactual Theory, Logic, and Evidence* (Cambridge: Cambridge University Press, 2012). Makes the case that the Iraq War would have happened even if Al Gore had won the 2000 election. Presents a list of all the steps that took the US to war and names all the Democrats who helped us climb them.

John Mueller, *War, Presidents, and Public Opinion* (New York: Wiley, 1973). An astute observer gives the numbers from Korea and Vietnam a close look.

David Rothkopf, *Running the World: The Inside Story of the National Security Council and the Architects of American Power* (New York: Public Affairs, 2005). You are right. Power does go to their head. And yes, they often don't know what they are doing.

11 Gaining intelligence

Intelligence accounts for approximately 10 percent of America's security effort.[1] Approximately is the correct modifier because intelligence is, of course, mostly a secret enterprise. The government only started releasing an official budget for the "Intelligence Community" in 2007, and it still does not release many details about the allocations to particular programs or activities within this total. The release indicates that it excludes some intelligence activities, but even so, the official numbers are huge, with $66.8 billion appropriated in 2015, down from a peak of $80.1 billion in 2010. Most of that reduction came in the part of the budget that supports the military's tactical operations, which scaled back as major combat operations stopped in Iraq but is sure to rise again through the ups and downs of US interventions. The annual budget for the National Intelligence Program, which accounts for most but not all activities other than tactical military intelligence, has held fairly steady around $50 billion after its substantial increases in the 2000s.[2]

Bouncing back from substantial cuts in the 1990s that followed the end of the Cold War, the Intelligence Community found new missions and popular support with the Global War on Terror. Most people assume that the future, with its terabytes of digital data and its complex, multifaceted threats, will be more intelligence-intensive than the past. Intelligence – gathering, interpreting, and transmitting information to fielded forces and policy-makers – is clearly a very big part of American national security.

It wasn't always so. On becoming secretary of state in the late 1920s, Henry Stimson closed down the "Black Chamber" joint code-breaking effort of the State and War Departments, famously proclaiming, "gentlemen do not open other gentlemen's mail."[3] But as with many other things in American defense policy, World War II changed intelligence. When Stimson was the secretary of war during World War II, breaking German and Japanese codes was crucial in the Allies' success, as were various other clandestine and covert operations. Just six months after the disastrous attack on Pearl Harbor, the US Navy reversed the tide in the Pacific at the Battle of Midway, thanks to its breaking of the Japanese naval codes.[4] And the Allies won the Battle of the Atlantic, the struggle to supply the European allies and to transport American forces past German submarines, in large part due to intelligence efforts, including breaking the Enigma code and monitoring German radio traffic.[5] The Office of Strategic Services (OSS), a civilian agency and the predecessor of the Central Intelligence Agency, conducted American clandestine operations during World War II.

The National Security Act of 1947 established the CIA as the government's main gatherer and analyzer of intelligence, openly and secretly obtained, and gave its director (the DCI, or Director of Central Intelligence) broad responsibility for coordinating the intelligence operations of other agencies, both civilian and military. Today, the IC comprises 17 agencies and directly employs more than 200,000 people, but the DCI does not run it anymore. Reformers

Figure 11.1 Sometimes people estimate facilities' level of effort by counting cars in the parking lot. NSA Headquarters has a lot

Source: National Security Agency.

blamed the failure to detect the 9/11 plot on insufficient coordination in the IC.[6] Perhaps the DCI was too distracted by the need to manage his own large organization or was too parochial and couldn't encourage real blending of insight across the many agencies. So they created a new, dedicated executive, the Director of National Intelligence (DNI), to "connect the dots" and advise the president. The head of the CIA became the D/CIA, and the title DCI no longer exists.

But even after that reorganization, the IC remains at best a loose coalition of agencies. The history shows both the continuing interest in centralization and the ever-present ability of different agencies, each promoting its own interest, to maintain some control of their own intelligence assets. The result seems at times to combine the worst pathologies of decentralization (expensive redundancy and inability for top policy-makers to control the activities of field agents many bureaucratic layers below) with those of centralization (groupthink that squelches creativity, prevalence of least-common-denominator reporting, and politicization rather than independent assessment). We can always hope, though, that a marketplace of ideas, of contending perspectives among the agencies, will protect against strategic surprises while providing enough tailored collection and analysis to support the operational needs of America's great range of military forces and other government agencies. Thankfully, if we don't hold the exaggerated expectation of perfect foresight, we might recognize that the Intelligence Community quietly succeeds in most of its work, despite its flaws. And if we recognize the eternal verities of American politics, we might notice that no other system is likely to work better.

Managing the information flow within the Intelligence Community is only one of the great challenges of intelligence. Even perfect intelligence analysis is not useful if it does not try to address the topics that interest its consumers. On the other hand, there is the ever-present fear of making intelligence products too easy for politicians to consume: "politicization" sometimes tells leaders what they want to hear rather than what they need to know, and the Intelligence Community needs checks and balances to prevent it. Holding a large, and largely secret, bureaucracy to account, both for the quality of its product and for the methods used to gain information, is a real challenge.

In addition to deciding the right balance between political and expert influence, we also have to decide on the correct balance between the public and the private in intelligence. As with the rest of the defense effort, more and more intelligence work is contracted out. Tens of thousands of contractors design, build, and operate various surveillance systems, translate and interpret data gathered through intelligence activities, and even interrogate prisoners, handle agents in the field, and fire weapons as part of covert actions.[7] Privatization may provide unique expertise and surge capacity, but it may come with economic costs and challenges to public accountability.

In the end, there is no satisfaction. There are continuous worries about how intelligence is gathered and used. You can never know enough, and there are persistent concerns about the political and moral costs of gathering and acting upon the knowledge that you do gain. Intelligence presents many of the same trade-offs as other areas of defense policy: calls to coordinate and centralize are politically popular, but efforts to implement them often don't turn out as promised, and impose some significant costs along the way.

It takes a community

There are several types of intelligence. Human intelligence, or HUMINT in the argot of the business, refers to information gained through personal contacts, ranging from diplomatic meetings to the high-stakes exploits of spies. Signals intelligence, or SIGINT, simply refers to the interception of signals, either communications between people (COMINT) or the electromagnetic radiations (ELINT) that an enemy's systems may give off, for example radars for surface-to-air missiles. Image intelligence, or IMINT, gathers information through images, which can be obtained via many means, though satellites and especially unmanned aerial vehicles are the headline-grabbers. GEOINT refers to geospatial intelligence, that is, information about the physical features of the Earth. It often includes IMINT, and has become a much more powerful tool in recent years. And MASINT represents measurement and signature information on militarily relevant targets, such as the distinctive sounds made by a particular submarine. There are lots of variations within these types and much overlap among them. Intelligence organizations are formed to gather a particular type or to assemble and interpret the information from them all for a particular customer.

The CIA has the broadest interest and jurisdiction of the intelligence agencies, with three core missions: producing all-source assessments, led by the Directorate of Analysis (DA), which used to be called the Directorate of Intelligence (DI); collecting HUMINT, led by the Directorate of Operations (DO);[8] and shaping the international security environment with covert operations, an activity that did not get its own directorate but that is supported by a smaller group, the Special Activities Center.[9] A third major subunit, the Science and Technology (S&T) Directorate, develops and acquires specialized systems to support the agency's core missions. The contemporary era's ubiquitous emphasis on technology might have increased the S&T Directorate's importance, but strangely it did not. In 2015, as part of a major CIA reorganization, D/CIA John Brennan created the first new CIA directorate in more than 50 years, the Directorate of Digital Innovation, a very public attempt to signal the CIA's continuing relevance in the cyber age. He did not explain what the S&T Directorate will do in the future. Presumably it will develop and acquire whatever non-digital systems the CIA needs.[10]

In fact, because of the media obsession with all things digital, the key change in Brennan's "Blueprint for the Future" got much less emphasis in major newspapers. Without eliminating the DO and the DA, Brennan apparently took them out of the day-to-day business of the CIA. The CIA's organization now mirrors the military's Unified Command Plan, with analysts and operators working together in six regional and four functional mission centers; the directorates of the future may be akin to the military services, responsible for recruiting, training, and acquiring equipment, but not for operations. This reorganization might improve some aspects of intelligence, putting analysts closer to agents, letting analysts target HUMINT collection efforts toward the most likely targets, encouraging agents to answer the most pressing questions, and giving analysts more insight into the reliability of particular sources. On the other hand, it might create a new kind of parochialism, in which analysts shade their product to favor sources from within their mission center – if the mission centers actually breed close ties among former DO and DA employees, who perform quite different tasks and have developed expertise in quite different tradecraft.[11]

More important, though, D/CIA Brennan's quest to eliminate "seams" between organizations is impossible: even if he can end the divide between the DO and the DA (desirable or not), the CIA will now have seams between the mission centers instead. Does a particular activity belong in a functional center for counterterrorism or in the regional center for Africa? Or does a source who moves around in the globalized world belong to the Near East or to South Asia? And can the CIA adjust the boundaries or replace an outmoded functional center with a newly emerging area of emphasis, or will these new organizations inhibit the agency's flexibility to adapt?[12]

Of course, the rest of the IC is also full of "seams," starting with the chasm between the CIA and the Defense Department. Defense manages its intelligence operations through an undersecretary for intelligence and operates several agencies that have Intelligence Community-wide responsibilities. The National Security Agency, which was formed in 1952, does a lot of listening globally, and has code-making and code-breaking responsibilities. The National Reconnaissance Office (NRO) was created in 1960 to develop satellites and reconnaissance aircraft; it is famous for internal competition, historically among its divisions that separately served the Air Force, the Navy, and the CIA. The Defense Intelligence Agency (DIA) was established in 1961, does analysis for the secretary of defense, and runs the Defense Clandestine Service. Finally, the National Geospatial-Intelligence Agency (NGA) was formed in 1996 and gathers information from a variety of sources to build detailed terrain maps for consumers throughout the US government. Each had predecessor organizations and thus is an amalgamation of one kind or another, and all have ended up with a quirky mission or two as a result. For example, the DIA holds responsibility for gathering information on medical facilities globally in case US forces deployed in a particular region need them.

Although these DoD agencies support fielded forces as well as the rest of government, each of the services has its own intelligence organization as well, mostly for operational needs. The intelligence relevant to military tactical decision-making is usually quite different from that relevant to political decision-making at the national level. For example, the Office of Naval Intelligence (ONI) catalogs the capabilities of foreign navies and monitors anti-ship weapons developments globally. During the Cold War, the ONI worked closely with several elements of the fleet to locate and track Soviet submarines. With one agency for each of the services, including the Coast Guard, plus the four central agencies (NSA, NRO, DIA, and

NGA), the DoD lays claim to 9 of the 17 components of the Intelligence Community and likely the bulk of its combined budget.

The rest of the Intelligence Community comprises the intelligence arms of other federal departments. The State Department works closely with the CIA but has its own intelligence unit, the Office of Intelligence and Research, which performs analysis and helps monitor treaty compliance, among other things. The Treasury's intelligence unit worries mainly about money flows, including efforts to intercept terrorist financing and enforce sanctions and export controls that might limit nuclear proliferation. Energy's is concerned primarily with nuclear weapons security and the technical side of proliferation. And the one at Homeland Security tries to prevent terrorism and smuggling into the United States. The Department of Justice also has two members of the Intelligence Community: the FBI, which is responsible for domestic counter-intelligence and for global counterterrorism investigations, and the Drug Enforcement Administration (DEA), which tracks narcotics networks globally.

The final member of the IC is its new, independent coordinator, the Office of the Director of National Intelligence. Freed from the supposedly crippling parochialism that comes with attachment to a single organization, the DNI is designated as the president's point person for all-source analysis. The DNI is to make sure that the president can "connect the dots" by understanding what different parts of the Intelligence Community are doing and where their judgments differ, but the DNI's staff, though growing fast, is not supposed to collect its own data or produce independent analyses; instead it tasks other agencies and integrates their products.

Although the DNI has authority by law, in practice his power has been limited, and there were five DNIs in the first five years the office existed. The DNI has tangled not only with the CIA, from whom it took the IC's leadership, but also with the Pentagon. Donald Rumsfeld created the post of undersecretary of defense for intelligence partly in reaction to the creation of the DNI – to ensure that the DoD would not become dependent on other agencies for important intelligence assessments and that the DoD would have a strong voice in presenting its view of intelligence issues to the president. The CIA, too, maintains great independence from the DNI. Its ever-growing operational role in chasing terrorists ensures as much.

In short, efforts to centralize and coordinate the Intelligence Community have not ended the organizational rivalries inherent to a fragmented and decentralized system.[13] In fact, one could argue that some of these rivalries are productive. Stovepipes and firewalls can hinder coordination, sometimes with fatal consequences, and those must be eased where possible. But there are multiple intelligence agencies for a reason. Much like the military services, they can seem redundant to the naked eye, yet their different identities, histories, and specializations also lead them to assess the world differently and prescribe different solutions, which can be beneficial. What the FBI ignores, the CIA may notice; what the civilian agencies may miss, the military ones may detect. Competition among the different organizations can stimulate better analysis and result in more options for the president – an especially important output in a policy area plagued by surprises. It is important that the president hear the different options, of course, which is part of what the DNI is supposed to ensure.

Pathologies and problems

Some of the fault lines in the Intelligence Community are obvious. Civilian agencies fear domination by the military, which is always richer and usually more disciplined, comparatively speaking. The military hierarchy within DoD clashes with the more intellectual and academic debating style of the civilian intelligence agencies. And civilians dislike the imperial expectations of senior officers, who are used to numerous and deferential assistants. In turn, the military worries that civilian agencies will be unresponsive to operational needs, favoring instead the analytical side and their role in top-level Washington policy-making. One of the main flashpoints in this bureaucratic rivalry is the allocation of scarce national assets such as satellites and surveillance ships, whose priorities are often set in discussions that take place far from military commanders operating in the field.

There are also some long-term organizational clashes within the civilian parts of the Intelligence Community, the one between the CIA and the FBI being the most prominent. The FBI's jurisdiction is broad, while that of the CIA explicitly excludes any domestic operations. But spying and counter-spying activities intentionally ignore borders, so conflicts between the two organizations cannot be avoided. The key division between the organizations, though, comes from their different missions: the CIA's critical task is to provide information that decision-makers need, often gathered by sources and methods that can never be made public, while the FBI's critical task is to gather evidence for judicial prosecutions, where the evidence will be subject to cross-examination and public discussion. Each organization has been known to take some pleasure in the failures of the other. The 9/11 problems between them were neither their first nor last.

The Intelligence Community is often accused of bias toward technical means of information gathering.[14] The success of the NRO in producing extraordinary aircraft and whole families of very capable reconnaissance and early warning satellites has set the pace for American intelligence. Segments of the aerospace industry are quite dependent on the support of the NRO and are its strong advocates.[15] Naval intelligence likewise achieved some storied results through technical means, for example using special submarines to tap Soviet phone lines, and technical means play an important role in counter-narcotics operations such as the successful hunt for Colombian drug kingpin Pablo Escobar in the early 1990s.[16] But the resources required to maintain the lead in technical capabilities tend to put pressure on the funding of other, perhaps less glamorous intelligence programs, and many people suggest that technical means are inherently less effective against insurgencies and terrorist threats.

Technical bias may explain the alleged weakness of American HUMINT and the apparent inability of the Intelligence Community to protect the nation's secrets. It is impossible, of course, for those outside the Intelligence Community to have a deep understanding of America's HUMINT capabilities. They are, after all, secret undertakings. We do know from the resulting criminal trials, however, that essentially every major US intelligence organization has been penetrated at one time or another by Soviet, Chinese, Cuban, and even Israeli spies. Some of the cases are staggering in their scope. During the Cold War, the Walker family handed the Soviet Union the keys to the US Navy's most classified communications for nearly two decades before they were caught. A high-ranking CIA official, Aldrich Ames, revealed to the Soviet Union the names and reports of US agents inside the Soviet government; the Soviets executed some of those American agents. And Robert Hanssen, who held key counter-intelligence positions at the FBI, also happened to work for years as a spy for the Soviet Union. The Soviets gained US atomic secrets and information on the best spy satellites, the Cubans discovered the inner workings of US policy toward them, and the Chinese and Israelis found access to some of America's most classified technologies.

It is not that the United States completely failed to pay attention to counter-intelligence: James Jesus Angleton held the job as the CIA's head of counter-intelligence for decades, and he so vigorously pursued a "mole hunt" looking for Soviet agents that he may actually have weakened the agency by making everyone inside distrust everyone else. He clearly bent or broke the rules in his zealotry.[17] But despite Angleton's power, the Intelligence Community's priorities were usually elsewhere. It is hard to make a strong case for the internal surveillance necessary to guard secrets in the libertarian-leaning United States. So some level of foreign penetration is likely just a cost of America's openness. In a democracy, some information is going to leak, and some misbehavior is going to go unnoticed or unpunished for long periods of time.

America's adversaries often fail to return the favor. It is harder to penetrate their closed societies and organizations. Reliance on technology is a logical response, especially given American culture's fascination with technology and the natural political support from contractors that build the expensive, high-tech intelligence systems. Americans tend to photograph, data mine, and cable tap wherever possible. Some of America's greatest intelligence successes over the years have stemmed from technical rather than human sources, though sometimes luck was involved, too. In a complex and secret operation, the United States partially salvaged a Soviet submarine, complete with code books and nuclear weapons, that had sunk in an accident in the Pacific.[18] And Osama bin Laden was found in large part by connecting many dots acquired through technical means.[19] So perhaps resources and organizational culture create a tension between HUMINT and technical intelligence or have even led to relative neglect of the former, but the United States actually has something positive to show for its choices – some real successes.

The Intelligence Community faces other trade-offs, including the classic dilemma of how to handle the relationship with political leaders. Politicization, which is the distortion of intelligence to fit a political agenda, is one of the most perplexing problems in intelligence. Intelligence purveyors want the pride of professionals, meaning that they want to be recognized (and even deferred to) for their expertise. The professional ideal for intelligence is to offer objective analysis of the threats facing the nation. But intelligence purveyors also want access to the nation's foreign policy and security decision-makers and to have an influential role in government, which requires being useful to those decision-makers.

Most simply, the quest for political relevance requires the Intelligence Community to offer insight into questions that policy-makers actually face, meaning that policy rather than some objective fact shapes what the decision-makers pay attention to. Furthermore, intelligence is rarely clear in its rawest state, especially since the picture of an adversary or the projection of a "likely" future event is inherently incomplete. In practice, the Intelligence Community integrates various pieces of partial and not fully verified information, and in the end it offers judgment calls about interpretation. The need for judgment is precisely what makes intelligence a profession rather than a simple technical skill or trade, but with judgment comes the opportunity for manipulation in order to fit political agendas.

In a competition for relevance among intelligence professionals – or in a collusive deal among intelligence professionals on what to report as the "key judgment" of the Intelligence Community – the president's known preferences might just creep into the "objective" reports. In fact, they almost have to, otherwise the president might simply ignore the reporting entirely for lack of interest.[20]

The challenge is similar to one of the problems in defense acquisition discussed in chapter 7: monopsony power. Many different government organizations need specific kinds of intelligence to do their jobs, and that diversity of demand rewards a variety of different perspectives for tactical and operational intelligence. But there is really only one "buyer" for strategic assessments and input to top-level US foreign policy, so all of the producers have an incentive to seek relevance by catering to that buyer's desires. That they do not always do so is a testament to the power of professional norms, including explicit discussion of the need to sometimes "speak truth to power," and to the strength of organizational culture in the separate agencies of the IC. Each agency's distinct way of seeing the world undercuts its analysts' ability to reach the same judgment as its competitors, even if the analysts find some clues that a particular judgment might be favorably received.

Presidents also understand the risks of politicized intelligence, and on many issues they have little desire to shape the analysis, But sometimes they will try to use intelligence to gain public support for their policy choices. If the evidence for their positions is weak, ambiguous, or hard to confirm, they may want the intelligence officials to imply it is strong, clear, and fully vetted. These officials may find it difficult to resist the presidential pressure, fearing not only the loss of personal influence or career advancement but also that their organization's place in the bureaucratic hierarchy may be jeopardized otherwise.

The intelligence blunders surrounding Saddam Hussein's supposed possession of weapons of mass destruction provide a useful illustration of these dynamics in practice. In the run-up to the Iraq invasion, the George W. Bush administration needed crucial allies, most especially the United Kingdom, to endorse the operation in order to build support for the war with the US public. But those allies needed the United Nations' endorsement of the invasion for their own domestic support. UN endorsement could be obtained only on grounds that Iraq had violated sanctions by acquiring WMD.[21] Thus, much came to depend upon very ambiguous intelligence on Iraq's nuclear, chemical, and biological weapons stocks. Conveniently, George Tenet, CIA director at the time, called the evidence "a slam dunk;" Secretary of State Colin Powell presented the intelligence case to the UN Security Council with conviction. Although the Security Council did not sanction the invasion, the willingness of the CIA and other intelligence agencies both in the US and in Europe to buttress the Bush administration claims about Iraq's WMD program greased the way to war.

The failure to find such weapons after the invasion helped erode public support for the war and accelerated the call for Intelligence Community reforms, specifically the creation of the aforementioned Office of the Director of National Intelligence. The DNI was to provide the coordination for the Intelligence Community that the CIA director had supposedly been unable to do. But a lack of coordination was not the problem leading up to the Iraq War. In fact, it would seem there was a lot of coordination to fit the administration's need for a consistent intelligence position that Iraq had chemical and biological weapons and was attempting to develop nuclear ones.

The problem was politicization. Joshua Rovner, who has studied politicization in the Iraq WMD case and several others, believes that the problem lies in using intelligence in political debates. He advocates adherence to the norm of secrecy – basically, avoiding the invocation of intelligence to make public arguments – to lessen the use of intelligence estimates for partisan advantage. But he ultimately holds out little hope that the temptation of politicization can be resisted.[22]

Intelligence in the Global War on Terror

Intelligence has been central to the war against terrorism, and so have been the controversies caused by intelligence-gathering operations. Early on, the CIA set up a global network of secret prisons and used what are described as enhanced interrogation techniques (a euphemism for torture, according to some) to extract information about possible follow-on attacks to 9/11 and the composition of al Qaeda and affiliated terrorist groups. It also transferred captives back to their home countries for interrogation, including sending some to destinations where torture is said to be common. The military created a prison for what were called "enemy combatants" at the US naval facility at Guantánamo Bay in Cuba, intentionally avoiding both the jurisdiction of US courts and the full legal protections afforded prisoners of war. Pictures of hooded, manacled captives in orange jumpsuits at Guantánamo and of mistreatment at the Abu Ghraib prison in Iraq inflamed critics at home and abroad, who called America's actions in the wake of 9/11 "human rights abuses."

The question, of course, is how to deal with combatants in an undeclared war with a non-state actor. Candidate Barack Obama pledged to close Guantánamo and return to the practice of treating terrorism as criminal rather than military behavior, even when terrorists target US military forces abroad. But President Obama's administration struggled to fulfill those promises: it's hard to find a good place to send alleged terrorists, especially those who can add years at Guantánamo to their list of grievances. Through great diplomatic effort, many detainees were sent home or discharged to third countries that committed to monitoring and humane treatment. But strong Republican-led opposition prevented the transfer of the last few to a US prison and made it difficult to hold criminal trials for them. For years, Obama's policy on Guantánamo looked remarkably like that of President George W. Bush, even as the number of detained enemy combatants dwindled.[23]

Perhaps even more ironically, the Obama administration has championed drone attacks, the CIA's use of armed UAVs to track and kill members of al Qaeda and its affiliates, especially in Pakistan, Somalia, and Yemen. These attacks handle potential threats without taking any prisoners, removing the challenge of deciding whether to send captives to Guantánamo or elsewhere. Of course, the drone strikes offer no potential for interrogation or to confirm that the target is "the right guy," but those are classic targeting problems in war. And as in past wars with imperfect intelligence and target discrimination, drone strikes also sometimes kill and wound civilians. The program is essentially one of aerial assassinations, tightly held within the administration, and has limited congressional oversight. It has been used to kill American citizens, starting with Anwar al-Awlaki and his son in Yemen.[24] Drones were used in Libya, too, and likely patrol elsewhere.

"Signature strikes" are the most controversial: missiles are fired at military-aged males in hostile regions who are acting suspiciously but who have not been specifically identified or linked to a particular terrorist plot or militant attack. It is easy to imagine that these strikes would have a higher rate of errors and would be more likely to kill bystanders, actually setting back the American effort to counter extremist rhetoric. Even though President Obama announced in a May 2013 speech that he planned to scale back drone strikes, especially signature strikes, and to shift command of many drone operations from the CIA to the military, the strikes continue, including CIA signature strikes.[25] It is especially hard to estimate "collateral damage" from signature strikes due to the government's practice of automatically labeling all military-aged males killed in certain regions of the world "militants." Well, foreign males, at least: it turns out that the United States was willing to admit a male death as collateral damage in a signature strike in April 2015, when it announced that an American aid worker held hostage in Pakistan had been killed in a drone strike. Or maybe the key factor was that he was 70 years old.[26] In the big picture, though, the alternatives to drone strikes are either sending conventional military forces, an expensive and dangerous effort fraught with its own political challenges, or scaling back the fight against far-away militants, anathema to many Americans.

In general, the last decade's wars have blurred the lines between the Intelligence Community and the military, with each playing an increasingly active role in areas once dominated by the other.[27] CIA paramilitary capabilities have grown, enabling it to conduct operations on a much greater scale than was true in the past. Perhaps such expansion was inevitable after the agency's forces became much more integrated into military operations in

Figure 11.2 Someone's Reaper UAV on watch somewhere
Source: US Air Force photo/Lt. Col. Leslie Pratt.

Iraq and Afghanistan. CIA operators were lauded as the leaders of the counter-attack against al Qaeda after 9/11, though some of them were actually US soldiers detailed to agency teams; the collaboration in the war on terror started very quickly.[28] Later, much of the work of counterinsurgency involved the identification and elimination of insurgent networks, a long-standing CIA specialty. Night raids became coordinated military and CIA operations to capture or kill insurgent leaders, exploit any intelligence gained on site, and use it to fuel the next round of action. Thousands of such raids were undertaken, resulting in increasingly close ties between civilian and military agencies whose missions once seemed distinct.

Meanwhile, just as the CIA has acquired its own weapons and operational capabilities, the military has grown more ambitious with respect to espionage. The DIA is now planning to build much larger spying networks overseas, comparable to those of the CIA: reports anticipate growth from roughly 500 operatives in 2012 to more than 1,000 by 2018, and eventually to 1,600 worldwide.[29] Instead of simply providing targeting information to battlefield commanders, the DIA now seeks to generate strategic and political intelligence on emerging threats more akin to what its civilian counterpart has long provided.

Perhaps nothing better symbolizes this increasing overlap between the two communities than recent high-ranking personnel assignments. During the first Obama administration a former combatant commander (General David Petraeus) was tapped to head the CIA, while the former CIA director (Leon Panetta) took up the top post in the Pentagon. Similarly, while DIA directors are three-star military intelligence flag officers, a career CIA officer, David Shedd, became acting director in 2014, moved at the end of his career into the military intelligence leadership, though *his* successor, General Vincent Stewart, had a more traditional career, rising through the military intelligence ranks to be the first Marine Corps director of the DIA.

But it is more than overlap. The seeds of future rivalry are being planted. The struggle against terrorism has, as Mark Mazzetti put it,[30] driven the Department of Defense to build its own CIA in the form of an undersecretary for intelligence and an enhanced DIA, and it has likewise driven the CIA to acquire its own army via contractors, expanded paramilitary forces, and close work with Special Operations Forces.

The wars in Iraq and Afghanistan and the Global War on Terror have brought other changes to intelligence as well, some in the form of new tools. Biometric identifiers are among the most controversial. Soldiers scan the irises of local military-age males encountered during raids and patrols, creating a database for identifying suspected terrorists. They also collect DNA samples to provide positive identification of captured or killed terrorist leaders. Before the raid that killed bin Laden, US agents created a fake public health campaign to collect DNA samples that would increase their confidence that bin Laden was actually hiding in that particular safe house in Pakistan. Critics fear that the widespread collection of biometric information offends honest citizens or that the databases might be shared with unsavory local governments that could use the information against their own people. Others point out that a connection between the CIA and a fake public health campaign may undermine locals' confidence in real public health efforts; distrust of the West is already a real problem for vaccination and disease surveillance efforts around the world.[31]

And of course the new technical methods like biometrics mainly supplement rather than replace the old ones, at least in time of war when the Intelligence Community is flush with resources. The US Intelligence Community still collects emails and records of financial transfers and intercepts and records phone calls all around the world. Shortly after 9/11, Section 215 of the Patriot Act allowed the FBI "to acquire records that a business has in its possession, as part of an FBI investigation, when those records are relevant to the investigation."[32] The government broadened the definition of "relevant" so far that it collected metadata on essentially all US phone calls and emails, because when you are data mining, training your system on "normal" interactions helps make the aberrant ones, the terrorist communications, stick out better. And the National Security Agency did the collection, not the FBI, operating under a broad grant of court authority at least on the borderline of a Constitutionally prohibited "general warrant" rather than under the oversight of a warrant specific to a particular case.[33] This overreach, conducted in secret for more than a decade, was one of Edward Snowden's key revelations when he gave thousands of stolen NSA documents to reporters. The leak may not have spurred the wide public discussion that Snowden claims he hoped for, but it eventually led to the 2015 passage of the USA Freedom Act, which imposed substantial restrictions on the bulk metadata collection program, among other constraints on the Intelligence Community.

Post-9/11, the jurisdictional and organizational barriers to exchanging information seem to have fallen away. Counterterrorism command centers, many newly built, are connected and staffed with representatives from throughout the Intelligence Community to facilitate collaboration and the sharing of information. But one vulnerability replaces another. The desire to be able to connect all the dots let Private Bradley Manning (now known as Chelsea Manning) have access to hundreds of thousands of classified reports, most unconnected to his job in Iraq – reports that the lowly intelligence soldier apparently downloaded and made public through Wikileaks. So now there are new layers of restriction on sharing data and new programs to monitor government employees, to ferret out leakers, and to block access to certain websites (including, naturally, Wikileaks, which is blocked for government employees, whether to upload material or simply read what has already been posted there). Similarly, the government has learned that trying to free up opportunities for information exchange has also opened opportunities for the spread of computer viruses and other "malware," and that, too, has bred new restrictions. Those who once rejoiced in the ever-improving networks used by the US military later found themselves ordered to fill all their USB ports with hot glue.

Private spies

The sudden need for a much larger intelligence effort after 9/11 involved a lot of outsourcing, with both positive and negative results. It was not the first time that the Intelligence Community had turned to the private sector for help – one of the corporate legends taught to employees at Booz Allen Hamilton is that Booz consultants helped track German U-boats early in World War II – but contractors' use in the war on terror significantly expanded in scale and scope.[34] As that happened, there was little public discussion of the appropriate balance between public and private activity in intelligence. The subsequent experience led to vigorous debate.

Government hiring is not nimble. To ensure that all applicants get fair consideration, the process involves many layers of red tape that slow it down. The government also generally hires only for entry-level positions, at least for staff jobs if not for its executives, partly as a way to protect the seniority privileges built into its Civil Service rules. And before the 9/11 attacks, the Intelligence Community had been shrinking, scaling back from its Cold War size, though in significant part by reducing hiring and waiting for people to retire rather than by firing no-longer-needed employees who had dedicated their careers to studying the now-defunct Soviet Union. It is hard to adjust the expertise of your workforce when you cannot shed older talent and your new applicant pool only contains a handful of people truly dedicated to public service or to the perceived excitement of a life in the clandestine world.

Hiring contractors was the answer. When Congress rapidly expanded the intelligence budget after 9/11, the fastest way to get employees was to offer contracts to services specialists such as Booz Allen Hamilton, SAIC, or Computer Sciences Corporation and to defense firms such as Lockheed Martin and Raytheon. Those firms knew their way around the government procurement regulations, and they could draw from the pool of intelligence workers who had left the government in the 1990s, had training in analysis procedures and collection tradecraft, and were ready to start working on the terrorism problem with sophistication beyond the entry level. Some reports suggested that in the mid-2000s as many as 50 percent of the people in the National Clandestine Service (a temporary name change for the CIA's Directorate of Operations) were contractors. Across the Intelligence Community, contractors were recruiting spies, controlling case officers, manning watch centers, and acting as regional desk officers, among other core functions.[35] Even though contractors are prohibited from performing "inherently governmental" work, the DNI's 2006 *Strategic Human Capital Plan* acknowledged that contractors performed "borderline 'inherently governmental'" tasks.[36]

Many contractor jobs were less exciting or less controversial. The IC may have spent 70 percent of its budget on contracts, but that figure includes a lot of systems contracting, such as the NRO buying intelligence satellites.[37] Even within services contracting, a lot of the money goes for routine installation and maintenance of IT systems – along with routine services such as lawn mowing, trash collection, and building maintenance.[38] The difficulty comes in two official categories that are subsets of the "commercial activities" that the government is formally allowed to privatize: functions that are "closely associated with inherently governmental" and "critical functions," meaning those that are "necessary to the agency being able to effectively perform and maintain control of its mission and operations."[39] How should we categorize case officers, collection managers, and other high-level operators – the kind of personnel that Booz Allen Hamilton, for example, specialized in providing?[40] While it is not illegal to contract out for those key functions, it may not be advisable, if you have a choice.

Besides the speed at which they can be brought on board, contractors have another advantage: they are temporary. When the government directly hires a civilian, the civilian is often signing on for a long career. This arrangement allows the government to train the person and inculcate him or her with agency culture and professional ethics, but it does not allow the government much leeway to deal with a short-term crisis. The contractors, on the other hand, build the risk that their working stint will be short into their contract price: contractors charge more than an equivalently skilled government employee for the years that they are working, in part because contractors expect some unemployment while looking for a new job when the contract ends.

When the contractors in question are former government employees, who "grew up" with the government's training and professionalization but had left the government for reasons other than to work as a contractor, contracting is a great solution.[41] Over time, though, government employees start to resent that contractors working with them, side-by-side, are paid more. The government workers realize that they can earn the higher, contractor wages, doing the same work that they are currently doing, simply by quitting the government, going to work for a private company, and getting hired back into their old job with a new badge. Especially when it seems as if the increased demand for intelligence is going to be sustained, the revolving door is very attractive – and threatens to bust the Intelligence Community budget. And of course critics of privatization also suggest that a revolving door at the executive level helps firms garner expensive contracts in the Intelligence Community the same way that they suspect that the revolving door is a key link in the broader military-industrial complex.

The government might also demand services for which there is not a ready pool of people in the private sector, waiting for a contract. On 9/11, there were analysts and operators who had left the Intelligence Community who could come back on contract. There were even Russian linguists. But the demand was for Arab linguists, Pashto linguists, and skilled interrogators who could handle the sudden flood of intercepts, captured documents, and prisoners and turn them into meaningful data for the analysts to work into intelligence products. The contractors ended up hiring modestly qualified people, sometimes with incomplete vetting, "often straight out of college and trained at corporate headquarters."[42] Later, CIA Director Leon Panetta and Secretary of Defense Robert Gates both openly worried about these contractors' loyalty to their paycheck rather than to the national interest.[43]

In principle, a well-written contract could provide clear conduct standards, but in practice, many hurriedly written contracts did not. Contract interrogators became the sad model. Before 9/11, the government had only a small number of people in the IC with expertise in questioning hostile agents – and no expertise at all in enhanced interrogation techniques. It initially got help from Air Force officers who worked to develop training designed to help captured American soldiers resist enemy interrogation, but at some point those psychologists left the Air Force and started their own company. They set the standards, involving very harsh treatment including waterboarding, and in the end, contractors performed 85 percent of all interrogations as part of the CIA's covert program.[44] One contract interrogator working for the CIA went to prison in 2003 when a prisoner in Afghanistan whom he had struck with a flashlight later died in his cell, but that kind of accountability for the contractors, who used more force than military or civilian government employees, was otherwise limited. The CIA stopped using contract interrogators in 2009, and the DoD stopped in 2010.[45] It turns out that politicians and the public think interrogation should be inherently governmental after all – even though the first phase of enhanced interrogation took place while the Air Force psychologists were still government employees. No matter who they work for, some people go too far, especially in a war.

Being intelligent about intelligence

We are always being surprised. Sometimes it is a surprise attack. Sometimes it is a surprising enemy capability. Sometimes it is a surprising failure on the part of an ally. Sometimes it is a surprise consequence of victory. We were surprised by the 1998 attack on our embassies in Africa, by the 9/11 attacks, by the refusal of the Turkish government to allow US forces to invade Iraq through Turkey, by the use of IEDs against our forces there and in Afghanistan, by the intensity of the civil war in Iraq, by the Arab Spring that toppled some of America's friends but also some of its enemies, by the brutal civil war in Syria and the rise of ISIS there and in Iraq, and by ISIS' decision to launch attacks in European capitals. Intelligence depends on information and judgment, and rarely is either perfect.

It is not surprising, then, that much of the academic literature on intelligence is about its pathologies, its limits, its failures. Enemies try to deceive us and hide their plans. We are never sure whether to believe our own eyes or our own spies. The outline of pending disaster may be buried in the noise, a flood of contradictory pieces of information. Agencies seeking influence may shape their interpretations to fit the policy preferences of leaders. Reforms are still offered, usually plaintive calls for more coordination and greater centralization.[46]

It would seem that less coordination and more decentralization is the more appropriate policy prescription in a world where your opponent seeks to catch you by surprise, at least for strategic-level assessments. More independent judgments rather than fewer seem wise. The US Army uses red teams to test for faults in operational plans.[47] In the Intelligence Community, multiple agencies sifting the same and different evidence are red teams for one another. In the end it is left to the judgment of the person whom President George W. Bush called "the Decider," the Commander-in-Chief, which is also why we have periodic, competitive elections for that office.

Questions for discussion

1   **How much should the Intelligence Community coordinate? Did the 2004 reforms go too far, or not far enough?**

2   **How are the challenges involved in organizing the Intelligence Community similar to or different from those that affect defense organization (i.e., the question of jointness)?**

3   **How do we assess whether the Intelligence Community is working well or not? Are some failures inevitable?**

4   **What are the constraints on the president's ability to make big decisions based on differing interpretations of intelligence? Can the president make those decisions without politicizing intelligence?**

5   **How has the relationship between the Intelligence Community and the Department of Defense evolved since 9/11? Do you think the changes are likely to be permanent?**

Notes

1 Richard K. Betts, *Enemies of Intelligence: Knowledge and Power in American National Security* (New York: Columbia University Press, 2007), p. 186.

2 "U.S. Intelligence Community Budget," *Office of the Director of National Intelligence*, available at: https://www.dni.gov/index.php/resources/intelligence-community-budget (accessed September 2, 2016). For example, domestic counterterrorism efforts don't count in the intelligence budget: Dana Priest and William M. Arkin, "A Hidden World, Growing Beyond Control," *Washington Post*, July 19, 2010.

3 William E. Odom, *Fixing Intelligence for a More Secure America* (New Haven, CT: Yale University Press, 2003), p. 29; see also p. xii.

4 Paul Stillwell, "The Lead Code-Breaker of Midway," *Proceedings of the US Naval Institute* (June 2012): 62–65.

5 W. J. R. Gardner, *Decoding History: The Battle of the Atlantic and Ultra* (Annapolis, MD: US Naval Institute Press, 1999).

6 *The 9/11 Commission Report: Final Report of the National Commission on Terrorist Attacks upon the United States* (New York: Norton, 2004).

7 Dana Priest and William M. Arkin, "National Security, Inc.," *Washington Post*, July 20, 2010.

8 The DO was renamed the "National Clandestine Service" from 2005 to 2015. Stories about WMD provided by a key HUMINT source, code-named Curveball, influenced the decision to launch the 2003 Iraq War, but the stories turned out to be fabrications designed by an Iraqi with a stake in encouraging the United States to depose Saddam Hussein. To try to protect the United States against such manipulation in the future, President George W. Bush sought to improve HUMINT tradecraft across the Intelligence Community by raising the profile of that part of CIA. Whether the effort succeeded or not, the new name was never popular at the CIA, and D/CIA John Brennan changed the name back. Of course, nothing substantive changed about the CIA's official role managing HUMINT.

9 Stephen Slick, "Measuring Change at the CIA," *Foreign Policy.com*, May 4, 2016.

10 Guy Taylor, "CIA Goes Live with New Cyber Directorate, Massive Internal Reorganization," *The Washington Times*, October 1, 2015.

11 Slick, "Measuring Change."

12 Paul R. Pillar, "The CIA and the Cult of Reorganization," *National Interest Online*, March 10, 2015.

13 See Odom, *Fixing Intelligence for a More Secure America*, for military complaints about the CIA.

14 R. A. Ratcliff, *Delusions of Intelligence: Enigma, Ultra, and the End of Secure Ciphers* (New York: Cambridge University Press, 2006), pp. 233–236.

15 In 1996, the NRO was caught with a $4 billion unreported reserve fund, some of which it used to build a lavish headquarters: Craig Eisendrath, *National Insecurity: U.S. Intelligence after the Cold War* (Philadelphia, PA: Temple University Press, 1999), p. 82.

16 See: Sherry Sontag and Christopher Drew, *Blind Man's Bluff: The Untold Story of America's Submarine Espionage* (New York: HarperCollins, 1998); Mark Bowden, *Killing Pablo: The Hunt for the World's Greatest Outlaw* (New York: Atlantic Monthly Press, 2001).

17 David Robarge, "'Cunning Passages, Contrived Corridors': Wandering in the Angletonian Wilderness," *Studies in Intelligence*, 53(4) (December 2009): 49–61.

18 Norman Polmar and Michael White, *Project Azorian: The CIA and the Raising of K-29* (Annapolis, MD: US Naval Institute Press, 2010).

19 Mark Mazzetti, *The Way of the Knife: The CIA, a Secret Army, and a War at the Ends of the Earth* (New York: Penguin, 2013).

20 Betts, *Enemies of Intelligence*, Chapter 4.

21 William Shawcross, *Allies: The U.S., Britain, Europe, and the War in Iraq* (New York: Public Affairs, 2004).

22 Joshua Rovner, *Fixing the Facts: National Security and the Politics of Intelligence* (Ithaca, NY: Cornell University Press, 2011).

23 Robert M. Chesney, "The Least Worst Venue," *Foreign Policy.com*, January 21, 2011; Spencer Ackerman, "Two Dozen Guantánamo Detainees Poised for Release under Obama Deals," *The Guardian*, May 23, 2016.

24 Charles G. Kels, "Mixed Messages on Targeted Killing," *Armed Forces Journal* (July/August 2012): 10–16, 32. Micah Zenko and Emma Welch, "Where the Drones Are," *Foreign Policy*, May 29, 2012, available at: http://www.foreignpolicy.com/articles/2012/05/29/where_the_drones_are/ (accessed September 2, 2016).

25 Paul D. Shinkman, "Obama, CIA Cornered into Troubling 'Signature Strikes,'" *US News and World Report*, June 18, 2015.

26 David Rohde, "What the United States Owes Warren Weinstein," *The Atlantic*, April 28, 2015.
27 Mazzetti, *The Way of the Knife*.
28 Thomas Gibbons-Neff, "After 13 Years, CIA Honors Green Beret Killed on Secret Afghanistan Mission," *Washington Post*, April 17, 2016.
29 Greg Miller, "DIA Sending Hundreds More Spies Overseas," *Washington Post*, December 1, 2012.
30 Mazzetti, *The Way of the Knife*.
31 David Sterman, "Pakistan's Health Workers under Attack," *Foreign Policy.com*, July 16, 2013.
32 Privacy and Civil Liberties Oversight Board, *Report on the Telephone and Records Program Conducted under Section 215 of the USA PATRIOT Act and on the Operations of the Foreign Intelligence Surveillance Court* (Washington, DC: January 23, 2014).
33 Laura K. Donohue, "Bulk Metadata Collection: Statutory and Constitutional Considerations," *Harvard Journal of Law and Public Policy*, 37(3) (2014): 759–900.
34 Drake Bennett, "Booz Allen, the World's Most Profitable Spy Organization" *Bloomberg Businessweek*, June 21, 2013.
35 R. J. Hillhouse, "Who Runs the CIA? Outsiders for Hire," *Washington Post*, July 8, 2007.
36 L. Elaine Halchin, *The Intelligence Community and Its Use of Contractors: Congressional Oversight Issues* (Washington, DC: Congressional Research Service, August 18, 2015), p. 15.
37 Halchin, *The Intelligence Community*, p. 1. The NRO might spend as much as 95 percent of its budget on contracts.
38 Bennett, "Booz Allen."
39 US Office of Federal Procurement Policy, "Policy Letter 11-01, Performance of Inherently Governmental and Critical Functions," Office of Management and Budget, September 12, 2011, p. 56,236.
40 Bennett, "Booz Allen."
41 Hillhouse, "Who Runs the CIA?"
42 Priest and Arkin, "A Hidden World."
43 Priest and Arkin, "National Security, Inc."
44 Joseph Tanfani and W. J. Hennigan, "Two Psychologists' Role in CIA Torture Program Comes into Focus," *Los Angeles Times*, December 14, 2014.
45 Hunter Stuart, "How We Outsourced Torture and Why It Matters," *Huffington Post*, December 16, 2014.
46 Dennis C. Blair, "Unfinished Business," *The American Interest* (Spring 2012): 70–79.
47 Micah Zenko, *Red Team: How to Succeed by Thinking Like the Enemy* (New York: Basic Books, 2015).

Recommended additional reading

Richard K. Betts, *Enemies of Intelligence: Knowledge and Power in American National Security* (New York: Columbia University Press, 2007). An intelligent assessment by one of the leading scholars on intelligence. Surprises cannot be avoided, so we should have modest expectations.

Robert Jervis, *Why Intelligence Fails: Lessons from the Iranian Revolution and the Iraq War* (Ithaca, NY: Cornell University Press, 2010). Insightful history, analysis, and comparison of two frequently cited intelligence failures by a leading international relations theorist and long-time Intelligence Community advisor.

William E. Odom, *Fixing Intelligence for a More Secure America* (New Haven, CT: Yale University Press, 2003). Analysis of the issues and structural problems from a senior military intelligence officer. Offers many suggestions for reforms that were subsequently adopted.

Jeffery T. Richelson, *The U.S. Intelligence Community* (Boulder, CO: Westview Press, 1999). A useful overview of the major players and their historical context.

Joshua Rovner, *Fixing the Facts: National Security and the Politics of Intelligence* (Ithaca, NY: Cornell University Press, 2011). Demand for transparency creates incentives for politicians to politicize intelligence.

12 Homeland security

America is a very secure nation. It is surrounded by two big oceans and two soft neighbors. It is rich and has a powerful, experienced military. The majority of its people believe in gun ownership and retribution. History demonstrates that there is no end to the violence it is capable of inflicting upon those who challenge its safety.

America is also a very vulnerable nation. It has dozens of big cities, hundreds of ports, and thousands of airfields. It has more than 20,000 miles of borders, and nearly 200,000 miles each of railroad track and natural gas pipeline. Each year, 12 million 20-foot containers, 12 million tractor-trailers, and nearly 50 million visitors cross its borders. There are more than 100 nuclear power plants, 450 50-plus-storey buildings, and 600,000 bridges to guard. The United States prides itself on being an open and free society. There is no national police or national identity card, and its 320 million-plus residents include millions of legal and illegal foreigners.

In this chapter, we examine the politics of America's attempt to provide homeland security, the defense of its people and borders. One would imagine that its 1.3 million-person armed forces, its million-person Reserve and National Guard, its tens and tens of thousands of border patrol and other federal agents, and its nearly 775,000 state and local police would provide sufficient protection, but apparently they do not. Instead, a mix of reorganization myths, organizational ambitions, expandable threats, and demagogic politicians assures Americans a continuing feeling of unease.

Recognizing threats to the homeland

The 9/11 attacks were the turning point in American discussions of homeland security. Before that day, experts knew not only that Osama bin Laden was plotting to attack the United States but also that his minions had carried out such attacks. He was a wanted man.[1]

He did not hide his intentions; instead, he made speeches declaring war on the United States and used jihadist websites to rally other extremists to his cause. Al Qaeda was not responsible for every spectacular anti-American bombing (e.g. most experts think that the Iranian-backed Saudi Hizballah perpetrated the 1996 attack on the Khobar Towers in Saudi Arabia that killed 19 American servicemen),[2] but bin Laden's followers attacked American embassies in Africa and a US Navy ship in port in Yemen, among other targets. Customs agents disrupted an al Qaeda plot to attack Los Angeles airport at the turn of the millennium, and the US military launched missile attacks against targets in Sudan and Afghanistan to retaliate against al Qaeda activities and to try to limit the terrorists' capabilities. We knew terrorists were after us before 9/11.

The CIA, FBI, and other agencies dutifully reported that they were working on the terrorist threat. The FBI even declared counterterrorism to be its number one priority in 1998.

National Security Council staffer Richard Clarke and some other government insiders focused hard on terrorism, and Clarke claims that then-CIA director George Tenet had his "hair on fire," a great image of his heightened level of concern. A series of major studies of the Intelligence Community, law enforcement agencies, and other organizations that we now associate with "homeland security" urged hundreds of reforms, major and minor, to improve America's defenses against terrorism.

But public concern about the terrorist threat only simmered until major attacks on American soil brought the issue home in every sense of the word. Remarkably few of the policy recommendations put forth by terrorism experts were adopted before 9/11.[3] Some probably faltered because they did not actually turn out to be good ideas when subjected to the checks and balances of the American policy-making process, but others were simply ignored because it is hard to make national security policy, especially in the United States, in the absence of a clear demonstration of a threat to the national interest. Spectacular events get attention, and 9/11 was indeed spectacular.

Before 9/11, few people had heard the phrase "homeland security."[4] Most people probably assumed, reasonably, that the Department of Defense had something to do with preventing attacks on the United States, but as the public discussion recognized a "new kind of war" – a hybrid between traditional war against foreign enemies and law enforcement against small groups of criminals that threaten social order – it also seemed reasonable to think about a new policy framework.

The crisis atmosphere that immediately followed the attacks persisted for a number of years. The next spectacular terrorist attack in the United States did not come until the 2013 Boston Marathon bombing, and even then it was a much smaller operation that killed and wounded many fewer people than 9/11. US Navy SEALs killed Osama bin Laden in 2012, but that great counterterrorism success did not have much impact on concerns about domestic security. The real and rhetorical links between terrorism and the wars in Afghanistan and Iraq perpetuated a policy discourse in which it was easier to propose and adopt policy initiatives than to analyze their results and calibrate the policy response.

The United States has adopted dozens of initiatives in the name of homeland security, some sensible and others less so. The terrorists used commercial aircraft as weapons on 9/11, and indeed extremists have shown a long-term fascination with aviation. So, one of the first reactions was to create a new federal agency, the Transportation Security Administration (TSA), to take over the job of screening passengers at airports and inspecting other parts of the US transportation infrastructure. Federal workers in police-style uniforms and operating various high-tech screening machines replaced private-sector contractors, mostly paid for by the airlines, because some people feared the private security screeners were not serious enough about their jobs. And although many experts (and some travelers) criticize the new screening techniques as more hassle than they are worth, stepped-up airline security might well make sense, given what we know about terrorists' habits.[5]

On the other hand, the argument that federal employees somehow perform airport checks more effectively than the private firms is weak: all screeners do a routine task, many aspects of which can be clearly described and monitored; private screeners can follow the same procedures as TSA employees and can be held to the same standards – as they are at a few airports, including San Francisco International.[6] The challenge is for any screener, no matter who pays him or her, to stay alert through a long, repetitive shift. In fact, in unannounced tests, the post-9/11 federal screeners perform at a similar level of effectiveness to pre-9/11 private screeners.[7] Even after years of effort to improve procedures, screeners routinely fail to find explosives and weapons that investigators try to bring through checkpoints in unannounced tests: for example, in 2015 reports surfaced that investigators got dangerous contraband past the TSA's government employees 67 out of 70 times.[8] The argument against privatization of airport security is a political one, not one based on operational analysis – not surprisingly, given how government makes defense policy.

Soon after the 2015 report on inspectors' ineffectiveness, the TSA ordered its employees to concentrate on finding contraband, no matter how long lines at security checkpoints got. Not surprisingly, lines became interminable: passengers were upset to find that they sometimes waited longer at the TSA checkpoint than they spent on the plane flying to their destination.[9] The inspectors' union, the American Federation of Government Employees, naturally seized on the "crisis" to blame its shrinking workforce (from 2011 to 2016, the number of screeners dropped from about 47,000 to about 42,000 even as the number of airline passengers increased) and to lambaste Congress for diverting funds from an airline ticket fee earmarked to fund the TSA to other national priorities.[10] Meanwhile, conservatives returned to their tried-and-true formula of calling for privatization to fix the delays.[11] And the TSA's head of security was fired.

All of this is the typical and predictable result of pressures for fast, visible crisis response in security policy-making. Spectacular events cause visible policy changes. Careful analysis and prioritization of various policy initiatives often do not. Few responses are efficient, trade-offs are often ignored, and policy entrepreneurs are tempted to leverage events to further preexisting agendas. Even so, not every new policy is a bad idea. The post-9/11 homeland security rubric cannot protect Americans against every threat, and the policy process has not carefully targeted its homeland security efforts. As it often does, the United States adopted a scattershot approach to policy change, trying a number of options to attack various aspects of the homeland security problem.

Box 12.1   The politics of protecting ports

Tens of thousands of standard-sized shipping containers enter American ports every day – filled with food, textiles, electronics, and every other imaginable product. Indeed, the inventions of the 20-foot container and inter-modal transport are some of the key technological underpinnings of the late twentieth-century surge in globalization. But now that dockworkers do not see all the cargo on its way into the United States, people naturally wonder if someone might slip something unpleasant across the border in a container. Could terrorists also smuggle in weapons?

Devious minds have explored many possibilities, but in one often-discussed nightmare scenario, terrorists would put a nuclear weapon in a container with a timer. The blast might harm huge numbers of people, since many container ports are near major American cities (including New York and Los Angeles). Of course, this assumes that, among other things, terrorists can get their hands on the nuclear materials, really want to use a nuclear bomb, can get their device to work properly, and can arrange to load their bomb into a shipping container. All of these steps are dubious.

People worry that the last task might be all too easy. Since 9/11, the US Customs and Border Protection Agency has worked with major port operators overseas to improve their security, especially with respect to containers bound for the United States. The idea is that as much of the security effort as possible should take place far from US ports – to keep the danger far from American shores. But working at a distance is more difficult and more expensive, and not every foreign port or shipper is eager to comply with American requests. The situation is even worse when you consider that container ships often stop in multiple ports on their way to their destination: you never know what's hidden on a ship, even if the last several ports on its itinerary were "secure," if it had previously stopped at an "insecure port."

Americans usually look for technological solutions, in this case radiation detectors and X-ray and gamma-ray scanners that inspectors can use to see what is inside containers without unpacking them. Companies are working hard on the container inspection problem (often at taxpayers' expense), but the machines are expensive, slow, cumbersome, and not as effective as anyone would like. As with fighter aircraft and other defense technologies, the government is asking for nearly miraculous innovations: it wants the scanners to be able to see all kinds of materials, regardless of what else is packed around them, and to differentiate even very low-level signatures. For example, nuclear bombs give off only a little bit of radioactivity, comparable to such innocuous substances as kitty litter.

Neither the technical problems nor the sovereignty issue has done much to stop politicians calling for a major expansion of container security regulations and investments. Of course, they have been reluctant to pay for a major initiative, and they have been sensitive to lobbying from the shipping industry and from importers, who fear the tremendous inefficiency that the political proposals would impose. Sometimes politicians benefit from making a lot of noise about a problem whether or not they can realistically solve it. In the summer of 2007, Congress passed legislation mandating a five-year transition to 100 percent screening. Just before the deadline in June 2012, Secretary of Homeland Security Janet Napolitano notified Congress that she would trigger a clause in the law allowing a two-year extension to the phase-in. Not surprisingly, the DHS missed the 2014 deadline, too, triggering another two-year extension. Meanwhile, congressional representatives still routinely call for 100 percent scanning: grandstanding doesn't cost them much of anything, even though experts, shipping interests, and the agency charged with executing the inspection task all say that it is impossible.[12]

"Don't just stand there, reorganize!"

Americans do not accept that some problems have no solution. When a crisis hits, American politicians are expected to have answers. After the 9/11 attacks, the government launched several investigations of their cause and of policy options intended to prevent similar attacks in the future. The most prominent such study was the bipartisan 9/11 Commission, according to which the basic failure in the lead-up to 9/11 was that no one "connected the dots."[13] Many in several agencies knew bits and pieces of the plot, but this knowledge stayed fragmented because of legal blockages, lack of a feeling of urgency, and various jurisdictional disputes. In other words, the people on those planes and where they crashed were victim of both al Qaeda and the normal life of bureaucracies. To the Bush administration, perhaps due to its own culpabilities, doing nothing seemed an acceptable response to the Commission's findings and recommendations, but to the Commission members and some of the politically organized families of 9/11 victims, action seemed imperative. They wanted solutions, something to make certain that this type of tragedy would never happen again – likely an impossibility. In parallel to the reorganization of the Intelligence Community described in Chapter 11, they pushed for centralization of the effort to defend the homeland.

Senator Joseph Lieberman sought to use homeland security as a springboard to propel his candidacy for the Democratic nomination in the 2004 presidential election. He led Congress' push to create a Department of Homeland Security (DHS), eventually an amalgamation of 22 agencies, numerous programs (not all of which are related to security), and a collection of very confused officials. The Bush administration initially resisted the expansion of the cabinet, which it argued would lead to more bureaucracy, bloated budgets, and congressional interference. The administration's idea was to appoint a special presidential advisor for homeland security issues who would guide national policy, relying on the president's authority to drive implementation – along the lines of other presidential advisors such as the national security advisor. But critics attacked the advisory office because it lacked budgetary and enforcement authority, forcing the administration's hand. In June 2002, the president proposed the new department, and Congress enacted a slight modification of that proposal.[14] By the January 2004 State of the Union address, President Bush was ready to lavish praise on the department (and critics still decried even the cabinet-level department as insufficiently robust).[15]

Forming this new department gave a strange result: it brought together the Coast Guard, the Secret Service, the Border Patrol, and the Federal Emergency Management Agency, among others, but it left out the FBI, which is the agency that coordinates the response to domestic attacks; the National Guard, which has equipment and personnel dispersed around the country to deal with emergencies; the CIA, which tracks terrorists overseas; the Centers for Disease Control (CDC), which worries about biological attacks and epidemics; and the Federal Aviation Administration (FAA) and the North American Air Defense Command (NORAD), which manage and protect national airspace. Homeland Security watches the borders and ports but not the skies. It protects against nuclear weapons, as long as they are not delivered on ballistic missiles.

Box 12.2   Bigger than the Pentagon: the Department of Homeland Security's new home

The managers of departments built by agglomeration are tormented by the desire to achieve unity, a common corporate identity for all of their component organizations. In the case of the Department of Homeland Security, some of its predecessors were well-known, relatively powerful entities on their own, such as the Coast Guard, the Secret Service, and the US Border Patrol. Trying to corral them into a single, integrated effort to protect the US homeland is not only a challenge at the planning level but costs a lot of money.

When the DHS was established, it was given a home for its own headquarters elements at a former Navy radar facility in Northwest Washington, DC, that was too small to accommodate anything else besides the headquarters. Many of the component agencies had their own headquarters scattered around Washington, some freestanding, others located in their previous home department's facilities. Soon the search began for a consolidated DHS headquarters, a search that ended up at the largely abandoned Southeast Washington site of St. Elizabeth's Hospital, formerly the national insane asylum. The DHS hopes to save money, improve morale, and enhance efficiency by moving to the large site on a commanding hill across the Potomac from Reagan National Airport.

As befits an expanding bureaucracy with the job of safeguarding America, plans call for the headquarters to exceed the Pentagon in total space by nearly a million square feet, although DHS' space is spread across several buildings in a campus-like setting rather than consolidated in one big building. There will be common purchasing and asset sharing but mostly an opportunity to meet around the same DHS flag pole or, better yet, command center. With costs spiraling, in 2016, the DHS proposed an "Enhanced Plan" for the new headquarters site that would cut the construction bill from $4.5 billion to $3.7 billion while promising to speed completion to 2021 compared to the old scheduled completion in 2026.[16] That's still a lot of money, even with the optimistic re-baselining of the costs, and the bill does not count the $2.6 billion to create a departmental communications network linking the campus and its agencies' widely dispersed field facilities.

The costs are high not just because of big ambitions but also because of the St. Elizabeth's site. It is a national heritage location due to its insane asylum history, and it happens to house a Civil War-era cemetery as well. The DHS promises to rehabilitate 52 of the hospital's 70 buildings, and it is the largest General Services Administration project ever.

Moving the project along requires promises to many other stakeholders – expensive and time-consuming efforts to buy off resistance to getting things done. That means spending hundreds of millions more on highway connector lanes and ramps, parking garages, and a new surface light rail line to accommodate the 12,000–14,000 employees coming to the site each day. But that kind of transit commitment threatens the environment, so to placate environmental groups, the project also seeks to surpass the latest environmental and energy-use standards, including putting plants on the roofs of the buildings, because "green roofs" are a "sustainable design best practice." Of course, those standards layered yet another requirement onto the complex undertaking. And finally, making the project politically acceptable requires compensating the poor, largely African-American neighboring community, which for decades has endured the 9-foot walled-off presence of the hospital but soon will have to live with the super-heightened security appropriate for the new National Homeland Security Operations Center and the new headquarters of the Coast Guard, US Immigration and Customs Enforcement, the Federal Emergency Management Agency, and the Border Patrol.

Despite the complexity and high costs, the project is slowly making progress. The Coast Guard moved its headquarters to St. Elizabeth's in 2013, and some of the site infrastructure improvement is done. But Congress chronically underfunded the overall project, appropriating no money for it in 2010 and only 25 percent of President Obama's budget request in each of the following two years.[17] As part of the 2015 budget deal that funded the DHS's Enhanced Plan for the headquarters consolidation, even the secretary's office is not scheduled to be ready until 2017 – a year after the entire project was initially projected to finish. Then Congress slashed the funding it had promised in the budget deal.[18]

The new plan also calls for only 12,800 desks across the campus, despite the fact that 17,000 DHS workers will relocate to the new facility. Even making heroic assumptions about how the next few years of the project will go will yield at best a partial solution. And partial in another important way: the Transportation Security Administration, perhaps the most visible part of the DHS, will not move its headquarters to St. Elizabeth's

(continued)

(continued)

after all, at least not for decades. Because of construction delays, the TSA's lease at its current headquarters is up before the new site is anywhere close to ready. Signing an indefinite short-term lease while the TSA waits to move into St. Elizabeth's would be extremely expensive. As a result, the TSA tried to sign a 15-year lease to move its headquarters to new site in Virginia, but its first effort was voided by a court order, because despite the plan's claimed cost savings, the new site was bigger than what Congress had authorized for the TSA. The upshot is that the TSA is extending its current lease, at great cost, until 2020, after which the TSA plans to move into another leased site – not to St. Elizabeth's, because there is no room for it in the St. Elizabeth's Enhanced Plan.[19]

The reorganization confusion is a result of what James Q. Wilson cogently described as the politically irresistible need for action.[20] Reorganization is the easiest though not necessarily the most effective political response. As Wilson noted, it is of course possible that a deep investigation might reveal some organizational changes that could improve governmental performance in a given area, but such work requires a full understanding of agency missions, and it is rarely attempted – especially in the immediate aftermath of a crisis or a perceived policy failure. Instead, a plan is quickly thrown together, mostly in secret so as not to allow mobilization of agency opposition, to be offered as a solution in the hope of calming the political storm. Given the period of months that is needed to bring agencies together, design a logo, and create common procedures, the reorganization ploy often buys time and thus allows the storm to pass, without a performance gain but at the cost of much wasted effort.

Crisis-driven reorganization plans tend to revolve around the call for czars. Americans' fascination with their absolute power is somewhat strange. The concept comes, after all, from the state that America defeated in the Cold War. Usually Americans believe that absolute power corrupts, so American government decentralizes authority and fragments power. When problems develop, the obvious, though usually false, solution is to blame the fragmentation and to centralize power in response: establishing a czar does not assure that the dots will be connected; remember, the Russian czar was surprised by his own overthrow.

Czars could be called kings or dictators if not for the fact that such titles are held in disrespect in the country that overthrew King George and fought Hitler and Stalin. "Czar," on the other hand, is exotic enough to be a symbol for Americans of a powerful though not tyrannical office-holder who will make the tough decisions that the previous system could not make. The fact that even that kind of authority is hard to assemble in American public administration matters little, as most politicians simply intend to offer a gesture of serious concern and the hope of future action.

Czars became the common solutions to difficult coordination problems during World War II, when there was a transportation czar, a manpower czar, and a production czar. President Nixon revived usage of the term when he appointed an energy czar in response to the first oil crisis in 1973. Ronald Reagan announced the first drug czar in 1986, and the position has been an executive office fixture since then. Bill Clinton followed with another permanent fixture, the AIDS czar, in 1993. Then George W. Bush appointed the first homeland security and intelligence czars. And Barack Obama has appointed more than a dozen czars, including ones for border control, climate change, and response to the Ebola crisis. Only Russia has had more czars.[21]

Of course, there is the problem of coordinating the czars, because there are so many of them, each with so many important tasks. Should the borders be watched to control illegal immigration, stop the smuggling of contraband drugs, ensure the safe passage of trade, or prevent the entrance of terrorists? The efforts at centralizing the response to so many important issues lead to a proliferation of organizations (and plans) – that is, centralizing reforms sometimes replicate the alleged problems of decentralization.

And then each czar also faces multiple challenges. Even if a homeland security czar could answer all of the border control questions, he would not be finished, because his organizations have other tasks, too. The Coast Guard adds boating safety and protecting American fishing waters from foreign fishing fleet intrusions to its concerns about port security. The Secret Service guards the currency as well as the president. And without the CDC, the FBI, and the National Guard, the Department of Homeland Security has big gaps, but with them it would be worrying about AIDS, bank robberies, and training for overseas military deployments in addition to trying to stop terrorists. The part of the DHS tasked with responding to emergencies, the Federal Emergency Management Agency (FEMA), got into huge trouble by focusing too much on recovery from terrorist attacks and not enough on the preparation for and recovery from hurricanes and floods; its response to Hurricane Katrina in 2005 created a serious scandal.[22] Government is full of contending priorities and conflicting tasks.[23] There is little that a czar can do to reconcile them.

When the czars in the American government actually try to act like tyrants, pushing through their priorities to try to achieve the missions with which they have been formally charged, they usually face determined resistance. Not only is there no rational answer to the political question of which government task should trump the others, but the American fear of absolute power also denies czars the opportunity to implement their choices by diktat. Civil libertarians mobilize to protect liberty, and established bureaucratic players use their institutional power to ignore the czar, subvert his directives, or defeat him in warfare over "turf." Czars' tenure in office can sometimes be short and unpleasant, if they are tempted by hubris to overreach their limited power; more sensible czars seek political accommodation.[24] Policy initiatives that hand out money are generally more palatable than ones that seek to command other government agencies or to infringe on citizens' freedoms.

Even in the aftermath of the 9/11 attacks, when Americans were gripped by a sense of national emergency, homeland security initiatives were tempered in practice by national resistance to the "garrison state."[25] The secretary of homeland security manages the unwieldy department, writes rafts of plans with which he or she is unlikely to enforce compliance, and hands out growing sums of money in the name of the department's mission.

More planning, please

A persistent belief in the value of planning parallels the infatuation with czars.[26] If a potential problem can be identified, people want the government to have a plan to deal with it. This is all very strange, because it is much easier to identify potential problems, especially those involving risks to homeland security, than it is to offer realistic responses that acceptably balance all the affected values. Nevertheless, commentators, national commissions, congressional committees, and oversight agencies such as the Government Accountability Office routinely admonish government for the lack of planning or, even better, the lack of a national strategy.

The result is a plethora of plans, never enough to cover all contingences, most of which are incompatible with one another and with available resources. The United States has a National Strategy for Homeland Defense, a National Infrastructure Protection Plan, a National Response Framework, a National Vaccine Strategy, a National Bio-terrorism Defense Plan, a

National Emergency Communications Plan, a DoD Strategy for Homeland Security and Civil Support, a National Military Strategic Plan for the War on Terror, a Military Transformation Strategy, a National Military Strategy, a National Defense Strategy, and a National Security Strategy. They all supposedly nest together as neatly as a Russian doll set, perhaps with the help of the National Homeland Security Planning Process and the Quadrennial Homeland Security Review. But does the National Bio-terrorism Defense Plan fit well with the Port Defense Plan and the Container Security Initiative? And are the Port Defense Plan and the Transportation Security Administration's air cargo screening plan compatible with national border protection plans? Even good faith efforts to comply with all of the plans are likely to fail. And a good faith effort by a plan's authors to consider its interfaces with other plans would probably miss some conflicts and certainly some deadlines. In practice, deconfliction efforts are unlikely to receive high priority among overworked officials struggling to achieve their own organization's objectives.

Despite the extraordinary and ever-growing number of plans, there are never enough, and the plans that exist are never up to date or fully developed. The possible dangers are everywhere and always changing. All the danger identification effort requires is a good imagination. It is the plague of "You Never Knowism."[27] What if terrorists hid nuclear weapons aboard ships in the ports of Long Beach, Baltimore, and New York? What if they blew up chemical cars on trains passing through St. Louis and Chicago? What if they used baby talcum powder containers to spread anthrax in Yankee Stadium or during the Super Bowl? What if they started using suicide bombers in shopping malls across the country? What if they struck while the National Guard was deployed to the Middle East and a flu epidemic was already taxing the capacity of the nation's hospitals? You never know what can happen.

If anything can happen, then supposedly you must be prepared for everything and have plans that cover all contingencies. But there are not enough resources to prepare all the plans, let alone to have the staff to carry them out. Priorities have to be set.

Unfortunately, planners are not good at setting priorities. Priorities are set politically in recognition of the distribution of power and interest. It may be rational to not defend the rail lines in Kansas or to ignore the malls in Vermont, but such choices are not usually possible in the American political system, especially officially, in formal plans. Kansas and Vermont each have two senators, and there are a lot of other small states. No state, large or small, wants to feel abandoned. The political solution provides a (small) bio-response team for every state, with the requirement that the teams can shift to aid each other as emergencies occur. Or Kansas gets an Anthrax Research Center, Vermont gets a Border Patrol Winter Training Center, and the bio-response teams are distributed regionally: perks of roughly equal size and importance are parceled out to each state. One way or another, everyone gets a cut of the overall pie.

Why, then, the great pressure to plan? Because it is hard for Americans to admit that key decisions are politically determined. They prefer the claim of technical analysis. They want policy to be apolitical, to be engineering rather than a political construct, even when there is no way to make the decisions without consulting values and interests of those affected. The messy path of politics is always to be denied, if not avoided.

Rise of the first responders

In the United States, state and local government are responsible for providing "first responders," the emergency personnel (usually police, firefighters, and emergency medical technicians) who rush to the scenes of accidents and other dangerous situations. They are usually local government employees, although private firms on contract provide some services and state governments provide others, especially in sparsely populated areas. Backup support for first responders is also locally provided in the form of mutual aid pacts among communities and state police and emergency management personnel. In the most difficult or widespread cases, a governor can mobilize the state's National Guard or request federal aid. Until the president accepts a governor's request to declare part or all of a state a "disaster area," state and local taxpayers bear the costs for helping those in need.

Over 400 first responders died in the 9/11 attacks, mostly New York City firefighters. The fires at the Pentagon, a federal facility, were largely fought by Arlington County, Virginia, emergency personnel, who clearly had more capabilities than the federal guards and firefighters on the scene. Although the federal government paid almost all of the billions of dollars required to deal with the attack and to manage the consequences at the sites, the disaster highlighted the value of local first responders. It also restarted a familiar struggle.

Many of the costs for services that were once entirely the problem of state and local officials have shifted over to the federal budget, often with a security rationale. The National Interstate and Defense Highway Act of 1956 set the precedent for increasing federal support for highway construction and other transportation system costs.[28] Initially focused on support for the development of "vital skills" for defense, the federal government has gained a huge role in higher education in the United States.[29] Primary and secondary education has followed, though slowly because of the recognition that with federal money comes the possibility of federal standards and controls, traditionally anathema to many Americans. And much of the cost of medical care for the poor and the indigent, long the charitable responsibility of local governments, is now shared by the federal and state governments via the Medicaid Program.[30]

The 9/11 fires were hardly out before some people saw the need for the federal government to share some or all of the nation's first responder costs on a continuing basis, because these state and local employees were indeed the nation's first line of defense in the age of terrorism. The Bush administration resisted. It pointed out that federal grants already supported some training and the development of standards for state and local firefighters and law enforcement officers. The FBI helped train local officers, as did the Bureau of Alcohol, Tobacco, Firearms, and Explosives (ATF). Airport and port security were in large part a federal responsibility. Federal support helped buy Special Weapons and Tactics (SWAT) team equipment. And the Drug Enforcement Administration was deeply involved in local efforts to interdict drug trafficking. The Bush administration feared that despite all this federal effort, Congress would do a big favor for local politicians by providing large-scale federal funding for local public safety in the name of homeland defense. One of the core reasons for the Bush administration's resistance to creating the DHS was the fear of creating another big grants program. But once the political debate began, resistance was futile.

Federal grants to state and local first responders had unintended negative consequences beyond the ballooning pork-barrel cost. Along with money, the federal government transferred military equipment, from MRAPs to bayonets. The federal government's donated equipment cultivated a taste among local police, who then used some of the money they were given to buy even more military-style materiel. The programs actually started at a small scale before 9/11, before the Iraq War, and before the Department of Homeland Security, but the events of the 2000s dramatically accelerated them. Terrorism seemed to prove that first responders needed heavy armor to compete with an ever-more-serious threat; the National

Guard that deployed to Iraq and Afghanistan has a lot of members who are first responders back home, who learned how to use the equipment overseas; and the DHS budget, along with the drawdown from Iraq and the need to dispose of all the equipment that the military hurriedly bought for the war but no longer needed, greased the skids of police militarization.

As a result, SWAT teams are involved in an increasing number of arrests, including those of a type that used to be handled by routine law enforcement officers. The relatively clear prohibition in the venerable Posse Comitatus Act against using the military in the United States for domestic law enforcement is breaking down. For the same reason that analysts questioned whether scary equipment such as big, heavily armored MRAPs would build trust in US forces engaged in counterinsurgency operations overseas, analysts now question whether that sort of equipment is further damaging relations between police departments and their communities, especially minority and poor communities, across the United States.[31]

But the politics of support for first responders – and for escalating expenditure and militarization for homeland security – are powerful. A favorite satire of an American state legislator or congressional representative begins with the line, "Mr. Speaker, how many more must die before we . . .?" One way to gain a headline for a representative or senator is to point out an obvious but difficult-to-deal-with security risk, for example: "Each day tens of millions of pounds of air cargo travels on passenger aircraft, but little of it is inspected." Of course, much of it is provided by trusted sources, so the risk involved is very low, and much of it is perishable and/or of high value, so inspections that delay delivery would be very costly. Moreover, the airlines and the shippers themselves have strong incentives to keep the system safe, even without federal inspections. And, of course, installing X-ray machines and other detectors at all loading points would require a multiyear, multimillion-dollar effort. But it is a no-risk strategy for the representative or senator to complain about the lack of inspections. If nothing happens, no one will remember the call for action beyond a day or two later. And if something goes terribly wrong, the politician can claim that his or her call for preparedness went unheeded, earning political points.

Normally, though, the politician's exaggerations are just another fear, another potential inadequacy of government, for citizens to uneasily ignore. To get apathetic voters' attention, political rhetoric often paints struggles in moral terms, with the consequences of not acting listed as catastrophic at best. After the 9/11 attacks, the Bush administration made security its key issue. Thus, President Bush was hardly in a position to moderate congressional demands for reorganization and budgetary expansion. The Department of Homeland Security became a conduit for money to state and local governments, distributed according to the political logic of the pork barrel, with little expectation of prioritizing threats. Optimists sometimes hope that after the immediate pressure of responding to a crisis fades, rational analysis of threats and responses might be able to guide and constrain programs.[32] Sadly, in a world of You-Never-Knowism and a world in which threats are used to provide cover for politicians' interest in sending resources home to their districts or to provide an opportunity for higher office, that is but a faint hope.

WMD

The tendency to exaggerate security threats leads to muddled and dangerous thinking. Fears of nuclear proliferation – and the expansion that broadened the discussion to "WMD proliferation" – offer a key example. After the end of the Cold War, in the 1990s, many defense experts worried that the United States would cut back its defense effort too much, though they could not discern particular threats that would justify continued spending. Russia still had thousands of nuclear weapons pointed at the United States, but the diminished former superpower seemed focused on a difficult political and economic transition. Russian weakness became pundits' new fear: perhaps collapse of Russian state capacity would leave their nuclear sites open to infiltration by evil non-state actors, who would steal a bomb, or perhaps Russia's underpaid nuclear scientists would be willing to go to work for rogue states and terrorist groups, presumably lured by high, reliable pay. To find a new threat worthy of the US defense effort, analysts shifted from the idea of talking about a great power with a large arsenal, which they could not credibly claim would likely be launched against the US homeland, to talking about irresponsible rogues and terrorists they alleged might well try to smuggle even a single weapon into the United States to carry out a dastardly plot. To make the threat big, they coined the term "Weapons of Mass Destruction (WMD)."

In response, in 1991 the United States started the Nunn–Lugar program, named for its bipartisan Senate co-sponsors, to secure and dismantle nuclear infrastructure by buying equipment and nuclear material, paying for heightened security at facilities in the former Soviet Union, and funding research projects to keep former Soviet scientists occupied on non-threatening activities. The program later spread to try to keep nuclear scientists in other countries such as Pakistan and Libya occupied with civilian research. The program has spent billions of dollars over the decades, and while "loose nukes" have not been the problem that advocates feared in 1991, a seeming success, the Nunn–Lugar efforts have struggled with implementation challenges and probably matched most of their effort with the scientists and facilities that were least likely to pose a proliferation risk.[33] It turns out that the logic of deterrence can apply to small arsenals, too, and pretty much everyone has an incentive not to give nuclear technology to terrorists and crazy people.[34]

Nuclear technology was also relatively easy to address, at least compared to chemical and biological weapons, and advocates of the defense effort had strong incentives to expand the size of the challenge that the United States faced. Nuclear weapons production requires a massive effort that has only been made by a handful of countries, and it leaves a trail of telltale markers visible to aerial surveillance and through other means. It also involves a long supply chain, and breaking any step of that chain will prevent construction of a bomb. In contrast, both chemical and biological weapons seem easy to make and easy to hide within the normal production activities of the chemical and medical products industries. If nuclear weapons concerns would not be enough to justify a massive non-proliferation effort, then perhaps expanding the issue to "WMD" would.

But as Owen Coté points out, there are important differences among the types of WMD, differences that lumping them all together obscures.[35] Although it is possible to concoct an exciting scenario or two for chemical and biological weapons, these weapons are not as dangerous or as militarily useful as nuclear weapons. To begin with, there is no viable defense against nuclear weapons. You can dig deep or try to shoot down missiles that might carry them, but mostly you pray intensively for a dud. For chemical and biological weapons there are masks, protective clothing, and vaccines. Armies can operate on battlefields where chemical and biological weapons have been used, but soldiers face vaporization when nuclear bombs explode. Wind and other environmental factors have a huge impact on the lethal effects of chemical and biological weapons. These factors affect nuclear weapons, too, but not anywhere near as much. Unless a target is protected by literally tens of feet of reinforced concrete and earth, a nuclear near-miss is almost as good as a nuclear hit. An adversary's threat to deploy any weapon of mass destruction will cause panic among the public, but only nuclear weapons strike fear in the hearts of generals.

Box 12.3   Secretary Cohen's five-pound bag of sugar

On Sunday, November 16, 1997, Secretary of Defense William Cohen made a guest appearance on ABC's *This Week* show during which he dramatically put a five-pound bag of sugar on the table and announced that this amount of anthrax, if aerially dispersed over Washington, DC, could kill at least half the population. This, of course, was not a spontaneous act on the secretary's part. According to newspaper reports, his press secretary said that in the weeks prior, they had experimented with bags of flour and sugar of varying sizes before settling on Domino's five-pounder. The Clinton administration wanted to prepare the public for possible military action against Iraq and believed that generating fears of Iraq's biological and chemical warfare capabilities would be an effective political tactic. A year later, under Operation Desert Fox, the United States hit Iraq with four days of bombing and cruise missile attacks to punish Iraq's failure to heed the UN resolution on WMD inspections. Hyped dangers of WMD played on a set of fears that would keep on giving. Less than six years later, the Bush administration would invade Iraq using the same justifications.

The five-pound bag story was a bit of a stretch. Experts questioned both the lethality of the amount shown and the ability of a terrorist group and/or Iraq to disperse anthrax properly. Perhaps the secretary and his staff thought that a 100-pound bag of sugar would be too hard for him to handle on the show without assistance. Ignoring the difficult details about weaponizing anthrax was also probably necessary: processing anthrax to get it "just right" to disperse over a city and to lodge in the lungs of hapless citizens who inhale the powder requires very sophisticated work.[36] The show did stimulate lots of false threats, as various cranks and teenagers enjoyed hearing the sounds of emergency vehicles racing to help evacuate government buildings and abortion clinics. And, of course, there were actual anthrax attacks in 2001 that demonstrated the agent's ability to kill a few people – five, including workers in postal sorting facilities. But those attacks also reconfirmed the technical difficulty of arranging an attack and the barriers to generating mass casualties.[37]

The calculated political hype plus the additional panic following the 2001 attacks has generated a multibillion-dollar vaccine production and storage program with mandatory vaccination for military personnel, needless courses of drug therapy for the potentially exposed, and much work on biological attack detection systems that may never be triggered. Buying a bag of sugar is a lot easier than building an effective biological weapon. Terrorists and rogue states seem to know this, and they spend their time working with explosives.

The WMD designation confuses policy priorities as well. Non-proliferation detection and verification regimes become exceedingly complicated and ultimately impossible to administer when they involve chemical and biological materials along with nuclear materials. Scarce resources needed to monitor or intercept nuclear shipments are wasted hunting common commodities. International attention is likely also to be misdirected. The United States attacked what was thought to be a biological weapons facility in Sudan, but it turned out that the building was probably an innocent aspirin factory.[38] Saddam's chemical weapons warehouses were not found. Meanwhile, domestic research and development programs (not loose nukes from the former Soviet Union) turned North Korea and Pakistan into nuclear weapon states, the United States failed to detect India's preparation to resume nuclear testing, and Iran accelerated its nuclear program.

A WMD sleight of hand also helped build the case for the Iraq War: almost every intelligence service agreed that Saddam probably had hidden away some chemical weapons, because they could not account for the final disposition of several hundred tons of the stockpile that Saddam had declared to the UN inspectors; therefore, people believed that Saddam had WMD; and everyone also knew that WMD were extremely dangerous, because a single nuclear weapon smuggled into an American city would cause untold devastation. Bush administration officials and even President Bush himself mentioned nuclear threats to the homeland many times.[39] To be sure, they did not only use the term "WMD." They spent a lot of effort building a case that Saddam Hussein specifically had a serious nuclear weapons program, from alleging that Iraq purchased a key nuclear precursor, called yellowcake, from Niger to alleging that special aluminum tubes intercepted en route to Iraq were parts for nuclear centrifuges. But these bits of nuclear-specific evidence all turned out to either be false leads or to have alternative explanations not linked to nuclear weapons, and many people knew it at the time.[40] Nevertheless, the case that the public came to understand was that the United States needed to stop a WMD program to prevent a nuclear attack, even though the best evidence for WMD was evidence of chemical weapons, not nuclear weapons.

But the biggest danger of imprecise, threat-inflating terminology is fomenting unnecessary fears domestically. Government needs to educate the public about the security risks the nation faces. Defense preparedness and foreign military action require public support – several decades' worth of support for the Cold War – but exaggerating the dangers and stimulating excessive fears also threatens American values. The sometimes hysterical hunt for Communists in education, government, and Hollywood during the early Cold War is one example. The internment of Americans of Japanese descent who lived on the West Coast during World War II is another.[41] Having the public fear developments in biotechnology or the nearby construction of biological research facilities may be the dangerous by-product of the effort to gain support for initiating otherwise sensible steps in homeland security.[42]

Some threats to homeland security are serious. Some terrorists, a small fraction of the universe of groups, may be hard to deter, especially religious groups whose members believe that salvation awaits those who attack their enemies. Once homeland security policy focuses on those really dangerous groups and the truly dangerous threats such as nuclear weapons, it should devote great effort to defending against them.

Preventing less deadly terrorism at a reasonable cost may be an impossible task. A modern, affluent society just has too much to defend. Terrorists should not find unlocked doors; private citizens and government policy should both contribute to reasonable precaution. But terrorists can rarely do much damage when they manage to break through simple safeguards. The 9/11 attack was most likely an outlier not easily duplicated once basic precautions are in place. Terrorism is unsettling, but not permanently. People still take buses in Israel, trains in Spain, and the Underground in London, even though recent history has shown the possibility of attacks in all of those locations. Terrorists should be hunted, and states should be punished if they offer sanctuary for them. But without a domestic base, terrorists can do little to alter the direction of a strong, moderately alert nation, much less threaten its survival.

Cyber attack – the new WMD?

Bored as people are with warnings of the danger of nuclear weapons, cyber threats have the advantage of novelty. The Internet has become part of normal life. Private citizens use it for banking, to check their door locks remotely, and as the backbone of their social lives; businesses use it to reach their customers, to handle supply chain and sales, and for huge, nearly instantaneous financial transactions; and the military routinely uses information systems (on the public Internet and in its own private networks) for intelligence, command-and-control, and kinetic operations. Those network connections are also now seen as a huge vulnerability: as recently as 2007, the Director of National Intelligence did not even mention cyber attack as part of the annual *Worldwide Threat Assessment of the U.S. Intelligence Community*, but since 2012, it has been listed as the number one threat to the United States.[43] Government officials and private-sector security experts pepper their speeches with reference to the "Cyber Pearl Harbor," a devastating surprise cyber attack, although that hyperbolic language surprisingly does not appear in the Department of Defense's official *DOD Cyber Strategy*, released in April 2015. The public finds the threats very believable, because evidence of the danger is at hand as government agencies and major retailers constantly confess of being hacked by Chinese army units, the Russian mafia, or unknown criminal entities.

It is clear that foreign governments and criminals regularly try to penetrate firewalls and steal your data. What is not discussed is how vulnerable the United States is, relatively speaking. We are told that networks are at risk, for example that Iranians and Russians have penetrated the operations networks of the US electric grid, and the Federal Energy Regulatory Commission has warned that a cyber attack could cause a months-long, coast-to-coast blackout.[44] The difficulty is in trusting those who are there to protect us, as it is in their interest to keep us frightened. Scaring people is a job requirement for some, a business model for others. There is almost no point of being the Director of National Intelligence, the Chairman of the Joint Chiefs, or the head of the Central Intelligence Agency if you can't frighten a Chamber of Commerce luncheon audience (or a Senate confirmation hearing, for that matter) with a list of things that supposedly keep you awake at night. Many of the private cyber security experts who warn of the dangers also work for companies that are selling cyber defense software and services.[45] Given the distractions of life, it would not be surprising if the protectors exaggerated a bit, as it is their responsibility to gain sufficient resources from us to keep us safe. But how would we know if they exaggerate too much?

Looking carefully at the US profile in cyber space suggests that the threats of cyber doom are easily inflated. The vast majority of cyber attacks turn out to be mere nuisances, certainly at the national level but often even for the specific target. Unlike other countries, America does not have just one city that is the center of national political and economic life. There isn't just one vulnerable banking network or electrical grid. There isn't one port or one coast or one technology hub. Companies compete, and agencies overlap and fight. An attack on one part of the system could be very painful, but American decentralization and diversification limit the potential devastation.

Meanwhile, the most common attacks are relatively mild cyber crime – graffiti defacing a particular website, or a "botnet-enabled distributed denial of service attack," in which an army of thousands of virus-infected computers are harnessed to simultaneously demand information from a particular website, over and over again, preventing legitimate traffic from being able to fit a word in edgewise. These attacks are soon remedied, at modest cost, by private-sector cyber defenders. Even in more serious incidents known as cyber espionage, in which password-protected networks are penetrated and a company's proprietary data or even government secrets are stolen, much of what is stolen is useless to the thieves, who lack the context and tacit knowledge to exploit the data.[46] Modern, complex products, whether business algorithms or classified aspects of weapon system plans, are hard to reverse engineer.[47]

The most devastating attacks that people imagine would take over industrial control systems and actually break expensive, vital machinery, such as the feared attack on the electric grid that the Federal Energy Regulatory Commission warned about. These attacks turn out to require incredible sophistication and detailed knowledge of the target system; they must be tailored, and the scenario-specific penetration strategy and custom software take vast time, resources, and expertise to develop.

Two examples of this sort of attack tell the tale. Russian cyber attackers caused a blackout in Ukraine in December 2015, but they had the advantage of tremendous insider knowledge, and even then the attack only lasted six hours. And the authors of the Stuxnet worm, which targeted the operation of finicky centrifuges spinning to enrich uranium in Iran, wrote very detailed, mission-specific code to accomplish their limited disruption of the Iranian nuclear program. Perhaps those attacks were intended as warnings rather than intended to cause maximum damage right away, but in other ways, their technical details reveal limits of cyber war, not just its potential.[48]

Of course, cyber attacks have caused real damage to some individuals whose identities have been stolen or whose computers have been held for ransom by cyber thieves. But media coverage of a particularly high-profile incident – the 2014 North Korean hack of Sony Pictures' computers that revealed nasty, personal emails about some celebrities – spurred a "crisis" response from the government. The Obama administration turned to various centralization initiatives, including some that it had previously resisted on the grounds of protecting citizens' privacy. The government's cyber security budget, already on a substantial growth trajectory, also shot through the roof: as part of a *Cybersecurity National Action Plan*, the president's budget proposal for fiscal year 2017 called for $19 billion in dedicated cyber security spending, a 35 percent increase from the year before.[49]

The cyber effort involves many departments. The Department of Homeland Security naturally has a major role on the civilian side, and the 2017 budget will enable it to expand from 10 to 48 "cyber response teams" that will "make house calls" to help businesses protect against attacks. At the same time, though, the FBI investigates cyber crime, the Department of Energy tries to protect the electric grid, and other civilian agencies have developed their own specialties. For its part, in 2010 the military established a US Cyber Command that reports to the joint Strategic Command. Each of the services has a cyber effort, as do many agencies of the Intelligence Community, led by the National Security Agency, which has decades of expertise with hacking to collect overseas signals intelligence and with advanced computer cryptography to try to defend US information. Even before President Obama's focused effort, there was little danger that cyber security would fall through the cracks: recognizing cyber's relevance to political leaders, nearly every government agency eagerly sought a role that was consistent with its established tasks. It is like the military service's response to the nuclear revolution, when each fought hard to ensure a role in the United States' most important defense effort in the 1950s by trying to build its own nuclear delivery systems. The competition among the efforts was productive then, and it probably will be in the cyber environment today.

As in the 1950s, though, politicians fear that uncoordinated effort won't yield the best results. Though it is hard (or in the nuclear case, nearly impossible) to suppress organizations' desire to stay involved, President Obama is trying to rationalize the government's efforts. In addition to releasing the Department of Defense's cyber strategy in 2015, President Obama created the Cyber Threat Intelligence Integration Center (CTIIC), an explicit effort to "connect the dots" regarding cyber threats. As part of the Intelligence Community, though, the CTIIC faces tight restrictions on its ability to work with data on US persons, so even though the CTIIC is a major presidential initiative, it cannot access data on actual attacks on

Americans and their resilience to them; analysis of that data, and policy reactions to it, must come from the Department of Homeland Security.[50]

Separately, the administration also reorganized the NSA to further centralize cyber activity on the military side, combining its offensive (Signals Intelligence) and defensive (Information Assurance) directorates into a single Directorate of Operations.[51] But while these organizations share a reliance on the same sort of technical skills – understanding computer security, in one case to keep out attackers and in the other to break in – their critical tasks are quite different. For example, the network defense operators work closely with industry, which has to trust them with quite sensitive access; linking the defenders to the offense team might hurt that relationship, because the industrial partners could reasonably fear that the offense side of the NSA would spy on them or might inhibit efforts to fix vulnerabilities because of a desire to keep exploiting them internationally. More likely, given the growth of cyber fears and the temptation to fight silent cyber wars against terrorists and others, the number of cyber bureaucratic empires will be expanded. There is even talk of a Cyber COCOM.

In the end, the Homeland Security part of cyber really is a question of the relationship between the public and the private. Businesses and individual citizens obviously have incentives to protect themselves, but perhaps the costs of disruption or the sophistication required for defense are too great, meaning that the public needs a role – or perhaps it is just that Americans think the government is supposed to be responsible for defending them from foreign threats, whether those threats are terrestrial or in the cyber domain. There is also an effectiveness argument for a significant government role: companies often resist revealing that they have been penetrated by a cyber attack, because they fear that the intrusion will hurt their reputation or otherwise damage their competitiveness. The Cybersecurity Act of 2015, which Obama signed into law as part of the budget agreement after resisting in previous years, tried to address this concern by granting liability protection to those companies that share data on cyber attacks with the Department of Homeland Security, allowing the DHS to develop national cyber defenses and to teach other businesses how to respond to threats, too.[52]

Even with that incentive for voluntary information-sharing, pressure continues to mount to make sharing legally required. Critics continue to resist, partly because such sharing threatens privacy (including of affected companies' customers' data), because it might reduce cyber defenders' ability to quietly respond to attacks without tipping off the attackers that they have been discovered, and because the flood of data may be uninterpretable and may distract companies and the government from more important "cyber hygiene" initiatives. As with other homeland security topics, cyber security must balance between an effort to connect all the dots, to understand everything that is out there, and an effort to focus on the most important threats, the ones that can really harm the United States or that the cyber defense can really prevent.

Questions for discussion

1   **Why does the United States need a Department of Homeland Security when it already has a Department of Defense?**

2   **How should the total homeland security budget and the distribution of these funds be determined?**

3   **What counts as vital infrastructure, and how is it best defended?**

4   **What organizational structure should the federal government select for homeland security and for foreign intelligence? How should they be linked?**

5   **Do we ever need to appoint "czars"?**

6   **How much effort to protect cyber space is enough?**

Notes

1 Pamela Constable, "Lower Profile Has Not Diminished bin Laden; Enemy of West Still a Hero to Many Muslims," *The Washington Post*, May 9, 2000, p. A20; Milt Bearden, "Making Osama bin Laden's Day," *New York Times*, August 13, 1999, p. A21.
2 David D. Kirkpatrick, "Saudi Arabia Said to Arrest Suspect in 1996 Khobar Towers Bombing," *New York Times*, August 26, 2015.
3 Amy Zegart, *Spying Blind: The CIA, the FBI, and the Origins of 9/11* (Princeton, NJ: Princeton University Press, 2007).
4 Jeremy Shapiro, *Managing Homeland Security: Develop a Threat-Based Strategy*, *Opportunity '08 Issue Paper* (Washington, DC: Brookings Institution, 2007).
5 Shapiro, *Managing Homeland Security*.
6 Ron Nixon, "Airport Security: What's Behind the Backups," *New York Times*, May 18, 2016.
7 John M. Doyle, "Ex-TSA Chief Suggests Novel Ways to Privatize Airport Screening," *Aviation Daily*, April 26, 2007; Amy Schatz, "Private Airport Screening Is off the Radar," *Wall Street Journal*, April 19, 2005, p. A4.
8 Jack Nicas, "Homeland Security Chief Orders Changes at TSA after Failed Tests," *Wall Street Journal*, June 1, 2015. See also Jeffrey Goldberg, "The Things He Carried," *The Atlantic*, November 2008.
9 Brian Naylor, "After a Season of Long Lines, Homeland Security Secretary Says He Feels Your Pain," *NPR's All Things Considered*, May 13, 2016.
10 "To Shorten Security Lines, Union Calls for More TSA Screeners," *NPR's Morning Edition*, May 24, 2016.
11 Rep. Darrell Issa (R-CA), "A Simple Solution to the TSA Breakdown," *CNN.com*, May 24, 2016.
12 Reynolds Hutchins, "US Legislators Highlight Dirty Bomb Threat in Appeal for 100% Container Screening," *Journal of Commerce*, October 27, 2015.
13 *The 9/11 Commission Report: Final Report of the National Commission on Terrorist Attacks upon the United States* (New York: Norton, 2004).
14 Ivo H. Daalder, I. M. Destler, David Gunter, James Lindsay, Michael E. O'Hanlon, Peter R. Orszag, and James B. Steinberg, *Protecting the American Homeland: One Year On* (Washington, DC: Brookings Institution, 2003), pp. xxi–xxii.
15 Michael Crowley, "Playing Defense: Bush's Disastrous Homeland Security Department," *The New Republic*, March 15, 2004, p. 17.
16 Bradley Saull, "TSA Is Moving to Alexandria – Not St. Elizabeth's?" *Security Debrief*, December 7, 2015.
17 Jonathan O'Connell, "Dept. of Homeland Security Headquarters May Actually Get Built," *Washington Post*, December 16, 2015.
18 Jory Heckman, "DHS Funding for New Headquarters Slashed in FY 2017 Bill," *Federal News Radio*, June 9, 2016.
19 Chris Teale, "New TSA Location Delayed until 2020," *Alexandria Times*, April 7, 2016.
20 James Q. Wilson, "Thinking about Reorganization," in Roy Godson, Ernest R. May, and S. Gary Schmitt (eds.), *U.S. Intelligence at the Crossroads* (Washington, DC: Brassey's, 1995), pp. 28–35.
21 Shannon Beckham, "Obama Appointed 45 Czars to Replace Elected Officials, Chain Email Claims," *PolitiFact*, June 25, 2014, available at: http://www.politifact.com/truth-o-meter/statements/2014/jun/25/chain-email/obama-appointed-45-czars-replace-elected-officials/ (accessed September 2, 2016).
22 Saundra K. Schneider, "Administrative Breakdowns in the Governmental Response to Hurricane Katrina," *Public Administration Review*, 65(5) (September/October 2005): 515–516.
23 James Q. Wilson, *Bureaucracy: What Government Organizations Do and Why They Do It* (New York: Basic Books, 1989).
24 Ivo H. Daalder and I. M. Destler, "Advisors, Czars, and Councils: Organizing for Homeland Security," *The National Interest* (Summer 2002), pp. 66–78.
25 Matthew Kroenig and Jay Stowsky, "War Makes the State, But Not as It Pleases: Homeland Security and American Anti-Statism," *Security Studies*, 15(2) (April–June 2006): 225–270.

26 See the classic Aaron Wildavsky, "If Planning Is Everything, Maybe It's Nothing," *Policy Sciences*, 4 (1973): 127–153.

27 Benjamin H. Friedman and Harvey M. Sapolsky, "You Never Know(ism)," *Breakthroughs*, 15(1) (Spring 2006): 3–11.

28 Mark H. Rose, *Interstate: Express Highway Politics, 1939–1989*, rev. edn. (Knoxville, TN: University of Tennessee Press, 1990).

29 Harvey M. Sapolsky, "The Truly Endless Frontier," *Technology Review* (November/December 1995): 37–43.

30 Hugh Heclo, "The Clinton Health Plan: Historical Perspective," *Health Affairs*, 14(1) (Spring 1995): 86–98.

31 Dexter Filkins, "'Do Not Resist' and the Crisis of Police Militarization," *The New Yorker*, May 13, 2016.

32 Shapiro, *Managing Homeland Security*.

33 Sharon K. Weiner, "Retooling Efforts to Stop the Proliferation of WMD Expertise," *Arms Control Today*, December 2, 2011.

34 Robert F. Trager and Dessislava P. Zagorcheva, "Deterring Terrorism: It Can Be Done," *International Security*, 30(3) (Winter 2005/2006): 87–123; Keir A. Lieber and Daryl G. Press, "Why States Won't Give Nuclear Weapons to Terrorists," *International Security*, 38(1) (Summer 2013): 80–104.

35 Owen R. Coté, Jr., "Weapons of Mass Confusion," *The Boston Review* (April/May 2003): 26–27.

36 Jeanne Guillemin, *Biological Weapons: From the Invention of State-Sponsored Programs to Contemporary Bioterrorism* (New York: Columbia University Press, 2006).

37 Marilyn W. Thompson, *The Killer Strain: Anthrax and a Government Exposed* (New York: HarperCollins, 2003).

38 James Risen, "To Bomb Sudan Plant or Not: A Year Later, Debates Rankle," *New York Times*, October 27, 1999, p. A1.

39 John B. Judis and Spencer Ackerman, "The Selling of the Iraq War: The First Casualty," *The New Republic*, June 30, 2003.

40 Chaim Kaufmann, "Threat Inflation and the Failure of the Marketplace of Ideas: The Selling of the Iraq War," *International Security*, 29(1) (Summer 2004): 5–48.

41 Japanese-Americans living on the West Coast of the United States were interned but not those living elsewhere, including Hawaii, where populations of Japanese-Americans were either too large to place in camps or too small to notice. Panic often leads to regret.

42 Kendall Hoyt and Stephen G. Brooks," A Double-Edged Sword: Globalization and Biosecurity," *International Security*, 28(3) (Winter 2003/2004): 123–148.

43 Amy Zegart, "Additional Thoughts on the DNI's Annual Threat Assessment," *Lawfare Blog*, March 2, 2015, available at: https://www.lawfareblog.com/additional-thoughts-dnis-annual-threat-assessment (accessed September 2, 2016).

44 Garance Burke and Jonathan Fahey, "US Power Grid Vulnerable to Foreign Hacks," *The Associated Press*, December 21, 2015.

45 Jerry Brito and Tate Watkins, "Loving the Cyber Bomb? The Dangers of Threat Inflation in Cybersecurity Policy," *Harvard Law School National Security Journal* 3(1) (2011): 67–73.

46 Jon R. Lindsay, "Stuxnet and the Limits of Cyber Warfare," *Security Studies*, 22(3) (August 2013): 369–371.

47 Andrea Gilli and Mauro Gilli, "Goodbye Gerschenkron: Complexity and the Waning Advantages of Backwardness in Military Technology," paper presented at the *International Studies Association Annual Conference*, March, 2016.

48 Kim Zetter, "Inside the Cunning, Unprecedented Hack of Ukraine's Power Grid," *Wired*, March 3, 2016; Lindsay, "Stuxnet and the Limits of Cyberwarfare," 378–384.

49 Aaron Boyd, "President's Budget Proposes $3.1 Billion Cybersecurity Revolving Fund, National Action Plan," *Federal Times*, February 9, 2016.

50 Steve Slick, "CTIIC – Learning from the Choices and Challenges that Shaped the National Counterterrorism Center," *Lawfare Blog*, March 4, 2015.

51 Ellen Nakashima, "National Security Agency Plans Major Reorganization," *Washington Post*, February 2, 2016.

52 Jack Detsch, "Is the Cybersecurity Act Really Government Spying in Disguise?" *Christian Science Monitor*, December 23, 2015.

Recommended additional reading

Mariano-Florentino Cuellar, *Governing Security: The Hidden Origins of American Security Agencies* (Stanford CA: Stanford Law Books, 2013). Explores the broadening of the definition of security via agency reorganizations that led to the cabinet departments of Health and Human Services and Homeland Security. Politics, sometime nefarious, shapes all.

Stephen Flynn, *America the Vulnerable: How Our Government Is Failing to Protect Us from Terrorism* (New York: HarperCollins, 2004). America is a big unprotected target.

Gregory D. Koblentz, *Living Weapons: Biological Warfare and International Security* (Ithaca, NY: Cornell University Press, 2009). Learn the role biological weapons played in the Cold War and how the threat has evolved.

Christopher A. Preble and John Mueller (eds.), *A Dangerous World: Threat Perception and U.S. National Security* (Washington DC: CATO, 2014). Exaggeration, the business plan for some, scares many Americans, even if the world is ever-safer for them.

13 Veterans and the costs of war

Wars end, but their costs linger on. Veterans, those who served and survived, have a hold on the federal budget that lasts through their return to civilian life, eventual retirement, and death, and the lives of their dependents as well. Veterans' benefits – the cost of the health care of veterans, their housing subsidies, further education and training, counseling, pensions, and survivors' support – approached $175 billion in 2015, nearly the same amount all the members of the European Union spent on defense in the same year. This cost is certain to grow, whereas the European defense expenditures are not. Nearly a hundred years after the end of World War I, the US government continues to pay veterans' benefits for that war.[1] And a hundred years from today, Americans will continue to pay for the veterans of the Global War on Terror, even if it ends tomorrow.

The costs are high because veterans, despite scandals that appear to point to the contrary, are especially well treated in the United States. The welfare state was slower to develop, and until recently was more limited, in the United States than in most other industrialized nations. But veterans have long been a privileged group in American society, considered to be the deserving because they have earned their society's support, as opposed to slackers seeking to live off others. Thus veterans were among the first to be offered publicly provided health care, pensions, and survivors' benefits. And given the price some have paid for their service, veterans are hard to portray in other than the most sympathetic terms, even when their benefit claims are beyond reason and proof. The great sacrifices of some are the political shield for all.

Support for veterans in part comes directly from the Department of Defense, but most of it comes from a dedicated agency. Once called the Veterans Administration, the Department of Veterans Affairs was given cabinet status and its name was changed in 1988. Today, it serves the nation's 23 million veterans, a shrinking number because of the passing of World War II and Korean War veterans. The recent wars in Afghanistan and Iraq, though, have brought new challenges, as public perceptions of veterans, veterans' organizations, and veterans' needs all evolve. Pressure to reform policies regarding veterans continues to raise questions about the appropriate care to provide for those who have served their country – and also about the proper role of expert medical judgment compared to political gratitude in deciding the type and amount of care. Reform proposals also raise the question of balance between public and private efforts in providing care.

In this chapter, we will also consider the pay and benefits for currently serving military personnel. Prior to the establishment of the AVF, military personnel were something of an exploited class, relatively poorly paid and housed and with not much attention given to their family obligations. Now the military competes for personnel, and politicians compete to show how much they care for those who serve and their dependents. Like veterans, members of the military are now a privileged group in society, but the costs for their benefits, unlike those of veterans, come directly out of the defense budget. A third of the defense budget goes to personnel costs, and as longevity increases for all, military pensioners will help make that share grow.

Money, especially the potential for gaining some, attracts interest and organization. Every possible interest in the pay and benefits for military personnel, retirees, veterans, and their dependents has an organizational presence in American politics. Lobbying organizations are difficult to create and sustain because the benefits achieved through legislation are available to all in the favored class, not just to those who organized and fought for the benefit. Like alliances, lobbies have a free-rider problem; some carry the burden that others avoid. In examining veteran organizations, we will discuss this dilemma, noting the different strategies used to sustain viable organizations.

Thank you for your service

Narratives, true or not, can be political weapons, shaping the public debate for advantage. One such narrative is that soldiers returning from Vietnam were poorly treated, even spat upon in airports and bus stations.[2] Another is that some Americans were left behind in Vietnam when the war ended, the hidden captives of a heartless enemy, even though prisoners were supposedly repatriated. To this day, black POW/MIA flags fly by state law over public buildings, police stations, schools, and the like, in Massachusetts, which was one of the more dissenting states in the time of the Vietnam War, showing that narratives can be disputed or modified subtly with effort.[3]

When the Global War on Terror began, there was an apparently spontaneous movement to "support our troops" that included bumper stickers and billboards. As the war progressed, volunteers greeted each returning planeload of troops, whatever the hour, with snacks and gifts. The clear message was that soldiers of this war weren't going to be abused or forgotten, as Vietnam veterans supposedly were. Moreover, with the All-Volunteer Force in place, the threat of involuntary service was absent. The expression of civilian guilt for avoiding service has shifted from opposition to "bad" wars to hyper appreciation of those who chose to wear the uniform. "Thank you for your service" became a constant and not always welcome refrain.[4]

Congress expressed its thanks by raising substantially the pay and benefits of the military. Of course, it seemed to make sense to raise the compensation for military service right after 9/11, because the risks of military service had increased substantially, though that was counterbalanced to some extent by an outpouring of patriotism and the increased sense of adventure that war brings. Over time, growing dissent over the conduct of the war, especially after its expansion to include fighting an insurgency in Iraq, posed a real recruitment and retention challenge, though again, there were counterbalancing factors, such as the great recession, which weakened alternative employment opportunities for young people. Nevertheless, throughout the 2000s, there was continuing bipartisan support for increasing the pay and benefits for service. No one in public life wanted to be seen as unappreciative of the military, even opponents of the war, and even if recruiting did not require expanded financial incentives.

To appreciate the appreciation, we need to start with the compensation for the currently serving.[5] Compensation can be divided into three parts: base pay and allowances, special compensation, and benefits. A four-star general or admiral gets a base pay of about $200,000 a year, a full colonel or Navy captain about $110,000, an Army captain or Navy lieutenant about $68,000, a senior enlisted soldier or sailor about $50,000, and a junior enlisted soldier or sailor about $30,000. Military personnel get additional allowances for meals, housing, clothing and dependents that can add a third or more to their base pay, depending on rank and location. This compensation, paid to all of the same rank and years of service regardless of military occupation, is now 20–30 percent higher than salaries for civilians with equivalent education and work experience.[6]

Military pay is not static, of course, and neither are comparable civilian wages. In some years when Congress did not specially adjust military pay, the relatively fixed cost-of-living adjustments that the government uses trailed civilian pay increases by a notable margin, but big pay boosts in the late 1970s and early 1980s, the late 1990s, and early 2000s drove up pay to soldiers.[7] In 1998, enlisted personnel earned more than about 75 percent of American workers with a high school education, while officers were generally paid at about the 75th percentile among male college graduates, although mid-career officers earned slightly less than that benchmark while senior officers earned somewhat higher relative pay. Recent surveys indicate the military is faring even better.[8]

Service personnel in especially hazardous locations and/or occupations get additional compensation. Being in a combat zone pays $225 more a month. Being a paratrooper, a member of an air crew, a diver, or assigned to a ship at sea can add several hundred dollars more a month. And being a submariner pays up to $835 extra a month. There are retention bonuses for nuclear-trained naval officers (up to $35,000 per year), judge advocates (up to a total of $60,000), medical doctors and dentists ($10,000 to $15,000 per year plus initial accession bonuses and repayment of educational loans), special warfare officers (up to $25,000 per year), and pilots (up to $25,000 per year). Becoming proficient in certain foreign languages earns a onetime bonus of up to $12,000. Some of these hazardous duty payments and bonuses are tax-free.

And then there are the benefits. Some who advocated for the establishment of the AVF before 1973 wanted soldier compensation to be primarily monetary, with pay to be determined by the market – up in time of war and down or steady in times of high unemployment. The military, however, wanted service to be more than just a job, a mercenary calling, and pushed hard for an expansion of benefits as the source of attraction and the reward for service, including medical care, housing, education, day care for children, and the like. Although pay increased significantly for service in the armed forces, the military won the argument, and benefits expanded even more. Today, the military is the most socialized segment of American society, the deepest welfare state within the welfare state, although it is hardly ever expressed that way. Instead, there is talk of the military family and earned benefits.[9]

The benefits are substantial. Service members and their families can shop for groceries, household goods, and clothing at base commissaries and exchanges, which sell items at a discount compared to civilian prices and whose profits fund recreational activities. Active-duty personnel and their dependents receive health care under the TRICARE program, which has various options that allow access to non-military hospitals and doctors as well as military medical facilities at no or low cost based on location and preferences. The maximum out-of-pocket expense is $1,000 per year under the main plan.[10] Dental care is free for active-duty personnel, with a subsidized plan for dependents. Prescriptions for the whole family are filled free at military treatment facilities.

Service in the military also can famously bring educational benefits. Many military personnel benefit from training and educational opportunities while on active duty; these benefits improve their job performance, to be sure, but they also can contribute to life satisfaction, a sense of achievement, and post-service employment opportunities and salary. Separately, the Post-9/11 GI Bill and related educational benefit legislation provide full college tuition and fees, a monthly housing allowance, a stipend, and money for books and supplies that has a total value of more than $90,000 and that is transferable to dependents. There is also Veterans Affairs assistance for the education of surviving children of veterans. Additional VA programs offer subsidized loans for housing purchases, counseling of all types, funeral expenses, and interment in national cemeteries. The United States is indeed a very appreciative nation.

Generous retirement benefits are also part of the package. All who leave the military with an honorable discharge – and nearly 200,000 men and women do each year – are veterans and, as such, are eligible for veterans' benefits. Military retirees and their families can continue to shop at base commissaries and exchanges, preserving that subsidy to reduce their cost of living. A pension comes after at least 20 years of service. For someone with 20 years, the monthly pension is half of the average of the highest 36 monthly paychecks; for soldiers who retire later, the fraction increases, up to 75 percent for those who stay in 30 years. The nominal pension subsequently increases with an annual cost of living adjustment. Members of the National Guard and the Reserves also are eligible for retirement based on a point system for their years of service.

More important, over time, retiree health care has also expanded. In the current system, in place since 2001, all retirees may continue their TRICARE benefits until age 65, after which TRICARE becomes a very generous Medicare (health care for the elderly) wrap-around policy under the TRICARE for Life (TFL) program. The TFL benefit adds billions of dollars of costs to the defense budget, which supported 2.3 million retirees in 2015. Including the cost of these retirees, health care for the military and dependents now costs nearly 10 percent of the defense budget.[11] Alternatively, veterans can receive free health care from a network of VA hospitals and clinics. Priority goes to veterans with service-connected injuries, major disabilities, and/or low income, but care is available to all, as resources permit. The system may seem complicated to some, but the government provides many options, and veterans successfully exercise those options, as we can see from the soaring cost of providing these services.

Veterans are also able to apply for disability ratings for injuries or illness that were incurred or were aggravated during active duty, regardless of whether the disability was related to the performance of military service. A limp acquired in combat, one resulting from falling down a ship ladder, or one from a motorcycle accident while on leave in Tijuana counts the same for a disability. Ratings convert to lifetime pensions, some or all of which may be tax-free, depending upon the level of the disability.

Retirement comes so young in the military that it provides an opportunity for a second career, especially as Americans' average lifespan has increased. Some work for defense contractors. Many go to work for the government, federal and state, where they receive preferential employment status, meaning that their job applications get bonus points when they are reviewed, helping them rise to the top of the stack. Jobs go to veterans over equally qualified non-veterans. Including those who leave the military early along with military retirees, veterans account for 30 percent of the federal workforce and nearly 50 percent of the DoD's.[12] This second employment creates a whole new set of benefits for veterans – double dipping, some call it – as federal pay and retirement benefits are also now competitive with those in the private sector, and veterans do not give up military retirement pay while gaining another government check. Generals and colonels have been particular beneficiaries of the second career opportunities. Besides working for defense contractors, some retired general officers are paid as consultants by the military to mentor serving general officers. The teaching staffs at the war colleges, supposedly heavily civilian, are so dominated by officer retirees that faculty searches are jokingly referred to as "the no colonel left behind program."

There is growing recognition that the military retirement policies exploit the short-termers, those many junior officers and enlisted personnel who serve one or two tours and then leave the military without accruing any military retirement benefits and those forced out in the military's up-or-out promotional system.[13] Currently, nearly 83 percent of service members leave before being eligible for any retirement benefits. Legislation passed in 2015 to accommodate the short-termers by shifting away from the defined-benefit system that vests after 20 years to an employee-directed, 401K-type defined-contribution retirement system, similar to the pensions that are increasingly common in the private sector. The new system's implementation does not start right away, however, and it will apply only to new enlistees.[14] Military retiree organizations are still strongly opposed to the military's use of a commercial-like retirement plan that requires participant contributions, which they claim is a breach of faith on the part of the government.[15]

Overall, the list of benefits is quite long and comprehensive. When you add it all together, the current package shows that the United States is indeed a very appreciative nation.

Marching for bonuses and more

It is not surprising that the interests of veterans have long had the attention of Congress. One of the first acts of the First Congress was to provide pensions for disabled veterans of the Revolutionary War. America's military strength was initially based on militias, local forces composed of adult males. Given the restrictions on the franchise – neither women nor slaves could vote – the militias were the core of the electorate. Moreover, the path to elected office often ran through the militia, which itself often elected its own leaders. Being a war veteran remained a sought-after status well into the twentieth century, with the designation sometimes appearing on state and local ballots next to a candidate's name.[16]

Veterans want things, not necessarily unreasonably. They want pensions when their wounds prevent them from earning a normal living, bonuses in recognition for their service in times of war, and support for their spouses and children when they die. And legislators generally want to accommodate them. But preferences for limiting the role of the federal government in American society made the accommodation a slow one, even though veterans were viewed as especially deserving and politically important. The states were often more willing to act, for example, establishing old soldiers' and sailors' homes as the Civil War veteran population aged.

Pressure grew on the federal government to act after World War I as veterans returned uniquely injured by poison gas and requiring specialized care. There were also more wounded than in past wars, because medicine could save more of those hurt on the battlefield or stricken with disease than in the past. In 1921, Congress consolidated the programs providing veterans' pensions and rehabilitative services into a separate Veterans Bureau, which also became responsible for a set of public hospitals that provided care for war-injured veterans.[17]

The highest-profile political mobilization was about money, not health care. Veterans of the war had been sent home with a train ticket and $60, which many of them considered too little. In 1924, after much wrangling with the administration, Congress passed the World War Adjusted Compensation Act, which provided a complicated scheme of bonuses of up to $500 for stateside service and $625 for overseas service: the veterans would receive a certificate designating their bonus eligibility on their next birthday, but they would not be paid actual money until twenty years later, in 1945. Politicians were reluctant to provide a more generous

Figure 13.1 Bonus Army shanties burning in sight of the US Capitol after the Army drove out
     the protestors

Source: National Archives.

benefit because of the high costs of Civil War benefits, accounting for at times a third of the
federal budget.[18] Under the law, veterans could use their certificates as collateral for loans, and
many did, but when the Great Depression hit in 1929, they clamored for immediate payment
and additional awards. The government agreed to partial payment, but as the Depression deep-
ened in 1932, veterans calling themselves the Bonus Army marched on Washington seeking
full payment. Rebuffed, some set up makeshift encampments in an attempt to embarrass
President Hoover and Congress into acting. After clashes with police and fears that unsanitary
conditions in the encampments were creating a public health hazard, troops with armored
vehicles and horses were called out to clear the city of the petitioning veterans and burn their
shanty towns. Public sentiment shifted decidedly toward the veterans.[19]

   President Franklin Roosevelt's New Deal, his response to the Depression, and World War
II vastly expanded the federal role in American life. The president and his mostly supportive
Congress were not about to disappoint the millions of new veterans the war was creating, having learned from Hoover's Bonus Army experience. As the war's tide turned with
the invasion at Normandy, they enacted the GI Bill of Rights, officially the Servicemen's
Readjustment Act of 1944, a comprehensive package of benefits, initially drafted by the
American Legion, which would await returning veterans. Included were a year of unemployment compensation, pensions, mortgage subsidies, cheap loans to start businesses, and most
famously, money for education and training. In the late 1940s and early 1950s, millions of
veterans bought houses and went to college or received vocational training, transforming
American society.

After the war, the government also had to face the task of restructuring and expand-ing the VA's medical services. VA hospitals had been deteriorating physically due to the budget restrictions imposed during the Depression and the war, and the overall care provided was thought to be of poor quality. Construction or acquisition of more than 50 hospitals in the decade after the war, although certainly needed, was not going to be enough to fix the problem. Private medicine also opposed the growth in this form of publicly provided care, particularly the expansion to include outpatient care to veterans through hospital-based clin-ics. To blunt the opposition and to deal with the quality issue, the government affiliated VA hospitals with the nation's medical schools, making them teaching hospitals and part of the physician-training system. Medical residents and medical school faculty affiliations would help staff the hospitals, supposedly assuring cutting-edge care for veterans and making the VA part of the local medical community, not an isolated federal appendage.

The affiliations, however, came with a cost. Medical schools are research-oriented, need-ing to work with the most difficult cases. The challenge of caring for the war-wounded may be quite intense initially, but it soon dissipates into routine-though-vital medical maintenance and social support. The majority of veterans then seeking care from the VA are the elderly, with the normal problems of aging, and the poor, including major substance abuse problems, neither group being particularly attractive to the medical schools. Moreover, teaching hos-pitals tend to develop a cold, indifferent manner of care in their constant quest to provide "clinical material" for the training of physicians and other health care professionals. Clashes with veterans and their families, given a growing sense of earned entitlement and the various organizations established to champion their cause, were inevitable.[20]

These problems are exacerbated by the need of the VA and its hospitals to adjust to a new generation of veterans after each war. For example, since the wars in Iraq and Afgh-anistan, a much higher percentage of VA care has been for women than in the past.[21] Newly prevalent types of injuries, such as traumatic brain injury, also provide challenges for the hospitals.

Not all heroes

The budget for the Department of Veterans Affairs has more than tripled since 2000. It employs some 365,000 people (50 percent growth since 2000) at 152 medical centers and 1,400 other community-based outpatient clinics, counseling centers, and community living facilities (nursing homes).[22] VA benefits are so varied and complex that state and local gov-ernments as well many veterans' organizations employ counselors to assist veterans through the maze. In a system this big, there are bound to be bad apples and bad policies, and there are certainly some of both.

Military service is hazardous. Nearly 7,000 US personnel have died in combat or accidents during the post-9/11 fighting in Iraq and Afghanistan. Another 50,000 have been wounded or injured, about half of whom required medical evacuation out of theater. About 1,650 lost one or more limbs, while thousands more suffered catastrophic burns and head injuries.[23] Still more experience post-traumatic stress disorder (PTSD) for the horrors they endured. It is right that there are benefits for the families of the fallen and disability payments for those who returned hurt.

It seems strange, though, that so many apply for disability payments after their service. Of the nearly two million who have left the service since 9/11, over 700,000, not all of whom deployed, have sought disability awards. Even among those deployed, most do not leave their bases or fire a weapon in combat; people "inside the wire" in Afghanistan and Iraq faced the threat of random mortar attacks and occasional bombings, but casualties from those kinds of events were relatively few. Of course, not all injury or illness occurs as a result of combat or in a combat zone, but the overall disability claim rate is increasing sharply. It was 15 percent after World War II and 25 percent after Vietnam. It is now about 37 percent. There are no time limits for applications, the awards are for life, and the benefits are tax-free. The cost of VA disability claims now exceeds $60 billion, tripling since 2000. Without the time limit and with the intervening recession, more than 1.2 million people have been added to the veteran disability rolls since 2000. The actual amount of benefit that a disabled veteran receives mainly depends on two factors: the "dependency level," which specifies how big a family the veteran's income is expected to support, and the "percentage of disability," which estimates what percentage of a non-disabled person's working time that veteran should to be able to perform.

The opportunity for fraud is built in. The number one disability claim, worth 10 percent, is tinnitus, a ringing or buzzing in the ears, a malady that is common with exposure to loud noises and is hard to measure.[24] Another is back pain, which is also a common and hard-to-measure complaint. Pilots often claim hemorrhoids from those long hours in the saddle. Processing for low-level claims is routine, without much documentation required. But claims are cumulative and can add up to the 50 percent mark and beyond, where the benefits become more significant. PTSD usually earns a higher percentage disability, though it, too, is hard to measure medically. The PTSD claim rates for Americans serving in Iraq or Afghanistan are much higher than they are for British personnel serving in the same conflicts.[25] Over 20 percent of 177,000 US service personnel officially diagnosed with some level of PTSD had not even deployed to either Iraq or Afghanistan.[26] Surely, there are cultural differences in the expression, treatment, and acceptance of particular disabilities.

Wars have developed signature wounds that test the ability of the medical community to respond quickly and effectively to the treatment challenge. For Iraq and Afghanistan, it has been traumatic brain injury (TBI), publicly associated with improvised explosive device attacks. The medical community, military as well as civilian, did step up for TBI, and real progress has been made in the care of victims.

But wars also have their medical mysteries, problems more for the politicians than for the doctors. In Vietnam, it was Agent Orange, an herbicide compound that was aerially sprayed along convoy routes to reduce the danger of ambushes (Operation Ranch Hand). In the Gulf War, it was a chronic fatigue disorder that was labeled the Gulf War Syndrome.[27] And for Iraq and Afghanistan, it is PTSD.[28] In these cases, the medical condition is hard to define, hard to treat, and hard even to measure the extent of the damage. They are ripe for politicization.

For politicians, the diagnosis is often whatever the claimants want. The answer to how much cure money to provide is, "lots of it." The response to the effects of Agent Orange provides a good example. From a medical perspective, focusing on problems for which there is substantial evidence that doctors can interpret with a high degree of confidence, Agent Orange at high levels of exposure is known to produce a severe-but-treatable form of acne. Such acne was observed among the ground and air crew handlers of the barrels of the product, identified by an orange stripe, barrels that occasionally broke open or spilled accidentally when attached to the spraying equipment. Disability claims were approved.

But critics of the Vietnam War sought to stop the military use of the herbicides, exploiting generalized fears of chemicals in the environment by asserting additional dangers for soldiers and civilians. In sorting out these claims, investigators found that Agent Orange often included dioxin, a highly toxic chemical, as a contaminant, and that there had been serious health consequences of the commercial use of Agent Orange-type herbicides elsewhere. Veterans who feared their own exposures while in Vietnam picked up on this information. Military records of troops passing through sprayed areas were incomplete, making it difficult to trace individual exposures. But after further investigation, the medical judgment was firm that there was no harm done beyond that to the Agent Orange handlers, who at times were covered in the defoliant.[29]

Private lawsuits produced little gain for the veterans, but veterans soon found champions in Congress. In 1991, Congress passed the Agent Orange Act, which authorized the VA to declare certain conditions to be presumptively due to exposure to the herbicide no matter the documentation. The Act also required continuous studies by the National Research Council as a basis for expanding the list of presumptive conditions. Successive VA secretaries anxious to please Congress and veterans presumptively attributed more and more diseases to Agent Orange exposure, now including lung cancer (even for smokers) and those conditions normally thought part of the aging process such as heart disease, type II diabetes, and prostate cancer. Any time spent in Vietnam, including even a brief air transit stopover in what was then Saigon, is now accepted as "exposure."[30] The Operation Ranch Hand aircraft, primarily C-123s, were cleaned and eventually ended up serving some years in the Air Force Reserve as transports. In 2015, the 2,000-plus Reservists and active duty personnel who tended or flew the aircraft after the war won full eligibility for any disability claims they may wish to make.[31]

The broader definitions for presumptive conditions came largely in the early 2000s, just about the time when the VA had to cope with the influx of veterans from Iraq and Afghanistan and the aging out of the World War II and Korean War veterans. As is typical after wars, the VA was hit by several scandals.[32] It had difficulty being responsive to a new wave of amputees and PTSD victims. The disability claims processing system built up a huge backlog. Medical appointment scheduling systems collapsed, and their problems were concealed in official reports. VA construction projects ran way over budget, the most publicized being the Denver VA Medical Center, contracted for $604 million and now likely topping out at $1.73 billion.[33] Some of this is undoubtedly due to old-fashioned corruption, but most of it is the product of a bureaucracy overburdened by excessive rules and given excessive discretion, and manned by a staff protected by civil service regulations and a management selected by patronage. That bureaucracy is trying to cope with a clientele that expects market-like responsiveness in a socialized medicine setting with academic overtones.[34] The medical schools and science pull in one direction, Washington in another, and the veterans in a third. And because of the civil service protection, some of the staff don't pull at all.

The scandals help reinforce a narrative that recent veterans are victims – victims of being sent to bad wars and victims of being ignored by their government or of receiving bad treatment and slipping into violent or self-destructive behavior.[35] Commentators often cite a VA report that 22 veterans a day commit suicide, a seemingly outrageous number, with the implication that this is the result of governmental failure either on the part of the military or the VA.[36] It turns out most of these veterans are older (average age is 60) and are facing serious personal problems such as terminal illness.[37] Most of the suicides are not veterans of the campaigns in Iraq or Afghanistan. Among Iraq and Afghanistan veterans, the number is about one a day, each no doubt a tragedy but likely with different origins than the headlines imply.[38] A comprehensive study by the Army of suicide among serving soldiers, which is trending upward, shows it is not linked to deployments and military occupation, but rather to disciplinary problems including drug use and criminality as well as to failed relationships and financial stress.[39]

The bad apples and the bad policies are unlikely to disappear. Congress may want to have the VA fire employees who lost or misstated appointment wait list reports, but it is not about to reduce civil service employment protection, which it established in the past for good reasons, such as efforts to reduce patronage and increase incentives to provide training that enhances the competence and morale of public servants. Those well-intentioned rules, though, make firing incompetent or dishonest public employees nearly a lifelong bureaucratic task for supervisors. Remember also that substantial numbers of federal employees are veterans.

Moreover, bad policies are often well-intentioned policies with loopholes or anomalies caused by other well-intentioned policies. For example, Congress created the Individual Unemployment Benefit that supplements the disability payments of low-income veterans rated 60–90 percent disabled and deemed unable to work, paying them at the 100 percent rate: an average monthly tax-free increase of $1,600 for a qualified, married veteran receiving a disability pension. It turns out, however, that over 60 percent of the 180,000 veterans receiving the Individual Unemployment Benefit are 65 or older – that is, likely to be retired rather than working, if they were not disabled. Several thousand of the new claimants were over 75 when the program began. But Congress is not likely to impose age limits on the employability of veterans when it has waived mandatory retirement requirements for civilians.[40] Doors are meant to be opened for veterans, not closed to them, even if the door is to the Treasury.

A frequent reform proposal is to give veterans gold-card access to private-sector health care. Some of this already occurs when veterans live more than 40 miles from a VA facility. And more is certain to come to give veterans flexibility in gaining specialized care. But the dedicated VA health system is not likely to be eliminated. Much of the purpose of the system is to show how much the society cares about its veterans. Politicians are certain to tread carefully. The VA is not going to be privatized, nor is the care it provides going to be outsourced, at least not while millions of veterans are among us. However, without the hammer of competition, making the system responsive to the needs of a population ever on the edge of decline is a very big policy challenge.

The many veterans organizations

As discussed in Chapter 9, lobbies suffer from a free-rider problem. It usually takes effort – someone's time, compensated or not – to present Congress and the administration with ideas for new programs, changes in existing ones, or increases in agency budgets, and to agitate for their adoption. For some interests with relatively concentrated groups of direct beneficiaries – say, shipyard companies building warships – members of the class understand the organizing problem and/or can be shamed into contributing to support a lobby by other members of the class. For veterans and those currently serving, though, the affected class can easily number in the tens of thousands, if not the hundreds of thousands or millions. Because everyone in the class gains the benefit of successful lobbies such as higher checks or future educational opportunities, lobbies need selective rewards, some incentive that can be denied to those who have not contributed to sustaining the effort to influence governmental policy.[41]

Of course, less effort is needed when the public strongly support a particular group or cause, as is now clearly the case for veterans and the military. Politicians do not need to be persuaded by lobbyists to believe that those who have served are worthy of assistance. Moreover, once the enterprise gets big, it has a momentum of its own. There are now well-staffed committees and subcommittees in both houses of Congress whose sole focus is on

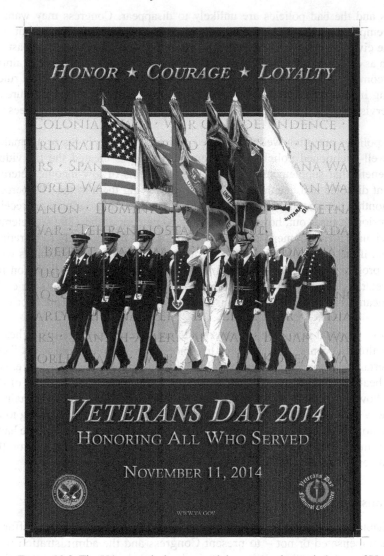

Figure 13.2 The VA commissions a special poster each year in honor of Veterans Day
Source: Department of Veterans Affairs. Reproduced with permission.

veterans and their needs. The VA itself is a mammoth organization with strong interests in protecting the benefits it provides to veterans – or in enlarging those benefits, especially if the new benefit comes from reducing the rate at which VA employees have to make a difficult choice to deny benefits to an applicant who is already in the VA system. One VA administrator admitted that he devoted considerable time on Capitol Hill to trying to counter proposals from VA professional staff that were running too far ahead of what the president was seeking for veterans or the VA itself.[42]

But in the years before the welfare state was so firmly embedded in the warfare state, veterans' groups advocating benefits for veterans and their dependents needed to have incentives for participation that could be denied to non-members. The best-known organizations are the Veterans of Foreign Wars, which was founded after the Spanish–American War, and the American Legion, which was founded after World War I. Mostly these organizations have used what Peter B. Clark and James Q. Wilson called solidarity incentives.[43] These incentives include the opportunity to join an after-hours local club to drink with friends, to sponsor sports teams, and to confer social status on one another by gaining local (e.g., post commander), state, and national Legion or Veterans of Foreign Wars offices. The national organizations in effect taxed the local affiliates' membership dues in exchange for the use of the national name, and then the national organization used the money to lobby nationally for benefits.[44] The organizations often further differentiated by ethnic ties (Italian-American Veterans, Jewish War Veterans of the USA, etc.), service affiliation (the Marine Corps League, Fleet Reserve Association), condition (the Disabled American Veterans), or volunteer urge (AMVETS), creating even stronger emotional reasons for an individual to join up and be part of the club.

By the Vietnam War, though, the traditional veterans' organizations were losing their appeal. Veterans' benefits were already well protected by politicians and professionals. The older World War II veterans dominated the organizations, but their preferences for garrison caps, ladies' auxiliaries, and conventional views did not fit well with the more rebellious veterans of the 1960s and 1970s. The most visible veterans of the era were those who protested the war by joining anti-war marches and offering congressional testimony that accused the military of war crimes. John Kerry, later a senator from Massachusetts, presidential candidate, and secretary of state, was among their leaders. Others helped form the Vietnam Veterans of America, which championed the Agent Orange cause along with seeking aid for homeless veterans. The strikingly dark Vietnam Veterans Memorial on the Mall in Washington, DC, is another legacy. It was politics – purposive incentives, in Clark and Wilson terms, where members joined because they cared about the group's policy goals – that motivated what little organizing occurred among Vietnam veterans.

The typical veteran-oriented organization in the Iraq/Afghanistan era is neither a social nor a political club; instead, it is a charity. Organizations such as the Gary Sinise Foundation, the Fisher Foundation, and the Wounded Warrior Project seek to assist injured veterans and their families. Even the one major membership organization, Iraq and Afghanistan Veterans of America, is primarily about soliciting funds for and providing service to needy veterans. All of these organizations thrive on the largely false public image that the government is neglecting or underserving the many severely damaged veterans of these conflicts and their burdened families. The danger is that the charity slips into being a racket that plays on the sympathies of the public while diverting donations into lavish salaries and plush surroundings for the charities' executives.[45] But because of publicly provided benefits, most veterans and their dependents will not notice.

Questions for discussion

1   What is fair compensation for military service?
2   How can Congress balance benefits for those who served with fairness to taxpayers?
3   How would you relate the growth of America's welfare system to the growth of veterans' benefits?
4   Should there be a separate set of hospitals for veterans?
5   Will either the changing demographics of the military or the changing nature of modern warfare impact the prospects for veterans' organizations?

Notes

1 Christopher Harress, "World War I Veterans' Benefits Continue to Be Paid 100 Years after Fighting Began," *International Business Times*, July 15, 2014.
2 Jerry Lembcke, *The Spitting Image: Myth, Memory, and the Legacy of Vietnam* (New York: NYU Press, 2000).
3 Douglas Clarke, *The Missing Man: Politics and the MIA* (Washington, DC: National Defense University Press, 1979).
4 Ken Harbaugh, "The Risk of Over-Thanking Our Veterans," *New York Times*, June 1, 2015, p. A17.
5 A good place to learn about military compensation is the very appropriately titled annual *The Military Advantage*: Terry Howell, *The Military Advantage: The Military.com Guide to Military and Veterans Benefits* (Annapolis, MD: US Naval Institute Press, 2015).
6 Philip Carter and Katherine Kidder, *Military Compensation and Retirement Modernization: A Primer* (Washington, DC: Center for a New American Security, January 2015), p. 13.
7 Cindy Williams, "The G.O.P.'s Pay Gap," *New York Times*, August 17, 2000.
8 James Hosek, Beth J. Asch, and Michael G. Mattock, *Should the Increase in Military Pay Be Slowed?* (Santa Monica, CA: RAND Corporation, 2012).
9 Jennifer Mittelstadt, *The Rise of the Military Welfare State* (Cambridge, MA: Harvard University Press, 2015).
10 Howell, *The Military Advantage*, p. 91.
11 See Alexis Lasselle Ross, "Legislating 'Military Entitlements': A Challenge to the Congressional Abdication Thesis," in Colton C. Campbell and David P. Auerswald (eds.), *Congress and Civil-Military Relations* (Washington, DC: Georgetown University Press, 2015), pp. 98–100.
12 "Veterans: What next?" *The Economist*, December 6, 2014, p. 29; Paige Hingle-Bowles, Deputy Assistant Secretary of Defense (Civilian Personnel Policy), DoD press release, June 9, 2015.
13 Tom Kane, "Military Retirement: Too Sweet a Deal?" *War on the Rocks*, March 2, 2015, available at: http://warontherocks.com/2015/03/military-retirement-too-sweet-a-deal/ (accessed June 11, 2016).
14 Leo Shane III, "Military Retirement Overhaul: Congress Is on Board—So What Comes Next?" *Military Times*, October 7, 2015.
15 Leo Shane III, "Advocates Expand Fight over Military Retirement Changes," *Military Times*, April 17, 2015.
16 Massachusetts, for one. Some states allow veterans to use the designation "veteran" on drivers' licenses so as to ease the collection of benefits and perhaps dodge a traffic ticket or two.
17 Michael Lipsky, Lawrence McCray, Jeffrey Prottas, and Harvey Sapolsky, "The Future of the Veterans' Health Care System," *Journal of Health Care Politics, Policy, and Law*, 1(3) (Fall 1976): 285–294.
18 Glenn C. Altschuler and Stuart M. Blumin, *The G.I. Bill: A New Deal for Veterans* (New York: Oxford University Press, 2009), pp. 18–25.
19 Roxanne Shirazi, "Bonus Army, 1932: A Bibliographic Essay," *Roxanne Shirazi*, November 2009, available at: http://roxanneshirazi.com/projects/bonus-army/ (accessed June 11, 2016).
20 Lipsky et al., "The Future of the Veterans' Health Care System."
21 Leo Shane III, "Survey: Women Struggle to be Seen as 'Real' Veterans," *Military Times*, June 9, 2015; Emily Wax-Thibodeaux, "One Female Veteran's Epic Quest for a 'Foot that Fits,'" *Washington Post*, September 9, 2015.
22 Anthony Principi, "Money Can't Cure What Ails Veterans Affairs," *Wall Street Journal*, May 26, 2016.
23 David Wood, "U.S. Wounded in Iraq, Afghanistan Includes More than 1,500 Amputees," *Huffington Post*, November 7, 2012; Bryant Jordan, "Report Obscures Extent of Combat-Related Traumatic Brain Injuries," *Military.com*, August 12, 2015, available at: http://www.military.com/daily-news/2015/08/12/report-obscures-extent-combat-related-traumatic-brain-injuries.html (accessed June 11, 2016).
24 Elizabeth Bass and Heidi Golding, *Veterans' Disability Compensation: Trends and Policy Options* (Washington, DC: Congressional Budget Office, August 2014), pp. 3–4.
25 Sarah Sloat, "The U.K. Understand How to Treat PTSD. Why Does the U.S. Lag Behind?" *The New Republic*, February 28, 2014.
26 Jordan, "Report Obscures Extent of Combat-Related Traumatic Brain Injuries." And less than 80 of the TBI cases are linked to a deployment.

27 Kelly Kennedy, "House Asks VA for Presumptive Conditions for Gulf War Vets," *USA Today*, March 18, 2014.
28 Eighty percent of TBI cases are said to be mild, hard to diagnose, and overlap with PTSD in described symptoms: Dewleen G. Baker, "Post-Traumatic Stress Disorder and Traumatic Brain Injury – Current Issues," undated PowerPoint presentation at the Idaho Traumatic Brain Injury Virtual Program, Idaho State University, available at: http://www.idahotbi.org/Portals/_AgencySite/pdf/DGB_Part%201_%20PTSD-TBI.pdf (accessed June 11, 2016).
29 Michael Gough, *Dioxin, Agent Orange: The Facts* (New York: Springer, 1986).
30 Anthony J. Principi, "Wounded Vets Deserve Better," *Wall Street Journal*, August 29, 2013, p. A-15; Principi was secretary of veterans affairs under George W. Bush.
31 Hope Yen, "US Agrees to Pay Millions for Agent Orange Claims," *ABC News*, June 22, 2015.
32 Tom Temin, "VA's Ongoing Problems Started at Top, and They Can End There," *Federal News Radio*, September 7, 2015.
33 Mark K. Matthews, David Olinger, and David Migoya, "Anatomy of a Calamity," *The Denver Post*, August 11, 2015; Leo Shane III, "Denver Vets Hospital Mistakes Echo Larger VA Issues," *Military Times*, April 15, 2015.
34 Harvey M. Sapolsky, "America's Socialized Medicine: The Allocation of Resources Within the Veterans' Health Care System," *Public Policy*, 25(3) (Summer 1977): 359–382.
35 Mackubin Thomas Owens, "Life after Wartime: Combating the Veteran-as-Victim Narrative," *The Weekly Standard*, June 2, 2014, pp. 21–24. Owens mostly focuses on Vietnam War veterans.
36 Gregg Zaroya, "VA study: 22 Vets Commit Suicide Every Day," *USA Today*, February 1, 2013. The report is Janet Kemp and Robert Bossarte, *Suicide Data Report, 2012*, Department of Veterans Affairs, Mental Health Services, Suicide Prevention Program, available at: http://www.va.gov/opa/docs/Suicide-Data-Report-2012-final.pdf (accessed June 11, 2016). See also Nancy A. Youssef, "As Iraq Winds down, U.S. Army Confronts a Broken Force," *McClatchyDC*, September 17, 2010, available at: http://www.mcclatchydc.com/news/nation-world/national/article24593521.html (accessed June 11, 2016).
37 The age figure is from Michelle Ye Hee Lee, "The Missing Context behind the Widely Cited Statistic that There Are 22 Veteran Suicides a Day," *Washington Post*, February 4, 2015. There were some elevated rates for first-term, never-deployed enlisted combat infantrymen and combat engineers that reversed for those deployed and having been deployed: R. C. Kessler, M. B. Stein, P. D. Bliese, E. J. Bromet, W. T. Chiu, K. L. Cox, L. J. Colpe, C. S. Fullerton, S. E. Gilman, M. J. Gruber, S. G. Heeringa, L. Lewandowski-Romps, A. Millikan-Bell, J. A. Naifeh, M. K. Nock, M. V Petukhova, A. J. Rosellini, N. A. Sampson, M. Schoenbaum, A. M. Zaslavsky, and R. J. Ursano, "Occupational Differences in U.S. Army Suicide Rates," *Psychological Medicine*, July 20, 2015, pp. 1–12.
38 Stacy Bare, "The Truth about 22 Veteran Suicides a Day," *Task & Purpose*, June 2, 2015, available at: http://taskandpurpose.com/truth-22-veteran-suicides-day/ (accessed June 11, 2016).
39 Note also Alan Zarembo, "Looking Closer at the Role of Life Insurance in Military Suicides," *Los Angeles Times*, September 8, 2013.
40 Bass and Golding, *Veterans' Disability Compensation*, p. 19.
41 Mancur Olson, *The Logic of Collective Action: Public Goods and the Theory of Groups* (Cambridge, MA: Harvard University Press, 1965).
42 Sapolsky, "America's Socialized Medicine," p. 364.
43 Peter B. Clark and James Q. Wilson, "Incentive Systems: A Theory of Organizations," *Administrative Science Quarterly*, 6 (September 1961): 129–168.
44 Harvey M. Sapolsky, "Organizational Competition and Monopoly," *Public Policy*, 17 (1968): 355–377.
45 Tim Mak, "'Wounded Warrior' Charity Fights – to Get Rich," *The Daily Beast*, June 8, 2015.

Recommended additional reading

Glenn C. Altschuler and Stuart M. Blumin, *The GI Bill: A New Deal for Veterans* (New York: Oxford University Press, 2009). The generous and comprehensive GI Bill, which helped transform post-World War II American society, was a reaction to the limited benefits offered to World War I veterans, itself a reaction to the generous benefits offered to Union veterans of the Civil War.
Douglas Clarke, *The Missing Man: Politics and the MIA* (Washington, DC: National Defense University Press, 1979). The National League of POW/MIA Families is dominated by parents rather than wives.

Wives want to get on with their lives, while parents are unwilling to let go. Benefits play a big part. In negotiations with the United States, Vietnamese exploited these emotions in not offering a full accounting, but they didn't get the reconstruction aid that the United States promised them, either.

Jerry Lembcke, *PTSD: Diagnosis and Identity in Post-Empire America* (Lanham, MD: Lexington Books, 2013). Murky diagnosis for murky wars. PTSD becomes a way to change the subject from bad wars to all the wounded veterans.

Jennifer Mittelstadt, *The Rise of the Military Welfare State* (Cambridge, MA: Harvard University Press, 2015). The Army wanted to make service something special, more than just a job for a mercenary. After loading on the benefits, it tried to find ways to reduce its costs and paternalism by outsourcing and preaching self-reliance, things Mittelstadt does not like but also does not examine very fairly or thoroughly.

14 Preparing for the next war

The famous quotation "Predicting is hard, especially about the future" is alternatively attributed to Yogi Berra and Niels Bohr, two quite different insightful men of history. One was an all-star baseball catcher, and the other was a father of nuclear weapons and a Nobel Laureate. Baseball is a sport where you cannot be certain of the outcome until the last out is made. Physics seeks predictions, but even an outstanding physicist like Niels Bohr was wrong about the future of nuclear weapons. Many try to predict what America's next war will be, but such prediction is hard for a nation that has neither a large, powerful enemy living nearby nor the willpower to resist trying to shape the global security environment.

Nevertheless, security policy and politics, the subjects of this book, are all about predicting what the next war will be like, with whom it will be fought, and how to prepare for it. The defense budget is a planning document and so, too, are many others: the war plans that fill the secure vaults in the Pentagon, the various reports that the Defense Department submits to Congress, the *National Security Strategy*, the *National Military Strategy*, and a hundred more documents like them. Decisions about what weapons to build, what training to give to troops, what stockpiles to hold, and what doctrines to adopt require predictions about which wars are, and are not, coming.

Of course, the prediction record is not good. No one expected that more than 60 years after the North's invasion, American forces would still be deployed in South Korea – especially after South Korea was left off a 1950 list of places to be defended. No one thought that America would be fighting an insurgency in Vietnam a mere decade after it bypassed the opportunity when the French were forced out in the 1950s. Meanwhile, the much-studied and heavily garrisoned Fulda Gap never saw military action during the Cold War, but the US armor units originally assigned there helped liberate Kuwait in one war and Iraq in another. The B-52 was designed as a strategic nuclear bomber but flew missions with conventional ordnance over Vietnam and Afghanistan. And the *Spruance*-class destroyers, designed as superb submarine hunters, never wound up chasing a submarine in anger, but they did patrol the waters of the Middle East and South Asia looking for small boats smuggling weapons and al Qaeda volunteers. Wars are mostly about surprise, adjustment, and improvisation.

This chapter draws out the lessons of the other chapters, returning to the four key axes on which policy debates are fought that we described at the beginning: (1) markets versus planning, (2) public versus private, (3) experts versus politics, and (4) centralization versus decentralization. It assumes that the United States will invest some effort in preparation for war, even if wars are very hard to predict. Responsible officials cannot explain away their tasks with academic theories, even proven ones. Choices have to be made. In offering advice, we will address the policy issues discussed in the first chapter, what we called the enduring questions of public policy. Grappling with these questions, policy-makers can find the framework for dealing with the uncertainties of national defense.

Markets versus planning

The advantage of a market is that it undermines hierarchy. Planners offer one answer, the answer they think best. Planners cannot control the future, but they want to control the efforts of an organization or society in its attempts to cope with uncertainty. Markets offer choices about the future, essentially the chance to bet on different plans, different ways for coping with whatever comes. Consumers, not the planners, make the key choices in commercial markets. In video recorders, the choice was between Beta and VHS. In computer operating systems, it has been between Mac and Windows. And in automobiles, it has been between domestic and foreign.

The American government could avail itself of formal or informal markets as it tries to prepare for an uncertain future, a future with the distinct possibility of the nation having to or choosing to fight wars of one kind or another. The United States has within it the armed services and other agencies (e.g., the CIA and the State Department) that have distinct identities, command of some resources, a concern for their own future, and unease about potential competition with other services and agencies. Fears about their own organizational fortunes spur them to think about the nation's security needs.[1] Organizations guaranteed a well-endowed future with influence at the highest levels of decision-making behave like the monopolists that they are, and they have little or no reason to think innovatively about how they can contribute to solving the nation's problems. Organizations that have to prove their relevance usually do so, or they wither away.

The informal competition among the services and agencies could be focused on defining security threats, and the diversity of answers to this question could be a good thing. The Navy is likely to see China as a threat because it has growing international trade interests, an expanding dependence on energy imports, concern about potential US coercion, and the resources to build a blue-water navy. The Army and Marine Corps likely will be concerned about a conventional warfare threat, though the Marines might stress future risks to friendly governments in Asia and Africa, while the Army might mention a resurgent Russia and the need to keep involved in Europe and the Middle East. The Air Force likely would see airpower as solving all or most of the possible threats. The competitors would try to persuade, but senior officials could choose not to sign up for any of these alternatives, listening instead to the State Department or CIA's descriptions of a different set of threats. Each organizational advocate would have to defend its potential contribution to national security and the view of the threat environment that went with it. The danger of ignoring one or another possible threat would be part of the ongoing debate. And as each real threat revealed itself in the future, the focus could shift toward methods for meeting it, likely benefiting the organization that first identified it and has thought longest about what to do in response.

The more formal competitions could be reserved for equipment and doctrine. Although there is much talk today of the need for joint procurement and centralization, historically there have been significant benefits in allowing redundancy.[2] For example, during the Cold War, the Air Force, despite valiant efforts, failed to keep the other services, the CIA, and NASA from sponsoring satellite development and independent schemes for using space for their own operations. As a result of this proliferation of organizations working on the development of spacecraft, the United States quickly gained a strong lead in the use of space for both civilian and military purposes. The same could be said for inter-service competition in aviation. Four air forces have indeed been better than one, and each of them is better because of the existence of the others. Competition has promoted innovation, increased the information available to the public and decision-makers, and given civilians leverage in dealing with the services.

This past should be kept in mind in today's defense debates. For example, the Air Force seeks to gain control over all development of unmanned aerial vehicles, citing its special expertise in flight, the need to coordinate airspace usage and the potential cost savings of joint procurement. The other services object, arguing that UAVs need to serve field commanders and have tailored missions that are different for ground, naval, and air forces.[3] If the United States' experiences with spacecraft and manned aircraft are any indication, decentralized UAV development across multiple services would be more conducive to innovation and would create a more diverse set of capabilities for the future.

The boundaries of competition need not stay fixed. Jointness, despite its limitations, has taken hold among the conventional forces and has enduring support among civilian officials. The cartel that protects the services from deep questioning has encouraged much sharing of responsibilities and a common preference for modularity, the interchangeability on an ad hoc basis of functionally similar units such as infantry battalions and fighter squadrons among the services as they operate in contingencies. However, this form of harmonization stands in contrast with Special Operations Forces, which favor combined arms units that work together on a long-term basis. Special Operations also has its own acquisition authority and global command structure. The opportunity then exists for contrasting, even competing, perspectives on security threats, equipment, and doctrine between the conventional forces team – the services – and Special Operations. These different perspectives will challenge decision-makers to recognize more options as they contemplate the use of force.

Indeed, if the security future is opaque, as it seems for the United States, and if the United States must nevertheless prepare for the future, as it must, then the United States should want always to hedge its bets. Most security expectations are going to go unfulfilled. Most plans are going to be inaccurate. If planners are likely to get it wrong, then it is best to have several sets of planners, each seeing the future from a different perspective. Listening to their arguments is a way to explore premises, identify policy options, and avoid very big, very unpleasant security surprises.

Public versus private

Government is not an admired institution in the United States. With the exception of military service and a few other governmental callings, public service is not a highly respected career choice. Although Republicans and Democrats agree on very little, there is a national political consensus that government is usually the problem, not the answer. Government often fouls up what it aspires to accomplish, and much of what government does is better done in the private sector. Even those who seek more funding for government programs often advocate disbursing this money to private actors as much as is possible. This is true for education; it is true for the delivery of health care services; it is true for the design and procurement of weapons; and it is even true for the provision of combat support services such as transport, food service, and communications. Save for what is "inherently governmental," Americans are ready to privatize, privatize, privatize, or so it seems.

Of course, what is inherently governmental is neither obvious nor much of a barrier to privatization. The widespread use of contractors makes such distinctions moot because contractors contribute to the government's staff, provide advice, and, in many cases, do everything except sign the official papers. For example, so much of the weapons acquisition system has been shifted to contractors that retention of official responsibilities within the civil service has become nearly meaningless. Contractors are so involved in designing the contracts, setting the points for evaluation, and recording the results that they are practically in charge.

The intent of outsourcing is often to reduce reliance on civil servants and military personnel on the promise of reduced costs and greater efficiency. But because costs are hard to define and efficiency can rarely be measured directly, privatization is not always the easy solution it seems.

Private companies and organizations performing public missions soon acquire public-sector attributes. Regulations and expectations limit their supposed flexibility. The contextual goals of government – the political constraints governing how things get done – are as much part of the organizational life of a private shipbuilder as of a government-owned yard. Military contractors learn to worry about the proportion of their employees who count as minorities, the appearance of excess in their executives' salaries and bonuses, and their recordable profits. Private arsenals have replaced many of the public arsenals, but it is still government work that is being done.

The distinction that counts may not be what is inherently governmental or what is formally public or private but rather how well the government's (the public's) interest is protected. This likely depends, in turn, on the quality of the information and personnel available to the government. Hiring and retaining highly trained technical specialists are especially difficult. Public service often does not attract these people, and military managers often lack the in-depth training and experience needed to manage the complex programs that the government is inclined to undertake. Such training and experience are available to contractors but are managed to reflect the interests of the stockholders rather than those of the government.

The answer may well be in the form of dedicated advisory organizations such as the Federally Funded Research and Development Centers (FFRDCs) and similar organizations – for example, the Aerospace Corporation, MITRE, Sandia, Draper Laboratory, Lincoln Laboratory at MIT, and the Applied Physics Laboratory at Johns Hopkins University.[4] These specialized not-for-profit organizations work exclusively for the government, become store-houses of technical knowledge and experience, and buttress the government's capabilities as it attempts to manage the large-scale programs that are so much part of the national security enterprise. Unfortunately, funding for these institutions is always under threat: for-profit firms argue that they can do the work more efficiently, and politicians periodically remember that these organizations are designed to privilege elite technocrats, which grates in the American policy environment.

The public and the private blend in providing America's defense. Private firms develop America's most advanced weapons and deploy personnel along with the troops to help them fight more effectively, while the defense agencies act as entrepreneurs – identifying, organizing, and promoting waves of innovation that change the way the nation lives as well as how it fights wars. For example, satellite communications and the Global Positioning System are DoD-managed innovations that have large military benefits, but they contribute even larger benefits to the rest of society. Government cannot provide these sorts of benefits, however, without being able to independently judge its needs and the potential of the relevant technologies. The FFRDCs and similar not-for-profit organizations dedicated to government service help agencies avoid becoming totally dependent on contractors' pitches. They provide another source of expertise, one that takes the government's perspective rather than the stockholders'.

Experts versus politics

The government needs to be technologically savvy, to have the advice of knowledgeable and trusted experts, but the government cannot and should not be run by "experts." There is too much uncertainty in governing, and especially in providing for the national defense, for experts to rule. History may repeat itself, but only partially. There may be laws of society and war just as there are laws of nature, but they are often too opaque and contingent for those who seek to understand them to claim the title of scientist. Rather, what is required is judgment – organizational judgment, domestic political judgment, technical judgment, and international relations judgment.[5]

As former Secretary of Defense Harold Brown pointed out, a secretary and the president need to appreciate the organizational lives of the armed services and other defense agencies.[6] These organizations are not simply about maximizing their budgets. They care about their standing relative to each other and with the nation, the ways in which their members' families are treated, and where their bases are located. The Marine Corps wants to be viewed as ever most heroic, the Army as ever most self-sacrificing, the Navy as ever most admired, and the Air Force as ever most effective. These "masks of war," as Carl Builder called them, motivate many a service decision, because they are deeply held self-images.[7] Providing benefits for military dependents is more than a personnel cost. It is also a symbol of national concern for the family costs of military service. Military retirees like to be near bases that have good medical and post exchange facilities in regions of the country that have lots of sun and no snow. Not surprisingly, the services tend to favor retaining bases in the South and West while closing them in the Northeast and Central States.

Sensitivity to organizational needs goes beyond letting the fleet move south or training fighter pilots near Las Vegas. It includes recognizing why the services want the fastest aircraft, the toughest tanks, and the best ships. Proud professionals want to meet the most difficult challenges, not just the most expected, and they want to work with the most advanced equipment at the cutting edge of their fields. Senior officials have to bargain with the services, not dictate to them. Sometimes that involves giving a service more fifth-generation fighters than analysts say are needed, or buying advanced-design destroyers when the old ones would do, in exchange for service concessions or support on other matters that are more important strategically.

The United States fights wars of choice. America is too powerful to be conquered and too rich and too large to notice much when it is at war. Only a small portion of its population needs to be in uniform or to run the risks of combat. What is usually a matter of life and death to opponents, a war with the US, is only a passing thought of distant conflict to many Americans. But ironically, this very distance makes it difficult for senior officials to mobilize and maintain public support. Threats have to be exaggerated to find support for the sacrifice of soldiers when danger seems so far from America's doorstep. Even once war begins, the American public quickly begin to wonder why the continuing toll is required. Over and over again since World War II, declining public support has made it difficult to find even the relatively few soldiers needed to sustain wars and to convince the untouched many that there is value in the killing conducted in their name. Not surprisingly in a tax-averse country, it is difficult to convince Americans that a war is worth financial contribution, sometimes even when that contribution is simply borrowed at very low interest rates. The public must continue to feel the fear that made them resort to war in the first place, and then must be convinced again and again, both that sufficient progress is being made against that threat and that the threat is still sufficient to justify continuing to fight.[8] Although many security specialists have said

Figure 14.1 An artist's rendering of the USS *Zumwalt* (DDG-1000)
Source: US Navy.

that the danger posed by al Qaeda did not end with the killing of Osama bin Laden, most Americans thought it had until ISIS began its wave of beheadings and shootings.

American diplomacy faces similar problems internationally. Most allies free-ride on our defense spending, knowing that the United States will take care of the big threats. Smaller threats include charitable efforts to stem the killing of innocents and the creation of refugees. The United States needs allies in these efforts to convince the American public that other nations assess the dangers to be as great as they have been described by the domestic advocates of intervention. Leaders in most developed nations, however, are unwilling or unable to hype the threat to the point at which their publics are willing to lose soldiers. War seems unnecessary, even obsolete, in a world where big threats do not exist or are taken care of by a big nation.[9]

Pity, then, the American politician who has to weave his or her way to gaining domestic and international support for military action that is less than a war to save civilization as we know it. Leaders need political support, but it is not easily obtained or maintained. Who is expert at forging the right message, making the threat big enough for military action, small enough for progress to be visible, and sustainable enough to survive either success or failure? Making these calls is an art, not a science. And we should not be surprised that justifying them likely will involve some overstatements and even an occasional near outright lie.

Centralization versus decentralization

Early in this book, we began our discussion of American defense policy and politics by examining the US framework for defense policy-making, embodied in the National Security Act of 1947. We noted its initial decentralized structure and the evolution toward a more centralized system, albeit at times contentiously. First the civilian secretariat-focused powers in the Office of the Secretary of Defense, and then the military side followed with the effort toward creating military jointness embodied in the Defense Reform Act of 1986 (often informally called Goldwater–Nichols). Today, the secretary of defense controls the service secretaries and their assistants via the OSD staff, which is responsible for budget, personnel, acquisition, and strategy, and for logistics, nuclear weapons, and other tasks directly (via the central defense agencies) or in conjunction with the services. Through the combatant commands, the secretary of defense controls the nation's operating forces, at the president's direction. On the military side, the chairman of the Joint Chiefs, who acts officially only as an advisor to the secretary and the president, uses the enlarged Joint Staff that he now controls to coordinate the views of the operating forces and the service chiefs to gain consensus that can counter civilian positions. In short, the Department of Defense comprises two power pyramids: one civilian and one military.

The clamor, as we pointed out, is always for more centralization, not less. Whenever there is a crisis, the first solution offered is the appointment of a czar to increase policy coordination, with the implicit, but usually false, assumption being that there is an agreed-upon policy to implement. Similarly, whenever there is a need to save resources, someone quickly proposes to consolidate agencies, as if such an action ensures lower expenditures and greater efficiency. These centralizing proposals should almost always be resisted. In a crisis, the need is to see the options, not to stifle them. The best way to find savings is to let the services and other agencies tell you why to eliminate or reduce the other guys' programs and to force each to defend its own. Again, the need is to see the options, but there are few when policy becomes centralized, standardized, and joint.

Decentralization encourages the development and presentation of new ideas, but it does not encourage the implementation of any.[10] It is great to have options, but is there not a need to choose among them? Centralization, to the extent that it can be accomplished in American society, would seem to be the way to get things done. In fact, American military organization inherently blends centralization and decentralization because America has four military services. Each of the four can develop and present its own ideas, and each has a hierarchy that can implement the ideas that civilian leaders choose.

What is unproductive is to divide the DoD up into civilian versus military camps. This type of division encourages the services to collude among themselves to protect their interests from being subordinated to civilian interests – often just the interests of the current presidential administration. Collusion does not produce better answers but rather the ones upon which agreement can be reached, usually those that share gains and losses proportionately. The wiser policy is to seek overlap and duplication among the services so that they are encouraged to promote ideas that offer them a chance of disproportionate gains or lower losses. This is what firms experience in competitive commercial markets. The same should happen in bureaucratic markets.

What about the need to make a choice among options? This is intentionally hard to do in American politics because the constitutional structure is intended to prevent the destruction of minority views by majority views. But as crises deepen, authority can be ceded to the center. This is often done in wars, although usually with some later regrets. Although not without some excesses, the American government had much leeway in the first decade of the Cold War to mobilize to meet the threat. But the very successes achieved during this period in ballistic missiles, anti-submarine warfare, and satellites undermined societal mobilization and public support as the Cold War ground on. The Iranian hostage crisis and the persistent campaigning by those who feared the Soviets' intentions allowed for a renewal of the mandate and the Reagan buildup. Similarly, the 9/11 attacks gave President Bush a mandate that

246 Preparing for the next war

the 2000 election did not. But the occupation experience in Iraq gradually wore away public support and the president's power. President Obama preferred the war in Afghanistan, but soon recognized that the public had tired of it. Decisions can be made when needed, but political power ebbs and flows in American politics. This is not necessarily a bad thing.

It is also not a bad thing that spending on defense has to compete for public funds with other governmental activities. Wars are often financed by borrowing as well as taxation. The attempts of Great Britain to tax its North American colonies to repay the costs incurred fighting the French and Indian War (the North American component of Britain's global Seven Years' War with France and Spain) was a precipitating cause of the American Revolution. "No taxation without representation" was the cry, but the main problem was actually paying. The colonists did not want to pay for the defense of the empire or even the defense of their own frontier. Since then, the costs of wars have played a crucial part in determining American public support for conflicts.

Almost always, taxes go up when the US is at war. That is surely why politicians prefer short wars. The Global War on Terror has been exceptional in a number of ways. It has been long. It has also been paid for entirely by borrowing. In fact, taxes were cut soon after 9/11 and not raised later as the war continued. No taxes and no draft tempered opposition, but the bill for the war will eventually come due in one fashion or another. Those trillion-plus dollars will be laid on top of the costs of the welfare state the US has been building for itself since the latter half of the Cold War.

After all, President Obama not only escalated the war in Afghanistan but also gained passage of universal health insurance. The war in Afghanistan will end one day, though that day keeps getting postponed. But the war against disease and death never will. Already the federal government's spending on health care is much larger than federal spending on defense, and even if the costs of the other parts of the welfare state are somehow moderated, health care costs are certain to grow. Soon perhaps, the restraint on the desire of America's political leaders to manage global security affairs may come from domestic pensioners rather than foreign insurgents. Welfare policy and security policy may seem to follow independent paths, but their advocates will likely discover that the two are on a collision course.

All hail confusion and indecision

It seems strange to praise confusion and indecision, but we must. Usually, systems that produce these conditions are condemned, but if uncertainty is the prevailing security condition, then confusion and indecision are to be both expected and accepted. Clarity comes when a threat is obvious, or at least is believed to be so. When threats are vague or contested, then the lack of clarity should not be thought of as wrong. In that situation, what is needed is a policy that preserves options, produces prototypes of various weapons designs, and experiments a lot to discover doctrinal flaws. If the services follow different paths, one of them may turn out to be the right one.

Unfortunately, too many security specialists are planners at heart. They want to control the future, to make it fit their perception of what dangers exist and how best to deal with them. Officials often want certainty, too. And some security specialists will help guide them towards the mirage, telling them that a particular set of policies offers security, based on clear statements of threats with clear solutions.[11] Wise leaders, however, will search out other planners and analysts for confirmation or, more importantly, for dissent. With the fragmentation of American political institutions and the variety of potential foreign policy advisors, American leaders are unlikely to find a consensus. Their best option is to encourage the pursuit of several policy options, postponing a commitment to a single view.[12]

Some people are indeed very prescient. Some warned correctly of the rise of non-state terrorist groups. A very few had even predicted the end of the Cold War and the collapse of the Soviet Empire. But to what extent should the United States allow its security to depend on having the most prescient analysts, generals, and decision-makers – on the ability to choose which forecasters are the best? It is better to see the evolving security world through several sets of eyes and to listen to the arguments for this course or that.

This is the way the American economy is run. It is the basis of the judicial system in which competing advocates try to persuade a jury. It is also the basis of American democracy, as parties and candidates compete for votes. And it is the way science advances and American universities stay at the top. Certainly, the armed services have much in common in their general approaches to problem-solving and in their outlooks on the world. But they also have many divergences in their diagnoses and solutions to problems – a diversity of views that is ultimately useful to the nation. It is also a boon to civilian control of the military. Politicians need to exercise judgment as representatives of the American people, choosing the defense policy that best fits the values of the time and the strategic environment. The greatest danger is to succumb to the advocates of total jointness and centralization. America should harness rather than suppress differences in views about national security.

Questions for discussion

1   **Has security policy-making been easier or harder since the end of the Cold War?**

2   **If redundancy is so good in public affairs, why is it so often opposed?**

3   **Which security decisions are best left to the military, and which are the responsibility of civilians?**

4   **How many different kinds of expertise are relevant to national security decision-making? How many organizations are involved?**

Notes

1 Sanford Weiner, "Resource Allocation in Basic Research and Organizational Design," *Public Policy*, 20 (Spring 1972): 227–255.
2 Stephen P. Rosen, "Service Redundancy: Waste or Hidden Capability?" *Joint Force Quarterly*, 1 (Summer 1993): 36–39.
3 "Unmanned and Dangerous: How UAV–Plane Collisions Are Changing U.S. Air Control," *Defense News*, June 11, 2007, p. 1; "Army Hoping to Keep UAVs from Air Force," *Huntsville Times*, August 13, 2007.
4 Eugene Gholz, "Systems Integration for Complex Defense Products," in Guy Ben-Ari and Pierre Chao (eds.), *Organizing for a Complex World: Developing Tomorrow's Defense and Net-Centric Systems* (Washington, DC: CSIS, 2009), pp. 50–65; Harvey M. Sapolsky, Eugene Gholz, and Allen Kaufman, "Security Lessons from the Cold War," *Foreign Affairs*, 78(4) (July/August 1999): 77–89.
5 Isaiah Berlin, "On Political Judgment," *New York Review of Books*, October 3, 1996, pp. 26–30.
6 Harold Brown, "Managing the Defense Department: Why It Can't Be Done," *Dividend*, magazine of the Graduate School of Business Administration, University of Michigan (Spring 1981): 10–14, available at: http://deepblue.lib.umich.edu/bitstream/2027.42/50728/2/1981-spring-dividend-text.pdf (accessed September 2, 2016).
7 Carl Builder, *The Masks of War: American Military Styles in Strategy and Analysis* (Baltimore, MD: Johns Hopkins University Press, 1989).
8 John Mueller, "The Iraq Syndrome," *Foreign Affairs*, 84(6) (November/December 2005): 44–54.
9 John Mueller, *Retreat from Doomsday: The Obsolescence of Major War* (New York: Basic Books, 1989).
10 James Q. Wilson, "Innovation in Organization: Notes Toward a Theory," in James D. Thompson (ed.), *Approaches to Organizational Design* (Pittsburgh, PA: University of Pittsburgh Press, 1966).

11 Jack Snyder, *The Ideology of the Offensive: Military Decision-Making and the Disasters of 1914* (Ithaca, NY: Cornell University Press, 1984), pp. 24–30.
12 James D. Thompson, *Organizations in Action: Social Science Bases of Administrative Action* (New York: McGraw-Hill, 1967).

Recommended additional reading

Richard Danzig, *Driving in the Dark: Ten Propositions about Prediction and National Security* (Washington, DC: Center for a New American Security, 2011). Explains why the DoD perpetually tries and fails to predict the future, and what to do about it.

Niall Ferguson, *Colossus: The Price of America's Empire* (New York: Penguin, 2004). There is much to do if America is going to manage global security.

Daniel Kahneman, *Thinking Fast and Slow* (New York: Farrar, Straus, and Giroux, 2011). A Nobel Laureate examines ways to think about uncertainty.

John Mueller, *The Remnants of War* (Ithaca, NY: Cornell University Press, 2004). Describes how for many people war is a forgotten enterprise, practiced only by thugs and thieves.

David Runciman, *The Confidence Trap: A History of Democracy in Crisis from World War I to the Present* (Princeton NJ: Princeton University Press, 2013). Democracies can't plan well, like to kick problems down the road, and thus tend to lurch from crisis to crisis, but they have the advantage over autocratic regimes in that they can adapt more easily.

Glossary

Acquisition   The entire process of designing, developing, producing, and supporting new military equipment.

All-Volunteer Force (AVF)   Method of recruiting through monetary and/or career incentives rather than coercion. Instituted in the United States in 1973 in response to the recommendations of the Gates Commission. The main alternatives for recruiting are forcing people to serve through conscription, also known as a draft, or drawing on able-bodied citizens within a particular geographic area for service in a militia.

Base Realignment and Closure (BRAC) Commission   A bipartisan, supposedly apolitical group that Congress established at the end of the Cold War to nominate military bases for realignment or closure. The goal was to increase efficiencies and reduce the defense budget. The BRAC process provides that Congress has to vote up or down on the commission's entire list of recommendations – accepting all or none. This approval mechanism was meant to bind Congress's hands, preventing the protection of local interests that might want bases to stay open or stay wedded to old and inefficient purposes.

Bush Doctrine   The post-9/11 American diplomatic and military policy that claimed that the United States should maintain military primacy and be willing to conduct preventive war against threats even when they are not yet imminent, especially those threats that link terrorism and weapons of mass destruction.

Buy-in   A process in which a contractor intentionally underbids or underestimates costs to persuade politicians to start a project. The contractor usually figures that it can convince the government to allocate additional resources later, when actual project costs escalate above the predicted amount.

Chairman of the Joint Chiefs of Staff   Position that has evolved into the main military advisor to the president. Serves as a conduit for the orders to US forces from the president and the secretary of defense.

CINCs and COCOMs   The Commanders-in-Chief, later called Combatant Commanders, of the United States' joint regional and functional commands that have operational control of American military forces around the globe. For example, US Strategic Command outside Omaha, Nebraska, is in charge of space operations, missile defense, global strike, and strategic deterrence, while US Central Command, headquartered in Tampa, Florida, has responsibility for the Middle East.

Concurrency   The practice of conducting development and production simultaneously – a formula for weapons acquisition disaster, as design details continue to change while the contractor attempts to produce the promised system.

Decade of neglect   Republican characterization of the defense policies of the 1970s that cut back American forces after the end of ground combat in Vietnam. Naturally, the Republicans generally blamed the Carter administration.

Director of National Intelligence (DNI)   The formal head of the US Intelligence Community. Established in 2004 through a series of post-9/11 reforms, the position was intended to displace the Director of Central Intelligence as the principal all-source intelligence provider to the president, ensuring decision-makers' access to unbiased and integrated intelligence from across the community. In practice, the DNI has proven much less powerful, in part because the office's authority greatly exceeds its funding, especially in comparison to well-established organizations such as the CIA and DIA.

"Don't ask, don't tell" (DADT)   The policy adopted early in the Clinton administration that allowed gay and lesbian military personnel to serve as long as their sexual orientation was not openly acknowledged. It also prohibited the military from seeking to find out soldiers' sexual orientation.

First responders   The firefighters, police, and paramedics who are first to arrive on the scene of a major incident such as a terrorist attack or a natural disaster.

Flexible response   The Kennedy administration's security strategy, which rejected the Eisenhower strategy's emphasis on massive retaliation as lacking credibility. Instead, flexible response promised that the United States would be ready to use both conventional and nuclear forces as needed to defend US interests. The practical implication of the strategy was to shift resources from the Air Force to the Army and the Navy.

Garrison state   The worry, first voiced by Harold Lasswell in the 1940s, that the United States would have to become an authoritarian state in order to marshal the defense resources needed to prevail in modern military competition. This became a major concern by the 1950s as the Cold War set in. The United States managed to prevail in the Cold War despite forsaking the "garrison state" approach – indeed, liberal US society and its free-market economy ultimately gave the United States a big advantage over the Communists.

Goldwater–Nichols/Defense Reform Act   A 1986 law that required more coordination among the US armed forces by giving additional authority to the Joint Staff, the Chairman of the Joint Chiefs, and regional commanders. Among other things, Goldwater–Nichols made experience in a joint billet – that is, working for a central staff rather than a service-specific one – a requirement for promotion to flag rank (general or admiral) and made the Chairman of the Joint Chiefs the president's principal military advisor.

Grand strategy   Distinct from particular strategies for dealing with specific situations, problems, and opportunities, grand strategy is a state's theory about how it can "cause" security for itself. It offers, or purports to offer, some theory about the ends a state seeks and the means by which it will achieve them – requiring an explanation of how the state will use its economic, military, political, diplomatic, geographic, and even demographic assets. Examples include the grand strategy of containment during the Cold War.

Intelligence Community (IC)   The collection of 17 different agencies and organizations within the executive branch responsible for collecting and analyzing intelligence provided to national security decision-makers. Members include the intelligence branches of each of the military services and the Coast Guard, the Central Intelligence Agency, the Defense Intelligence Agency, the Drug Enforcement Administration, the National Security Agency, the Federal Bureau of Investigation, the National Geospatial Intelligence Agency, the National Reconnaissance Office, the Office of the Director of National Intelligence, and intelligence arms within the Departments of State, Treasury, Energy, and Homeland Security. After 9/11, Congress passed a law intended to increase centralization of the Intelligence Community, which gave it this composition.

Jointness   The idea that the military services should work closely together, recognizing that national security comes from their combined efforts; the opposite of "servicism" or "parochialism." Cooperation during peacetime on planning, acquisition, and training may prepare the forces and develop a culture that enables cooperation during wartime. Operational jointness refers to the ability of forces from different services to fight together effectively in battle and is often achieved by having them train together and by equipping the services with compatible systems (especially for communications). Doctrinal jointness involves agreeing, formally, that certain concepts or procedures will govern service interactions. Managerial jointness, including at the very highest levels of decision-making, posts members of each of the armed services to staff positions to plan, acquire weapons, and prepare the budget for the Department of Defense.

Key West Agreement   A foundational deal negotiated at a meeting in Key West, Florida, in 1948 that allocated certain roles and missions to each of the military services.

Lead Systems Integrator (LSI)   Approach to defense acquisition in which the government buyer delegates control of the acquisition process for an entire weapon system to one defense contractor. Associated with large-scale, highly complex projects such as the Army's Future Combat Systems and intended to allow the integrator full insight to make necessary design choices and technical trade-offs during system development. In practice, this contracting form over-stretched technical and managerial competence, and the National Defense Authorization Acts of 2008 and 2009 tried to ban its future use. See also: *Total package procurement.*

Logrolling   The swapping of political favors to build a powerful coalition behind a policy initiative, especially one that benefits particular or "special" interests. A common practice in the conduct of democratic government.

MacArthur, Douglas (General)   American Army general who was the UN Commander in the Korean War. He was eventually relieved of his command by President Truman for insubordination and later made a failed bid for the Republican presidential nomination. Also served as World War I combat leader, Commandant of West Point, Governor General of the Philippines, Commander of US Forces in the South West Pacific during World War II, and Commander of the Occupation of Japan.

McNamara, Robert S.   The longest-serving secretary of defense (1961–1967). Before serving as secretary, McNamara was president of the Ford Motor Company. He was noted for his skill in mastering the complexity of defense programs, his mismanagement of the Vietnam War, his persuasiveness in debate, and his arrogance. He was admired by the presidents he served and intensely disliked by many senior military officers and defense contractors of his time.

Massive retaliation   A strategic emphasis during the Eisenhower administration on the threatened use of nuclear weapons to deter Soviet aggression. A key component of Eisenhower's New Look security strategy.

Military-industrial complex   A term first used in the 1960s to describe the close and nefarious relationship among defense contractors, the military, and supportive groups, including local business interests and universities doing defense research, to promote and protect an expanding defense budget and its component programs.

Missile gap   The supposed lag in the fielding of US nuclear missiles in comparison with Soviet deployments during the late 1950s. President Eisenhower correctly thought that the United States actually had a lead in deployment of strategic weapons, but he did not publicly rebut then-candidate John F. Kennedy's claims to the contrary.

Monopsony   A market structure in which there is only one buyer.

National Security Act of 1947   The foundational federal law for the organization of authority in national security affairs. It sought to improve coordination through the establishment of the Department of Defense and the National Security Council, among other entities. Amended in the Defense Reorganization Act of 1958, which gave the secretary of defense greater control over the activities of the services.

Nuclear freeze movement   A political campaign begun in the initial years of the Reagan administration that sought to halt the Cold War arms race through comprehensive rejection of nuclear weapons, especially additional deployments, rather than through opposition to particular weapon programs.

Parochialism   The notion that military services act based on a narrow set of interests benefiting their organizations more than the national interest. Sometimes called "servicism" or "corporatism" and often contrasted with jointness. Considered a dirty word at the Pentagon.

Peace dividend   The not-always-fulfilled expectation that money will be freed up for non-defense expenditures after the end of a war.

Planning, Programming, and Budgeting System (PPBS)   A system of defense planning created under Secretary McNamara, based on five-year plans that grouped programs by military missions (strategic attack, sealift, etc.) rather than by service, so that output comparisons (targets destroyed, tons delivered) and program investment decisions could be made more logically. Secretary Rumsfeld later renamed the framework to stress implementation, calling it the Planning, Programming, Budgeting, and Execution System (PPBES).

Powell, Colin (General)   Reserve Officers' Training Corps graduate who served in Vietnam and became National Security Advisor to President George H. W. Bush, Chairman of the Joint Chiefs of Staff during the Gulf War, and secretary of state for President George W. Bush during his first term, which included the diplomatic effort to build and maintain a coalition for the Iraq War. Gave his name to the famous "Powell Doctrine" (see below).

Powell Doctrine   The assertion, first articulated by Secretary of Defense Caspar Weinberger during the Reagan administration, that US forces should go to war only when vital interests are at stake, when the United States is willing to use overwhelming force, when clear goals and an exit strategy are defined, and when strong public and congressional support has been mobilized.

Private arsenals   Defense contractors on which the armed services depend for vital equipment and which, in turn, depend on the services for most of their revenues.

Procurement   The buying of military equipment under government acquisition rules.

Readiness   The capacity of armed forces to perform their military missions if called upon.

Reagan buildup   The major recapitalization and expansion of US forces that began in the late 1970s and continued through 1986. It is usually at least partly credited with convincing the Soviet Union's leadership that continuing competition with the United States was too expensive to maintain. Key elements of the buildup included the MX missile, the Trident submarine, and the Strategic Defense Initiative.

Republicanization of the military   The contestable belief that the US military, and especially the officer corps, identifies with and favors the policies of the Republican Party.

Reserve Component   Includes the Army Reserve, Navy Reserve, Air Force Reserve, Marine Corps Reserve, and Coast Guard Reserve, plus the Army National Guard and Air National Guard. Together these form the backup to the active-duty military. The Reserve units are federal creations and are under sole federal control; the Guard units are controlled by state government, subject to call-up by the federal government in times of emergency.

Revolt of the admirals   A political maneuver attempted by the Navy's leadership in the late 1940s to prevent the Truman administration from favoring the Air Force strategic bomber force over the development of a new class of larger aircraft carriers capable of launching nuclear strike aircraft. The maneuver failed, the secretary of the Navy and the chief of naval operations both lost their jobs, and several senior officers had their careers curtailed or threatened. Although the Navy lost this round, the "supercarriers" were built in the 1950s.

Revolution in military affairs (RMA) A somewhat vague term that generally refers to the cluster of significant changes in military technology after the Vietnam War. The RMA enabled a style of warfare based on highly networked forces that rely more on information and speed than mass and armor for their effectiveness. Key changes include the ability to gain greater intelligence about targets on the battlefield through the use of satellites, unmanned aerial vehicles, and other reconnaissance technologies; and the ability to conduct precision attacks against these targets through the use of laser-guided and GPS-guided munitions.

Ridgway, Matthew (General) Army general who replaced MacArthur in Korea. Later served as Chief of Staff of the Army and led opposition to the Eisenhower administration's "New Look" posture that emphasized nuclear weapons rather than conventional forces. President Eisenhower appointed General Maxwell Taylor to replace General Ridgway as Chief of Staff when Ridgway made his policy objections public.

Shinseki, Eric (General) US Army commander in Europe during the Bosnian conflict who became Chief of Staff of the Army. Secretary Rumsfeld marginalized Shinseki for warning in congressional testimony that troop levels planned for the Iraq occupation were inadequate. Later appointed secretary of veterans affairs by President Obama, and eventually forced to resign from that post in one of the many intense rounds of criticism of the VA's purported lack of responsiveness to veterans' needs.

Sputnik The world's first artificial satellite, launched by the Soviet Union in 1957. Its launch shook the confidence of the American public in the government's ability to protect the nation through leadership in the advancement of militarily relevant technologies.

Strategic bombing A doctrine that involves long-range bomber attacks on an opponent. It seeks to force the enemy's capitulation by breaking its will or industrial capability rather than by defeating its armed forces in the field through invasion or conquest of territory.

Sunk costs Preexisting investments in projects. From an economic perspective, the resources have already been spent, so decision-makers cannot get them back whether or not the project continues; standard economic advice is that sunk costs should not influence forward-looking decisions about continuing investments. However, in the practical politics of government decision-making, sunk costs are often used as a reason to continue a project.

Systems analysis An analytical technique that grew out of the operations research efforts of World War II. The general idea was to measure inputs and outputs of various processes, looking for correlations that analysts could use to optimize military effort. Secretary McNamara imported these tools to the Pentagon for use in defense planning during the 1960s. Like all analytical tools, however, systems analysis and the broader field of quantitative defense analysis have their limits.

Taylor, Maxwell (General) Author of *The Uncertain Trumpet*, which critiqued US strategy under Eisenhower. President Kennedy recalled Taylor from retirement to be Chairman of the Joint Chiefs of Staff and later appointed him ambassador to South Vietnam as the insurgency grew there. General Taylor had previously also served as a World War II Commander and Chief of Staff of the Army during the Eisenhower administration.

Title X A section of law that describes the powers and functions of the military departments (services) in their roles as the providers of training and equipment for the US armed forces.

Total force policy   Policy instituted after the Vietnam War in which all active-duty Regular forces were tied tightly to the Reserves. Many units like the military police, medical service, and truck companies needed to sustain overseas forces in the field were stripped out of the active force and placed in the Reserves, while the Regulars focused on the combat arms. This distribution of labor meant that any large or long-term military operation required the mobilization of the Reserves. The policy was intended to put a political brake on the use of force by requiring a disruption to larger US society and the workforce in the event of war.

Total package procurement (TPP)   A contracting format initiated by Secretary of Defense Robert McNamara that included in a single procurement competition the contract award for the development, production, and logistical support of a weapon system. TPP was a precursor to the Lead Systems Integrator approach seen in the 1990s and 2000s. Neither process adequately recognizes the technological and political uncertainty built into the acquisition process: contractors cannot know everything they need to know in order to make reasonable bids entirely up-front, and the government cannot know in advance whether any bid that it receives makes reasonable provisions for development, manufacturing, and support costs or for likely changes in the political and strategic situation over the likely 30-year lifespan of the weapon system.

Transformation   The name given to Secretary of Defense Donald Rumsfeld's ambitious and rather vague program of Pentagon reform. Typically associated with efforts to make the US military operate "lighter" by leveraging advances in speed, precision, stealth, and networking technology that are sometimes referred to as the "revolution in military affairs." Also associated with greater use of Special Operations Forces.

Weapons of mass destruction (WMD)   A term used to refer to nuclear, biological, and chemical weapons, sometimes also extended to include radiological weapons known as "dirty bombs." WMD were invented after conventional explosives, and it is generally more difficult to make them and use them effectively, although the basic scientific explanations for how they work are now well known around the world. Discussion of the spread of WMD has also had a useful political resonance, particularly when politicians can stress the relative ease of acquiring chemical weapons and the huge destructive potential of nuclear weapons – linking the two types of weapons via the category "WMD" even though acquiring chemical weapons does not make it any easier to wreak destruction with nuclear weapons. Politicians used the fear that Saddam Hussein had WMD in Iraq to drum up support for the US-led invasion. For terrorists, even chemical weapons have proven a challenge, so they have focused on using conventional high explosives in their attacks.

Index

Page numbers in italics refer to illustrations